New Canadian Readings

RETHINKING CANADA:

THE PROMISE OF WOMEN'S HISTORY

Edited by
Veronica Strong-Boag and Anita Clair Fellman

Copp Clark Pitman Ltd.
Toronto

To our colleagues — the students, staff, and faculty
members of the Women's Studies Program at Simon
Fraser University

ISBN 0-7730-4601-1

Editing: Barbara Tessman
Design: Kathy Cloutier
Typesetting: Compeer Typographic Services
Printing and Binding: Webcom Ltd.

Canadian Cataloguing in Publication Data

Main entry under title:
Rethinking Canada : the promise of women's history

(New Canadian readings)
Bibliography: p.
ISBN 0-7730-4601-1

1. Women — Canada — History — Addresses, essays,
lectures. 2. Women — Canada — Social conditions —
Addresses, essays, lectures. I. Strong-Boag,
Veronica Jane, 1947– II. Fellman, Anita Clair.
III. Series.

HQ1453.R47 1986   305.4'0971   C86-093462-4

Copp Clark Pitman Ltd.
495 Wellington Street West
Toronto, Ontario
M5V 1E9

Printed and bound in Canada

FOREWORD

New Canadian Readings is an on-going series of inexpensive books intended to bring some of the best recent work by this country's scholars to the attention of students of Canada. Each volume consists of ten or more articles or book sections, carefully selected to present a fully-formed thesis about some critical aspect of Canadian development. Where useful, public documents or even private letters and statistical materials may be used as well to convey a different and fresh perspective.

The authors of the readings selected for inclusion in this volume (and all the others in the series) are all first-rank scholars, those who are doing the hard research that is rapidly changing our understanding of this country. Quite deliberately, the references for each selection have been retained, thus making additional research as easy as possible.

Like the authors of the individual articles, the editors of each volume are also scholars of note, completely up-to-date in their areas of specialization and, as the introductions demonstrate, fully aware of the changing nature of the debates within their professions and genres of research. The list of additional readings provided by the editor of each volume will steer readers to materials that could not be included because of space limitations.

This series will continue into the foreseeable future, and the General Editor is pleased to invite suggestions for additional topics.

J.L. Granatstein

CONTENTS

INTRODUCTION

History is a retelling of the human experience. To give meaning to that experience, we focus the beams of memory and research on certain events, people, and places, leaving others in the shadows. From time to time, influenced in part by what seems to be important in our own lives, we move the beams to illuminate unfairly obscured aspects of the human past.

Until recent years the telling of Canadian history has focussed most on the economic and political origins of the two founding cultures, and on the winning of nationhood. The primary actors in these dramas were seen to be fur traders, merchants, lumberjacks, and politicians. Many historians, assuming that the kernel of Canadian history lay there, chose to concentrate on a small number of males of European origin whom they identified as the critical pioneers, leaders, and trendsetters. Ontario and Quebec, especially Ottawa, Toronto, and Montreal, supplied the most common settings for prominent figures like the Jeans/Johns — Talon, Simcoe, Macdonald, Lesage, and Diefenbaker — and Roberts — Baldwin, Borden, Stanfield, and Bourassa — who monopolize most textbooks. It was taken for granted that this view of the past included all that was truly important about Canada and Canadians. Left in the shadows were native peoples, non-charter ethnic groups, geographical areas outside central Canada, the inner lives of Canadians, most members of the working class, and almost all women. The focus on public figures fed a particular view of time as well. Chronological signposts, such as changes in political regimes or prime ministers, were assigned to designate important transitions in Canadian life, but in fact they were neither universal nor inevitable, and may very well have had less meaning to most Canadians than shifts in domestic technology, economic organization, or fertility patterns.

Today these conventions engage our scrutiny and criticism. Events in our own times have prompted us to rethink Canadian history to understand more fully the participation and importance of groups and areas previously slighted. Pushed by the contemporary women's movement to become more conscious of gender as a category of analysis, and aided by a resurgence of interest in social history, which broadened the range of legitimate historical topics, researchers have begun exploring the history of Canadian women. They do so for two basic reasons. Inasmuch as we as human beings need to place ourselves in time, to tie ourselves to those who came before us, it is only just that women — and men too — know as much as possible about the lives of their female ancestors. To be denied a sense of one's own history, indeed to be informed that there exists no history worth recounting, is to have an essential part of one's humanity denied. The second reason that historians have begun to study women is the gradual realization that we cannot pretend to reconstruct a reasonable history of the

Canadian people by ignoring the lives and participation of half of them. History without women is, of necessity, a distorted history. Even in areas in which they would seemingly not figure — on the battlefield, for example — women are part of the total picture. Unless it includes the contributions of women, any portrait of the past is essentially incomplete and finally inexplicable.

Women became a majority of the Canadian population in the second half of the twentieth century, but long before the arrival of Europeans they were major participants in the creation of their communities. Like the males they worked alongside, loved, bore, and frequently struggled with, the land's female inhabitants cannot be reduced to any single portrait. They are distinguished by race, ethnicity, and class, and by a wide range of individual differences. The patterns of variety, are not constant. The percentage of all women who may be, for instance, immigrant or rural or Caucasian or in waged labour or single mothers has shifted, often markedly, over time.

Yet, while their experiences have differed from group to group and time to time, in some ways women's lives resemble each other's as much or more than they resemble those of the men with whom they are closely associated. As a group women have been defined and delimited, not so much by any lesser capacity for work or determination or thought, but by patriarchal custom and male authority. Each successive socio-economic stage in Canada, from seigneurialism to liberal capitalism, has allocated substantial advantages to males within every rank and class. Men's sisters, however privileged relative to other women, encountered more confined horizons then their brothers.

To be sure, there is much else to say about women's lives, but this discrepancy in formal power and authority between males and females has strongly marked the lives of both. The state, for instance, far from neutral, has through legislation and fiscal policies reinforced asymmetrical gender relations. While women and men in Canada have occasionally, and in some periods even frequently, breached the barriers that separated them, they have always lived in a society whose customs and institutions have been largely predicated on presumed differences between the sexes. The tension between the ways in which women share with male contemporaries prevailing economic, social, and political realities and the ways in which women reap different consequences supplies a dynamic as fundamental to the shaping of Canadian history as the influence of the great water routes proposed by the Laurentian thesis of national development.

Moved by a sense of common interest, women have collaborated with men as associates, subordinates, and superiors in causes as varied as opposition to and support for wars, the right to unionize, the preservation of particular cultural identities, and the defence of the region and the family farm against encroaching metropolitan powers and urban interests. On a daily basis women have guaranteed alongside men the survival of family, firm, organization, and state. Yet for all the tug of heterosexual loyalties these male-female alliances make up only one dimension of the female experience. Women's awareness of the common elements of their situation, whether it be in their special responsibility for domestic management, their peril in childbirth, or their lack of autonomy in comparison to males, has prompted collective as well as individual responses. Their prominence in food riots in the eighteenth century, their special enthusiasm for alcohol prohibition and sexual purity, their struggle for the vote and the rights of married women in waged labour in the nineteenth and twentieth centuries all supply clear instances of gender politics based on women's distinctive experience, just as do their creation today of transition houses for battered women, the demand for equal rights for native women, and the movement in favour of midwifery.

More subtle but no less effective has been the elaboration of what has been termed women's culture. Rooted in friendships and family ties this culture includes a broad range of rituals and traditions — anything from help in childbirth, advice on dealing with husbands, the exchange of recipes and folk remedies, to sharing strategies for confounding troublesome bosses and organizing needed community services. Such customs, repeated dozens of times over a lifetime, help assign a distinctive texture to female experience, and give women a particular past that cannot be presumed to mirror the portion of male reality that most historians have chosen to highlight.

The reconstruction of Canadian women's history is still in its infancy. Little can be taken for granted and contributions come from many quarters. Choosing material for a general text was difficult. A number of different criteria had to be satisfied. As much as possible we wanted the selections as a group to cover the entire course of Canadian history, to suggest the range of female experience and initiative, to reveal some of the particularities of class, race, and culture. We also wished the contributors to address many of the major issues in Canada's development, and to demonstrate a variety of ways that women's lives may be investigated and comprehended. Our final choice brought together senior and junior historians and graduate students, anthropologists, sociologists, and political scientists, independent researchers and scholars attached to institutions, those writing in traditional scholarly solitude and in married collaboration. Their ambitious interrogation of the past helped us realize many of our hopes.

We could have used many more pages to do the job as well as we would have liked. We particularly regret the omission of investigations focussing more specifically on women's relationships to the worlds of medicine, science, technology, education, and literature. We wish we could have dealt more fully with sexuality and sexual preference. Pioneer and rural life also received much less attention than we would have liked. To some extent interested readers can compensate for these omissions through the bibliographic suggestions we include and by paying attention to feminist journals like *Atlantis*, *Resources for Feminist Research*, and *Canadian Women's Studies*, which regularly note recent work in women's history.

Whether one chooses to add women to the study of the past simply because their lives are unexplored territory, historically speaking, or from a feminist urge to see the past through women's eyes, a narrow disciplinary focus and traditional sources of information are rarely sufficient or satisfactory. Historical sources have traditionally been defined by a focus on the public realm where women's influence has been more indirect. No wonder women frequently seem not to exist as historical actors. Crossing conventional disciplinary boundaries, often desirable in studying male historical figures, is inescapable when studying women. Historians of women need access to other disciplines both to broaden the range of questions they are accustomed to asking and to acquire data that they otherwise would not have. Hence some of the essays in this volume integrate history with other disciplines — with anthropology in the case of Eleanor Leacock's discussion of the separate but roughly equal spheres of men and women among the Montagnais-Naskapi, with historical sociology in Graham Lowe's investigation of the feminization of clerical work, with psychology in Patricia Rooke and Rudy Schnell's assessment of the impact of a midlife crisis on Charlotte Whitton's thought, or with political science in Sylvia Bashevkin's identification of two frequently conflicting traditions: women going it alone or integrating themselves into male institutions.

While applying the methods and questions of other disciplines is often essential, historians of women cannot abandon traditional historical sources, which, when reconsidered, are also invaluable. Women's lives have intersected with men's and with the public sphere at many points, and even if the beam of the public chroniclers has not been focussed on women, historians must re-examine, from new angles if necessary, long-familiar documents. Many of the abundant records generated by churches, the state, the military, and the economy, deal with women only obliquely, despite women's participation in these sectors of Canadian life. However, a careful reading of the religious press, royal commission reports, army regulations, labour force and demographic data, and business records is frequently extremely revealing, if not always for plentiful detail on women's lives, then at least for assumptions, both explicit and implied, about women and their roles. When fresh questions are asked of familiar data, they will sometimes elicit new answers. This is a process at which many of the contributors to this volume are adept. For instance, through an impressive compiling and reinterpretation of available information, Jan Noel has managed, in "Les femmes favorisées," to turn on its head the traditional view of women in New France.

As Susan Mann Trofimenkoff demonstrates in "One Hundred and Two Muffled Voices," the historian of women must become skilled at "squeezing every drop of information from every kind of source." Informed by a new perspective, Trofimenkoff uses documents gathered by the state, as do Joan Sangster, Graham Lowe, and Julie White, to reveal unappreciated information about women. Individual lives may be fleshed out in much the same way. Since her subject lived at a time when women often played an active role in family businesses, Lilianne Plamondon has been able to sketch a picture of the Widow Fornel's life through the use of routine legal and judicial documents; business contracts and family wills convey a remarkable sense of Fornel's economic activity and personal authority. Once the historian has identified women as subjects of interest, then the records of a wide range of institutions and organizations can also be made to yield very worthwhile information. Sylvia Van Kirk's mining of the Hudson's Bay Company records and Eleanor Leacock's use of the reports of the Jesuits in New France are two good examples of what can be learned about women from studying ostensibly all-male organizations. A rich cache of data in which women's voices are more directly heard, is to be found within specifically female institutions, as Christina Simmons discovered for Halifax's Jost Mission.

Historians are also accustomed to using the published record — books, newspapers, and magazines — as sources. Yet they have tended to ignore women's presence, whether as subjects or as authors, in many publications. This is changing. Readily available newspapers provided Joan Sangster with part of the means to reconstruct a significant early twentieth-century labour struggle featuring female strikers. The published writings of Nellie McClung and Charlotte Whitton permitted fruitful interpretation of their thought by Veronica Strong-Boag and Rooke and Schnell respectively. Sylvia Bashevkin applied the insights of the political scientist to the publications of historians and others and discovered in "women's politics" a recurring tension between independence and partisanship. Published accounts may be usefully re-examined by the investigator who turns on them a critical eye.

Yet for all such successes, much of female experience has gone unrecorded in easily recognizable or accessible form. Of necessity historians of women have had to tap some previously unused, even uncollected, sources. A new sensitivity, often feminist in inspiration, to the frequency with which women's lives and beliefs have been interpreted for them by men has led to a search for documents in which the historical subjects themselves describe their own experiences. In her article on women in Atlantic Canada, Margaret Conrad is explicit about the need for uncovering women's points of view. She maintains that without using the diaries and letters of ordinary women, the historian misses a complex female culture that left virtually no trace in conventional historical documents. Sara Brooks Sundberg also uses letters and diaries as well as autobiographies in order to vary the picture of downtrodden prairie frontierwomen. Again in the belief that women may be their own best chroniclers, historians are now turning to oral testimony. Simmons' depiction of the interplay between groups of women at the Jost Mission utilizes interviews as a corrective to sources frequently dominated by a male agenda. Talks with birth controller Vivian Dowding permit Mary Bishop to challenge our assumptions about the availability of birth control in the 1930s. Anne Woywitka's treatment of the Ukrainian activist Teklia Chaban suggests that giving women's voices their due may result in a finer appreciation for the interconnections between public and private spheres.

Coming gradually is a further broadening of the definition of what constitutes an historical source. Historians are now beginning to use recipes, songs, and aspects of material culture such as cooking and cleaning equipment, quilts, and wearing apparel to make serious analyses of women's positions in any given society. They look at the names women chose for their daughters — often those of their own sisters and of their close friends — to help them interpret a female culture and sense of family. Photographs and other visual materials are viewed with an increasingly sophisticated eye for the clues they provide for sense of self, and for patterns of interaction among family members and co-workers.

Although our selections cover a wide range in time and space, they reflect a shared view of Canadian women as actors rather than merely as the acted-upon. The authors do not ignore the structures or ideas that affect women's well-being and limit the expression of female talents and autonomy. Nonetheless they acknowledge, whether explicitly or implicitly, female resilience, energy, and ingenuity in situations where women might have wished the ground rules to be more equitable. While recognizing women's subordinate status in Canadian life, the contributors to this volume tend to move away from the "woman as victim" motif that so often preoccupied investigators in the 1960s and 1970s. Their stance argues for the significance and the richness of female experience.

The goal of this history is a fundamental reconstruction of our knowledge of the past. For the first time light is to fall on a full cast of Canadian women and men with all their potential for interplay and isolation. Susan Mann Trofimenkoff's chapter, "Feminism, Nationalism, and the Clerical Defensive", like her *Dream of Nation* itself, provides a preview of just what a more balanced history might look like. To the usual discussion of the alarmed response of early twentieth-century Quebec nationalists and clerics to the disruptions to traditional family life brought by urbanization and industrialization, Trofimenkoff adds analysis of the feminist response to this issue. In so doing she compels us to rethink the very nature of the intellectual ferment of the time. Her reformulation of a key historical debate encourages still further speculation about the comparable English Canadian response at the turn of the twentieth century, for many of the same phenomena and similar sorts of commentators were present. Possibly among the socially-conscious élite in both French and English Canada there was a certain set of shared presumptions about the family and sex roles that lies directly at the heart of the emerging Canadian state. Today, ideas of national identity and concerns about male-female relationships remain linked. Trofimenkoff's suggestive interpretation may well help to explain the depth of commitment present in the 1980s among both feminist and anti-feminist forces; both sides sense that they are not dealing with trivial social arrangements.

Correcting the historical record to embrace the experience of both sexes has just begun. It is not a small task and the consequences are considerable. For going as it does to the core of the way we think about ourselves, as with the debates over the future of the family and sex roles, the history of women invites the rethinking of Canada itself. We hope this volume will contribute to that process.

MONTAGNAIS WOMEN AND THE JESUIT PROGRAM FOR COLONIZATION†

ELEANOR LEACOCK[1]

Since the native peoples residing in what became Canada had no written language, we are dependent upon the observations of Europeans for our knowledge of Indian life and history at the point of contact. In this article, Eleanor Leacock, utilizing the records of the Jesuit missionaries sent to convert them, assesses the status of Montagnais-Naskapi women of the St. Lawrence valley roughly one hundred years after the Indians' first dealing with Europeans. We are not, then, getting a picture of Indian life before it was affected by Europeans, nor are we looking at it through Indian eyes — sources do not permit that.

Although she here uses historical documents, Leacock is an anthropologist, applying to a culture of the past, the concerns of her discipline: courtship, marriage, child-rearing practices, access to subsistence, expressions of influence in a nonstatus society. She suggests that under some social arrangements, namely nonhierarchical societies with little distinction between the public and private spheres, separate activities for women and men may not imply inequality for women. The splitting of tasks along gender lines did not mean that Montagnais females were helpless without males, or vice versa. While women and men exchanged products of their labour in ways that emphasized their mutual dependence, each also controlled the terms and arrangements of his or her own work.

Indeed, personal autonomy for every individual, rather than obedience to a leader, was central to the organization and ethics of Montagnais society. This lack of hierarchy, whether in the nuclear family or within the larger group, troubled the French who urged the Montagnais to appoint leaders and to put wives firmly under their husbands' control. Montagnais-Naskapi culture changed gradually over time, largely in response to pressure from European colonizers, but more isolated Montagnais groups retained large elements of respect for the autonomy of women as well as men at least until the middle of the twentieth century. Anthropologists' reminder of such alternatives to the dominant European form of social organization is instructive for historians who might be tempted to see universals in relationships that are, in fact, peculiar to a certain time and place.

During the sixteenth century, the St. Lawrence valley was the scene of French and English competition for furs, especially for beaver which was used in the manufacture of hats. Sporadic trade of furs between native peoples and European fishermen was old, possibly preceding Columbus's first voyage; for when Cartier sailed up the St. Lawrence in 1534, the people he met were familiar with European vessels, products, and interest in furs. By mid-century, ships were coming to the area for the sole purpose of trading, and during the latter part of the century several companies competed unsuccessfully for a monopoly of the trade.

In 1559, a permanent French trading post was established at Tadoussac, downriver from Quebec, chosen by Champlain to be the headquarters of New France and founded in 1608. Three Rivers, further up the St. Lawrence, was

†Mona Etienne and Eleanor Leacock, eds., *Women and Colonization. Anthropological Perspectives* (New York: Praeger, 1980): 25–41.

established in 1617. Champlain was welcomed by the Algonkins and Montagnais.[2] They saw in him an ally in their warfare with the Iroquois, who, armed with weapons obtained from the Dutch, were raiding north and west for furs. Champlain's main interest was in gaining access to the interior trade through making alliances with Huron and Algonkin middlemen. He agreed to join the Algonkins and Montagnais in a retaliatory expedition against the Iroquois and was led, in the process, to the "discovery" of Lake Champlain. His way west, however, was persistently blocked by friendly noncooperation on the part of both Algonkins and Hurons. They were not eager to relinquish a middleman status that yielded a steady supply of iron tools, utensils (especially copper kettles), clothing, grain, and dried fruit.

Meanwhile, the number of trading vessels sailing up the St. Lawrence increased. Champlain wrote in 1611 that the Indians waited until several arrived before bringing out their furs, so that competition for them would push up their price. An average annual harvest of 15,000 to 20,000 beaver in the first years of the seventeenth century rose to 80,000 by 1670. By that time, the Iroquois had defeated and virtually annihilated the Hurons, the French were about to cede Canada to the English, and the English "company of adventurers" was opening up another route to the west with its post, Rupert's House, on Hudson's Bay. As the interest in furs pushed west, the northern and eastern parts of the Labrador Peninsula remained relatively distant from its influence. Not until the nineteenth century did the Hudson's Bay Company begin setting up posts in the Labrador interior.

Several missionaries accompanied Champlain on his first trips, but missionizing did not begin in earnest until 1632, when Quebec, temporarily occupied by the English, had been regained by the French. The traders were interested in the Indians as a source of furs. By contrast the mission, under the able leadership of the Jesuit Paul Le Jeune was committed to converting them to Christianity, resocializing them, and transforming them into settled farmers, citizens of New France. The Jesuits first worked intensively with the Montagnais-Naskapi, but soon began to pin their hopes on the populous, agricultural Hurons. When the Iroquois decimation of the Hurons dashed these hopes, some Jesuits remained to work with their Montagnais converts, but the main missionizing drive was over.

What was the status of Montagnais-Naskapi women in the early seventeenth century when the French were establishing a foothold in the upper St. Lawrence valley? As is often the case, a look through accounts written at the time yields contrasting judgements. One may read that "women have great power . . . . A man may promise you something and if he does not keep his promise, he thinks he is sufficiently excused when he tells you that his wife did not wish him to do it."[3] Or one may read that women were virtual slaves.

> The women . . . besides the onerous role of bearing and rearing the
> children, also transport the game from the place where it has fallen; they
> are the hewers of wood and drawers of water; they make and repair the
> household utensils; they prepare food; they skin the game and prepare the
> hides like fullers; they sew garments; they catch fish and gather shellfish

for food; often they even hunt; they make the canoes, that is skiffs of marvelous rapidity, out of bark;[4] they set up the tents wherever and whenever they stop for the night — in short, the men concern themselves with nothing but the more laborious hunting and the waging of war . . . . Their wives are regarded and treated as slaves.[5]

Fortunately, the ethnohistorical record for the Montagnais-Naskapi is full enough so that contradictions between two statements such as these can be resolved. The view that the hard work of native American women made them slaves was commonly expressed by European observers who did not know personally the people about whom they were writing. The statement about female authority, however, was written by a man who knew the Montagnais-Naskapi well and recognized that women controlled their own work and made decisions accordingly. Paul Le Jeune, superior of the Jesuit mission at Quebec, had spent a winter in a Montagnais lodge in order to learn the language and understand the culture of the people he was supposed to convert and "civilize." He commented on the ease of relations between husbands and wives in Montagnais society, and explained that it followed from "the order which they maintain in their occupations," whereby "the women know what they are to do, and the men also; and one never meddles with the work of the other".[6] "Men leave the arrangement of the household to the women, without interfering with them; they cut and decide and give away as they please without making the husband angry. I have never seen my host ask a giddy young woman that he had with him what became of the provisions, although they were disappearing very fast".[7]

Le Jeune sought to change this state of affairs, and he reported to his superiors in Paris on his progress in "civilizing" the Montagnais-Naskapi through what became a fourfold program. First, he saw permanent settlement and the institution of formally recognized chiefly authority as basic. "Alas!" he wrote, "If someone could stop the wanderings of the Savages, and give authority to one of them to rule the others, we would see them converted and civilized in a short time".[8] Second, Le Jeune stressed the necessity of introducing the principle of punishment into Montagnais social relations. Third, central to Le Jeune's program was education of Montagnais-Naskapi children. "How necessary it is to educate the children of the Savages," he stated. "We shall have them at last if they see that we do not send them to France."[9]

> If we had a good building in Kebec, we would get more children through the very same means by which we despair of getting them. We have always thought that the excessive love the Savages bear their children would prevent our obtaining them. It will be through this very means that they will become our pupils; for, by having a few settled ones, who will attract and retain the others, the parents, who do not know what it is to refuse their children, will let them come without opposition. And, as they will be permitted during the first few years to have a great deal of liberty, they will become so accustomed to our food and our clothes, that they will have a horror of the Savages and their filth.[10]

As the quotation suggests, Montagnais-Naskapi culture posed a stumbling block for the Jesuits, in that the Montagnais did not practice corporeal punishment of children. Le Jeune complained, "The Savages prevent their instruction; they will not tolerate the chastisement of their children, whatever they may do, they permit only a simple reprimand".[11] Le Jeune's solution was to propose removing the children from their communities for schooling: "The reason why I would not like to take the children of one locality in that locality itself, but rather in some other place, is because these Barbarians cannot bear to have their children punished, even scolded, not being able to refuse anything to a crying child. They carry this to such an extent that upon the slightest pretext they would take them away from us, before they were educated".[12]

Fourth, essential to Le Jeune's entire program was the introduction of European family structure, with male authority, female fidelity, and the elimination of the right to divorce. Lecturing a man on the subject, Le Jeune said the man "was the master and that in France women do not rule their husbands".[13] The independence of Montagnais women posed continual problems for the Jesuits. Le Jeune decided that:

> . . . it is absolutely necessary to teach the girls as well as the boys, and that we shall do nothing or very little, unless some good household has the care of this sex; for the boys that we shall have reared in the knowledge of God, when they marry Savage girls or women accustomed to wandering in the woods will, as their husbands, be compelled to follow them and thus fall back into barbarism or to leave them, another evil full of danger.[14]

Le Jeune's account of his problems, successes, and failures in introducing hierarchical principles into the ordering of interpersonal relations among the Montagnais-Naskapi affords a clear record of the personal autonomy that was central to the structure and ethics of their society — and autonomy that applied as fully to women as to men.

Montagnais-Naskapi Economy and Decision Making

The Montagnais-Naskapi lived by hunting and trapping wild game — caribou, moose, beaver, bear, hare, porcupine and water fowl — by fishing, and by gathering wild berries and other vegetable foods. Like foraging peoples everywhere, they followed a regular pattern of seasonal movement according to the provenience of the foods on which they depended. The Montagnais with whom Le Jeune worked summered on the shores of the St. Lawrence River, where groups of several hundred people gathered to fish, socialize, and make and repair canoes, snowshoes, and other equipment. In the fall, groups of some 35 to 75 people separated out to ascend one or another of the rivers that emptied into the St. Lawrence. During the winter hunting season, these bands might split up into smaller groups in order to spread out over a wide area in search of game. However, they kept in touch with each other so that if some were short of food, they could turn to others for help.[15]

The smallest working unit was the group that lived together in a large conical lodge — some ten to twenty people, or, in Western terms, several nuclear families. In early times, as later, residential choices were probably flexible, and people moved about in accord both with personal likes and dislikes and with the need for keeping a reasonable balance in the working group between women and men and young and old. Upon marriage, however, a man ideally moved into his wife's lodge group.[16] Accordingly, mentions of a Montagnais man's family might include the man's wife's sister, or a son-in-law, or a father-in-law.[17] Yet three brothers and their wives shared the lodge in which Le Jeune lived. Le Jeune is silent about the relationships among the wives who, judging from hunting-group compositions in recent times, could easily have been sisters or parallel cousins.[18] In any case, Le Jeune's diary shows that the arrangement was not permanent.

Ethnographic evidence as well as the *Jesuit Relations* indicates that decisions about movements were made by the adult members of whatever group was involved. There is no question about women's importance in making such decisions. In fact, one recorder stated that "the choice of plans, of undertakings, of journeys, of winterings, lies in nearly every instance in the hands of the housewife".[19] Individuals might be chosen as spokespersons to mediate with the French, but such "chiefs" held no formal authority within the group. Le Jeune noted that "the Savages cannot endure in the least those who seem desirous of assuming superiority over the others; they place all virtue in a certain gentleness or apathy".[20]

> They imagine that they ought by right of birth, to enjoy the liberty of wild ass colts, rendering no homage to anyone whomsoever, except when they like. They have reproached me a hundred times because we fear our Captains, while they laugh at and make sport of theirs. All the authority of their chiefs is in his tongue's end; for he is powerful insofar as he is eloquent; and, even if he kills himself talking and haranguing, he will not be obeyed unless he pleases the Savages.[21]

Le Jeune was honest enough to state what he saw as the positive side of Montagnais egalitarianism:

> As they have neither political organization, nor office, nor dignities, nor any authority, for they only obey their Chief through good will toward him, therefore they never kill each other to acquire these honors. Also, as they are contented with a mere living, not one of them gives himself to the Devil to acquire wealth.[22]

In his final judgement, however, Le Jeune remained bound by his culture and his missionizing commitment: "I would not dare assert that I have seen one act of real moral virtue in a Savage. They have nothing but their own pleasure and satisfaction in view".[23]

The Jesuit Program for Changing Montagnais Marriage

As indicated above, Le Jeune's original assumption — that he could win the Montagnais to Christianity through converting the men — changed when he learned how far Montagnais family structure was from that of the French. He realized that he would have to give special attention to women as well as men if he was to eliminate the Montagnais' unquestioned acceptance of divorce at the desire of either partner, of polygyny, and of sexual freedom after marriage.

"The young people do not think that they can persevere in the state of matrimony with a bad wife or a bad husband," Le Jeune wrote. "They wish to be free and to be able to divorce the consort if they do not love each other".[24] And several years later: "The inconstancy of marriages and the facility with which they divorce each other, are a great obstacle to the Faith of Jesus Christ. We do not dare baptize the young people because experience teaches us that the custom of abandoning a disagreeable wife or husband has a strong hold on them".[25]

Polygamy was another right that women as well as men took for granted: "Since I have been preaching among them that a man should not have more than one wife, I have not been well received by the women; for, since they are more numerous than the men, if a man can only marry one of them, the others will have to suffer. Therefore this doctrine is not according to their liking."[26] And as for the full acceptance of sexual freedom for both women and men, no citation can be more telling of the gulf between French and Montagnais society than Le Jeune's rendition of a Montagnais rebuff.

> I told him that it was not honorable for a woman to love any one else except her husband, and that this evil being among them, he himself was not sure that his son, who was there present, was his son. He replied, "Thou hast no sense. You French people love only your own children; but we all love all the children of our tribe." I began to laugh, seeing that he philosophized in horse and mule fashion.[27]

Converts to Christianity wrestled with the dilemmas posed by the French faith. A recently married young man wished to be faithful to his wife, but felt himself "inclined toward infidelity." Deeply disturbed by his criminal wish, he entreated to be imprisoned or publicly flogged. When his request was refused, "He slips into a room near the Chapel and, with a rope that he finds, he beats himself so hard all over the body that the noise reaches the ears of the Father, who runs in and forbids so severe a penance".[28] The adoption of severe punitiveness both towards the self and others was reported by Le Jeune.

> The most zealous Christians met during the winter, unknown to us, in order to confer together upon the means of keeping themselves in the faith. One of them, in making an address, said that he thought more highly of prayers than of life, and that he would rather die than give them up. Another said that he wished he might be punished and chastised in case he forfeited the word he had given to God. A third claimed that he who should fall into any error must be put into prison and made to fast for four days without eating or drinking. The acts of justice that they see from time to time exercised on delinquents give them these ideas.[29]

Upon hearing the news, the fathers informed the converts that "they proceeded with too much severity; that mildness had more power over souls than force." The zealots argued, however, that the first among them who commited a fault, "however inconsiderable, should suffer imprisonment and fasting." This so frightened "the weak," Le Jeune continued, that "the report spread among the unbelievers that the Christian Savages had chains and bonds all ready to bind the refractory." Le Jeune concluded, "Some pagans told us they were risking the ruin of everything and that the Savages would kill one another. All this consoled us much, for we took pleasure in seeing the union of the Christians; it is much easier to temper fervor than it is to kindle it".[30]

Women and children alike suffered punishment at the hands of converts. "A young Christian, getting into a passion, beat his wife, who had insolently provoked him," Le Jeune wrote. The man then repented of his sin and went to the chapel to pray to God for mercy. Le Jeune had the couple brought to him. "They were properly reprimanded," he reported, "especially the woman, who was more guilty than her husband".[31] As for the children,

> they are all in an incredible state of satisfaction at having embraced the
> Faith. "We punish the disobedient" said they. A young girl who would
> not go to the nets, where her father sent her, was two days without food as
> a punishment for her disobedience. Two boys, who came late to prayers in
> the morning were punished by having a handful of hot cinders thrown
> upon their heads with threats of greater chastisement in case the offenses
> were repeated.[32]

Several Christians even had a drunken, young, pagan relative thrown into prison — in Le Jeune's view, "an act fit to astonish all those who know the customs of the Savages, who cannot endure that any one should touch their kinsmen; but God has more power than nature".[33]

In 1640, eight years after Le Jeune's arrival in New France and the setting up of a Jesuit mission, the governor called together a group of influential Montagnais men, and "having recommended to the Christians constance in their marriages — he gave them to understand that it would be well if they should elect some chiefs to govern them".[34] Accordingly, the Montagnais sought advice from the Jesuits, who supervised the election of three captains. The men then "resolved to call together the women, to urge them to be instructed and to receive holy Baptism." The women were used to holding councils of their own to deal with matters of concern to them and reported surprise at being lectured to by the men.

> Yesterday the men summoned us to a council, but the first time that
> women have ever entered one; but they treated us so rudely that we were
> greatly astonished. "It is you women," they said to us, "who keep the
> Demons among us; you do not urge to be baptized . . . . [W]hen you pass
> before the cross you never salute it, you wish to be independent. Now
> know that you will obey your husbands and you young people know that
> you will obey your parents, and our captains and if any fail to do so, we
> will give them nothing to eat.[35]

Women's responses ranged from zealous compliance to rebelliousness. An incident illustrating compliance with a husband's wishes, and suggesting the internalization of guilt, occurred when a Christian woman joined some "games or public recreation" of which her husband did not approve.

> Having returned, her husband said to her, "If I were not a Christian, I
> would tell you that, if you did not care for me you should seek another
> husband to whom you would render more obedience; but having promised
> God not to leave you until death, I cannot speak to you thus, although
> you have offended me." This poor woman asked his forgiveness, without
> delay, and on the following morning came to see the Father who had

baptized her, and said to him, "My Father, I have offended God, I have not obeyed my husband; my heart is sad; I greatly desire to make my confession of this".[36]

Other women continued to have lovers, to solicit married men to take a second wife, and to defy or leave their husbands. One convert complained, "My wife is always angry; I fear that the Demons she keeps in my cabin are perverting the good that I received in holy Baptism." Le Jeune wrote of this man,

> Another time his wife aimed a knife at his thigh, and he, evading the blow, had only his robe injured, in which this Megera made a great slash. Thereupon he came to us; meeting some Savages on the way, he began to laugh. "See," said he, "the anger of her who considers me her servant; she thought she would be able to irritate me, but I have more power over myself than to fall into passion at the anger of a woman."

Le Jeune added, "It is strange what Enemies the Savages are of anger, and how this sin shocks them," and continued,

> I know not what this simple man has done to win her over to God. "If thou wilt believe," he said to her, "I will love thee above all things; I will wait upon thee in all they needs, I will even perform the little duties that the women do, I will go for water and wood; I will love thee more than myself." He pinched his arm and said to her, "Dost thou see this flesh? I do not love it; it is God whom I love, and those who believe in him. If thou are not willing to obey him thou must go away from me; for I cannot love those who do not love God."
> His wife derided him: "Dost thou not see that we are all dying since they told us to pray to God? Where are thy relatives? Where are mine? The most of them are dead. It is no longer a time to believe".[37]

Another particularly revealing incident offers an important comment on Montagnais ethics, and indicates the growing distance between the missionized Montagnais, with their acceptance of corporeal punishment, and the unconverted. A Jesuit called some "chief men" together and, after commending them on putting a stop to "the disorderly conduct that occasionally occurred among them," expressed astonishment at their permitting a young baptized woman to live apart from her husband. The captain responsible for her replied that "he had tried all sorts of means to make her return to her duty and that his trouble had been in vain; that he would, nevertheless, make another effort." The Jesuit Father counseled him to consult his people and decide upon what was to be done for such disobedience. "They all decided upon harsh measures. 'Good advice,' they said, 'has not brought her to her senses; a prison will do so.' Two Captains were ordered to take her to Kebec and . . . have her put in a dungeon." The woman fled, but they caught her and tied her to take her by canoe to Kebec. At this

> some Pagan young men, observing this violence, of which the Savages have a horror, and which is more remote from their customs than Heaven is from Earth, made use of threats, declaring that they would kill any one who laid a hand on the woman. But the Captain and his people, who were Christians, boldly replied that there was nothing that they would not do

or endure, in order to secure obedience to God. Such resolution silenced the infidels.

To avoid being imprisoned, the woman "humbly begged to be taken back to Saint Joseph, promising thence forward she would be more obedient." Le Jeune stated,

> Such acts of justice cause no surprise in France, because it is usual there to proceed in that manner. But, among these peoples . . . where everyone considers himself from birth, as free as the wild animals that roam in their great forest . . . it is a marvel, or rather a miracle, to see a peremptory command obeyed, or any act of severity or justice performed.
> Some Savages, having heard that in France, malefactors are put to death, have often reproached us, saying that we were cruel — that we killed our own countrymen; that we had no sense. They asked us whether the relatives of those who were condemned to death did not seek vengeance. The Infidels still have the same ideas; but the Christians are learning, more and more, the importance of exercising Justice.[38]

Shortly afterwards, another act of violence towards a woman again threatened to provoke conflict between Christian and "pagan" Montagnais, and again called for commendation on the part of the recorder (in this instance, not Le Jeune, but Bartholemy Vimont). The Christian relatives of a young woman agreed in family council to beat her for speaking to a suitor against her parents' wishes: "We are taught that God loves obedience. We see the French practicing it; they have such a regard for that virtue that, if any one of them fail in it, he is punished. Parents chastise their own children, and masters their servants."

One of the relatives beat the girl and lectured other girls who had gathered: "This is the first punishment by beating that we have inflicted upon anyone of our Nation. We are resolved to continue it, if any one among us should be disobedient." Vimont commented:

> During the previous year the new Christians had a Savage put in prison. This year they have done more, for this last punishment seems to me very severe to be the first. Those who know the freedom and independence of these peoples, and the horror they have of restraint or bondage, will say that a slight touch of Heaven and a little grace are stronger and more powerful than the cannons and arms of kings and monarchs, which could not subdue them.

The angry suitor appealed to his father, who threatened the Christian Indians. They defended their action, saying this his son had not been affronted and that he should be satisfied with the girl's punishment. At this, Governor Montmagny had the suitor called in and, through an interpreter, warned the young man to be careful, saying he would consider any attack on the Christian Indians to be a personal attack upon him.[39]

Long-Range Impact of the Jesuit Program

One must ask how fairly the *Jesuit Relations* can be used to evaluate the success of the Jesuit program for conversion and resocialization of the Montagnais-Naskapi. After all, the Jesuit fathers were, in effect, soliciting continued support for their work, and they spent many pages describing the piety of their converts. Furthermore, they drew heavily on second-hand reports from adherents to the mission who doubtless presented themselves in a favorable light when repeating conversations and describing incidents. However, as seen by quotations above, both Jesuits and converts reported fully and convincingly on the views and actions of the unconverted. There is no reason to doubt the evidence the *Relations* offer of the conflicting ideologies that caused profound social disruption for the group as a whole and deep psychological turmoil for those individuals, both women and men, who made an often agonizing decision to give up traditional beliefs and practices and adhere to new codes of conduct and commitment. Therefore, although they do not reveal the actual extent of conversion that took place among the Montagnais-Naskapi during the seventeenth century, the *Jesuit Relations* document in detail what is more significant: the nature of responses to the Jesuit program, ranging from zealous dedication, through formal conversion, that might well involve backsliding, to indifference, and finally, to active hostility.

With respect to female-male relations, premarital chastity, male courtship, monogamy, and marital fidelity became accepted as ideal behavioral norms by dedicated converts. In 1639, Le Jeune wrote of the "evil custom" whereby a man who was courting a woman would go to her to make love at night, and he advised the girls to refer their suitors to the Jesuits.[40] Several years later Vimont reported that an old woman, "touched by the fear of God," gave the names of young unmarried lovers, who protested that such "suits of marriage" were "customary among them." The young people were lectured by their elders to "declare your affections to your parents; take their advice and that of the Father . . . . Make your visits by day and not by night; the faith and the prayer forbid this custom."[41] Some people, Vimont reported, had already adopted a new form of courtship, whereby a suitor would send a girl a bark painting of a young couple "holding each other by the hand, in the position that they assume in Church when they get married." A girl who was rejecting her suitor would send the drawing back.[42]

In keeping with the reciprocity of Montagnais-Naskapi female-male relations, converted men accepted the same standards as were enjoined on women. Le Jeune wrote that he had heard on good authority "that some shameless women, who have approached some men at night and solicited them to do evil in secret, received for answer only these words: "I believe in God, I pray to him every day; he forbids such actions, I cannot commit them".[43] Nor would a "worthy captain" take a second wife, even when solicited by the woman herself, but answered, "You come too late, I have given my word to God I cannot gainsay it. I will obey him; I have said to him, 'I will obey thee' and I will do it".[44]

The influence, direct and indirect, of formulating such ideals as these was enhanced by the Jesuit work with children. Le Jeune wrote,

> We have done so much for these poor unbelievers that they have given us some of their daughters, which seems to me an act of God . . . . These little girls are dressed in the French fashion; they care no more for the Savages than if they did not belong to their Nation. Nevertheless, in order to wean them from their native customs, and to give them an opportunity

of learning the French language, virtue and manners, that they may afterwards assist their countrywomen, we have decided to send two or three to France, to have them kept and taught in the house of hospital nuns . . . . Oh if we could only send a certain one who is to remain in the house of which I have spoken . . . . The child has nothing savage about her except her appearance and color; her sweetness, her docility, her modesty, her obedience, would cause her to pass for a wellborn French girl, fully susceptible of education.

Le Jeune followed this entry with a reference to his wish for a building in Quebec, where three classes could be lodged, "the first of little French children, of whom there will be perhaps twenty or thirty Pupils; the second, of Hurons; the third, of Montagnes".[45]

For their part, the Montagnais expressed resentment that their presentation of children to the French was not reciprocated. A "captain" complained "One does not see anything else but little Savages in the houses of the French; there are little boys there and little girls, — what more do you want? . . . You are continually asking for our children, and you do not give yours; I do not know any family among us which keeps a Frenchman with it".[46]

The contrast between the Montagnais attitude towards sharing children and that of the French was expressed by Le Jeune's statement that "they think they are doing you some great favor in giving you their children to instruct, feed and dress".[47] Perhaps no incident in the *Relations* more poignantly reveals the cultural distance to be spanned by Montagnais converts than that in which a French drummer boy hit a Montagnais with his drumstick, drawing blood. The Montagnais onlookers took offense, saying, "Behold, one of thy people has wounded one of ours; thou knowest our custom well; give us presents for this wound." The French interpreter countered, "Thou knowest our custom; when any of our number does wrong, we punish him. This child has wounded one of your people; he shall be whipped at once in thy presence." When the Montagnais saw the French were in earnest about whipping the boy,

> they began to pray for his pardon, alleging he was only a child, that he had no mind, that he did not know what he was doing; but as our people were nevertheless going to punish him, one of the Savages stripped himself entirely, threw his blanket over the child and cried out to him who was going to do the whipping; "Strike me if thou wilt, but thou shalt not strike him," And thus the little one escaped.[48]

This incident took place in 1633. How was it possible that scarcely ten years later, adults could be beating, withholding food from, and even, if the report is accurate, doing such things as throwing hot ashes on children and youths? Above, I have referred to the punitiveness toward the self and others that accompanied the often tormented attempt on the part of converts to reject a familiar set of values and replace it with another. This psychological response is familiar. To say this, however, merely presses the next question: Why did some Montagnais feel so strongly impelled to make this attempt? The answer is that the Jesuits and their teachings arrived in New France a full century after the economic basis for unquestioned cooperation, reciprocity, and respect for individual autonomy began to be undercut by the trading of furs for European goods. On the basis of new economic ties, some Montagnais-Naskapi were interested in attaching themselves to the mission station and the new European settlement, thereby availing themselves of the resources these offered. By the same token, some were prepared to accept the beliefs and ritual practices of the newcomers, and to adopt — or attempt to adopt — new standards of conduct.

Elsewhere, I have documented the process whereby the stockpiling of furs for future return, to be acquired when the trading ships arrived, contradicted the principle of total sharing based on subsistence hunting, fishing, and gathering.[49] The process has subsequently been well described for the Canadian sub-Arctic generally, and it has been pointed out that parallel processes are involved when a horticultural people becomes involved in exchange relations with a market economy.[50]

At the same time that the fur trade was undercutting the foundation for Montagnais-Naskapi values and interpersonal ethics, the terrible scourge of epidemic disease, the escalation (or introduction) of warfare, and the delusion of relief from anxiety offered by alcohol were also undermining Montagnais-Naskapi self-assurance. Alfred Goldsworthy Bailey[51] has described the effects of these developments in a review of the conflict between European and eastern Algonkian cultures during the sixteenth and seventeenth centuries. Fear of disease, particularly smallpox which raged in the decade after the priests' arrival, was only equaled by fear of the Iroquois. The prolonged and intricate torture of Iroquois prisoners, into which women entered with even more zeal than men, was a grim expression of profound fearfulness and anger. Alcohol, which temporarily elated the spirits, led to fights around the European settlement; in 1664 there is reference to a case of rape committed under its influence.[52]

This is not to say, however, that Montagnais-Naskapi society as a whole was thoroughly disrupted. The violence that occurred around the European settlement contrasts not only with the friendliness, gaiety, and lack of quarreling that Le Jeune described during the winter he spent in the interior in 1633–34, but also with the general cooperativeness and good will — albeit laced with raucous banter and teasing — that characterized Montagnais-Naskapi life in later centuries in the rest of the Labrador Peninsula. Quebec was, after all, a gateway to the North American interior, and fur-trading posts and mission stations pushed ever westward. The nonracist policy of building a French colony in part with resocialized Indians was abandoned and replaced by a hardening color line. In time, all Montagnais-Naskapi became Catholic, but without the close supervision of the Jesuits, they retained established religious practices and added Catholic sacraments and prayer. During the summer of 1951, the "shaking-tent rite," in which a religious practitioner converses with the gods, both gaining useful information and entertaining an audience in the process, was still being practised in eastern Labrador.

The pace of change in most of the Labrador Peninsula was slow, as Indians living far from centers of early settlement and trade gradually became drawn into a fur-trapping economy. In the summer of 1950, I was able to document the final stages of transition in southeastern Labrador, at a time when the next major change was about to transform life for French and English fishermen and fur-trappers as well as Montagnais-Naskapi hunter-trappers; a railroad was being built into a huge iron mine deep in the north-central part of the peninsula. When I was there, conditions in the north woods were still such that the traditional Montagnais-Naskapi ethic of cooperativeness, tolerance, and nonpunitiveness remained strong.

What about the relations between women and men? As in seventeenth-century accounts, one can still find contrasting judgements. Burgesse has written that:

> labour is fairly equitably divided between the sexes under the economic system of the Montagnais. Each sex has it own particular duties but, within certain limits, the divisions between the types of work performed are not rigid. A man would not consider it beneath his dignity to assist his wife in what are ordinarily considered duties peculiar to the woman. Also, women are often enough to be seen performing tasks which are usually done by men. On being questioned in regard to this aspect of their economics, the Montagnais invariably reply that, since marriage is an union of co-equal partners for mutual benefit, it is the duty of the husband to assist his wife in the performance of her labors. Similarly, it is the duty of the wife to aid the husband . . . .
>
> The Montagnais woman is far from being a drudge. Instead she is a respected member of the tribe whose worth is well appreciated and whose advice and counsel is listened to and, more often than not, accepted and acted upon by her husband.[53]

Earlier, and by contrast, Turner had written:

> The sexes have their special labors. Women perform the drudgery and bring home the food slain by their husbands, fetching wood and water, tanning the skins, and making them into clothing. The labor of erecting the tents and hauling the sleds when on their journey during the winter falls upon them, and, in fact, they perform the greater part of the manual labor. They are considered inferior to men, and in their social life they soon show the effects of the hardships they undergo.[54]

One could take these statements at face value as reflecting differences between two Montagnais-Naskapi bands, for the first statement refers to the southerly Lake St. John people and the second to the Ungava people of the north. However, the continuation of Turner's account reveals realities of Ungava life that contradict his formal statement.

> An amusing incident occurred within a stone's throw of Fort Chimo. An Indian had his clothes stripped from him by his enraged wife. She then took the tent from the poles, leaving him naked. She took their property to the canoe, which she paddled several miles upstream. He followed along the bank until she relented, whereupon their former relations were resumed, as though nothing had disturbed the harmony of their life. The man was so severely plagued by his comrades that for many days he scarcely showed his head out of the tent.[55]

Translating the incident into the terms of political economy, women retained control over the products of their labor. These were not alienated, and women's production of clothing, shelter, and canoe covering gave them concomitant practical power and influence; despite formal statements of male dominance that might be elicited by outsiders. In northern Labrador in the late nineteenth century, dependence on trading furs for food, clothing, and equipment was only beginning. Band cohesion was still strong, based on the sharing of meat, fish, and other necessities and on the reciprocal exchange of goods and services between women and men.

By the middle of this century, the economic balance had tipped in favor of ultimate dependence upon the fur trade (and in many cases, wage labor) throughout the entire Labrador Peninsula. The Montagnais-Naskapi lived in nuclear family units largely supported by the husband and father's wages or take from the trap line. Nonetheless, the resources of the land were still directly used, were still available to anyone, were acquired cooperatively insofar as it was most practical, and were shared. Furthermore, partly through their own desire and partly in accord with the racist structure of Western society, the Montagnais-Naskapi maintained their status as a semi-autonomous people and were not separated into an elite minority versus a majority of marginal workers. Thus, a strong respect for individual autonomy and an extreme sensitivity to the feelings of others when decisions were to be made went with a continuing emphasis on generosity and cooperativeness, which applied to relations between as well as within the sexes.

In my own experience living in a Montagnais-Naskapi camp, I noted a quality of respectfulness between women and men that fits Burgesse's characterization. I also observed such behavior as an ease of men with children, who would take over responsibility even for infants when it was called for, with a spontaneity and casual competence that in our culture would be described as "maternal". Nonetheless, men were "superior" in ways commonly alluded to in anthropological literature. The few shamans who still practised their art (or admitted practicing it to an outsider) were men; band chiefs were men; and patrilocality was both an ideal and statistically more common among newlyweds than matrilocality. In short, Montagnais-Naskapi practice at this time fitted what is considered in the anthropological literature to be usual for people who live (or have recently lived) by direct acquisition and use of wild products: strongly egalitarian, but with an edge in favor of male authority and influence.

Seventeenth-century accounts, however, referred to female shamans who might become powerful.[56] So-called "outside chiefs," formally elected according to government protocol to mediate with white society, had no more influence within the group than their individual attributes would call for;[57] and matrilocality had only recently given way to patrilocal postmarital residence.[58] As markedly different as Montagnais-Naskapi culture continued to be from Western culture, the ethnohistorical record makes clear that it had been constantly restructuring itself to fit new situations and that the status of women, although still relatively high, had clearly changed.

Notes

1. This article is based in large part on a paper written in collaboration with Jacqueline Goodman (Eleanor Leacock and Jacqueline Goodman, "Montagnais Marriage and the Jesuits in the Seventeenth Century: Incidents from the Relations of Paul le Jeune," *Western Canadian Journal of Anthropology* 6, 3

(1976): 77–91). An ethnohistorical summary of Montagnais-Naskapi culture in the seventeenth century can be found in Eleanor Leacock, "The Montagnais-Naskapi of the Seventeenth Century: Social Relations and Attitudes, from the Relations of Paul le Jeune" in *Handbook of North American Indians* vol. 6 *Subarctic,* edited by June Helm (Washington: Smithsonian Institute, 1981).

2. The anthropological term for the native population of the Labrador Peninsula, exclusive of the Eskimo, is "Montagnais-Naskapi." At times I shall use the simpler "Montagnais," a name applied by the French to the various groups that summered on the north shore of the St. Lawrence river. Like the Algonkins, the Montagnais are an Algonkian-speaking people.

3. R.G. Thwaites, ed., *The Jesuit Relations and Allied Documents,* 71 vols. (Cleveland: Burrows Brothers Co., 1906), 5: 179.

4. Actually, men usually made canoe frames, and women covered them, though either sex could do both if necessary.

5. Thwaites, *The Jesuit Relations,* 2: 77.

6. Ibid., 5: 133.

7. Ibid., 6: 233.

8. Ibid., 12: 169.

9. Ibid., 5: 137.

10. Ibid., 9: 103.

11. Ibid., 5: 197.

12. Ibid., 6: 153–55.

13. Ibid., 5: 179.

14. Ibid., 5: 145.

15. Eleanor Leacock, "The Montagnais-Naskapi Band" in *Contributions to Anthropology: Band Societies,* edited by David Damas, National Museums of Canada Bulletin 228 (Ottawa: Queen's Printer, 1969).

16. Thwaites, *The Jesuit Relations,* 31: 169.

17. Ibid., 6: 125, 9: 33, 14: 143–45.

18. Parallel cousins are the children of two sisters or two brothers (and their spouses). Children of a brother or sister (and their spouses) are called "cross-cousins." As is common in many kin-based societies, the Montagnais-Naskapi terms for parallel cousins were the same as for siblings, while the terms for cross-cousins, who were desirable marriage partners, connoted something like "sweetheart" (William Duncan Strong, "Cross-cousin Marriage and the Culture of the Northeastern Algonkian," *American Anthropologist* 31: 277–88).

19. Thwaites, *The Jesuit Relations,* 68: 93.

20. Ibid., 16: 165.

21. Ibid., 6: 243.

22. Ibid., 6: 231.

23. Ibid., 6: 239–41.

24. Ibid., 16: 41.

25. Ibid., 22: 229.

26. Ibid., 12: 165.

27. Ibid., 6: 255.

28. Ibid., 22: 67.

29. Ibid., 20: 143.

30. Ibid.

31. Ibid., 18: 155.

32. Ibid., 18: 171.

33. Ibid., 20: 153.

34. Ibid., 18: 99.

35. Ibid., 18: 107.

36. Ibid., 18: 35.

37. Ibid., 20: 195–97.

38. Ibid., 22: 81–85.

39. Ibid., 22: 115–27.

40. Ibid., 16: 61.

41. Ibid., 24: 139.

42. Ibid., 22: 71.

43. Ibid., 16: 61.

44. Ibid., 16: 145.

45. Ibid., 9: 103.

46. Ibid., 9: 233.

47. Ibid., 5: 197.

48. Ibid., 5: 219.

49. Eleanor Leacock, "The Montagnais 'Hunting Territory' and the Fur Trade", *American Anthropological Association Memoirs* 78 (1954).

50. Robert F. Murphy and Julian H. Steward, "Tappers and Trappers: Parallel Processes in Acculturation," *Economic Development and Cultural Change* 4 (1955): 335–55.

51. Alfred Goldsworthy Bailey, *The Conflict of European and Eastern Algonkian Cultures, 1504–1700* (Toronto: University of Toronto Press, 1969).

52. Thwaites, *The Jesuit Relations*, 48: 227.

53. J. Allan Burgesse, "The Woman and the Child Among the Lac-St-Jean Montagnais," *Primitive Man* 17, 102: 4–7.

54. Lucien Turner, *Ethnology of the Ungava District, Hudson Bay Territory*, 11th Annual Report, Bureau of American Ethnology, 1894, 271.

55. Ibid.

56. Thwaites, *The Jesuit Relations*, 6: 61, 14: 183.

57. Eleanor Leacock, "Status Among the Montagnais-Naskapi of Labrador," *Ethnohistory* 5 (1958): 200–9.

58. Eleanor Leacock, "Matrilocality in a Simple Hunting Economy (Montagnais-Naskapi)," *Southwestern Journal of Anthropology* 11 (1955): 31–47.

NEW FRANCE: LES FEMMES FAVORISÉES[†]

JAN NOEL

In contrast to other periods of Canadian history, New France has always appeared well populated with imposing female figures. Jeanne Mance, Marguerite Bourgeoys, Madeleine Verchères, and Mme de la Tour, to name only a few, stand at the centre of the religious, economic, political, and military life of the colony. Such a remarkable phenomenon has not entirely escaped notice but rarely has New France itself been systematically interpreted as providing a promising environment for female talent. In a provocative synthesis of published materials Jan Noel attributes women's prominence directly to the flexibility of ancien régime *thinking on sex roles, the logic of colonial demography, and the pressure of economic necessity. Women benefited, as they did in Montagnais-Naskapi society, from the close integration of private and public life. Family, church, and state were intimately, but atypically, connected in ways that offered women, even in comparison to other colonial regimes in North America, maximum opportunity to demonstrate ability and exercise authority.*

This propitious conjunction of influences did not survive the nineteenth century intact. British North America saw women constrained by a middle-class ideology that stressed their domestic responsibilities, by a greater, more diverse and more sexually balanced population, and by the development of a more mature economy in which household and labour force were more distinct and in which labour shortages could rarely be used to female advantage. The very sources that Noel cites, however, suggest that the memory of a time when women too "strutted through life" did not entirely disappear from popular consciousness. In a later day it would help inspire, both in French and English Canada, women's claims to a more prominent role in every part of their community.

> You constantly behold, with renewed astonishment, women in the very depths of indigence and want, perfectly instructed in their religion, ignorant of nothing that they should know to employ themselves usefully in their families and who, by their manners, their manner of expressing themselves and their politeness, are not inferior to the most carefully educated among us.[1]

> Women surpass men in beauty, vivaciousness, cheerfulness and sprightliness; they are coquettish and elegant and prefer Europeans to the local folk. Gentle and polite manners are common, even in the countryside.[2]

> . . . the women there are very pleasant but extremely proud.[3]

> . . . they are witty, which affords them superiority over men in almost all circumstances.[4]

Many a man, observing the women of New France, was struck by the advantages they possessed in education, cultivation, and that quality called *esprit* or wit. Even an unsympathetic observer of colonial society, such as the French

---

†Alison Prentice and Susan Mann Trofimenkoff, eds. *The Neglected Majority. Essays in Canadian Women's History*, vol. 2 (Toronto: McClelland and Stewart, 1985): 18–40.

military officer Franquet, who visited New France in 1752–53, admitted that its women "surpass men in wit; generally they all have a great deal of it and speak in refined French, without the least accent. They also like finery, are pretty, generous and even genteel."[5] He notes, albeit with disapproval, that women very commonly aspired to stations above those to which they were born.[6] The Swedish naturalist Peter Kalm, who deplored the inadequate housekeeping of Canadian women, nevertheless admired their refinement.[7]

Those for whom history is an exercise in statistics have taught us caution in accepting the accounts of travellers, which are often highly subjective. However, the consensus (particularly that of seasoned observers such as Charlevoix and Kalm) on the superior education and wit of women in New France suggests that their views are founded on something more than natural male proclivity toward *la différence*. Moreover, historians' accounts of society in New France offer considerable evidence that women did indeed enjoy an unusually privileged position in that colony. It is difficult to think of another colony or country in which women founders showed such important leadership — not just in the usual tending of families and farms but in arranging financing, immigration, and defences that played a major role in the colony's survival. It is unusual for girls to receive a primary education better than that of the boys — as many evidently did in New France. One is also struck by the initiative of *canadiennes* in business and commerce. In sum, with respect to their education, their range and freedom of action, women in New France seem in many ways to compare favourably with their contemporaries in France and New England, and certainly with the Victorians who came after them.

Two cautions are in order. First, to arrive at a full appreciation of the position of women in New France would require detailed comparisons with their contemporaries in other Western countries and colonies. The study of *ancien régime* businesswomen, in particular, is a nascent enterprise. In this paper some twenty outstanding figures in business and politics will be examined and hypotheses put forward about what facilitated their rise to positions of influence. To what degree these women were outstanding in the context of their times one cannot yet say with precision. Second, it is not intended to portray New France as some sort of utopia for women. Women, like men, suffered from disease, privation, class inequalities, and the perennial scourge of war. There were also women's particular hardships, such as the dangers of childbirth and the difficulties of assuming double duty when the men were away. A definitive study of women in New France, which will plumb the primary sources and range the continents for useful comparisons, remains to be made. The purpose of this paper is to marshal the fairly extensive evidence that can be found in published works on New France in support of the thesis that women there enjoyed a relatively privileged position, and to discuss why they might have done so.

Why did the women of New France assume leadership positions? How did they acquire a superior education? How did they come to be involved in commerce? There is no single answer. Three separate elements help account for the situation. First, as studies of Western Europe under the *ancien régime* have indicated, ideas about women's roles were surprisingly flexible and varied at the time New France was founded. Second, the particular demographic configuration of the colony gave female immigrants a number of advantages not available to their counterparts in Europe. Third, the colonial economy, with its heavy emphasis on war and the fur trade, seems to have presented women with a special set of opportunities. Thus, as we shall see, the French cultural heritage and demographic and economic conditions in the colony combined to create the situation that so impressed contemporary observers.

Women and the Family under the *Ancien Régime*

The notion of "woman's place" or "women's role," popular with nineteenth-century commentators, suggests a degree of homogeneity inappropriate to the seventeenth century. It is true that on a formal ideological level men enjoyed the dominant position. This can be seen in the marriage laws, which everywhere made it a wife's duty to follow her husband to whatever dwelling place he chose.[8] In 1650, the men of Montreal were advised by Governor Maisonneuve that they were in fact responsible for the misdemeanours of their wives since "the law establishes their dominion over their wives."[9] Under ordinary circumstances the father was captain of the family hierarchy.[10] Yet, it is clear that this formal male authority in both economic and domestic life was not always exercised. Of early seventeenth-century France we are told that

> if the masculine pre-eminence has lost none of its prestige, if it has not had to defend itself against any theoretical claim . . . it has often had to . . . be content with appearances and abandon, in the face of expediency and public opinion, the substance of its claims.[11]

The idea of separate male and female spheres lacked the clear definition it later acquired. This is in part related to the lack of communication and standardization characteristic of the *ancien régime* — along sexual lines or any other. Generalizations about women are riddled with exceptions. Contradicting the idea of female inferiority, for example, were the semi-matriarchal system in the Basque country and the linen workers' guild, in which a 1645 statute prevented a worker's husband from engaging in occupations unrelated to his wife's business, for which he often served as salesman or partner. More important, because it affected a larger group, was the fact that noblewomen were frequently exempt from legal handicaps affecting other women.[12]

One generalization, however, applies to all women of the *ancien régime*. They were not relegated to the private, domestic sphere of human activity because that sphere did not exist. Western Europeans had not yet learned to separate public and private life. As Philippe Ariès points out in his study of childhood, the private home, in which parents and children constitute a distinct unit, is a relatively recent development. In early modern Europe most of domestic life was lived in the company of all sorts of outsiders. Manor houses, where all the rooms interconnect with one another, show the lack of emphasis placed on privacy. Here, as in peasant dwellings, there were often no specialized rooms for sleeping, eating, working, or receiving visitors; all were more or less public activities performed with a throng of servants, children, relatives, clerics, apprentices, and clients in attendance. Moliere's comedies illustrate the familiarity of servants with their masters. Masters, maids, and valets slept in the same room and servants discussed their masters' lives quite openly.[13]

Though familiar with their servants, people were less so with their children. They did not dote on infants to the extent that parents do today. It may have been, as some writers have suggested, that there was little point in growing attached to a fragile being so very apt, in those centuries, to be borne away by accident or disease. These unsentimental families of all ranks sent their children out to apprentice or serve in other people's homes. This was considered important as a basic education.[14] It has been estimated that the majority of Western European children passed part of their childhood living in some household other than their natal one.[15] Mothers of these children — reaching down, in the town, as far as the artisan class — might send their infants out to nursemaids and have very little to do with their physical maintenance.[16]

This lack of a clearly defined "private" realm relates vitally to the history of women, since this was precisely the sphere they later were to inhabit.[17] Therefore it is important to focus on their place in the pre-private world. To understand women in New France one first must pass through that antechamber which Peter Laslett appropriately calls "the world we have lost." Its notions of sexuality and of the family apply to France and New France alike.

In this public world people had not yet learned to be private about their bodily functions, especially about their sexuality. For aid with their toilette, noblewomen did not blush to employ *hommes de chambre* rather than maids. The door of the bed-chamber stood ajar, if not absolutely open. Its inhabitants, proud of their fecundity, grinned out from under the bedclothes at their visitors. Newlyweds customarily received bedside guests.[18] The mother of Louis XIV held court and chatted with visitors while labouring to bring *le Roi Soleil* into light of day. Humbler village women kept lesser court among the little crowd of neighbours who attended the midwife's efforts.[19] On the other side of the ocean, Franquet, arriving at Trois-Rivières in 1753, enjoyed the hospitality of Madame Rigaud de Vaudreuil who, feeling poorly, apparently received her visitors at bedside; farther west, he shared a bedroom with a married couple at Fort St. Jean.[20] From the seventeenth century to the colony's last days, clerics thundered more or less futilely against the *décolletage* of the *élite*.[21] Lesser folk leaned toward short skirts[22] and boisterous public discussion of impotent husbands.[23] Rape cases also reveal a rather matter-of-fact attitude. Courts stressed monetary compensation for the victim (as if for trespass on private property) rather than wreaking vengeance on the lustful villain.[24] There was not the same uneasiness in relations between the sexes which later, more puritanical, centuries saw, and which, judging by the withdrawal of women from public life in many of these societies, probably worked to their detriment.

Part of the reason these unsqueamish, rather public people were not possessive about their bodies was that they did not see themselves so much as individuals but as part of a larger, more important unit — the family. In this world the family was the basic organization for most social and economic purposes.[25] As such it claimed the individual's first loyalty.[26] A much higher proportion of the population married than does today.[27] Studies of peasant societies suggest that, for most, marriage was an economic necessity:

Work, particularly in rural areas, was at that time, based on a division of labour between the sexes: sailors and pedlars were absent for several months, their wives worked the land; the fishermen of the marsh-lands went to the market, the women went fishing; the labourer worked in the fields, his wife worked in the home but it was she who went to market; in the Auge region "the men looked after the livestock and the women attended to the cheese". In order to live, therefore, they had to be a couple, a man and a woman.[28]

The family was able to serve as the basic economic unit in preindustrial societies because the business of earning a living generally occurred at home. Just as public and private life were undifferentiated, so too were home and workplace. Agricultural and commercial pursuits were all generally "domestic" industries. We see this both in France and in New France. Removal of the man from home for most of the working day, an event that Laslett describes as the single most important event in the history of the modern European family,[29] was only beginning. The idea of man as breadwinner and woman as homemaker was not clearly developed. Women's range of economic activity was still nearly as wide as that of their husbands. Seventeenth-century France saw women working as bonesetters, goldbeaters, bookbinders, doubletmakers, burnishers, laundresses, woolfullers, and wigmakers. Aside from their familiar role in the textile and clothing industries, women also entered heavy trades such as stoneworking and bricklaying. A master plumber, Barbe Legueux, maintained the drainage system for the fountains of Paris. In the commercial world, women worked as fishmongers, pedlars, greengrocers, publicans, money-lenders, and auctioneers.[30] In New France, wives of artisans took advantage of their urban situation to attract customers into the taverns they set up alongside the workshop.[31] It was in farm work, which occupied most of the population, that male and female tasks differed the least of all. *Habitantes* in New France toiled in the fields alongside the men, and they almost certainly — being better educated than their French sisters — took up the farm wife's customary role of keeping accounts and managing purchases and sales.[32] Studies of Bordeaux commercial families have revealed that women also took a large role in business operations.[33] Marie de l'Incarnation's background as manager of one of France's largest transport companies[34] shows that the phenomenon existed in other parts of France as well.

Given the economic importance of both spouses, it is not surprising to see marriage taking on some aspects of a business deal, with numerous relatives affixing their signatures to the contract. We see this in the provisions of the law that protected the property rights of both parties contracting a match. The fact that wives often brought considerable family property to the marriage, and retained rights to it, placed them in a better position than their nineteenth-century descendants were to enjoy.[35]

In New France the family's importance was intensified even beyond its usual economic importance in *ancien régime* societies. In the colony's early days, "all roads led to matrimony. The scarcity of women, the economic difficulties of existence, the danger, all tended to produce the same result: all girls became wives, all widows remarried."[36] Throughout the colony's history there was an exceptionally high annual marriage rate of eighteen to twenty-four per thousand.[37] The buildup of the family as a social institution perhaps came about because other social institutions, such as guilds and villages, were underdeveloped.[38] This heightened importance of the family probably enhanced women's position. In the family women tended to serve as equal partners with their husbands, whereas women were gradually losing their position in European guilds and professions.[39] We see this importance of the family in the government's great concern to regulate it. At that time, the state *did* have a place in Canadian bedrooms (whose inhabitants we have already seen to be rather unconcerned about their privacy). Public intervention in domestic life took two major forms: the operation of the legal system and governmental attempts at family planning.

The outstanding characteristic of the legal system in New France — the *Coutume de Paris* — is its concern to protect the rights of all members of the family. The *Coutume de Paris* is considered to have been a particularly benevolent regional variation of French law.[40] It was more egalitarian and less patriarchal than the laws of southern France, which were based on Roman tradition. The *Coutume* reinforced the family, for example, by the penalties it levied on those transferring family property to non-kin.[41] It took care to protect the property of children of a first marriage when a widow or widower remarried.[42] It protected a woman's rights by assuring that the husband did not have power to alienate the family property (in contrast to eighteenth-century British law).[43] The Canadians not only adopted the Parisian *coutume* in preference to the Norman *coutume*, which was harsher,[44] they also implemented the law in a way that maximized protection of all family members. Louise Dechêne, after examining the operation of the marriage and inheritance system, concludes that the Canadian application of the law was generous and egalitarian:

> These matrimonial conventions do not resemble a "marriage market" in which two groups confront each other, but rather an unbiased agreement between the families aiming to create a new community, to help it, if possible, to erect some barriers around it in order to protect it. . . .[45]

The criminal law, too, served to buttress family life with its harsh punishments for mistreatment of children.[46]

The royal administration, as well as the law, treated the family as a matter of vital public concern. The state often intervened in matters that later generations left to the individual or to the operations of private charity. Most famous, of course, is the policy of encouraging a high birth rate with financial incentives. There were also attempts to withdraw trading privileges from voyageurs who showed reluctance to take immigrant women to wife.[47] Particularly in the seventeenth century, we see the state regulating what modern societies would consider intimate matters. However, in a colony starved for manpower, reproduction was considered a matter of particularly vital public concern — a concern well demonstrated in the extremely harsh punishments meted out to women who concealed pregnancy.[48] We see a more positive side of this intervention in the care the Crown took of foundlings, employing nurses at a handsome salary to care for them and making attempts to prevent children from bearing any stigma because of questionable origins.[49]

State regulation of the family was balanced by family regulation of the state. Families had an input into the political system, playing an important role in the running of the state. Indeed, it might be argued that the family was the basic political unit in New France. In an age when some members of the *noblesse* prided themselves on their illiteracy, attending the right college was hardly the key to political success. Marrying into the right family was much more important. Nepotism, or rewarding one's kin with emoluments, seemed a most acceptable and natural form of patronage for those in power.[50] In this sense, a good marriage was considered a step upward for the whole family, which helps to explain why choice of spouse was so often a family decision.[51] These family lines were particularly tightly drawn among the military élite in New France. Franquet remarked that "all those of a certain class are linked by kinship and friendship in this country."[52] In fact, with top military positions passing down from generation to generation, by the eighteenth century this élite became a caste.[53]

In this situation, where the *nom de famille* was vastly more important than that of the individual, it was apparently almost as good for political (though not military) purposes to be an Agathe de Repentigny as a LeGardeur de Repentigny. Moreover, women's political participation was favoured by the large role of entertaining in political life. For the courtier's role, women were as well trained as men, and there seems to have been no stigma attached to the woman who participated independently of her husband. Six women, Mesdames Daine, Péan, Lotbinière, de Repentigny, Marin, and St. Simon, along with six male officers, were chosen by the Intendant to accompany him to Montreal in 1753.[54] Of the twelve only the de Repentignys were a couple. It is surprising to see women from the colony's first families also getting down to what we would today consider the "business" end of politics. Madame de la Forest, a member of the Juchereau family, took an active role in the political cliques that Guy Frégault describes.[55] Mme. de la Forest's trip to France to plead the cause of Governor de Ramezay was inconsequential, though, in comparison with that of Mme. de Vaudreuil to further Governor Vaudreuil's cause in 1709. "Gifted with a very shrewd political sense,"[56] she soon gained the ear of the Minister of Marine. Not only did she secure the Governor's victory in the long conflict with the Intendants Raudot (father and son) and win promotion for his patrons; she appears to have gone on to upstage her husband by becoming the virtual director of colonial policy at Versailles for a few years. Vaudreuil's biographer discusses the influence Madame de Vaudreuil exerted with the Minister Pontchartrain who so regularly sought her comments on colonial patronage that supplicants began to apply directly to her rather than to the minister.[57] Contemporaries agreed that her influence was vast:

> Pontchartrain, Ruette d'Auteuil reports, refuses her nothing, "she has all the jobs in Canada at her disposal; she writes splendid letters from ports of call everywhere, about the good and the bad that she can do by using her influence with him", and the minister "does everything necessary to support her and justify her claims". Riverin confirms that . . . "there is no longer anyone but a woman in charge and she reigns whether she is present or absent."[58]

Governor Frontenac's wife (though not a *Canadienne*) also played an important role at court, dispelling some of the thunderclouds that threatened her husband's stormy career.[59]

As for the common folk, we know less about the political activity of women than that of men. That women participated in a form of popular assembly is hinted at in a report of a meeting held in 1713 (in present-day Boucherville), in which Catherine Guertin was sworn in as midwife after having been elected "in the assembly of the women in this parish, by a majority of votes, to practice as a midwife."[60] Were these women's assemblies a general practice? If so, what other matters did they decide? This aspect of habitant politics remains a mystery. It is clear, though, that women were part of what historians have called the "pre-industrial crowd."[61] Along with their menfolk, they were full-fledged members of the old "moral economy" whose members rioted and took what was traditionally their rightful share (and no more) when prices were too high or when speculators were hoarding grain.[62] The women of Quebec and Montreal, who rioted against the horsemeat rations and the general hunger of 1757–58, illustrate this aspect of the old polity.[63]

In sum, women's position during the *ancien régime* was open-ended. Although conditions varied, a wide range of roles were available to women, to be taken up or not. This was so because the separate spheres of men and women in *ancien régime* societies were not so clearly developed as they later became. There was as yet no sharp distinction between public and private life: families were for most purposes the basic social, economic, and political unit. This situation was intensified in New France due to the underdevelopment of other institutions, such as the guild, the seigneurie, and the village. The activities of breadwinner and homemaker were not yet widely recognized as separate functions belonging to one sex or the other. All members of the family also often shared the same economic functions, or at least roles were interchangeable. Nor had the symbolic honorific aspects of government yet been separated from the business end of politics and administration. These conditions, typical of most of pre-industrial France, were also found in New France, where particular demographic and economic conditions would enable the colony's women to develop the freedoms and opportunities that this fluid situation allowed.

Demographic Advantages

Demography favoured the women of New France in two ways. First, the women who went there were a highly select group of immigrants. Second, women were in short supply in the early years of the colony's development, a situation that worked in their favour.

The bulk of the female immigrants to New France fall into one of two categories. The first was a group of extremely well-born, well-endowed, and highly dedicated religious figures. They began to arrive in 1639, and a trickle of French nuns continued to cross the ocean over the course of the next century. The second distinct group was the *filles du roi*, government-sponsored female migrants who arrived between 1663 and 1673. These immigrants, though not as outstanding as the *dévotes*, were nevertheless privileged compared to the average immigrant to New France, who arrived more or less threadbare.[64] The vast majority of the women (and the men) came from the Île-de-France and the northwestern parts of France. The women of northern France enjoyed fuller legal rights and were better educated and more involved in commerce than those in southern France.[65] When they set foot on colonial soil with all this auspicious baggage, the immigrants found that they had yet another advantage. Women constituted a small percentage of the population. As a scarce resource they were highly prized and therefore in an excellent position to gain further advantages.

The first *religieuses* to arrive in New France were the Ursulines and Hospitallers who landed at Quebec in 1639. These were soon followed by women who helped establish Montreal in 1642. Their emigration was inspired by a religious revival in France, which is thought to have arisen in response to the widespread pauperism following the French civil wars of the sixteenth century. The seventeenth-century revival distinguished itself by tapping the energies of women in an unprecedented way.[66] Among its leaders were Anne of Austria and a number of the leading ladies at court.[67] In other parts of France, women of the provincial élite implemented the charity work inspired by Saint Vincent de Paul.[68] Occurring between 1600 and 1660, this religious revival coincided almost exactly with the period when the fledgling Canadian colony, besieged by English privateers and by the Iroquois, was most desperately in need of an injection of immigrants, money, and enthusiasm.[69] It was at this moment that the Jesuits in Quebec appealed to the French public for aid. Much to their surprise, they received not a donation but a half-dozen religious zealots, in person. Abandoning the centuries-old cloistered role of female religious figures these nuns undertook missionary work that gave them an active role in the life of the colony.[70] Thus the great religious revival of the seventeenth century endowed New France with several exceptionally capable, well-funded, determined leaders imbued with an activist approach to charity and with that particular mixture of spiritual ardour and wordly *savoir-faire* that typified the mystics of that period.[71] The praises of Marie de l'Incarnation, Jeanne Mance, and Marguerite Bourgeoys have been sung so often as to be tiresome. Perhaps, though, a useful vantage point is gained if one assesses them neither as saints nor heroines, but simply as leaders. In this capacity, the nuns supplied money, publicity, skills, and settlers, all of which were needed in the colony.

Marie de l'Incarnation, a competent businesswoman from Tours, founded the Ursuline Monastery at Quebec in 1639. Turning to the study of Indian languages, she and her colleagues helped implement the policy of assimilating the young Indians. Then, gradually abandoning that futile policy, they turned to the education of the French colonists. Marie de l'Incarnation developed the farm on the Ursuline seigneurie and served as an unofficial adviser to the colonial administrators. She also helped draw attention and money to the colony by writing some 12,000 letters between 1639 and her death in 1672.[72]

An even more prodigious fund-raiser in those straitened times was Jeanne Mance, who had a remarkable knack for making friends in high places.[73] They enabled her to supply money and colonists for the original French settlement on the island of Montreal, and to take a place beside Maisonneuve as co-founder of the town.[74] The hospital she established there had the legendary wealth of the de Bullion family — and the revenues of three Norman domains — behind it. From this endowment she made the crucial grant to Governor Maisonneuve in 1651 that secured vitally needed troops from France, thus saving Montreal.[75] Mance and her Montreal colleague Margeurite Bourgeoys both made several voyages to France to recruit settlers. They were particularly successful in securing the female immigrants necessary to establish a permanent colony, recruiting sizable groups in 1650, 1653, and 1659.[76]

Besides contributing to the colony's sheer physical survival, the nuns raised the living standards of the population materially. They conducted the schools attended by girls of all classes and from both of the colony's races. Bourgeoys provided housing for newly arrived immigrants and served in a capacity perhaps best described as an early social worker.[77] Other nuns established hospitals in each of the three towns. The colonists reaped fringe benefits in the institutions established by this exceptionally dedicated personnel. The hospitals, for example, provided high-quality care to both rich and poor, care that compared favourably with that of similar institutions in France.[78] Thus, the *dévotes* played an important role in supplying leadership, funding, publicity, recruits, and social services. They may even have tipped the balance toward survival in the 1650s, when retention of the colony was still in doubt.

In the longer run, they endowed the colony with an educational heritage, which survived and shaped social life long after the initial heroic piety had grown cold. The schools that the *dévotes* founded created a situation very different from that in France, where education of women in the seventeenth century lagged behind that of men.[79] The opinion-setters in France sought to justify this neglect in the eighteenth century and a controversy began over whether girls should be educated outside the home at all.[80] Girls in Montreal escaped all this. Indeed, in 1663 Montrealers had a school for their girls but none for their boys. The result was that for a time Montreal women surpassed men in literacy, a reversal of the usual *ancien régime* pattern.[81] The superior education of women that Charlevoix extolled in 1744 continued until the fall of New France (and beyond) — a tendency heightened by the large percentage of soldiers, generally illiterate, among the male population.[82] The Ursulines conducted schools for the élite at Quebec and Trois-Rivières. This order was traditionally rather weak in teaching housekeeping (which perhaps accounts for Kalm's famous castigation of Canadian housewifery). Nevertheless they specialized in needlework, an important skill since articles of clothing were a major trade good sought by the Indians. Moreover, the Ursulines taught the daughters of the élite the requisite skills for administering a house and a fortune — skills which, as we shall see later, many were to exercise.[83]

More remarkable than the Ursuline education, however, was that of the *Soeurs de la Congrégation*, which reached the popular classes in the countryside.[84] Franquet was apparently shocked by the effect of this exceptional education on the colonial girls. He recommended that the *Soeurs'* schools be suppressed because they made it difficult to keep girls down on the farm:

> These sisters are spread out across the countryside, in seigneuries where they have gone to educate the girls; their usefulness seems to be evident,

but the harm which results is like a slow poison which leads to a depopulation of the countryside, given that an educated girl become a young lady, puts on airs, wants to set herself up in the city, sets her sights on a merchant and looks upon the circumstances of her birth as beneath her.[85]

The second distinct group of female immigrants to New France was the famous *filles du roi*, women sent out by the French government as brides in order to boost the colony's permanent settlement. Over 900 arrived between 1663 and 1673.[86] If less impressive than the *dévotes*, they, too, appeared to have arrived with more than the average immigrant's store of education and capital. Like the nuns, they were the product of a particular historical moment that thrust them across the sea. The relevant event here is that brief interlude in the 1660s and 1670s when the King, his Minister Colbert, and the Intendant Talon applied an active hand to colonial development.[87]

There has been much historical controversy about whether the *filles du roi* were pure or not.[88] More relevant to our discussion than their morality are their money and their skills. On both these counts, this was a very selective immigration. First of all, the majority of the *filles du roi* (and for that matter, of seventeenth-century female immigrants generally) were urban dwellers, a group that enjoyed better access to education than the peasantry did.[89] Moreover, the *filles du roi* were particularly privileged urbanites. Over one-third, some 340 of them, were educated at the Paris Hôpital Général. Students at this institution learned writing and such a wide variety of skills that in France they were much sought after for service in the homes of the wealthy. Six per cent were of noble or bourgeois origin. Many of the *filles* brought with them a 50–100 *livres* dowry provided by the King;[90] some supplemented this with personal funds in the order of 200–300 *livres*. Sixty-five of the *filles* brought considerably larger holdings, in the range of 400 to 450 *livres*, to their marriages.[91] The Parisian origins of many *filles du roi*, and of the nuns who taught their children, probably account for the pure French accent that a number of travellers attributed to the colony's women.[92]

These two major immigrant groups, then, the nuns and the *filles du roi*, largely account for the superior education and "cultivation" attributed to the colony's women. Another demographic consideration also favoured the women of New France. As a result of light female emigration, men heavily outnumbered women in the colony's early days.[93] It might be expected that, as a scarce commodity, women would receive favoured treatment. The facility of marriage and re-marriage, as well as the leniency of the courts and the administrators toward women, suggests that this hypothesis is correct.

Women had a wider choice in marriage than did men in the colony's early days. There were, for example, eight marriageable men for every marriageable woman in Montreal in 1663. Widows grieved, briefly, then remarried within an average of 8.8 months after their bereavement. In those early days the laws of supply and demand operated to women's economic advantage, as well. Rarely did these first Montreal women bother to match their husband's wedding present by offering a dowry.[94] The colony distinguished itself as "the country of the *douaire* not of the *dot*."[95]

In the social and legal realm we also find privileges that may have been attributable to the shortage of women. Perhaps it is due to the difficulties of replacing battered wives that jealous husbands in New France were willing to forgo the luxury of uncontrolled rage. Some of the intendants even charged that there were libertine wives in the colony who got away with taking a second husband while the first was away trading furs.[96] Recent indications that New France conformed rather closely to French traditions make it unlikely that this was common.[97] But the judgements of the Sovereign Council do offer evidence of peaceful reconciliations such as that of Marguerite Leboeuf, charged with adultery in 1667. The charge was dismissed when her husband pleaded before the Sovereign Council on her behalf. Also leaving vengeance largely to the Lord was Antoine Antorche, who withdrew his accusation against his wife even after the Council found her doubly guilty.[98] In this regard the men of New France differed from their Portuguese brothers in Brazil, who perpetrated a number of amorous murders each year; also from their English brethren in Massachusetts, who branded or otherwise mutilated their errant wives and daughters.[99] When such cases reached the courts in New France the judges, too, appear to have been lenient. Their punishments for adulterous women were considerably lighter than those imposed in New England. A further peculiarity of the legal system in New France, which suggests that women were closer to being an equal footing with men than in other times and places, was the unusual attempt to arrest not only prostitutes but their clients as well.[100]

Another indication of the lenient treatment Canadian women enjoyed is the level of insubordination the authorities were willing to accept from them. There was a distinct absence of timidity vis-à-vis the political authorities. In 1714, for example, the inhabitants of Côte St. Leonard violently objected to the Bishop's decision to cancel their membership in the familiar church and enrol them in the newly erected parish of Rivière-des-Prairies. A fracas ensued in which the consecrated altar breads were captured by the rebellious parishioners. An officer sent to restore order was assailed by angry women:

> The officer who was sent to put down the rebellion relates that all the women were waiting for him "with rocks and sticks in their hands to kill me" and that they chased him yelling "stop, thief, we want to kill you and throw you in the swamp."[101]

Other women hurled insults at the Governor himself in the 1670s.[102] An even more outrageous case of insubordination was that of the two Desaulniers sisters, who by dint of various appeals, deceits, and stalling tactics continued to run an illegal trading post at Caughnawaga for some twenty-five years despite repeated orders from governors, intendants, and the ministry itself to close it down.[103]

A further indication of women's privileged position is the absence of witchcraft persecution in New France. The colony was founded in the seventeenth century when this persecution was at its peak in Western Europe. The New Englanders, too, were burning witches at Salem. Not a single *Canadienne* died for this offence.[104] It is not — as Marie de l'Incarnation's account of the 1663 earthquake makes clear[105] — that the Canadians were not a superstitious people. A scholar of crime in New France suggests that this surprising absence of witchcraft hysteria relates to the fact that "in the early days of the colony, women were scarce, prized, and protected from mass persecution."[106]

Thus, on the marriage market, and in their protection from physical violence, women seem to have achieved a favourable position because of their small numbers. Their relatively high wages and lighter court sentences may also have related to the demographic imbalance. Moreover, the original female immigrants arrived in the colony with better than average education and capital, attributes that undoubtedly helped them to establish their privileged status.

Economic Opportunities

Even more than demographic forces, the colonial economy served to enhance the position of women. In relation to the varied activities found in many regions of France, New France possessed a primitive economy. Other than subsistence farming, the habitants engaged in two major pursuits. The first was military activity, which included not only actual fighting but building and maintaining the imperial forts and provisioning the troops. The second activity was the fur trade. Fighting and fur trading channelled men's ambitions and at times removed them physically from the colony. This helped open up the full range of opportunities to women, whom we have already seen had the possibility of assuming a wide variety of economic roles in *ancien régime* society. Many adapted themselves to life in a military society. A few actually fought. Others made a good living by providing goods and services to the ever-present armies. Still others left military activity aside and concentrated on civilian economic pursuits — pursuits that were often neglected by men. For many this simply meant managing the family farm as best as one could during the trading season, when husbands were away. Other women assumed direction of commercial enterprises, a neglected area in this society that preferred military honours to commercial prizes. Others acted as sort of home-office partners for fur-trading husbands working far afield. Still others, having lost husbands to raids, rapids, or other hazards of forest life, assumed a widow's position at the helm of the family business.

New France has been convincingly presented as a military society. The argument is based on the fact that a very large proportion of its population was under arms, its government had a semi-military character, its economy relied heavily on military expenditure and manpower, and a military ethos prevailed among the elite.[107] In some cases, women joined their menfolk in these martial pursuits. The seventeenth century sometimes saw them in direct combat. A number of Montrealers perished during an Iroquois raid in 1661 in which, Charlevoix tells us, "even the women fought to the death, and not one of them surrendered."[108] In Acadia, Madame de la Tour took command of the fort's forty-five soldiers and warded off her husband's arch-enemy, Menou D'Aulnay, for three days before finally capitulating.[109]

The most famous of these seventeenth-century *guerrières* was, of course, Madeleine de Verchères. At the age of fourteen she escaped from a band of Iroquois attackers, rushed back to the fort on her parents' seigneurie, and fired a cannon shot in time to warn all the surrounding settlers of the danger.[110] Legend and history have portrayed Madeleine as a lamb who was able, under siege, to summon up a lion's heart. Powdered and demure in a pink dress, she smiles very sweetly out at the world in a charming vignette in Arthur Doughty's *A Daughter of New France, being a story of the life and times of Magdelaine de Verchères,* published in 1916. Perhaps the late twentieth century is ready for her as she was: a swashbuckling, musket-toting braggart who extended the magnitude of her deeds with each successive telling, who boasted that she never in her life shed a tear, a contentious thorn in the side of the local curé (whom she slandered) and of her *censitaires* (whom she constantly battled in the courts).[111] She strutted through life for all the world like the boorish male officers of the *campagnard* nobility to which her family belonged.[112] One wonders how many more there were like her. Perhaps all trace of them has vanished into the wastebaskets of subsequent generations of historians who, with immovable ideas of female propriety, did not know what on earth to do with them — particularly after what must have been the exhausting effort of pinching Verchères' muscled frame into a corset and getting her to wear the pink dress.

By the eighteenth century, women had withdrawn from hand-to-hand combat, but many remained an integral part of the military élite as it closed in to become a caste. In this system, both sexes shared the responsibility of marrying properly and of maintaining those cohesive family ties which, Corvisier tells us, lay at the heart of military society. Both also appealed to the ministry for their sons' promotions.[113]

What is more surprising is that a number of women accompanied their husbands to military posts in the wilderness. Wives of officers, particularly of corporals, traditionally helped manage the canteens in the French armies.[114] Almost all Canadian officers were involved in some sort of trading activity, and a wife at the post could mind the store when the husband had to mind the war. Some were overzealous. When Franquet rode into Fort Saint Frédéric in 1752 he discovered a terrific row among its inhabitants. The post was in a virtual state of mutiny because a Madame Lusignan was monopolizing all the trade, both wholesale and retail, at the fort; and her husband, the Commandant, was enforcing the monopoly.[115] In fact, Franquet's inspection tour of the Canadian posts is remarkable for the number of women who greeted him at the military posts, which one might have expected to be a male preserve. Arriving at Fort Sault Saint Louis he was received very politely by M. de Merceau and his two daughters. He noted that Fort Saint Frédéric housed not only the redoubtable Madame Lusignan but also another officer's widow. At Fort Chambly he "spent the whole day with the ladies, and visited Madame de Beaulac, an officer's widow who has been given lodging in this fort."[116]

The nuns, too, marched in step with this military society. They were, quite literally, one of its lifelines, since they cared for its wounded. A majority of the invalids at the Montreal Hôtel-Dieu were soldiers, and the Ursuline institution at Trois-Rivières was referred to simply as a *hôpital militaire.*[117] Hospital service was so vital to the army that Frontenac personally intervened to speed construction of the Montreal Hôtel-Dieu in 1695, when he was planning a campaign against the Iroquois.[118] In the colony's first days, the Ursulines also made great efforts to help the Governor seal Indian alliances by attempting to secure Iroquois students who would serve as hostages, and by giving receptions for Iroquois chiefs.[119]

Humbler folk also played a part in military society. In the towns female publicans conducted a booming business with the thirsty troops. Other women served as laundresses, adjuncts so vital that they accompanied armies even on the campaigns where wives and other camp followers were ordered to stay home.[120] Seemingly indispensable, too, wherever armies march, are prostitutes. At Quebec City they plied their trade as early as 1667. Indian women at the missions also served in this capacity.[121] All told, women had more connections with the military economy than is generally noted.

While warfare provided a number of women with a living, it was in commerce that the *Canadiennes* really flourished. Here a number of women moved beyond supporting roles to occupy centre stage. This happened for several reasons. The first was that the military ethos diverted men from commercial activity. Second, many men who entered the woods to fight or trade were gone for years. Others, drowned or killed in battle, never returned.[122] This left many widows who had to earn a livelihood. This happened so often, in fact, that when women, around the turn of the eighteenth century, overcame their early numerical disadvantage, the tables turned quickly. They soon outnumbered the men and remained a majority through to the Conquest.[123] Generally speaking, life was more hazardous for men than for women[124] — so much so that the next revolution of the historiographic wheel may turn up the men of New France (at least in relation to its women) as an oppressed group.

At any rate, women often stepped in to take the place of their absent husbands or brothers. A surprising number of women traders emerge in the secondary literature on New France. In the colony's earliest days, the mere handful of women included two merchants at Trois-Rivières: Jeanne Enard (mother-in-law of Pierre Boucher), who "by her husband's own admission" was the head of the family as far as fur-trading was concerned; and Mathurine Poisson, who sold imported goods to the colonists.[125] At Montreal there was the wife of Artus de Sully, whose unspecified (but presumably commercial) activities won her the distinction of being Montreal's biggest debtor.[126] In Quebec City, Eleonore de Grandmaison was a member of a company formed to trade in the Ottawa country. She added to her wealth by renting her lands on the Île d'Orleans to Huron refugees after Huronia had been destroyed. Farther east, Madame de la Tour involved herself in shipping pelts to France. Another Acadian, Madame Joybert, traded furs on the Saint John River.[127]

With the onset of the less pious eighteenth century, we find several women at the centre of the illegal fur trade. Indian women, including "a cross-eyed squaw named Marie-Magdelaine," regularly carried contraband goods from the Caughnawaga reserve to Albany.[128] A Madame Couagne received Albany contraband at the other end, in Montreal.[129] But at the heart of this illegal trade were the Desaulniers sisters, who used their trading post on the Caughnawaga reserve as an *entrepôt* for the forbidden English strouds, fine textiles, pipes, boots, lace, gloves, silver tableware, chocolate, sugar, and oysters that the Indians brought regularly from Albany.[130] Franquet remarked on the power of these *marchandes*, who were able to persuade the Indians to refuse the government's request to build fortifications around their village.[131] The Desaulniers did not want the comings and goings of their employees too closely scrutinized.

The *commerçants*, honest and otherwise, continued to play their part until the Conquest. Marie-Anne Barbel (*Veuve* Fornel) farmed the Tadoussac fur trade and was involved in diverse enterprises including retail sales, brickmaking, and real estate.[132] On Franquet's tour in the 1750s he encountered other *marchandes* besides the controversial "Madame la Commandante" who had usurped the Fort Saint Frédéric trade. He enjoyed a restful night at the home of Madame de Lemothe, a *marchande* who had prospered so well that she was able to put up her guests in splendid beds that Franquet proclaimed "fit for a duchess."[133]

A number of writers have remarked on the shortage of entrepreneurial talent in New France.[134] This perhaps helps to account for the activities of Agathe de St. Père, who established the textile industry in Canada. She did so after the colonial administrators had repeatedly called for development of spinning and weaving, with no result.[135] Coming from the illustrious Le Moyne family, Agathe St. Père married the ensign Pierre Legardeur de Repentigny, a man who, we are told, had "an easy-going nature." St. Père, of another temperament, pursued the family business interests, investing in fur trade partnerships, real estate, and lending operations. Then in 1705, when the vessel bringing the yearly supply of French cloth to the colony was shipwrecked, she saw an opportunity to develop the textile industry in Montreal. She ransomed nine English weavers who had been captured by the Indians and arranged for apprentices to study the trade. Subsequently these apprentices taught the trade to other Montrealers on home looms that Madame de Repentigny built and distributed. Besides developing the manufacture of linen, drugget, and serge, she discovered new chemicals that made use of the native plants to dye and process them.[136]

Upon this foundation Madame Benoist built. Around the time of the Conquest, she was directing an operation in Montreal in which women turned out, among other things, shirts and petticoats for the fur trade.[137] This is a case of woman doing business while man did battle, for Madame Benoist's husband was commanding officer at Lac des Deux Montagnes.

The absence of male entrepreneurs may also explain the operation of a large Richelieu lumbering operation by Louise de Ramezay, the daughter of the Governor of Montreal. Louise, who remained single, lost her father in 1724. Her mother continued to operate the sawmill on the family's Chambly seigneury but suffered a disastrous reverse due to a combination of flooding, theft, and shipwreck in 1725. The daughter, however, went into partnership with the Seigneuress de Rouville in 1745 and successfully developed the sawmill. She then opened a flour mill, a Montreal tannery, and another sawmill. By the 1750s the trade was flourishing: Louise de Ramezay was shipping 20,000-*livre* loads, and one merchant alone owed her 60,000 *livres*. In 1753 she began to expand her leather business, associating with a group of Montreal tanners to open new workshops.[138]

Louise de Ramezay's case is very clearly related to the fact that she lived in a military society. As Louise was growing up, one by one her brothers perished.

Claude, an ensign in the French navy, died during an attack on Rio de Janeiro in 1711. Louis died during the 1715 campaign against the Fox Indians. La Gesse died ten years later in a shipwreck off Île Royale. That left only one son, Jean-Baptiste-Roch; and, almost inevitably, he chose a military career over management of the family business affairs.[139] It may be that similar situations accounted for the female entrepreneurs in ironforging, tilemaking, sturgeon-fishing, sealing, and contract building, all of whom operated in New France.[140]

The society's military preoccupations presented business opportunities to some women; for others, the stress on family ties was probably more important. Madame Benoist belonged to the Baby family, whose male members were out cultivating the western fur trade. Her production of shirts made to the Indians' specifications was the perfect complement. The secret of the Desaulniers' successful trade network may well be that they were related to so many of Montreal's leading merchants.[141] The fur trade generally required two or more bases of operation. We saw earlier in our discussion that this society not only placed great value on family connections but also accepted female commercial activity. It was therefore quite natural that female relatives would be recruited into business to cover one of the bases. Men who were heading for the west would delegate their powers of attorney and various business responsibilities to their wives, who were remaining in the colony.[142]

We find these husband-wife fur trade partnerships not only among "*Les Grandes Familles*" but permeating all classes of society. At Trois-Rivières women and girls manufactured the canoes that carried the fur trade provisions westward each summer. This was a large-scale operation that profited from fat government contracts.[143] In Montreal, wives kept the account-books while their husbands traded. Other women spent the winters sewing shirts and petticoats that would be bartered the following summer.[144]

The final reason for women's extensive business activity was the direct result of the hazards men faced in fighting and fur-trading. A high proportion of women were widowed; and as widows, they enjoyed special commercial privileges. In traditional French society, these privileges were so extensive that craftsmen's widows sometimes inherited full guild-master's rights. More generally, widows acquired the right to manage the family assets until the children reached the age of twenty-five (and sometimes beyond that time). In some instances they also received the right to choose which child would receive the succession.[145] In New France these rights frequently came into operation, and they had a major impact on the distribution of wealth and power in the society. In 1663, for example, women held the majority of the colony's seigneurial land. The *Veuve* Le Moyne numbered among the twelve Montreal merchants who, between 1642 and 1725, controlled assets of 50,000 *livres*. The *Veuve* Fornel acquired a similar importance later on in the regime. Some of the leading merchants at Louisbourg were also widows. The humbler commerce of tavernkeeping was also frequently a widow's lot.[146]

Thus, in New France, both military and commercial activities that required a great deal of travelling over vast distances were usually carried out by men. In their absence, their wives played a large role in the day-to-day economic direction of the colony. Even when the men remained in the colony, military ambitions often absorbed their energies, particularly among the upper class. In these situations, it was not uncommon for a wife to assume direction of the family interests.[147] Others waited to do so until their widowhood, which — given the fact that the average wife was considerably younger than her husband and that his activities were often more dangerous — frequently came early.[148]

Conclusion

New France had been founded at a time in Europe's history in which the roles of women were neither clearly nor rigidly defined. In this fluid situation, the colony received an exceptionally well-endowed group of female immigrants during its formative stage. There, where they long remained in short supply, they secured a number of special privileges at home, at school, in the courts, and in social and political life. They consolidated this favourable position by attaining a major role in the colonial economy, at both the popular and the directive levels. These circumstances enabled the women of New France to play many parts. *Dévotes* and traders, warriors and landowners, smugglers and politicians, industrialists and financiers: they thronged the stage in such numbers that they distinguish themselves as *femmes favorisées*.

Notes

1. F.-X. Charlevoix, *History and General Description of New France* (New York, 1900), vol. 23, 28.
2. Cited in R.L. Séguin, "La Canadienne aux XVIIᵉ et XVIIIᵉ siècles," *Revue d'histoire de l'Amérique français* (hereafter *RHAF*), 13 (mars, 1960), 492.
3. Séguin, "La Canadienne," 500.
4. Ibid.
5. L. Franquet, *Voyages et mémoires sur le Canada* (Montréal, 1974), 57, recording a tour in 1752–53.
6. Ibid., 31.
7. Séguin, "La Canadienne," 492, 505.
8. G. Fagniez, *La Femme et la société française dans la première moitié du XVIIᵉ siècle* (Paris, 1929), 154.
9. Marcel Trudel, *Montréal, la formation d'une société* (Montreal, 1976), 216–17.
10. John F. Bosher, "The Family in New France," in *In Search of the Visible Past*, edited by Barry Gough (Waterloo, Ont., 1976), 7.
11. Fagniez, *Femme et société française*, 121.
12. Ibid., 149, 104, 193.
13. Philippe Ariès, *Centuries of Childhood* (New York, 1962), 392–406.
14. Ibid., 365–66.
15. Peter Laslett, "Characteristics of the Western Family Considered over Time," *Journal of Family History* 2 (Summer 1977): 89–115.
16. Richard Vann, "Toward a New Lifestyle: Women in Preindustrial Capitalism," in *Becoming Visible: Women in European History*, edited by R. Bridenthal and C. Koonz (Boston, 1977), 206.
17. Ibid., 206–08; Ariès, *Centuries of Childhood*, 397–406.
18. Fagniez, *Femme et société française*, 122–23, 179.
19. Vann, "Women in Preindustrial Capitalism," 206.
20. Franquet, *Voyages*, 135, 61.
21. Séguin, "La Canadienne," 499; R. Boyer, *Les Crimes et châtiments au Canada française du XVIIIᵉ au XXᵉ siècle* (Montreal, 1966), 391.

22. Séguin, "La Canadienne," 506
23. Boyer, *Crimes et châtiments*, 351.
24. Ibid., 344–46.
25. Laslett, "Western Family," 95.
26. I. Foulché-Delbosc, "Women of Three Rivers, 1651–1663," in *The Neglected Majority*, edited by A. Prentice and S.M. Trofimenkoff (Toronto, 1977), 26.
27. Bosher, "The Family," 3, found the marriage rate in New France to be about three times that of modern-day Quebec.
28. This information is taken from a study of Normandy, which was the birthplace of many of the Canadian colonists. J.M. Gouesse, "La Formation du couple en Basse-Normandie," *XVIIe Siècle*, nos. 102–3 (1974), 56.
29. Laslett, "Western Family," 106.
30. Fagniez, *Femme et société française*, 99–104, 108, 111, 114–16.
31. Louise Dechêne, *Habitants et marchands de Montréal au XVIIe siècle* (Paris, 1974), 393.
32. Fagniez, *Femme et société française*, 101; Séguin, "La Canadienne," 503; also G. Lanctôt, *Filles de joie ou filles du roi* (Montreal, 1952), 210–13.
33. Cf. Paul Butel, "Comportements familiaux dans le négoce bordelais au XVIIIe siècle," *Annales du Midi* 88 (1976), 139–57.
34. M.E. Chabot, "Marie Guyart de L'Incarnation, 1599–1672," in *The Clear Spirit*, edited by M. Innis (Toronto, 1966), 28.
35. Bosher, "The Family," 7; H.B. Neatby, *Quebec, The Revolutionary Age* (Toronto, 1966), 46.
36. Foulché-Delbosc, "Women of Three Rivers," 15.
37. Bosher, "The Family," 3. I have rounded his figures.
38. Dechêne, *Habitants et marchands*, 434; Bosher, "The Family," 5.
39. Vann, "Women in Preindustrial Capitalism," 205; cf. Alice Clark, *Working Life of Women in the Seventeenth Century* (London, 1968), chs. V, VI; and Fagniez, *Femme et société française*, for the scarcity of women's guilds by the seventeenth century.
40. Fagniez, ibid., 168ff.
41. Y. Zoltvany, "Esquisse de la Coutume de Paris," *RHAF* (décembre 1971).
42. Foulché-Delbosc, "Women of Three Rivers," 19.
43. Neatby, *Quebec*, 46.
44. Fagniez, *Femme et société française*, 147.
45. Dechêne, *Habitants et marchands*, 423–24.
46. A. Morel, "Réflexions sur la justice criminelle canadienne au 18e siècle," *RHAF* 29 (septembre 1975): 241–53.
47. Lanctôt, *Filles de joie*, 219.
48. Boyer, *Crimes et châtiments*, 128–29.
49. W.J. Eccles, "Social Welfare Measures and Policies in New France," *Congreso Internacional de Americanistas* IV (1966), Seville, 9–19.
50. J. Bosher, "Government and Private Interests in New France," in *Canadian History Before Confederation*, edited by J.M. Bumstead (Georgetown, Ont., 1972), 122.
51. Bosher, "The Family," 5–7; Fagniez, *Femme et société française*, 182.
52. Franquet, *Voyages*, 148; cf., also Frégault, *Le XVIIIe siècle canadien* (Montréal, 1968), 292–93.
53. W.J. Eccles, "The Social, Economic and Political Significance of the Military Establishment in New France," *Canadian Historical Review* LII (March 1971): 8–10.
54. Franquet, *Voyages*, 129–30. For another, similar trip, see 140–42.
55. Frégault, *Le XVIIIe siècle*, 208–09, 216–21.
56. Ibid., 229–30.
57. Y. Zoltvany, *Philippe de Rigaud de Vaudreuil* (Toronto, 1974), 110, 217.
58. Frégault, *Le XVIIIe siècle*, 228–30.
59. W.J. Eccles, *Frontenac: The Courtier Governor* (Toronto, 1959), 29.
60. *Rapport de l'archiviste de la province de Québec*, 1922–23, 151.
61. For example, George Rudé, *The Crowd in the French Revolution* (New York, 1959).
62. Superbly described in E.P. Thompson, *The Making of the English Working Class* (London, 1976), ch. 3.

63. Cited in T. Crowley, " 'Thunder Gusts': Popular Disturbances in Early French Canada," *Canadian Historical Association Report* (hereafter *CHAR*) (1979), 19–20.

64. Jean Hamelin, "What Middle Class?" in *Society and Conquest*, edited by D. Miquelon (Toronto, 1977), 109–10; and Dechêne, *Habitants et marchands*, 44, who concludes that the largest contingents of male immigrants arriving in seventeenth-century Montreal were *engagés* and soldiers.

65. H. Charbonneau, *Vie et mort de nos ancêtres* (Montréal, 1975), 38; A. Burguière, "Le Rituel du mariage en France: Pratiques ecclésiastiques et pratiques populaires, (XVIᵉ–XVIIIᵉ siècle)," *Annales E.S.C.*, 33ᵉ année (mai–juin 1978), 640; R. Mousnier, *La famille, l'enfant et l'éducation en France et en Grande-Bretagne du XVIᵉ au XVIIIᵉ siècle* (Paris, 1975); Fagniez, *Femme et société française*, 97. Commercial activities, however, also prevailed among the women of Bordeaux, an important port in the Canada trade. Ibid., 196.

66. Fagniez, *Femme et société française*, 267, 273–74, 311–12, 360–61.

67. Claude Lessard, "L'Aide financière de l'Eglise de France à l'Eglise naissante du Canada," in *Mélanges d'histoire du Canada français offerts au professeur Marcel Trudel*, edited by Pierre Savard (Ottawa, 1978), 175.

68. Fagniez, *Femme et société française*, 311–21.

69. Marcel Trudel, *The Beginnings of New France* (Toronto, 1973), for a gloomy assessment of the neglected colony during this period.

70. G. Brown et al., eds., *Dictionary of Canadian Biography* (hereafter *DCB*) (Toronto, 1966–), 1: 118; J. Marshall, ed., *Word from New France* (Toronto, 1967), 2.

71. Fagniez, *Femme et société française*, 320–33, 358. Of course, not all *religieuses* were competent as leaders. Madame de la Peltrie, for example, patron of the Ursuline convent, appears to have been a rather unreliable benefactress. Despite her first-hand knowledge of the difficulties under which the Ursulines laboured, her "charity" was quixotic. In 1642, she suddenly withdrew her support from the Ursulines in order to join the colonists setting off to found Montreal. Later she again held back her funds in favour of a cherished chapel project, even though the Ursulines' lodgings had just burned to the ground.

72. Chabot, "Marie Guyart de l'Incarnation," 27, 37; *DCB*, 1: 353; Lessard, "Aide financière," 169–70.

73. *DCB*, 1: 483–87; also Lessard, "Aide financière," 175.

74. This is the interpretation given by G. Lanctôt in *Montreal under Maisonneuve* (Toronto, 1969), 20–24, 170.

75. Ibid., 188.

76. Lanctôt, *Filles de joie*, 81; Trudel, *Montréal*, 21. The Hôtel-Dieu de Montreal also sponsored immigrants from 1655 to 1662 (Lanctôt, *Filles de joie*, 81).

77. Trudel, *Montréal*, 84.

78. Eccles, "Social Welfare Measures," 19; F. Rousseau, "Hôpital et société en Nouvelle-France: l'Hôtel-Dieu de Québec à la fin du XVIIᵉ siècle," *RHAF* 31 (juin 1977), 47.

79. Mousnier, *La Famille, l'enfant et l'éducation*, 319–31.

80. Vann, "Women in Preindustrial Capitalism," 208.

81. Trudel, *Montréal*, 276, 87; P. Goubert, *The Ancien Régime* (New York, 1974), 262.

82. Neatby, *Quebec*, 237; French soldiers had a literacy rate of three to four per cent. A. Corvisier, *L'Armée française de la fin du XVIIᵉ siècle ou ministère de Choiseul* (Paris, 1964), 862.

83. Fagniez, *Femme et société française*, 191.

84. Séguin, "La Canadienne," 501, lists nine of these schools in addition to the original one in Montreal.

85. Franquet, *Voyages*, 31–33.

86. According to Lanctôt (*Filles de joie*, 121–30), there were 961. Silvio Dumas counts only 774 (*Les Filles du roi en Nouvelle France* [Quebec, 1972], 164). Other estimates have ranged between 713 and 857.

87. J.N. Fauteux, *Essai sur l'industrie au Canada sous le Régime Français* (Quebec, 1927), "Introduction."

88. For the record, it now seems fairly well established that the females sent to New France, unlike those sent to the West Indies, were carefully screened, and any of questionable morality were returned by the authorities to France. Lanctôt (*Filles de joie*) and Dumas (*Filles du roi*) agree on this. See also Foulché-Delbosc, "Women of Three Rivers," 22–23.

89. Dechêne finds a majority of Parisiennes among the Montreal *filles* (*Habitants et marchands*, 96). Lanctôt states that one-half of the 1634–63 emigrants were urbanites and that two-thirds of the *filles* were

from Île-de-France (*Filles de joie*, 76–79, 124). On education in France, see Mousnier, *La Famille, l'enfant et l'éducation*, 319–25.

90. Lanctôt, *Filles de joie*, 110–30, 202.

91. Dumas, *Filles du roi*, 39, 41, 51–54, 56, 59.

92. Séguin, "La Canadienne," 492; Franquet, *Voyages*, 57.

93. J. Henripin, *La Population canadienne au début du XVIIIe siècle* (Paris, 1954), 120. The overall population was 63 per cent male in 1663 (Trudel, *Beginnings*, 261), an imbalance that gradually declined.

94. Trudel, *Montréal*, 45–47, 108, 113.

95. Foulché-Delbosc, "Women of Three Rivers," 19.

96. Cole Harris, *The Seigneurial System in Early Canada* (Quebec, 1968), 163.

97. The richest single source for evidence along these lines is Dechêne's *Habitants et marchands*.

98. Boyer, *Crimes et châtiments*, 326.

99. Toronto *Globe and Mail*, 29 October 1979, 1; Boyer, *Crimes et châtiments*, 329, 340. Cf. N. Hawthorne's novel, *The Scarlet Letter*, based on an actual occurrence.

100. Boyer, *Crimes et châtiments*, 329, 350, 361–62; also Morel, "Justice criminelle canadienne." See also the more recent discussion of women and crime by A. LaChance, "Women and Crime in Canada in the Early Eighteenth Century," in *Crime and Criminal Justice in Canada*, edited by L. Knafla (Calgary, 1981), 157–78.

101. Dechêne, *Habitants et marchands*, 464.

102. Séguin, "La Canadienne," 497–99.

103. Jean Lunn, "The Illegal Fur Trade Out of New France 1713–60," *CHAR* (1939), 61–62.

104. Boyer, *Crimes et châtiments*, 286–87.

105. Marshall, *Word from New France*, 287–95.

106. Boyer, *Crimes et châtiments*, 306.

107. Eccles, "The Social, Economic and Political Significance of the Military."

108. Charlevoix, *New France*, 3: 35.

109. Ethel Bennett, "Madame de la Tour, 1602–1645," in *The Clear Spirit*, edited by M. Innis (Toronto, 1966), 21.

110. *DCB*, 3: 308–13.

111. Ibid; Boyer, *Crimes et châtiments*, 338–39.

112. For a splendid description of the attitudes and lifestyle of this class in France, see P. de Vaissière, *Gentilhommes campagnards de l'ancienne France* (Paris, 1903).

113. G. Frégault, *Le Grand Marquis* (Montréal, 1952), 74–75; Corvisier, *L'Armée française*, 777.

114. Ibid., 762–63, 826.

115. Franquet, *Voyages*, 56, 67–68, 200.

116. Ibid., 35, 76, 88.

117. Dechêne, *Habitants et marchands*, 398; Franquet, *Voyages*, 16.

118. *DCB*, 2: 491.

119. Marshall, *Word from New France*, 27, 213, 222–23, 233.

120. Dechêne, *Habitants et marchands*, 393; Franquet, *Voyages*, 199; Foulché-Delbosc, "Women of Three Rivers," 25; Corvisier, *L'Armée française*, 760.

121. Boyer, *Crimes et châtiments*, 349–51; Dechêne, *Habitants et marchands*, 41. Dechêne concludes that, considering Montreal was a garrison town with a shortage of marriageable women, the degree of prostitution was normal or, to use her term, *conformiste* (437–38).

122. Eccles, "The Social-Economic and Political Significance of the Military," 11–17; Dechêne, *Habitants et marchands*, 121.

123. J. Henripin, *Trends and Factors of Fertility in Canada* (Ottawa, 1972), 2; Séguin, "La Canadienne," 495, 503.

124. Trudel, *Montréal*, 30–33; Charbonneau, *Vie et mort*, 135.

125. Foulché-Delbosc, "Women of Three Rivers," 25.

126. Trudel, *Montréal*, 163.

127. Bennett, "Madame de la Tour," 16; Madame Joybert was the mother of the future Madame de Vaudreuil. *DCB*, 1: 399. For E. de Grandmaison, see *DCB*, 1: 345.

128. Lunn, "Illegal Fur Trade," 62.

129. Eccles, *Canadian Society*, 61.

130. Lunn, "Illegal Fur Trade," 61–75.

131. Franquet, *Voyages*, 120–21.

132. Lilianne Plamondon, "Une femme d'affaires en Nouvelle-France: Marie-Anne Barbel, Veuve Fornel," *RHAF* 31 (septembre 1977).

133. Franquet, *Voyages*, 156–58.

134. For example, Hamelin in "What Middle Class?" The absence of an indigenous bourgeoisie is also central to the interpretation of Dechêne in *Habitants et marchands*.

135. Séguin, "La Canadienne," 494.

136. For accounts of Agathe de Saint-Père, see *DCB*, 3: 580–81; Fauteux, *Industrie au Canada*, 464–69; Massicote, *Bulletin des Recherches historiques* (hereafter *BRH*) (1944): 202–07.

137. Neatby refers to this activity in the early post-Conquest era (*Quebec*, 72–73); Franquet encountered Madame Benoist in 1753 (*Voyages*, 150).

138. For discussion of the De Ramezays' business affairs, see Massicote, *BRH* (1931), 530; Fauteux, *Industrie au Canada*, 158–59, 204–15, 442.

139. *DCB*, 2: 548.

140. Fauteux, *Industrie au Canada*, 158, 297, 420–21, 522; P. Moogk, *Building a House in New France* (Toronto, 1977), 60–64.

141. Lunn, *Illegal Fur Trade*, 61.

142. See Moogk (*Building a House*, 8) for one case of a husband's transfer of these powers.

143. Franquet, *Voyages*, 17.

144. Dechêne, *Habitants et marchands*, 151–53, 187, 391; Séguin, "La Canadienne," 494.

145. Charbonneau, *Vie et mort*, 184; Fagniez, *Femme et société française*, 111, 182–84. A recent study by Butel ("Comportements familiaux") has documented the phenomenon of widows taking over the family business in eighteenth-century Bordeaux.

146. Trudel, *Beginnings*, 250. This was largely due to the enormous holdings of Jean Lauzon's widow. Dechêne, *Habitants et marchands*, 209, 204–05, 393; Plamandon, "Femme d'affaires." W.S. MacNutt, *The Atlantic Provinces* (Toronto, 1965), 25.

147. This happened on seigneuries as well as in town, as in the case M. de Lanouguère, "a soldier by preference," whose wife, Marguerite-Renée Denys, directed their seigneury (*DCB*, 1: 418).

148. The original version of this paper was written as the result of a stimulating graduate seminar conducted by Professor William J. Eccles at the University of Toronto. My thanks to him, and to others who have offered helpful comments and criticisms, particularly Professors Sylvia Van Kirk and Allan Greer at the University of Toronto. The revised version printed here has benefited from the detailed response of Professor Micheline Dumont to the original version published in the Spring 1981 volume of *Atlantis*. For Professor Dumont's critique of the article, and my reply, see *Atlantis* 8, 1 (Spring 1982): 118–30.

A BUSINESSWOMAN IN NEW FRANCE: MARIE-ANNE BARBEL, THE WIDOW FORNEL[†]

LILIANNE PLAMONDON

Most of Canada's widows historically have been over-represented among impoverished mothers and the destitute aged. There were examples of both groups in New France but the fact that family life in this pre-industrial society frequently coincided in location and personnel with economic pursuits gave women a decided advantage. Lilianne Plamondon's biographical treatment of the widowed businesswoman, Marie-Anne Barbel, demonstrates how economic organization could combine with legal regimes, in this case the Coutume de Paris, *to promote a potentially high level of female independence. After the death of her husband, the forty-one-year-old mother of five living children used her on-the-spot knowledge of his exten-sive dealings in real estate and trade to expand operations and enlarge the family fortune. More than thirty years of remarkable entrepreneurial effort guaranteed Marie-Anne a comfortable social position and good marriages for her children.*

After the Conquest, French-Canadian entrepreneurs, female or male, found it difficult to preserve their position in the face of better-connected English-speaking rivals. In Britain's Atlantic and Canadian colonies some widows continued to manage family operations, every-thing from farms to stores to hotels. Such women would never entirely disappear, but less advantageous inheritance laws and economic developments that increasingly separated home and work and required larger outlays of capital, while simultaneously restricting women's access to credit, ensured that women as a group remained marginal in business. Shorn of substantial legal and economic advantages, widows in nineteenth-century Canada were all the more vulnerable to the cold charity of poorhouses, jails and les hôpitaux généraux. *Their special vulnerability continued well into the twentieth century as their continuing over-representation among the ranks of the poor suggests.*

The image that comes to mind of women at the time of the French Regime is that of a saint, a heroine, a woman of virtue or, at the other extreme, that of a flirtatious woman of easy virtue. And yet, it was not only women such as Mar-guerite Bourgeoys, Marie de l'Incarnation, Jeanne Mance, Madeleine de Verchères, and Madame de Péan who left their mark on colonial life. Some women took on commercial and financial endeavours both with their husbands and on their own initiative, but few historians have subjected such businesswomen to sustained analysis. Nevertheless, the lives of women such as Thérèse de Couagne, the widow Poulin de Francheville, Louise de Ramezay, the Misses Desaulniers, Agathe de Saint-Père Legardeur de Repentigny, and Marie-Anne Barbel, the widow Fornel, reveal a new aspect of female participation in the development of colonial society.

As an active businesswoman, Marie-Anne Barbel did not represent an exception for the period. In France, wives of middle-class merchants often assisted in

---

[†]"Une femme d'affaires en Nouvelle-France: Marie-Anne Barbel, veuve Fornel," *Revue d'histoire de l'Amérique française* 31, 2 (septembre 1977): 165–185. Translated by Barbara Krever with thanks to Veronica Strong-Boag.

business, and, even in the colonies, women were engaged in industry and trade. The historian Louise Dechêne tells us, moreover, that this type of woman existed as early as the seventeenth century in Montreal:

> Left on their own, they often proved to be excellent administrators, which indicates that they were already deeply involved in the family enterprise, whether a rural estate or a business.[1]

Marie-Anne was such a person. Her economic behaviour was dependent on her social position, on the legal system, and on the commercial and financial life of New France. As she had cause to know well, the favour of those influential in the colonial administration could be of enormous benefit to the ambitious. Managing trading posts in the west and along the Labrador coast was an attractive proposition to many merchants, and trading privileges could be much more easily obtained through the good offices of a friendly intendant or governor. Since the legal framework established by the *Coutume de Paris* provided single women above the age of majority and widows with a certain degree of independence, they too might take advantage of opportunities to translate social relationships with the powerful into opportunities to make money.

As will be demonstrated, Marie-Anne Barbel's social and economic situation before her husband's death was critical in establishing her subsequent career. As a widow, she took the initiative in a number of substantial business activities. Only old age and the worsening situation of the colony brought about her retirement from an active commercial and financial life. An examination of the liquidation of her estate points to the wealth of the Fornels, which Marie-Anne Barbel helped establish during her fifteen- to twenty-year stint as a businesswoman.

Social and Economic Environment

In December 1723, at the age of twenty, Marie-Anne Barbel married Jean-Louis Fornel. Their union brought together families representing two important sectors of colonial life, administration and commerce. At the time of the marriage, the bride's father, Jacques Barbel, held the positions of *juge sénéschal*[2] of Lauson, royal notary in Quebec City, bailiff of the seigneury of Beaupré and *greffier de l'Officialité*[3] and was well-known to the colony's leaders. His future son-in-law, Jean-Louis Fornel, described himself, as did his father, as a middle-class merchant.

The wedding guests represented a rather prestigious social network and included some of the most important people in the colony: the governor, the Marquis de Vaudreuil; the Intendant Bégon and his wife; the *contrôleur de la marine*, Eustache Lanouillier de Boisclerc and his wife, a cousin of the groom; the *commissaire de la marine*, François Clairambault Daigremont; the secretary to the intendant, Nicholas Gaspard Boucault, and François Daine, senior clerk of the Superior Council. Mingling with these distinguished guests were the bride's and groom's friends and family . . . .[4] By virtue of their family and social contacts the couple belonged to what may be termed the commercial middle class. Their ties with the colonial administration would prove very useful to the husband and later to his widow.

The financial situation of the young couple, as revealed in the marriage contract, ranked them among the well-to-do. In accordance with the provisions of the *Coutume de Paris*, the couple was wedded under a community property regime. The husband was the master of the estate and managed the property. The only restriction on his power involved his wife's possessions: he could "dispose of the fruit of the possession, such as the harvest of a field, or the interest accrued on an annuity, but not of the possession itself without his wife's consent." This was her sole legal say in the running of family finances. She could neither "go to court nor go into business without her husband's permission."[5] As a married woman she suffered nearly total legal incapacity.

The marriage contract signed in 1723 included all the clauses normally found in this sort of agreement.[6] Jean-Louis Fornel placed 2,000 *livres* of the property that he was due to inherit from his deceased parents in the joint estate.[7] Anything beyond that amount would become his personal property. Joachim Fornel, a priest, gave his brother 3,000 *livres* in coin of the realm with the condition that, if Jean-Louis were to die childless, he would retrieve this contribution from the estate. Marie-Anne brought to the marriage, 1,500 *livres* from her inheritance from her mother, Marie-Anne LePicard, from a gift from her uncle, the reverend Pierre LePicard, and from what she would receive from her father's will. Anything beyond the 1,500 *livres* would become her personal property.

Jean-Louis settled on his bride her choice of the customary widow's dower or 4,000 *livres*. There was provision for an equitable marriage settlement of 1,000 *livres* in cash or in personal estate determined by the inventory estimates. Furthermore, the surviving spouse would be entitled to his or her wardrobe and personal effects and to the furniture of the bedroom as it was at the time of the spouse's death. The contract's last clauses provided Marie-Anne with the right to accept or relinquish the joint estate, and if she relinquished, she would be allowed to keep what she brought to the marriage as well as any possessions inherited by dowry and settlement. Finally, she could not be liable for any debt or mortgage incurred during the marriage.

The marriage lasted until the death of Louis Fornel in 1745. Nine of the fourteen children born between 1723 and 1741 died at an early age. Four girls and one boy reached adulthood.[8] Only two daughters married, both to merchants, well after their father's death.

During his twenty-two year marriage, Fornel was profitably engaged in commerce. Between 1723 and 1745 he took on two kinds of business activities. From 1723 to 1737, he operated as a retail merchant; from 1737 to 1745 he was a tradesman, entrepreneur, and explorer. With the successful establishment of his Quebec City store, Fornel turned to the fur trade. In 1737 he formed a company with Louis Bazil and François Havy to take up the rights to "fishing, hunting, the fur trade and the coastal seal industry in the baye des Chasteaux."[9] Havy and Fornel were the mainstay of the business; Bazil and his wife only obtained the privilege of exploiting the region from the Crown. Faced with Bazil's lack of interest, Fornel wrote to the Governor of New France, Charles Beauharnois, and the Intendant, Gilles Hocquart, in 1742 to obtain sole rights. In his request, he emphasized that, if he gained this concession from the King, he would undertake, at his own expense, the exploration of the baie des Esquimaux from his base in the baie des Chateaux.[10] Without granting Fornel the sole rights to the area, Beauharnois and Hocquart gave the businessman permission to explore. Thanks in part to his influential supporters,[11] Fornel was able to set off in the spring of 1743. In the last years of his life Jean-Louis concentrated his energies on the running of trading posts along the Labrador coast. During his absences he left the entire running of his Quebec City affairs to his wife.[12] As his proxy, Marie-Anne enjoyed the same rights as Fornel; she was authorized to carry on all financial and legal business.

Even when tempted by the lure of exploration, Fornel remained a prudent businessman, investing his money, or at least part of his profits, in property, a safer investment than commerce. Between 1733 and 1745, Fornel acquired several Quebec City houses and land in the vicinity. He inherited and then improved his father's house in Place Royale, adding vaults to store merchandise.[13] In 1731, he purchased a plot of land along the shore for 2,100 *livres*,[14] and then, in April 1733, a 30-foot front lot on the rue Saint-Louis in Quebec City.[15] In 1734, his brother Joachim gave him two houses, one on the rue Sous-le-Fort, the other, which he would rent out, on the rue Sault-au-Matelot.[16]

In May 1741, Beauharnois and Hocquart granted him a seigneury behind the Neuville seigneury.[17] Then in 1742, Fornel began to take steps to purchase the neighbouring house in Place Royale; his widow would complete the transaction. The last property acquired by Fornel came from the auction of land known as "La Briqueterie" for 12,000 *livres*.[18] This list of properties is rather impressive: five houses and lots in the colonial capital. Taking into consideration the purchase prices, the value of Fornel's holdings amounted to approximately 40,000 *livres*.

After a two-year illness Jean-Louis Fornel died on 30 May 1745. His wife buried him as befitted a man of his rank, at a cost of about 300 *livres*.[19] She was alone at age forty-one with five children ranging in age from six to nineteen. For some time she had acted as her husband's authorized representative: running a business was not new to her. The property she inherited from her husband,[20] the situation of her family, and her own temperament influenced the choices she had to make as a widow.

The Businesswoman

Community property is usually terminated at the death of either spouse. The division of the estate leaves one-half the property to the survivor and divides up the remainder among the other heirs. As a widow Marie-Anne had two options: prolonging the joint estate for some time or proceeding with the division of the property among her underage children. At the time of his death, Louis Fornel's business was booming. His wife was familiar with his affairs and was still young and healthy. Her children were, moreover, not yet in a position to administer their inheritance and they would remain in her care for some time. Marie-Anne therefore decided to prolong the community property.

Since the *Coutume de Paris* set out the status of women as dependent on marriage, the rights of single or widowed women were only indirectly addressed. "Women being 'sui juris' and mistresses of their possessions, rights and actions, they fall upon marriage under the influence and authority of their husbands . . . ."[21] In the case of a woman separated from her husband, "there is nothing to stop her from disposing of her possessions at her will, just as if her husband were no longer alive."[22] Widows had the same rights, as did spinsters.

Thus as a widow, Marie-Anne Barbel had a civil status that imposed no restriction on her ability to carry on her husband's thriving business. At first she moved cautiously and merely kept up her husband's operations. Over time she seized the initiative on substantial enterprises, although she continued to invest part of her profits in property. She managed the Place Royale store and carried on, with Louis Bazil and the merchant François Havy, operating the trading post on the baie des Chateaux. From 1745 to 1748, the post made no profit, largely due to the English privateers. When, in 1748, things seemed to be under control the widow and her associates learned that the right to operate the post had been taken over by Dr. Gaultier, the king's physician, who alleged that they had abandoned the post and thus lost the right to the concession. They protested to the *ministre de la marine*, asking that the post be returned for six years, and, if that be refused, that they be compensated 30,000 *livres* for losses incurred by the facilities, rowboats, and tackle that they had left there.[23] Despite their protest the doctor continued to run the post.

However, Intendant Bigot asked the *ministre de la marine* to grant the widow the trading rights to the baie des Esquimaux explored by her husband.[24] . . . In 1749, the President of the *Conseil de la Marine* authorized Bigot and Governor LaJonquière to grant the concession to Marie-Anne Barbel for a space of twelve years,[25] a favour which Fornel had unsuccessfully requested in 1742 . . . . His widow also offered 7,000 *livres* for the Tadoussac fur trading lease. Intendant Bigot, who was hostile to the existing lease-holder, whom he suspected of making inordinate profits, was quick to accept her offer.[26]

Bigot, the *contrôleur de la marine* Bréard, and the widow Fornel drew up the Tadoussac lease on 9 September 1749. The contract was binding for a period of six years at a price of 7,000 *livres* per year, and included various expenses, clauses, and conditions. The widow assumed responsibility for loans made to the Indians at trading posts, the houses, implements, furnishings, and animals as well as the necessary repairs. She would reimburse the former lease-holder for goods already there and for the last shipments. The value of beaver, oil, pelts, and other goods at the posts would be added to the payment of 7,000 *livres*. The next lease-holder would reimburse the widow for investments made during the last year of her lease, 1756. All beaver pelts obtained in trade would be handled by the government-established monopoly. Finally, the widow Fornel agreed to maintain and increase the trade in Tadoussac and to manage the lease as profitably as possible. Otherwise she might lose the concession.[27] Matters did not, however, rest there. The king reprimanded Bigot for granting the Tadoussac lease and ordered him to put it up for auction. The intendant, however, managed the situation sufficiently skilfully to enable the widow to hold the rights until 1755 . . . .

The normal running costs for one year included the value of unsold merchandise in the trading post stores, goods to be shipped to Quebec, the wages and the freight charges for the buildings, and finally the expense of the lease itself. The amount invested in the first year was 125,766 *livres*. Income depended on oils and furs — beaver, lynx, fox, sable, mink, and others — and the latter brought in 50,428 *livres*. The deficit was high reflecting the start-up costs . . . .[28]

In October 1755 the widow's lease was terminated when the Crown took back the concession and a notary inventoried the trading posts at Tadoussac.[29] Fornel and her associates made improvements to the different posts. Counsellor Guillemin valued these posts at 44,686 *livres* in 1750; by 1755, inventories indicated a value of 71,069 *livres*. The king reimbursed the widow 26,383 *livres*.[30]

No document sheds any light on the management of the fur lease from 1751 to 1755. However, an estimate of beaver pelt sales each year from the posts at Tadoussac, Chicoutimi, Islets Jeremie, Rivière Moisy, and Sept-Îles places the average revenue between 18,000 and 20,000 *livres*. In 1755 this rose to 20,930 *livres*.[31] Furthermore, the amount invested in property by Marie-Anne — in 1753 she paid 8,000 *livres* for a house and purchased for 16,000 *livres* her sister's share of their property in Sainte-Anne de Beaupré — suggests that the Tadoussac concession was turning a tidy profit.

As well as being shopkeeper and manager for the Tadoussac posts, the widow Fornel turned her hand to another business venture when, about 1746, she set up a pottery works at "La Briqueterie."[32] However, she ran into numerous difficulties with the potters and production remained erratic. After a series of legal wrangles with the potters she gave up the venture around 1752.

Among her contemporaries Marie-Anne Barbel had a reputation as a good businesswoman. From 1746 on, she expanded her operations, secured the support of those with power, notably of the Intendant Bigot, and maintained her ties with the solid businessmen Havy and Lefebvre. Nor was she hesitant in defending her rights. Her most protracted defence involved legal proceedings (1745–56) between herself as *censitaire* or tenant and the Jesuits who were seigneurs or landlords of the property known as La Briqueterie. The lawsuit dealt with approximately nineteen *arpents* that had been washed away by the St.-Charles River. Marie-Anne demanded that the Jesuits restore that amount of land to her or pay 6,000 *livres* in damages. The Jesuits refused, arguing that they had granted to the former tenants an additional fifty *arpents* as compensation in April 1689.[33] The dispute lasted eight years, going from one court to another and requiring four land surveys. An out-of-court settlement was reached in August 1756 when the Jesuits agreed to relinquish to Madame Fornel the entire property. She in turn would pay 50 *livres*, 17 *sols*, 6 *deniers* outstanding balance on ten years' arrears of rents.[34]

Land purchases continued to contribute to the widow's financial security in these years. In March 1746 she acquired a tract of timber measuring two *arpents* by twenty in Charlesbourg at a price of 60 *livres* in cash,[35] and in November 1747 she was granted three *arpents* by thirty of land in the seigneury of Neuville.[36] Between 1746 and 1754 she completed the purchase of neighbouring properties in Place Royal. In order to build a new house on the adjacent lot and to repay a debt, Marie-Anne borrowed 8,000 *livres* at 400 *livres* interest per year,[37] a testament to her good financial standing in the community. In March 1753, the widow bought at auction a lot and house on the rue du Cul-de-Sac and Champlain for 8,000 *livres*.[38] She already owned another building on the rue du Cul-de-Sac and the rue du Meule.[39] Finally, she rented out the house and land on rue Saint-Louis for seventy *livres* a year.[40] All these investments brought in a healthy income. In addition, she shared the profits of two estates, one in Sainte-Anne de Beaupré, the other in Saint-Joachim, with her sister Marguerite. The land had been left them by their mother but Marie-Anne assumed the management. In May 1753, she bought out her sister's share in the Saint-Anne property for 1,600 *livres*.[41]

This pattern of property holding revealed an investment strategy geared to the fluctuations of an uncertain economy. The same sort of investments lured other businesspeople as well. In the case of Havy and Lefebvre, Mme Fornel's business associates, "Much of their capital was invested in houses and properties in and around Quebec and in mortgages providing them with some immunity against the fickle ups and downs of trade."[42]

Marie-Anne's substantial business operations helped ensure good marriages for her children. The first daughter to marry was the youngest, Louise, who wed in January 1758 Charles Parent, a merchant like his father. The guests at the wedding were mostly of the commercial class, a reflection of the community in which the Fornels moved so comfortably. However, the marriage contract occurred at a particularly unfavourable point in Madame Fornel's affairs. Final financial arrangements had to await the arrival of the spring fleet from France when Marie-Anne promised to value the entire estate for Louise's settlement.[43] In fact the inventory waited until 1765 after the separation of the young couple. Another daughter, Françoise, married Antoine-Florent Meignot in the early 1760s, and, a few years after his death, she became the wife of Alexandre Dumas. The two remaining daughters and the only son, Jean-Louis, remained single.

Throughout these years Marie-Anne maintained the community property established between herself and her late husband and increased it through a variety of income-producing activities. The foundations of her prosperity were, however, to be shaken. In 1755 the lease on the Tadoussac concession came to an end. The pottery was abandoned. The economic and military situation of the colony deteriorated as the English presence in the Gulf of the St. Lawrence hampered trade. War worsened matters still further.

The Liquidation of her Business

The Conquest ended many commercial and financial careers, including that of Marie-Anne Barbel. Following the shelling of Quebec City, which damaged many of her properties, including the store in Place Royale, Marie-Anne Barbel's name disappears from notarial deeds. Evidently after 1759 she was no longer engaged in any business deals. She concluded the joint estate she had carried on since her husband's death but the settlement itself spread over many years. Despite her advanced age Marie-Anne remained alert. She kept her commercial acumen and defended her right to a fair share of the estate. Even her children could not take advantage of her.

In 1765 she inventoried her possessions. Three of her daughters still lived with her: Joachim Charles (or Charlotte[44]), Anne Claire, both unmarried, and

Louise, who was separated. Her son-in-law, Antoine-Florent Meignot, helped her settle her debts and cash in various bills of exchange. The inventory of properties was lengthy:[45] first, the house left to her by Jean-Louis Fornel in Place Royale; the house next door built by Marie-Anne between 1753 and 1755; a 130-foot lot along the waterfront called La Canoterie — the buildings on it had been destroyed in a fire in 1759; a 60-foot front lot on rue Saint-Louis in Quebec's Upper Town. As well she possessed a 30-foot by 20-foot front lot on rue Sous-le-Fort, given her by Joachim Fornel in return for a lifelong pension. Finally, she owned a house and lot on rue du Cul-de-Sac and rue de Meulles.

Along with these city properties there were country estates. In 1741 a seigneury of 2¾ by 3 leagues behind the seigneury of Neuville had been granted to Jean-Louis. This land was never developed. In 1744, Fornel bought in an auction an estate and residence 6 *arpents* by 40 in the seigneury of Notre-Dame-des-Anges, on the small Saint-Charles river. This included a single storey 60 by 24-foot stone house, a barn attached to a stable, a small pigsty, a shed, a brick furnace, and a small 30 by 20-foot house. The list of holdings was completed with a 2 by 20-*arpent* lot of standing timber in the seigneury of Notre-Dame-des-Anges. Two other properties just missed the list. The lot and house she had purchased in 1753 on rue du Cul-de-Sac and Champlain were sold in April 1764 for 5,600 *livres*[46] and the lot of timber in the seigneury of Neuville, purchased in 1747, reverted to its seigneur in 1765.[47] Marie-Anne's personal property — including silver, domestic animals, tools, furniture, dinnerware, linen, money in bills of exchange and notes from the account of the *ministre de la marine* — was estimated at 8,800 *livres*. The silver alone accounted for 1,105 *livres*.

Mme Fornel's ledgers had obviously been updated before 1765. Almost all debts owing to the joint estate had been received before inventory was taken. The accounts payable seemed to be more significant; the more extensive debts had been incurred before the Conquest. Construction of the house next to her own in Place Royale had been made possible by a loan from Charles Berthelot. Debts to François Havy had been run up during their association in business. Accounts payable reached 24,320 *livres*, an imposing sum, but Mme Fornel had no difficulty in repaying it. Prior to the Conquest the Fornels had been well-off and following the French defeat they were still left with substantial reminders of their former wealth, as was obvious from the division of goods carried out in 1777.

In June 1765 furniture from the Barbel-Fornel estate was auctioned off for 3,985 *livres* although it had been valued at only 2,095 *livres*.[49] The liquidation of the estate continued as Marie-Anne, with her children's permission, parted with personal possessions. She also sold the two estates shared with her brother and sister, bringing in 4,250 *livres* in provincial currency.[50] As had been the case for many years she retained the upper hand in the running of family affairs. In 1771 she gave her children an account of her management of the joint estate since 1765.[51] Interestingly, she preferred the assistance of her son-in-law, the experienced businessman, Antoine-Florent Meignot, to that of her forty-six-year-old son.

TABLE 1

Accounts payable and receivable[48]

Dettes actives

par les héritiers de feu Mess. Chardon vivant cure de la paroisse de Beauport la somme de	311	
par M. Duplessis faber la somme de suivant son billet du 1ᵉʳ avril 1754 laquelle somme sad. Dame veuve a esté obligé d'accepter en payement de la nommée sanson pour loyer	636	15s
par le S. Michel Riverin neg. t la somme de pour fournitures a luy faites de divers effets in 1758 and 1759	152	

Dettes passives

au S. Charles berthelot, neg. t la somme de pour un Constitut par Elle consenti au profit dudit S. Berthelot suivant la grosse dud. contrat de constitution passé devant Me Dulaurent no. royal	8 000	
au S. Berthelot la somme de pour les arrerages de lad. rente depuis 1759 compris jusqu'au 1ᵉʳ octobre prochain	2 400	
a Mr françois havy residant a Bordeaux la somme de pour restant de plus grosse due par lad. communauté suivant la trans-action faite avec le S. L'Evesque negociant de cette ville au nom et comme fonde de procuration dud. S. havy lad. transaction passée devant Me Panet	12 000	
au S. Gaudet negociant de Montreal la somme de pour argent qu'il a presté a lad. Dame veuve pour le rétablissement des maisons apres l'incendie	1 000	
aux S. Chartier et Bondfield negociants a Quebec la somme de pour solde de compte suivant leur memoire du 10 du present mois	29	18s
plus la somme de pour fourniture de serrure qu'il a faite pour la maison dependant de la communauté suivant son memoire du 18 juin 1763	29	8s
au S. Jean Baptiste Charpentier negociant a Quebec la somme de pour argent par lui presté a lad. veuve pour payer les divers ouvriers qui ont travaillé au retablissements des deux maisons sizes sur la place du marché et rue Saint-Pierre suivant les differents reçus des ouvriers.	870	

The division of property from the Barbel-Fornel estate took place thirty-two years after the husband's death, twelve years after the inventory was taken, and six years after the widow's report to her children. Instances in which the joint estate was maintained for such a time were quite rare and presume special conditions or a special determination. The explanation for the twelve years between the inventory and the division of property is given in the deed itself: "After such a mediocre inventory and sale, the children of M. Fornel remained with their mother, who supports them as best she could, and did not dare to ask her for their share, being in ignorance of whether they would have to pay the debt of 30,000 *livres*: they were satisfied to live together on the money received from the rent of the various houses."[52] If they had not made this choice, the Fornel offspring might well have lost their inheritance. As it was, after twelve years, their inheritance was to be quite substantial.

. . . . Before the division of goods there remained 22,252 *livres* in the joint estate. Half the money went to the widow and the other half to the children. However, before the amount was divided among the offspring, funeral and mourning expenses for their father were deducted, as well as half the price of the seigneury as it was Louis' birthright.[53] There remained 10,176 *livres* to be divided among the five children. As the son, Louis Fornel received 2,335 *livres*; his sisters received 2,100 *livres* each.

TABLE 2

Summary of Each Child's Share

child	description of goods	sub-total	total
Louis	birthright for the seigneury of Bourg Louis	300	
	share in the estate	2 035	8 259
	1/5 of "*propres fictifs*"	2 022	
	share in selling price of the house and		
	remaining revenue	3 902	
Each of the four girls	share in the seigneury of Bourg Louis	65	
	share in the estate	2 035	
	1/5 of "*propres fictifs*"	2 022	8 024
	share in selling price of the house and		
	remaining revenue	3 902	

The goods were also divided up. Marie-Anne retained half of the rent of the house that was her husband's property, or 2,451 *livres*, as an annuity for the customary dower; the other half went to the children. Each child's share in "*propres fictifs*" amounted to 2,022 *livres*. The entire purchase price of the house together with the rent of other properties provided each child with 3,902 *livres*. In all, each daughter received 8,024 *livres* and Louis 8,259. The three children still at home reimbursed their mother 1,310 *livres* for their expenses. The very slight difference in receipts suggest that the principle of equality was respected as far as the children were concerned.

Before the division of the goods various house went up for auction. The widow kept the house on rue Sous-le-Fort and moved in with three of her children. Jean-Louis, Anne-Claire, and Joachim Charles acquired the Place Royale house. Antoine Panet became seigneur of Bourg Louis and Alexandre Dumas purchased the house on the corner next to the Fornels in Place Royale. These sales contributed to each heir's share in the estate. The clauses in the 1723 marriage contract were honoured with the widow choosing the customary dower set at 4,679 *livres*.

TABLE 3

Final Share of Goods

Actual assets	50 130
Louis Fornel	6 939
Anne Claire Fornel	6 714
Joachim Charles Fornel	6 714
Marie-Françoise Fornel, the widow Meignot	8 024
Louise Fornel, separated spouse of Charles Parent	8 024
Marie-Anne Barbel, the widow Fornel	13 713

For Marie-Anne, the years 1777–1793 brought old age marked by the trials of Louis's death in 1784 and that of Anne-Claire in September 1793. A few days after her daughter's death, the widow wrote her will, leaving 300 *livres* to Françoise, Dumas's wife, and 150 *livres* to Louise, the widow Parent. Joachim Charles was made sole legatee of all other possessions and property.[54] Their mother died at the age of 90 on 16 November 1793.

After the death of her husband, Marie-Anne left her mark on the family business. Not only did she obtain the posts in the baie des Esquimaux but also the lease for the Tadoussac concession . . . . She operated a pottery for several years although this provided more judicial harassment than it did earthenware pieces for the Place Royale store shelves. From 1755 on, the pace of her business operations slowed down. The Tadoussac lease was not renewed and François Havy returned to France to look after his business interests. Fornel's property investments, nevertheless, kept her financial position healthy. The estate's numerous houses were rented out and the land from her own inheritance provided an annuity. However, the war and the shelling of Quebec caused serious damage to her affairs.

Jean-Louis Fornel's estate did not place his widow among the most influential business people in the colony. She could not be compared, for example, to a

Jacques Perreault senior[55] or to the members of the *"Grande Société"*. Yet alongside the representatives of big business were found a large number of more modest merchants whose operations were nevertheless quite substantial. Marie-Anne Barbel belonged to this group. Her connections proved very useful for this skillful entrepreneur. She was able to secure assistance indispensable for winning concessions from the Crown as was the case with the Tadoussac lease.

Several other women were as active in commerce as the widow Fornel. The financial activities of the familiar saints and heroines, of women such as Marie de l'Incarnation, Jeanne Mance, Marguerite Bourgeoys, and Marguerite d'Youville deserve serious study. Such familiar figures would become a good deal more comprehensible and much less mystical if more were known about the financial activity and resources of women's religious communities during the French Regime. Our understanding of the role of women in New France has much to gain from the study of business women in the young colony.

Notes

1. Louise Dechêne, *Habitants et marchands de Montréal au XVIIe siècle* (Montréal: Plon, 1974), 439.

2. A royal officer who, in certain provinces or colonies, exercised functions analogous to those of bailiff.

3. A. Vachon, "Jacques Barbel", *Dictionnaire biographique du Canada*, II (Québec: P.U.L., 1969), 44–45. *L'Officialité* was a court of an ecclesiastical judge to which a bishop delegated the right to dispense justice in his stead.

4. Archives nationales du Québec (hereafter ANQ), J.C. Louet père, 31 décembre 1723, Contrat de mariage entre Jean-Louis Fornel et Marie-Anne Barbel.

5. Yves Zoltvany, "Esquisse de la Coutume de Paris", *Revue d'histoire de l'Amérique française* 25, 3 (décembre 1971): 369.

6. ANQ, J.C. Louet père, 31 décembre 1723, Contrat de mariage entre Jean-Louis Fornel et Marie-Anne Barbel.

7. The estate of Jean Fornel, father of Jean-Louis, was not entirely settled.

8. C. Tanguay, *Dictionnaire généalogique des familles canadiennes depuis la fondation de la colonie jusqu'à nos jours* (Montréal, Eusèbe Sénécal et fils, 1887), IV, 84.

9. ANQ, C. Barolet, 3 mai 1737, Société entre le Sr François Havy, Louis Fornel et Louis Bazil pour la pêche aux loups-marins.

10. ANQ, Fonds Fornel, lettre de Louis Fornel à MM. Beauharnois et Hocquart pour obtenir la concession de la baie des Châteaux pendant neuf ans, Québec, 1742.

11. "Apparently, from the time of their arrival in Canada as Dugard and Company's permanent representatives, Havy and Lefebvre were to be reckoned as part of that inner circle of resident metropolitans who dominated the colony's import-export trade." D. Miquelon, "Robert Dugard and the *Société du Canada* of Rowen, 1729–1770," (Ph.D. dissertation, University of Toronto, 1973), 171.

12. ANQ, C.H. Dulaurent, 15 mai 1743, Procuration par le Sr Louis Fornel à Marie-Anne Barbel, son épouse.

13. Michel Gaumond, *La maison Fornel, Place Royale, Québec* (Québec: Ministère des Affaires culturelles, 1965), 25.

14. ANQ, C.H. Dulaurent, 1 mai 1740, Concession et vente par les dames de l'Hôtel Dieu aud. Louis Fornel.

15. ANQ, J.C. Louet père, 19 avril 1733, Vente par Jacques Barbel à Louis Fornel et son épouse.

16. ANQ, J.C. Louet père, 14 mai 1734, Donation de Joachim Fornel à Louis Fornel.

17. ANQ, NF-4, Registre d'Intendance, no 9, fol. 8, 14 mai 1741.

18. ANQ, NF-25, Collection de pièces judiciaires et notariales, no 1426, Louis Fornel vs Jean Larchevêque.

19. ANQ, A.J. Saillant, 28 septembre 1771, Compte rendu de Madame Ve Fornel à ses enfants.

20. The author found no trace of Jean-Louis Fornel's will.

21. C. Ferrière et S. D'Aramond, *Commentaires sur la Coutume de la Prévôté et vicomté de Paris* (Paris: Les Libraires Associés, 1788), I, 105.

22. Ibid., 57.

23. A. Col., Série C 11 A, vol. 92, fol. 187–191, 10 novembre 1748, Representations respectueuses de la Dlle Fornel et les Srs Havy et Lefebvre à Monsieur le comte de Maurepas.

24. A. Col., Série C 11 A, vol. 92, fol. 229, 8 novembre 1748, Bigot au ministre.

25. A. Col., Série C 11 A, vol. 93, fol. 241, 25 septembre 1749, Bigot au ministre.

26. Ibid.

27. ANQ, Fonds veuve Fornel, Bail de la ferme de Tadoussac à la Vve Fornel, 9 septembre 1749.

28. A. Col., Série C 11 A, vol. 96, fol. 104v–108. Ètat et Compte des Traittes de Tadoussac . . . pendant la présente année 1750.

29. ANQ, NF-2, Ordonnances des Intendants, vol. 42, fol. 2r–3v, 18 juillet 1755.

30. Ibid., fol. 9–10, 28 décembre 1755.

31. A. Col., Série C 11 A, vol. 100, fol. 338 v, "Memoire sur l'Exploitation des Traittes . . . , Reflexion sur lad.(e) Exploitation", 19 novembre 1755.

32. ANQ, C.H. Dulaurent, 6 novembre 1747, Engagement de Michel Choret à Ve Fornel.

33. ANQ, NF-20, Documents de la Prévôté de Québec, dossier no 1445.

34. ANQ, C.H. Dulaurent, 9 août 1756, Acte d'accord et transaction avec solde de tous comptes entre la Dlle Ve Fornel et les R.P. Jésuites.

35. ANQ, C.H. Dulaurent, 29 mars 1746, Vente par Jacques Loiselle à M.A. Barbel, veuve Louis Fornel.

36. ANQ, C.H. Dulaurent, 6 novembre 1747, Vente par André Campagne à M.A. Barbel.

37. ANQ, C.H. Dulaurent, 15 octobre 1750, Constitution de 400 livres de rente au principal de 8 000 par Ve Fornel à Charles Berthelot.

38. ANQ, NF-19, Registres de la Prévôté de Québec, vol. 96, fol. 46r et v, 20 mars 1753.

39. There is no trace of any document concerning the acquisition of this house, but it is mentioned in another document: J.B. Decharnay, 7 avril 1758, Bail de la Ve Fornel à la Ve de Jacques Marseron.

40. ANQ, NF-25, CPJN, no 1586, Dlle Ve Fornel vs Blaise Perrot.

41. ANQ, J.C. Panet, 4 mai 1753, Vente de Pierre Costé et son épouse à M.A. Barbel veuve Fornel.

42. D. Miquelon, "Havy and Lefebvre of Quebec: A Case Study of Metropolitan Participation in Canadian Trade, 1730–60", *Canadian Historical Review* LVI, 1 (March 1975), 17.

43. ANQ, C.H. Dulaurent, 14 décembre 1757, Dépôts des articles du mariage de Louise Fornel et Ant. Charles Parent.

44. There remains a mystery surrounding Joachim Charles, or Charlotte: why was she given a boy's name at birth? And why, years later, was she called Charlotte, even when she signed the notarial deeds as Joachim Charles?

45. ANQ, Claude Louet fils, 10 mai 1765, Inventaire de biens de Dlle Marie-Anne Barbel et S. Louis Fornel.

46. ANQ, J.C. Panet, 2 avril 1764, Vente de M.A. Barbel à George Borne.

47. ANQ, S. Sanguinet, 1(er) août 1765, Abandon et déguerpissement de M.A. Barbel à N.M. Renaud d'Avaines Desmeloizes.

48. ANQ, Claude Louet fils, 10 mai 1765, Inventaire Barbel-Fornel.

49. ANQ, Claude Louet fils, 10 juin 1765, Procès-verbal de la vente de meubles de Dlle Ve Fornel.

50. ANQ, Claude Louet fils, 23 août 1765, Vente par M.A. Barbel à Jacques Talon.

51. ANQ, A.J. Saillant, 28 septembre 1771, Compte rendu de Mme Ve Fornel à ses enfants.

52. ANQ, J.A. Panet, 21–24 octobre 1777, Compte et partage des biens de feu Sr Louis Fornel.

53. Birthright is the rule by which the eldest son received a larger share of so-called "noble" inheritance in order to avoid its division. See Zoltvany, "Esquisse de la Coutume de Paris," 378.

54. ANQ, P.L. Deschenaux, 7 et 8 février 1794, Compte de succession de Joachim Charles Fornel à ses soeurs.

55. Jacques Mathieu, "Un négociant à Québec à l'époque de la Conquête, Jacques Perreault l'aîné", *Rapport des Archives nationales du Québec* 48 (1970): 29–81.

THE ROLE OF NATIVE WOMEN IN THE FUR TRADE SOCIETY OF WESTERN CANADA, 1670–1830[†]

SYLVIA VAN KIRK

Until recently the fur traders who explored the interior of North America were viewed almost as the epitome of frontier masculinity: transient, largely independent, engaged with native peoples in an inherently limited and exploitative fashion, and unencumbered by family. The work of Sylvia Van Kirk, to which this article is only a brief introduction, has dramatically altered this familiar stereotype. Native women and their Mixed Blood and Métis daughters now emerge as critical to the profits and ambitions of both independent operators and great corporations like the Hudson's Bay Company. On the Canadian frontier, collaboration with the tribes was necessary to European survival until at least the mid-nineteenth century. Women became key players in the meetings of white and native men. Their skills in diplomacy and trade maximized their attraction for traders far from home. This promise of fruitful co-operation, so different from that antagonistic relationship described by Eleanor Leacock, lasted for many decades but fell victim finally to rising levels of anti-native prejudice, the expansion of European influence, and the decline of tribal societies. The ideal of a bi-racial community as a permanent legacy of the fur trade disappeared irrevocably with the downfall of the Riel Rebellions. Women of partial or full Indian origin shared in full the consequences of this historic defeat. The operations of the federal Indian Act into the 1980s would further penalize those women and their children who continued old associations with white men. The ties, which during the fur trade had set the boundaries of the future Canadian state, came in time to exclude many native women from their own communities without giving in return the full benefits of meaningful citizenship in white Canadian society.

In essence the history of the early Canadian West is the history of the fur trade. For nearly 200 years, from the founding of the Hudson's Bay Company in 1670 until the transfer of Rupert's Land to the newly created dominion of Canada in 1870, the fur trade was the dominant force in shaping the history of what are today Canada's four western provinces.

This long and unified experience gave rise in western Canada to a frontier society that seems to me to be unique in the realm of interracial contact. Canada's western history has been characterized by relatively little violent conflict between Indian and white. I would like to suggest that there were two major reasons why this was so. First, by its very nature the Canadian fur trade was predicated on a mutual exchange and dependency between Indian and white. "The only good Indian" was certainly not "a dead Indian," for it was the Indian who provided both the fur pelts and the market for European goods. New research has revealed that not just Indian men but also Indian women played an active role in promoting the fur trade. Although the men were the hunters of beaver and large game animals, the women were responsible for trapping smaller fur-bearing animals, especially the marten whose pelt was highly prized.[1] The notable cases of Indian women emerging as diplomats and

†*Frontiers* VII, 3 (1984): 9–13.

peacemakers also indicate that they were anxious to maintain the flow of European goods, such as kettles, cloth, knives, needles, and axes, that helped to alleviate their onerous work role.[2]

The second factor in promoting harmonious relations was the remarkably wide extent of intermarriage between incoming traders and Indian women, especially among the Cree, the Ojibwa, and the Chipewyan. Indian wives proved indispensable helpmates to the officers and men of both the British-based Hudson's Bay Company and its Canadian rival, the North West Company. Such interracial unions were, in fact, the basis for a fur trade society and were sanctioned by an indigenous rite known as marriage *à la façon du pays*.

The development of marriage *à la façon du pays* underscores the complex and changing interaction between the traders and the host Indian societies. In the initial phase of contact, many Indian bands actively encouraged the formation of marital alliances between their women and the traders. The Indians viewed marriage in an integrated social and economic context: marital alliances created reciprocal social ties that served to consolidate their economic relationships with the incoming strangers. Thus, through marriage, many a trader was drawn into the Indian kinship circle. In return for giving the traders sexual and domestic rights to their women, the Indians expected reciprocal privileges such as free access to the posts and provisions.[3]

The Indian attitude soon impressed upon the traders that marriage alliances were an important means of ensuring good will and cementing trade relations with new bands or tribes. The North West Company, a conglomerate of partnerships that began extensive trading into the West in the 1770's, had learned from its French predecessors of the benefits to be gained from intermarriage, and it officially sanctioned such unions for all ranks, from *bourgeois* (officer) down to *engagé* (laborer). The Hudson's Bay Company, on the other hand, was much slower to appreciate the realities of life in Rupert's Land (the name given to the chartered territory of the Hudson's Bay Company encompassing the vast drainage basin of Hudson Bay). Official policy formulated in faraway London forbade any intimacy with the Indians, but officers in the field early began to break the rules. They took the lead in forming unions with women related to prominent Indian leaders, although there was great variation in the extent to which their servants were allowed to form connections with native women.

Apart from the public social benefits, the traders' desire to form unions with Indian women was increased by the absence of white women. Although they did not come as settlers, many of the fur traders spent the better part of their lives in Rupert's Land, and it is a singular fact in the social development of the Canadian West that for well over a century there were no white women.[4] The stability of many of the interracial unions formed in the Indian Country stemmed partly from the fact that an Indian woman provided the only opportunity for a trader to replicate a domestic life with wife and children. Furthermore, although Indian mores differed from those of whites, the traders learned that they trifled with Indian women at their peril. As one old *voyageur* (canoeman) explained, a man could not just dally with any native woman who struck his fancy. There was a great danger of getting his head broken if he attempted to take an Indian girl without her parents' consent.[5]

It is significant that, just as in the trade ceremony, the rituals of marriage *à la façon du pays* conformed more to Indian custom than to European. There were two basic aspects to forming such a union. The first step was to secure the consent of the woman's relations; it also appears that the wishes of the woman herself were respected, for there is ample evidence that Indian women actively sought fur trade husbands. Once consent was secured, a bride price had then to be decided; though it varied considerably among the tribes, it could amount to several hundred dollars' worth of trade goods. After these transactions, the couple were usually ceremoniously conducted to the fort where they were duly recognized as man and wife.[6] In the Canadian West marriage *à la façon du pays* became the norm for Indian-white unions, which were reinforced by mutual interest, tradition, and peer group pressure.[7] Although ultimately "the custom of the country" was to be strongly denounced by the missionaries, it is significant that in 1867, when the legitimacy of the union between Chief Factor William Connolly and his Cree wife was tried before a Canadian court, the judge declared the marriage valid because the wife had been married according to the customs and usages of her own people and because the consent of both parties, the essential element of civilized marriage, had been proved by twenty-eight years of repute, public acknowledgment, and cohabitation as man and wife.[8]

If intermarriage brought the trader commercial and personal benefit, it also provided him with a remarkable economic partner. The Indian wife was possessed of a range of skills and wilderness know-how that would have been quite foreign to a white wife. Although the burdensome work role of the nomadic Indian woman was somewhat alleviated by the move to the fur trade post, the extent to which the traders relied upon native technology kept the women busy.

Perhaps the most important domestic task performed by the women at the fur trade posts was to provide the men with a steady supply of "Indian shoes" or moccasins. The men of both companies generally did not dress in Indian style (the buckskinned mountain man was not part of the Canadian scene), but they universally adopted the moccasin as the most practical footwear for the wilderness. One wonders, for example, how the famed 1789 expedition of Alexander Mackenzie would have fared without the work of the wives of his two French-Canadian *voyageurs*. The women scarcely ever left the canoes, being "continually employ'd making shoes of moose skin as a pair does not last us above one Day."[9] Closely related to her manufacture of moccasins was the Indian woman's role in making snowshoes, without which winter travel was impossible. Although the men usually made the frames, the women prepared the sinews and netted the intricate webbing that provided support.

Indian women also made a vital contribution in the preservation of food, especially in the manufacture of the all-important pemmican, the nutritious staple of the North West Company's canoe brigades. At the posts on the plains, buffalo hunting and pemmican making were an essential part of the yearly routine, each post being required to furnish an annual quota. In accordance with Indian custom, once the hunt was over, the women's work began. The women skinned the animals and cut the meat up into thin strips to be dried in the sun or over a slow fire. When the meat was dry, the women pounded it into a thick flaky mass, which was then mixed with melted buffalo fat. This pemmican would keep very well when packed into ninety-pound buffalo-hide sacks, which had been made by the women during the winter. But pemmican was too precious a commodity to form the basic food at the posts themselves. At the more northerly posts the people subsisted mainly on fish, vast quantities of which were split and dried by the women to provide food for the winter. Maintaining adequate food supplies for a post for the winter was a precarious business, and numerous instances can be cited of Indian wives keeping the fur traders alive by their ability to snare small game such as rabbits and partridges. In 1815, for example, the young Nor'Wester George Nelson would probably have starved to death when provisions ran out at his small outposts north of Lake Superior had it not been for the resourcefulness of his Ojibwa wife who during the month of February brought in fifty-eight rabbits and thirty-four partridges.[10] Indian women also added to the diet by collecting berries and wild rice and making maple sugar. The spring trip to the sugar bush provided a welcome release from the monotony of the winter routine, and the men with their families and Indian relatives all enjoyed this annual event.

As in other preindustrial societies, the Indian women's role also extended well beyond domestic maintenance as they assisted in specific fur trade operations. With the adoption of the birchbark canoe, especially by the North West Company, Indian women continued in their traditional role of helping in its manufacture. It was the women's job to collect annual quotas of spruce roots, which were split fine to sew the seams of the canoes, and also to collect the spruce gum that was used for caulking the seams. The inexperienced and understaffed Hudson's Bay Company also found itself calling upon the labor power of Indian women, who were adept at paddling and steering canoes. Indeed, although the inland explorations of various Hudson's Bay Company men such as Anthony Henday and Samuel Hearne have been glorified as individual exploits, they were, in fact, entirely dependent upon the Indians with whom they traveled, being especially aided by Indian women. "Women," marveled one inlander, "were as useful as men upon Journeys."[11] Henday's journey to the plains in 1754, for example, owed much of its success to his Cree female companion, who not only provided him with a warm winter suit of furs, but also with much timely advice about the plans of the Indians. The Hudson's Bay Company men emphasized to their London superiors that the Indian women's skill at working with fur pelts was also very valuable. In short, they argued that Indian women performed such important economic services at the fur trade posts that they should be considered as "Your Honours Servants."[12] Indian women were indeed an integral part of the fur trade labor force, although, like most women, because their labor was largely unpaid, their contribution has been ignored.

The reliance on native women's skills remained an important aspect of fur trade life, even though by the early nineteenth century there was a notable shift in the social dynamic of fur trade society. By this time, partly because of the destructive competition between rival companies that had flooded the Indian country with alcohol, relations between many Indian bands and the traders deteriorated. In some well-established areas, traders sometimes resorted to coercive measures, and there were cases where their abuse of Indian women became a source of conflict. In this context, except in new areas such as the Pacific Slope, marriage alliances ceased to play the important function they had once had. The decline of Indian-white marriages was also hastened by the fact that fur trade society itself was producing a new pool of marriageable young women — the mixed-blood "daughters of the country." With her dual heritage, the mixed-blood woman possessed the ideal qualifications for a fur trader's wife: acclimatized to life in the West and familiar with Indian ways, she could also make a successful adaptation to white culture.

From their Indian mothers, mixed-blood girls learned the native skills so necessary to the functioning of the trade. As Governor Simpson of the Hudson's Bay Company emphasized in the 1820's, "It is the duty of the Women at the different Posts to do all that is necessary in regard to Needle Work,"[13] and the mixed-blood women's beautiful bead work was highly prized. In addition to performing traditional Indian tasks, the women's range of domestic work increased in more European ways. They were responsible for the fort's washing and cleaning; "the Dames" at York Factory, for example, were kept "in Suds, Scrubbing and Scouring," according to one account.[14] As subsistence agriculture was developed around many of the posts, the native women took an active role in planting and harvesting. Chief Factor John Rowand of Fort Edmonton succinctly summarized the economic role of native women in the fur trade when he wrote in the mid-nineteenth century, "The women here work very hard, if it was not so, I do not know how we would get on with the Company work."[15] With her ties to the Indians and familiarity with native customs and language, the mixed-blood wife was also in a position to take over the role of intermediary or liaison previously played by the Indian wife. The daughters of the French-Canadian *voyageurs* were often excellent interpreters; some could speak several Indian languages. The timely intervention of more than one mixed-blood wife was known to have saved the life of a husband who had aroused Indian hostility.[16] Indeed, in his account of fur trade life during the Hudson's Bay Company's monopoly after 1821, Isaac Cowie declared that many of the company's officers owed much of their success in overcoming difficulties and maintaining the Company's influence over the natives to "the wisdom and good counsel of their wives."[17]

In spite of the importance of native connections, many fur trade fathers were most concerned to introduce their mixed-blood daughters to the rudiments of European culture. Since the place of work and home coincided, especially in the long winter months, the traders were able to take an active role in their children's upbringing, and they were encouraged to do so. When the beginnings of formal schooling were introduced at the posts on the Bay in the early 1800's, it was partly because it was felt to be essential that girls, who were very seldom sent overseas, should be given a basic education that would inculcate Christian virtue in them. Increasingly fathers also began to play an instrumental role in promoting the marriage of their daughters to incoming traders as the means to securing their place in fur trade society. In a significant change of policy in 1806, the North West Company acknowledged some responsibility for the fate of its "daughters" when it sanctioned marriage *à la façon du pays* with daughters of white men, but now prohibited it with full-blooded Indian women.[18]

As mixed-blood wives became "the vogue" (to quote a contemporary), it is notable that "the custom of the country" began to evolve more toward European concepts of marriage. Most importantly, such unions were definitely coming to be regarded as unions for life. When Hudson's Bay Company officer J.E. Harriott espoused Elizabeth Pruden, for example, he promised her father, a senior officer, that he would "live with her and treat her as my wife as long as we both lived."[19] It became customary for a couple to exchange brief vows before the officer in charge of the post, and the match was further celebrated by a dram to all hands and a wedding dance. The bride price was replaced by the opposite payment of a dowry, and many fur trade officers were able to dower their daughters quite handsomely. Marriage à la façon du pays was further regulated by the Hudson's Bay Company after 1821 with the introduction of marriage contracts, which emphasized the husband's financial obligations and the status of the woman as a legitimate wife.

The social role of the mixed-blood wife, unlike that of the Indian wife, served to cement ties within fur trade society itself. Significantly, in the North West Company there were many marriages that cut across class lines as numerous Scottish bourgeois chose their wives from the daughters of the French-Canadian engagés who had married extensively among the native people. Among the Hudson's Bay Company men, it was appreciated that a useful way to enhance one's career was to marry the daughter of a senior officer. Whatever a man's initial motivation, the substantial private fur trade correspondence that has survived from the nineteenth century reveals that many fur traders became devoted family men. Family could be a particular source of interest and consolation in a life that was often hard and monotonous. As Chief Factor James Douglas pointedly summed it up, "There is indeed no living with comfort in this country until a person has forgot the great world and has his tastes and character formed on the current standard of the stage . . . habit makes it familiar to us, softened as it is by the many tender ties which find a way to the heart."[20]

However, the founding of the Selkirk Colony in 1811, the first agrarian settlement in western Canada, was to introduce new elements of white civilization that hastened the decline of an indigenous fur trade society. The chief agents of these changes were the missionaries and the white women. The missionaries, especially the Anglicans who arrived under the auspices of the Hudson's Bay Company in 1820, roundly denounced marriage à la façon du pays as immoral and debased. But while they exerted considerably pressure on long cohabiting couples to accept a church marriage, they were not in any way champions of miscegenation. In fact, this attack upon fur trade custom had a detrimental effect upon the position of native women. Incoming traders, now feeling free to ignore the marital obligations implicit in "the custom of the country," increasingly looked upon native women as objects for temporary sexual gratification. The women, on the other hand, found themselves being judged according to strict British standards of female propriety. It was they, not the white men, who were to be held responsible for the perpetuation of immorality because of their supposedly promiscuous Indian heritage. The double standard tinged with racism had arrived with a vengeance.

Both racial prejudice and class distinctions were augmented by the arrival of British women in Rupert's Land. The old fabric of fur trade society was severely rent in 1830 when Governor Simpson and another prominent Hudson's Bay Company officer returned from furlough, having wed genteel British ladies.[21] The appearance of such "flowers of civilization" provoked unflattering comparisons with native women; as one officer observed, "This influx of white faces has cast a still deeper shade over the faces of our Brunettes in the eyes of many."[22] In Red River especially, a white wife became a status symbol; witness the speed with which several retired Hudson's Bay Company factors married English schoolmistresses after the demise of their native wives. To their credit, many Company officers remained loyal to their native families, but they became painfully anxious to turn their daughters into young Victorian ladies, hoping that with accomplishments and connections the stigma of their mixed blood would not prevent them from remaining among the social elite. Thus, in the 1830's a boarding school was established in Red River for the children of Company officers; the girls' education was supervised by the missionary's wife, and more than one graduate was praised for being "quite English in her Manner."[23] In numerous cases, these highly acculturated young women were able to secure advantageous matches with incoming white men, but to some extent only because white ladies did not in fact adapt successfully to fur trade life. It had been predicted that "the lovely, tender exotics" (as they were dubbed) would languish in the harsh fur trade environment,[24] and indeed they did, partly because they had no useful social or economic role to play. As a result, mixed marriages continued to be a feature of western Canadian society until well into the mid-nineteenth century, but it was not an enduring legacy. Indian and mixed-blood women, like their male counterparts, were quickly shunted aside with the development of the agrarian frontier after 1870. The vital role native women had played in the opening of the Canadian West was either demeaned or forgotten.

Notes

1. Unless otherwise noted, the historical detail in this article may be found in my book, *"Many Tender Ties": Women in Fur Trade Society in Western Canada, 1670–1830* (Winnipeg: Watson and Dwyer, 1980), where it is given more extensive treatment.

2. The most outstanding example of Indian women who, although not married to whites, were active peacemakers and diplomats are Thanadelthur, a Chipewyan, and "Lady Calpo," a Chinook.

3. The few cases of violent conflict that did occur, such as the Henley House Massacre of 1752, were caused by the traders' failure to respect this bargain.

4. After an ill-fated venture involving women in 1686, British wives were officially prohibited from traveling to Hudson Bay. It was not until 1812 with the Selkirk settlers that women were again officially transported to Hudson Bay. A French-Canadian woman in 1806 was the first and one of the few white women to come west in the North West Company canoes.

5. "Johnstone *et al.* vs Connolly, Appeal Court, 7 Sept. 1869," *La Revue Legale* I, 280 (hereafter cited as "Connolly Appeal Case, 1869").

6. For a discussion of the motivation of the Indian women, see Van Kirk, ch. 4.

7. This does not mean that sexual exploitation of Indian women was unknown in the Canadian West. Prostitution certainly existed, and the marriage relationship could be abused as in white society.

8. "Connolly vs Woolrich, Superior Court, Montreal, 9 July 1867," *Lower Canada Jurist* XI, 230, 248.

9. W. Kaye Lamb, ed., *The Journals and Letters of Sir Alexander Mackenzie* (Cambridge: Cambridge University Press, 1970), 220.

10. George Nelson Papers, Journal 29 January-23 June 1815, Toronto Public Library. See also Van Kirk, 58–59.

11. J.B. Tyrrell, ed., *Journals of Samuel Hearne and Philip Turnor, 1774–1792* (Toronto: Champlain Society, XXI, 1934), 252–53.

12. Hudson's Bay Company Archives, B. 239/b/79, fols. 40d–41.

13. R.H. Fleming, ed., *Minutes of Council of the Northern Department of Rupert's Land, 1821–31* (London: H.B.R.S., III, 1940), 378.

14. Hargrave to Christie, 13 June 1832. James Hargrave Correspondence, vol. 21, Public Archives of Canada.

15. Hudson's Bay Company Archives, D. 5/18, fols. 535d–36.

16. One of the most famous cases was that of James Douglas. As a clerk in northern British Columbia, his highhanded treatment so outraged the Carrier Indians that he might have been killed without the intervention of his mixed-blood wife Amelia and the wife of the interpreter.

17. Isaac Cowie, *The Company of Adventurers* (Toronto: n.p., 1913), 204.

18. W.S. Wallace, ed., *Documents relating to the North West Company* (Toronto: Champlain Society, XXII, 1934), 211.

19. "Connolly Appeal Case, 1869," 286.

20. G.P. deT. Glazebrook, ed., *The Hargrave Correspondence, 1821–1843* (Toronto: Champlain Society, XXIV, 1938), 381.

21. They also violated "the custom of the country" by callously casting aside their former mixed-blood partners after the fact. For a full discussion of the episode, see Sylvia Van Kirk, "The Impact of White Women on Fur Trade Society," in *The Neglected Majority: Essays in Canadian Women's History*, edited by Alison Prentice and Susan Mann Trofimenkoff (Toronto: McClelland and Stewart, 1977), 27–48.

22. Hargrave to Charles Ross, 1 December 1830, Hargrave Correspondence, vol. 21.

23. Glazebrook, 229.

24. Glazebrook, 310–11.

"SUNDAYS ALWAYS MAKE ME THINK OF HOME": TIME & PLACE IN CANADIAN WOMEN'S HISTORY†

MARGARET CONRAD

The first historians to take a renewed interest in the history of women in the late 1960s and 1970s, focussed on women's neglected activities in the public sphere: the fight for the vote and women's labour force and trade union participation. By the mid-1970s, historians became fascinated as well by the worlds inhabited solely or largely by women. If from the late eighteenth or early nineteenth centuries, women and men had indeed occupied increasingly separate spheres in Canada as has been argued, then it was also important to study women's area of influence, the domestic sphere. This is being explored now with regard, not only for patterns of relations with male family members, but also for the female experiences, networks, and values that form the basis of distinct women's cultures.

Margaret Conrad, who writes about the women of Atlantic Canada, maintains that studies of such cultures compel us to question traditional historical sources and approaches. In this field, public documents become less important than personal and private ones such as diaries and letters. Even time and place look different when viewed through women's eyes. Thus the nineteenth-century household was not so much the place from which the other family members went off to lead their real lives, as the centre to which they returned again and again from their periodic excursions to the periphery. Time was measured less by the change of political regimes than by family and community anniversaries. Family time even affected people's participation in the world outside the home. Children went to school or later to work on a schedule determined by family resources. Young people married when their parents could spare their labour.

On a more mundane level, the letters and diaries that form much of the data for women's culture, also contain housework schedules, laundry lists, and daily menus. These help us discover how women organized their households and passed their days, which tasks they enjoyed least or most, when they gave up specific forms of domestic production for purchased goods or services. Information of this sort contributes to filling in the picture of work in the home to match the slowly emerging picture of labour in the workforce.

As enthusiasm for women's history gained momentum in the 1970s, scholars moved beyond the discussion of suffrage and labour force exploitation to describe the features of women's culture as it changed over time. The products of this research — studies of women's domestic labour, child-rearing practices, friendship networks, lifespan choices[1] — have revolutionized not only the way that we see the roles of women in the past but also how we assess the past generally. The study of women's culture is based on the assumption that "women have distinct experiences and values and that these must be studied as unique contributions to culture."[2] It assumes, as Eliane Silverman has recently argued, that

---

†Barbara K. Latham and Roberta J. Pazdro, eds., *Not Just Pin Money: Selected Essays on the History of Women's Work in British Columbia* (Victoria: Camosun College, 1984), 1–16. Portions of this paper will be incorporated in a forthcoming book entitled *Recording Angels, Diaries of Nova Scotia Women, 1775–1939*, written in collaboration with Donna E. Smyth and Toni Laidlaw.

women have historically lived dual lives: "one in the male culture where they are controlled by tradition, fear, loyalty and love; the other in a parallel society of women where their actions could range from intimacy to power."[3] Viewed from this perspective, tracing the contours of women's culture becomes central to writing women's history. Of course, women's culture is not a monolith. There are many women's cultures that must be studied if we are to understand the complexity of women's lives. Indeed, a major goal of those working in the field of women's history is to make it impossible for historians ever again to resort to over-simplifications which hide or trivialize women's past experience; in short, to make it impossible to write history without accounting for the active role of half the human race.[4]

The linking of gender with what Mary O'Brien has termed those other "commatized" categories of research — class, ethnicity, region — has already given birth to major achievements in the field of Canadian women's history.[5] Pioneering studies such as *Women at Work: Ontario, 1850–1930*,[6] *L'Histoire des femmes au Québec depuis quatre siècles*[7] and *In Her Own Right: Selected Essays on Women's History in British Columbia*[8] focus fruitfully on "limited" Canadian identities. The work on Western Canada by Jennifer Brown, Sylvia Van Kirk, Susan Jackel, Eliane Silverman and Meg Luxton has demonstrated the unique contribution made by women to a resource frontier too-long described exclusively in masculine terms.[9] The possibilities of gender and region are not yet fully exhausted. Little, for example, has been published on the women of Atlantic Canada and the North; ethnic minorities such as Oriental women in British Columbia or Anglo-Québécois women tend to have fallen through the cracks of larger general categories; class and culture in the context of Canadian women beg further consideration.[10]

An elaboration of the varieties of women's culture is more than an academic exercise for professional historians or an amusement for idle amateurs. It is an act of political awakening. As long as we continue to define our past only in terms of American or European research or even in terms of developments in other regions of Canada, we remain alienated from our own historical reality. I am continually reminded as I speak on local history in Nova Scotia how grateful women are to learn about their foremothers. More than at any time in our history, we need to make sense of our past and feel in touch with local traditions which have all-too-often been neglected in our pursuit of the "larger" forces explaining women's experiences. I would further argue that because women's lives have been dominated historically by the domestic and community context, it is doubly important that we analyze women's culture as it reproduces and modifies itself in specific places and specific times.

The pursuit of women's culture will transform not only how we study women historically but also how we "do" history generally. Demographic studies will expand to include analyses of women's unique experiences such as the changing ages of menstruation and menopause; economic and technological history will incorporate women's domestic production in its romp from fish, fur and wheat to railways and industry; political and legal history will account for the differential treatment of women in politics and law. Virtually every historical topic is evaluated differently when seen through the eyes of women.

It is frequently noted, for example, that Nova Scotia was, in 1848, the first colony in the British Empire to win responsible government. It is almost never recorded that only three years later the male victors in this political struggle deliberately disenfranchised women.[11] In any political history of Nova Scotia written from a woman's perspective, the fact that 50% of the population was robbed of its citizenship by a public act of parliament would constitute a significant historical event.

Similarly, our immigrant experience takes on a different complexion when seen from the point of view of its female contingent. That much-studied group, the Loyalists, for instance, included not only soldiers, men of principle and fortune seekers but also women and children. As described by diarist Sarah Frost, women experienced special difficulties associated with emigration:

> Our women with their children all came on board today, and there is
> great confusion in the cabin. We bear it pretty well through the day, but as
> it grows toward night, one child cries in one place and one in another,
> whilst we are getting them to bed. I think sometimes I shall be crazy.
> There are so many of them if they were still as common there would be a
> great noise amongst them. I stay on deck tonight until nigh eleven
> o'clock, and now I think I will go down and retire for the night if I can
> find a place to sleep.[12]

This passage takes on added meaning when we realize that Sarah is eight months pregnant. This condition may have influenced her reaction upon arrival in Saint John harbour on 29 June 1783: "This morning it looks very pleasant on the shore. I am just going ashore with my children to see how I like it. Later — it is now afternoon and I have been ashore. It is, I think, the roughest land I ever saw." Since many Loyalist women left their homes because of political decisions made by their husbands, they may well have been less than enthusiastic about their enforced exile. Any balanced account of the Loyalist experience must consider how these women reproduced their culture in the British North American environment and how their values and attitudes influenced the society which they helped to build.[13]

In taking up the issue of women's culture we are addressing fundamental questions of sources and methodology. We are shifting the focus of analysis from the world of men to that of women. If public and published documents are few and macro studies difficult, then we must investigate personal and private sources with greater seriousness. If women's participation in politics is peripheral and labour force activity is muffled then we turn to local and family histories where women have figured prominently both as participants and as chroniclers. When approaching history from a woman's angle of vision the question becomes not "Why did women not protest their deliberate disenfranchisement in the era of responsible government," but "What characterized the lives of middle-class British North American women in the nineteenth century?" Not "Why are women marginalized in the early trade union movement?" but "What are the essential features of working-class women's lives?" Not "Why have women been relegated to the private sphere in industrial societies?" but "How has women's sphere been transformed by the emergence of industrial society?" The answers to questions such as these will allow us to transcend the less ambitious queries and lay the foundation for a genuine human history.

My own research interests, which are presently being conducted in cooperation with Toni Laidlaw and Donna Smyth, focus on the women of Atlantic Canada.[14] Published and public documents on women in these four seaboard provinces are rare. Fortunately, other evidence of women's activity is abundant: handwritten memoirs, diaries, family letters, scrapbooks, genealogies, local histories, minutes of meetings, recipes, samplers, poems, quill baskets,[15] quilts and rugs comprise the material legacy which these women have bequeathed to us and with which we must come to terms.

Handwritten memoirs, diaries, personal letters, scrapbooks, genealogies, local histories and minutes of meetings — the very texture of these documents testifies to the role of women in recording events, keeping in touch and selecting information to be passed on to succeeding generations. The subjectivity of memoirs, diaries and autobiographical letters appealed to us as did the volume of information they offered on women's daily lives and life span choices. As we eventually realized, the sheer bulk of these chronicles was itself significant. Outmigration has been a constant feature of Atlantic Canada's history.[16] The diaries and letters chronicling this diaspora were not only a means whereby women kept in touch with extended kinship networks but were also a way of making sense of their highly mobile and surprisingly literate lives.

While the majority of the chroniclers in Atlantic Canada were native born Canadians and came from rural villages and small towns, it is obvious that they shared aspects of common North Atlantic culture. Since most of these women were descendants of British and American immigrants, this came as no surprise. What did surprise us was the extent to which women of various class and ethnic groups felt compelled to preserve their life stories. Many left behind diaries or memoirs; others, autobiographical letters, often written to the same person, describing in meticulous detail the rhythms of daily life. Such documents are extremely valuable tools for learning how the larger historical forces intersect with women's daily realities — how "census time" intersects with "women's time." They help us to understand what it means to be a mother of 4.6 children and have a life expectancy of 58.4 years or to be a sixteen year old teacher in a one-room school house on a salary of $200 a year. Learning to read these often tantalizingly elusive sources makes them no longer the boring and insignificant documents that archivists and bibliographers have led us to believe. Instead, they enable us to construct life stories that reveal much about the women who are conspicuously absent from our public records. The life stories of Maritime women raise many fascinating questions about women's culture but I want to focus on time and place in women's history.

Recent scholarship has given us a whole new vocabulary for discussing changes in time and place as they relate to women. "Industrial time," "family time," "social maps," "genealogical space" are concepts which help us to describe various components of women's culture.[17] Though Canadian women have not been like the Matapuguio of Peru for whom time and place are so intertwined that they have the same word for both concepts,[18] we can understand how they interact when we consider the ideal place of women in pre-industrial society: childhood and adolescence in a father's home; marriage and mother-hood in a husband's home; widowhood in a son's home. In each stage of life, women were confined by domestic space identified with the male head of household. Major turning points in a woman's life were defined by the change in home ownership and often, though not always, by a change in domicile.

The roles of daughter, wife/mother and widow reflect "family time" which is punctuated by such events as marriage and death of a parent or husband. These in turn were constrained by specific events in "women's time", most notably menstruation, motherhood and menopause. Such deeply entrenched roles were neither easily cast aside nor wholly useless in adapting to new environments. Tamara Hareven has brought to our attention the extent to which particular concepts of family time, nurtured in rural preindustrial settings, were adapted and idealized in urban industrial ones; how the well-worn rhythms of the household became consoling rituals in the paid workplace; and how women's concept of family and community were creatively reproduced over time in vastly different circumstances.[19] While this cultural continuity may have suited patriarchal husbands and was easily exploited by greedy capitalists, it also reflected the desperate attempt of women to emerge from the trauma of social change with something familiar still intact.

Though much research still needs to be done on women's culture in colonial British North America, we know that the time and place of women in rural pre-industrial societies were often regulated on a weekly and seasonal basis. Consider for instance, these passages from the phonetically written diary of twenty year old Phoebe Collins of Halifax County, who was writing in 1815:

> 15 August 1815
> The dairy as ushal takes up most of my morning on Fridays and after finishing there I picked a basket of black currents for Miss Beamish — in the afternoon I sowed a little while and then went out and raked hay. I wrote a note to my friend Harriet this evening. . . . Mama is know tying up her radishes and turnips for market tomorrow morning. As that don't belong to my part of the work I have left her to her self.
> 16 Sept. 1815
> It is Saturday this morning and as usual cleaning house — after that was over I went to spinning and spun a large ball. . . . I took a run before night and got a few blackberries. . . . I have been sitting by the kitchen fire knitting this evening, I am preparing for winter.
> 6 October 1815
> This morning I was very busy in my dairy churning and making butter; Harriet was helping me churn; the remainder of the day we sit up stares reading and knitting. Patience and Perseverence is the tital of the book we are perusing. I think it a very good thing. The weather has bin rather dul to day which prevented us from taking a walk. I have left them all seated around the table at their domestic employments, sum sowing and others knitting, and Pappa at the head reading. . . .[20]

Or this passage describing an annual housecleaning, written by seventy-nine year old Mary Smith of Cape Breton on June 22, 1891:

> A verry dry high easterly wind. The first tub Butter full 22 lbs. The little mare very sick. The boys hear helping doctor her. Flora washed her weeks

washing. I washed breakfast dishes then cleared the kitchen cupboard and washed all the things that was in it and after that the men moved it out of the clothes room into the kitchen. I washed dinner dishes and then had a rest and Sarah moved everything out of the dining room took up the carpet and swept and dusted and I washed the windows. The two girls washed up the floor and Sarah got tea ready and after tea she churned. Flora picked the geese and then put them down in the calf pasture; the children and G.P. finished picking stone a little while after dinner and then the men fixed the fence to keep the geese in. Sarah cleaned up the milk house all ready to wash the shelf and the floor and Flora and the girls finished it up.[21]

The ideal of women's place had been brought to the eastern colonies of British North America by British and American settlers and was well entrenched by the time Phoebe Collins was reading *Patience and Perseverance*. As with most ideals, the prescribed role of women was based on a domestic reality that had long included elements of specialization and routine as well as responsibilities assigned by age and gender. Phoebe Collins and Mary Smith lived in a domestic world of creative production and busy social intercourse. Though fathers sat at the head of the table, daughters and wives had their own practical timetable of social and productive activity.

The pattern of these activities changed slowly during the nineteenth century. We do not know when the spinning and weaving which occupied so much of Phoebe's time finally gave way to the consumption of factory-made cloth, though we have diarists in parts of Nova Scotia making cloth at home as late as the 1890s. On the other hand, canning of fruit and vegetables is not mentioned as a domestic chore until the first decade of the twentieth century, when glass bottles became readily available at reasonable prices. The tasks of house-cleaning, cooking, sewing and making butter persisted throughout the nine-teenth century among our rural diarists and most housewives, like Phoebe Collins' mother, sold a surplus of home production to local markets. One of our diarists, forty-five year old Rebecca Ells of Port Williams, Nova Scotia, notes proudly that in the year 1902 she churned 1363¼ pounds of butter.[22] She also raised hens and pigs for market and, in the absence of her husband who disappeared to the Klondike for twelve years, helped her son run a mixed commercial farm. Time for Rebecca Ells was money, and place was a close-knit community:

> Tues. 29 Jan. 1901
> And it has been a busy day for me. I cleaned mince meat this morning and cooked it, make cake etc. Just hurried all morning—Father came in to dinner. Then this afternoon I went to Kentville with my butter and eggs, did several errands and home again. It was beautiful sleighing. After tea Lee and I went to the Port and he got a suit of clothes all through from head to foot. Then we went up to Mary's. Found her in bed but she soon got up and we staid near an hour.

With the support of a dutiful son and a protective father, Rebecca Ells could get along without a husband, though she clearly found his absence an embar-rassment. Other women pulled their husbands out of debt by their exertions. Mary Bradley early in the nineteenth century found a lucrative market for her cloth.

Accordingly, I set up my loom, and notified my neighbours, and I soon had plenty of work. I exerted myself to the utmost of my power. I took my pay in such trade as was suitable for our family's use, which made the payment easy to my customers. I soon got into the way of helping ourselves greatly.[23]

Later, she ran a grocery store and kept boarders to supplement the family wage.

For many women, Sundays represented a welcome rest from domestic schedules. Mary Michener of Hantsport described her Sunday activity of 13 May 1849 this way:

This is the Sabbath day. . . . We have been to meeting this morning. Rev. Vaughan preached sacrement followed; it is always a solemn season to me. In the afternoon we went up to see about a Sunday School. . . . After talking the matter over it was arranged for a S. School to be held each Sabbath at nine o'clock. After we were dismissed we went up to Father's and took tea. . . . When we came home, Sam and Mary were at Mr. Michener's; they called here awhile and then went home.[24]

Sunday for a devout Baptist like Mary Michener offered an opportunity for spiritual and intellectual nourishment as well as social intercourse with friends and relatives. The idealization of Sunday is a regular refrain in many of our nineteenth-century diaries.

As industrialization encroached on domestic production, women's place gradually expanded beyond the domestic sphere to include the paid labour force but *ideally* only for a specific period of time — between the age of leaving school and marriage — and in specific occupations designated feminine. Despite its limitations, the paid labour force offered women an alternative to marriage and, for a few, prolonging "adolescent" work patterns was preferable to the "double poverty" of wedded dependence.[25]

Paid labour had its own rhythms but women invariably brought domestic rituals to the workplace. Ella Liscomb, a secretary in the Bank of Montreal in Sydney, reported on 16 April 1935:

Great housecleaning going on in the office. Drawers ransacked with great shaking of head on the part of Davidson [manager]. Things will be more satisfactory when it is finished, however. All the boys were assisting in the campaign — Eric not so good. I heard him ask Floyd which side of the cabinet was the woman's.[26]

Worked virtually as a "slave" — a term she herself used — during her six-day work week, Ella found Sundays less inspiring than women who remembered them as one day of rest in their domestic routines: "Always blue on Sundays," Ella wrote. "I don't know why it is, unless I just naturally slump after a busy week." Women in the paid labour force invariably reckoned time by the hands of the clock even if the work hours reflected domestic rather than industrial rhythms. "Enough excitement for one day," Ella concluded. "In the bank from 9:00 this morning until 11:30 tonight with an hour off at 6:30 when I went to Aunt Clara's and had shrimps, salad and cake." Women who worked in the home, in contrast, rarely mentioned a specific time of the day.

Women in the domestic sphere continued to reckon time by family and community anniversaries well into the twentieth century. "Just 50 years ago today since Father and Mother were married in the house where Levi Clark lives now," Rebecca Ells recorded in her diary on 12 March 1901. On 2 May 1901 she noted:

> Just eight years ago this morning our darling Willie closed his precious blue eyes forever — Oh how I miss him yet — That dear sweet face — but God knows best and I am sure he is better off — But O I miss him all the time — Churned 12¼ pounds.

Ella Liscombe remembered the boss's birthday because it was the same day as her own. He did not return the courtesy. Industrial time and family time, for him, belonged to strictly separate spheres.

In pre-industrial agrarian societies women were the primary agents of family and community welfare. As the factory system began to transform production and formal education altered child-rearing practices women continued to drop out of school to help a sick mother or widowed father, and quit paid labour to care for aged parents or to marry. Family time thus determined length of schooling, work-force participation, age of marriage and the resources of widows until the welfare state — which women did much to build — began to take over aspects of family welfare. Hannah Richardson, working in a Lynn shoe factory in 1872, found her yearly routine regulated by the work stoppages at the P.P. Sherry Shoe Company and her summer holiday in Yarmouth. Her brief foray into the lucrative paid labour force was terminated when she returned to Nova Scotia to marry in 1873. Similarly, forty year old Lucie Borden, a secretary in the offices of Perry Mason Co. in Boston, was forced to abandon her career to take care of her aged parents in Kingsport, Nova Scotia, even though a married brother lived nearby.[27]

Generally speaking, our early office and factory workers are curiously silent on matters relating to their paid labour. Instead, their diaries describe the social activities related to their work day and details of shopping, visiting, washing and sewing which dominated evenings and weekends. "This is one of Mark Twain's days on board ship," Lucie Borden noted on 14 April 1905. " 'Got up, dressed, ate and went to bed' with the slight variation of 8 hours work for Perry Mason Company." Whether such an entry reflects women's alienation in the workplace, a preoccupation with women's sphere, or both, is difficult to say, but the end result is that the diaries of single working women are surprisingly similar in content to those of their homebound counterparts. A day in the life of factory worker Hannah Richardson in 1872 was described in this typical diary entry:

> 17 January 1872
> Cold and snowy. To the shop. May in a while in the morning. Jennie Smith in in the afternoon. I ran over to the boys room a while after tea, came back went to work on Than's shirt. Nehemiah McCs wife died this morning 9 o'clock.

What Hannah did in the shop all day other than receive two friendly visits is never revealed.[28]

Women in the paid labour force, then, often carried domestic traditions such as housecleaning, the celebration of anniversaries and personal friendships into the workplace. One wonders how industrial society would have evolved had women claimed a larger voice in its organization. Obviously, they would have eliminated some of the frustrations from their work. "A very disgruntled day, rather unhappy morning," Ella noted on 3 January 1935.

> Felt discouraged and peeved. Some little thing that Basil said upset me for the entire day. It's the little things that take the toll. I really seem to be getting nowhere at the Bank of Montreal though, and if I try to do my work well and speedily nobody seems to notice. Pride! Pride! Why should I worry whether work is done to my own satisfaction. But that's just the trouble. I really have no fondness at heart for my work and it has become merely a matter of routine day after day.

Of course, as Ella herself noted on 28 February after receiving a paltry raise of $25.00 a year, "they seem to expect the women to work harder than the men." But instead of acting upon the contradictions of her absurd working conditions she "Became very brave and proceeded to have my desk moved". A retreat into domestic routine offered defiance of the inequitable business world in which she found herself.

Those women who followed the traditional course of marriage and motherhood often found their domestic base disrupted as men moved in search of a family wage. Significantly, no married women in our diary samples ever worked outside the home. When confronted with an alien environment they found comfort in performing domestic rituals. Annie Butler resorted to this alternative to despair when as a bride she accompanied her sea captain husband on a voyage from Yarmouth to South America in 1871:

> 8 April 1871
> I dreamed of Nellie last night helping her put her house to rights.
> 18th. April
> John has gone ashore and I am into housecleaning strong. I have got one of the men helping me. We have got everything cleaned out of our room and I have got Tom whitewashing and got things so he can go right ahead with the cleaning, so all I shall do now is look on and see he does it well. . . .I presume everybody at home is beginning to prepare for housecleaning, how I long to be at home once more.[29]

Women's work rhythms continued on board ship much, I suspect, to the dismay of the conscripted mate who was set to whitewashing to please the captain's wife. Each day seemed to have significance for the homesick. Annie who noted on 5th May: "This is the first Friday in May. I long to spend a Friday at home." Similarly, Mary MacDonald of Gore, Hants County, who with her new husband moved to California in 1873, found significance in days of the week: "Sunday always makes me think of home more than any other day," she noted. "Sunday was always a pleasant day at home; how I would like to be there now."[30] Singing hymns on Sunday with fellow migrants helped to wake memories of time and place:

> Sunday 7 September (1873)
> Sandy Gordon came in the evning and we had a sing. O, it reminds me so much of home when I hear our good old tunes sung again that we used to sing away in the dear old home with brothers and sisters.

Even the seasonal rhythm became more meaningful in the harsh glare of the California sun. When visiting a photographic exhibition, Mary noted:

> There was among every variety of other thing some very handsome engravings — one I thought perfection; it was a picture of a New England farmhouse and grounds just after a light skiff of snow had fallen.

A New England landscape in winter was the next best thing to a picture of home. World-reknowned author Lucy Maud Montgomery, following her parson husband from Prince Edward Island to Leaskdale, Ontario, in 1912, missed her island home terribly:

> Leaskdale is a very pretty country place — would be almost as pretty as Cavendish if it had the sea — which by the way I miss heartbreakingly at times. . . . Yes, I *like* Leaskdale very much. But yet I do not love it. Perhaps, I shall in time. But so far the only spot on earth I really *love* is that seaward looking slope where I lived and dreamed and worked for so many years. At times — generally in the winter twilight — I would exchange all the kingdoms of the world and the glory thereof for a sunset ramble in Lovers' Lane.

Eleven years later, "the island" was still the writer's spiritual home. "There is nothing like it in smug, opulent Ontario," she declared after a summer visit to Prince Edward Island in 1923. "I was at home — heart and soul and mind I was at home."[31]

Migration also made women more dependent upon their husbands, a situation conducive to feelings of helplessness and homesickness. "I feel saddened today on account of my evil disposition last night. To think I could so far lose control of myself and get so angry at my dear husband. . . . I wonder if Rie ever got that angry at Rob," Anne Butler confided to her diary on 6 August 1871. Mary MacDonald finally resorted to poetry to express her loneliness on 10 September 1873:

> Farewell my childhood's home and friends
> I bid you all adieu
> Twas hard to leave my native land
> But harder still to part with you
> This land seems very strange to me
> So different from my own
> And I feel so like a stranger here
> So far away from home. . . .
> I am not sorry that I came
> For him I'd go this world around
> For husband is the dearest soul
> That ere on earth was found
> The folks are very good and kind
> And the sun is shining bright today
> But O I feel so lonely now
> Whenever he's away
> It must be that I love him so
> I feel so different then
> Whenever he's away my sunshine's gone
> Until he comes home again.

"Home" had particularly poignant connotations for an unwed mother banished from Fredericton to Boston to carry her pregnancy to term. "I certainly feel bad to have to leave home and go among strangers," she wrote. "But if I had my life to live over I would do very different. I often feel, and especially now, that I haven't a friend in the world."[32]

The domestic ideal eluded many Maritime women in the nineteenth and twentieth centuries. For some women this constituted a failure sufficient to blunt all personal ambition. Others found ways of pursuing fulfillment both within and outside marriage. Religious enthusiasm, literary pursuits, female friendships, and kinship networks offered enriched social intercourse and a valuable safety net when the domestic ideal failed. Mary Bradley's early nineteenth-century prescription for psychological survival in a childless unhappy first marriage was particularly appropriate to her domestic setting:

> I contracted a habit of awakening and rising early at the hour of five in the morning, both summer and winter. My place of private devotions was an underground dairy room — which in the winter was used for a cellar for vegetables; protected from the frost by an outhouse over it, with a door to go downstairs — and this was my place of devotion in winter. . . . and when the door was shut down after me, all timidity and fear was dispelled, and my soul would be so happy, and enjoyed so much of the presence of God, that I sometimes felt as if the place was full of happy spirits who met with me.
> . . . With my heart full of love and truly alive to God, I returned from this Bethel to resume my domestic duties with great delight.

Community churches also offered women scope for teaching, social reform and female friendships. Later in the century, Maritime women would use religious conviction to justify the most audacious claims to education and career. "Next to Truro, Bobbili is now the dearest place on earth to me," Mathilda Churchill wrote from her mission station in India where she spent nearly fifty years of her life as a teacher and administrator. ". . . [I]t is Home in India and home wherever it may be is a loved spot to a woman" she declared somewhat ingenuously.[33]

Others, like Phoebe Collins, retreated into "novils" and day dreaming. On 24 October 1815 Phoebe noted:

> I don't think I shall git the rhumatism in my fingers for want of exercise, for I have bin in my spinning room all day; now one intrudes on my solitude, my mind has free scope of thinking — if it were not for hope and anticipation, time indeed would pass heavily on.

Margaret Michener, recently widowed, found solace in female frienships, English literature and the natural beauty of the seaboard village of Hantsport in 1850.

> I have come tonight to my lonely habitation. It is not the same as it has been all summer, for hope has departed. I was looking forward to winter when Simeon would be home. I took a walk down to the Halfway River bridge and sat on the fence by the marsh to watch the flowing tide. I sat there till it came all around me as the tides are high — and ebbed again. I read while there Pope's "Messiah" which Simeon had learned and wrote it off for me before we were married. It sounds so like him, I almost think I hear him repeat it. I seem to envy Maria the hope she has of Curry coming

home, but why should I? Let me give up and wish others all good success. Maria is here now; my friends are all very kind. I wrote to Rebecca Elder today. I find some consolation in scribbling. . . .

Female friendships are a well documented feature of women's culture. Less studied because they are so obvious are the strong bonds of sibling sisterhood that sustained women in earlier times. Older sisters in large families virtually raised younger children and sisters close in age shared intimacies that were denied even to husbands. "Dear sister Rie's birthday," the seaborne Annie Butler noted on 15 February 1871: "How I would like to be near her. I wonder what she is doing. Frying donuts maybe. Wouldn't I like to have one or two dozen to eat. . . ." On 13 May she pined: "I have got better of my dreary feelings but the desire to see my precious sister is just as strong but I am going to try to be cheerful and patient until I do." Leaving sisters for husbands, careers, or both, was often a difficult experience for women.

"Sister Lizzie and I had our farewell last night," Mathilda Faulkner Churchill reported before departing for the mission fields in 1873:

Hours we spent together, far into the night, talking over old childhood days at Stewiacke, the girlhood days here in Truro, her sickness and the long weary period of pain and retirement, my teaching and mission work, my wedding-day and the new life now stretching out for me ahead. She was very brave. We did not weep. It was rather a retrospect to record our joys and our mercies, the seal of mutual love.

Letters and even diary exchanges between sisters testify to the special support that siblings provided in good times and bad. Of all the features of women's culture revealed in our sources this is the most fleeting as modern family patterns take their toll on natural sisterhood.

Though the domestic ideal in the twentieth century had lost much of its glamour both in the home and in the workplace, women still struggled to keep their domestic networks. Ella Liscombe, who lived with her widowed mother and unmarried sister, found home ownership burdensome not only because of taxes but because the bank manager might conclude that she did not need a raise if she owned her own home. "It would be cheaper to board somewhere," she recorded in her diary on 20 January 1935, "but it is not like having your own home and we are still comfortable and warm."[34] Even more remarkable is the determination of Mary MacQuarrie, mother of twelve, to maintain the bonds among three generations of women, after the death of her husband.

We were left, the younger girls and I, fairly comfortable. However, when the war was over the three girls were married; thus leaving my old mother and me to face the world. The prospect was not very bright in Glace Bay and I had nobody belonging to me there; I sold all my property and bought a home in Sydney, because I had to make a home for my mother while she lived. When she died four years ago I rented my house, sold all my things and started out to visit my scattered family. I sometimes wish I had kept up my old home, but if I were by myself I wouldn't be able to stand the loneliness after always having a full house, and it would be more than I could bear to have to sit at a lonely table and not have people coming in at night. So here I am, at the age of 74, going about from place to place. At present I'm here with Katie in Halifax. I have been with Ethel in Baltimore, three winters and one summer; and with Flora in Buffalo and Syracuse; and with Alice in Montreal. I hope to be for awhile with Flora in Sydney where she is going to live for the next five years.[35]

Mary MacQuarrie felt that her place was with her family but her children were scattered all over North America. Moreover, sons no longer took precedence in caring for widowed mothers; only daughters figured in Mary MacQuarrie's wanderings. Genealogical maps had contracted while family space had expanded far beyond household and community. Despite these challenges, women's support networks continued to re-create themselves and take on new forms.

The women in our diaries clearly experienced time and place differently than many of us do today. Very few spoke of place in political or even larger geographical terms. Place for most women was represented by home, kin and community, spaces in which women's role was clearly defined and highly valued. Similarly, time was reckoned through the prism of the family and even the time and place of work were assigned according to the gender role expectations of daughters, mothers and widows. As has been noted elsewhere, "timely" action in the nineteenth century consisted of helpful responses in times of crises rather than adherence to a schedule; and, for women, personal life course decisions were directed by family expectations long after most men began to make choices based on individual and economic considerations.[36]

These generalizations are obviously not valid for all women at all times. Even certain women in Atlantic Canada — native Indian, Acadian and upper-class women for instance — would not always conform to such norms. However, given the close ties with New England and their high level of literacy, Anglo-Saxon women in Atlantic Canada eagerly subscribed to the cult of domesticity as the production and reproduction of the domestic sphere increasingly became the exclusive preserve of women in the nineteenth century.[37] Since all of the women cited above were products of this culture, their devotion to the domestic ideal is not surprising. Not only were they urged to conform to it by prescriptive literature, novels and community standards; they were taught it by their mothers' example. However, the post-Second World War generation of women would move into the labour force in larger numbers and the welfare state would shoulder some of the burden of domesticity. A casualty of this process and the revolution in communications which accompanied it was the custom of diary keeping and the art of private letter writing — the very sources which, for over a century, chronicled the fate of so many women in Atlantic Canada.

Notes

1. See, for instance, Susan Strasser, *Never Done: A History of American Housework* (New York: Pantheon Books, 1982); Diana Gittens, *Fair Sex: Family Size and Structure, 1900–39* (London: Hutchinson, 1982);

Lillian Faderman, *Surpassing the Love of Men* (New York: William Morrow, 1981); Beth Light and Alison Prentice, eds., *Pioneer and Gentlewomen of British North America, 1713–1867* (Toronto: New Hogtown Press, 1980); Beth Light and Joy Parr, eds., *Canadian Women on the Move, 1867–1920* (Toronto: New Hogtown Press and OISE, 1983).

2. Gayle Kimball, ed., *Women's Culture: The Women's Renaissance of the Seventies* (Metuchen, N.J.: Scarecrow Press, 1981): 3.

3. Eliane Leslau Silverman, "Writing Canadian Women's History, 1970–82: an Historiographical Analysis," *Canadian Historical Review* LXIII, 4 (December 1982): 521.

4. Ruth Pierson and Alison Prentice, "Feminism and the Writing and Teaching of History," *Atlantis* 7, 2 (Spring 1982): 43.

5. Mary O'Brien et al., "Feminism and Education: A Critical Review Essay," *Resources for Feminist Research* XII, 3 (Nov. 1983): 6.

6. Edited by Janice Acton, Penny Goldsmith and Bonnie Shepard (Toronto: Women's Press, 1974).

7. By Marie Lavigne, Jennifer Stoddart, Micheline Dumont and Michèle Jean (Montréal: Les Quinze, 1982).

8. Edited by Barbara Latham and Cathy Kess (Victoria: Camosun College, 1980).

9. Jennifer Brown, *Strangers in Blood: Fur Trade Company Families in Indian Country* (Vancouver: University of British Columbia Press, 1980); Sylvia Van Kirk, *"Many Tender Ties": Women in Fur Trade Society, 1670–1870* (Winnipeg: Watson and Dwyer, 1980); Susan Jackel, *A Flannel Shirt and Liberty* (Vancouver: University of British Columbia Press, 1982); Eliane Leslau Silverman, *The Last Best West: Women on the Alberta Frontier, 1880–1930* (Montreal: Eden Press, 1984); Meg Luxton, *More than a Labour of Love* (Toronto: Women's Press, 1980).

10. Comparative regional analysis offers a particularly valuable approach to women's history. See, for example, Claudette Lacelle, "Les domestiques dans les villes canadiennes au XIXe siècle: effectifs et conditions de vie," *Histoire sociale/Social History* XV, 29 (mai 1982): 181–207; Gordon Darroch and Michael Ornstein, "Family Life-Cycles, Occupations and Networks of Mutual Aid," *Historical Papers* (Canadian Historical Association, Vancouver, 1983): 30–55.

11. John Garner, *The Franchise and Politics in British North America, 1755–1867* (Toronto: University of Toronto Press, 1969), 155–56.

12. Sarah Frost, "Diary" published in Walter Bates, *Kingston and the Loyalists of 1783*, edited by W.O. Raymond, 1889 rept. (Woodstock: Non-entity Press, 1980): 26–30.

13. Mary Beth Norton, *Liberty's Daughters: The Revolutionary Experience of American Women, 1750–1800* (Boston: Little, Brown, 1980).

14. Margaret Conrad, *Recording Angels: The Private Chronicles of Women from the Maritime Provinces of Canada, 1750–1950* (Ottawa: CRIAW, 1982); Donna Smyth, "Mothers, Grandmothers and Young Wives Tales," unpublished play based on "Recording Angels" chronicles.

15. Ruth Holmes Whitehead, *Micmac Quillwork* (Halifax: Nova Scotia Museum, 1982).

16. Alan A. Brookes, "Out-migration from the Maritimes, 1860–1900: Some Preliminary Considerations," *Acadiensis* V, 2 (Spring 1976): 25–55; "The Golden Age and the Exodus: The Case of Canning, Kings County," *Acadiensis* XI, 1 (Autumn 1981): 57–82; Patricia Thornton, "Some Preliminary Comments on the Extent and Consequences of Out-Migration from the Atlantic Region, 1870–1920," in *Merchant Shipping and Economic Development in Atlantic Canada*, edited by Lewis R. Fischer and Eric Sager (St. John's: Memorial University, 1982).

17. Tamara K. Hareven and Maris A. Vinovskis, eds., *Family and Population in Nineteenth Century America* (Princeton: Princeton University Press, 1978); Shirley Ardener, *Women and Space: Ground Rules and Social Maps* (London: Croom Helm, 1981).

18. Ardener, *Women and Space*, 15.

19. Tamara K. Hareven, *Family Time and Industrial Time* (Cambridge: Cambridge University Press, 1982).

20. Public Archives of Nova Scotia, Phoebe Collins Diary, 1815–16.

21. Beaton Institute, University College of Cape Breton, Mary Smith Diary, 1891.

22. Acadia University Archives, Rebecca Ells Diary, 1901–05.

23. Mary Bradley, *A Narrative of the Life and Christian Experience of Mrs. Mary Bradley* (Boston: Strong

and Brodhead, 1849) reprinted in part as "Mary Bradley's Reminiscences: A Domestic Life in Colonial New Brunswick," *Atlantis* 7, 1 (Autumn 1981): 92–101.

24. Margaret Dickie Michener McCulloch Diary, *Wolfville Acadian*, December 1923–November 1929.

25. Albert Kennedy, "The Provincials," *Acadiensis* IV (Spring 1975): 94.

26. Beaton Institute, University College of Cape Breton, Ella Liscombe Diaries, 1915–1938.

27. Private, Hannah Richardson diary, 1872; Private, Lucie Borden Diary, 1905–09.

28. On shoemakers in Lynn, see Alan Dawley, *Class and Community: The Industrial Revolution in Lynn* (Cambridge: Harvard University Press, 1976).

29. Public Archives of Nova Scotia, Annie Butler Diary, 1871.

30. Private, Mary MacDougall MacDonald Mason Diary, 1873.

31. Francis W.P. Bolger and Elizabeth Epperly, eds. *My Dear Mr M: Letters to G.B. MacMillan from L.M. Montgomery* (Toronto: McGraw-Hill Ryerson, 1980), 65–115.

32. Anonymous, 22 May 1893. Letter supplied courtesy Alan A. Brookes.

33. Mrs. George Churchill, *Letters from My Home in India* (New York: George H. Doran Company, 1916), 92.

34. On the office situation see Graham S. Lowe, "Women, Work and the Office: the Feminization of Clerical Occupations in Canada, 1901–1931," *Canadian Journal of Sociology* 5 (1980): 361–381, and in this volume;"Class, Job and Gender in the Canadian Office," *Labour/Le Travailleur* 10 (Autumn 1982): 11–37.

35. Beaton Institute, University College of Cape Breton, Mary Killam MacQuarrie Memoir, 1929.

36. Tamara K. Hareven, "Family Time and Historical Time," in *The Family*, edited by Alice Rossi, Jerome Kagen and Tamara K. Hareven (New York: Norton, 1978), 63–4.

37. Nancy F. Cott, *The Bonds of Womanhood: Woman's Sphere in New England, 1780–1835* (New Haven: Yale University Press, 1977). Leonore Davidoff, Jean L'Esperance and Howard Newby, "Landscape with Figures: Home and Community in English Society" in *The Rights and Wrongs of Women*, edited by Juliet Mitchell and Ann Oakley (Harmondsworth: Penguin, 1976), 155.

ONE HUNDRED AND TWO MUFFLED VOICES: CANADA'S INDUSTRIAL WOMEN IN THE 1880's†

SUSAN MANN TROFIMENKOFF

While hard work has been a fact of life for most Canadians, its precise character has altered markedly over time in response to technological change, management initiative, and worker pressure. Women workers in nineteenth-century Canada were caught up, as Susan Mann Trofimenkoff demonstrates in this article, in the consequences of accelerated economic change. Although domestic and personal service remained the largest single category of female employment well into the twentieth century, public attention and many women's hopes for a better future focussed on newer professional, clerical, and manufacturing jobs. Women flocked to such opportunities, ignoring warnings about the preservation of morality and femininity alike. As the report of the Royal Commission on the Relations between Capital and Labour revealed, factory work was initially considered especially unsuitable for women by middle-class observers. The numbers of female workers who eagerly deserted traditional jobs, such as domestic service, for employment on the factory floor, however, tell a different story. Such recruits were rarely asked for their opinion of conditions, but not all passively endured twelve-hour days, unsafe machinery, and stern discipline. We may suspect, from studies done of comparable industries employing large numbers of female hands in the United States and Great Britain — cotton, boot and shoe, food processing, and clothing for instance — that, gagged as they might be in the public record, women found ways of subverting at least part of the industrial system that so discriminated against them. Workplaces became less intimidating with the emergence in song and ritual of new expressions of female culture, as with, for example, the ragging and teasing of girls "walking out" with male employees in the same concern. Factories, like offices later on, changed, if never enough, under pressure from female employees. Shortly after the near-silence noted by Trofimenkoff, blue-collar women, no longer neophytes in industrial employment, began to seize those forms of protest — notably sabotage, boycott, and union action — that male workers with their longer industrial history often practised. In response, strategies of employer control had to become much more subtle than the resort to physical intimidation reported by the Royal Commission.

The Royal Commissioners studying the relations between Capital and Labour searched diligently but in the end they could only find Georgina Loiselle. Since the Commissioners were well aware of enquiries similar to their own in the United States and in Great Britain, they fully expected to find many cases like Georgina's.[1] But after months of roving Canada's four eastern provinces, persistently questioning workingmen and their employers, they found only the one. And even that one had occurred some five years before, in the early 1880s, when "modern" factories were just beginning in Canada and when one might expect the accompanying tensions to burst into flagrant abuse. Still, it was too bad that only the one case could be found. The Commissioners, all of whom were political appointments[2] and most of whom shared solidly middle class values, somehow expected the lower orders to misbehave, particu-

†*Atlantis* 3, 1 (Fall 1977): 66–82.

larly when those lower orders were sexually mixed in the new factories. But there was only Georgina.

Mademoiselle Georgina Loiselle was an apprentice in Fortier's cigar factory in Montreal. She was one of a number of children supporting a widowed mother. But sometimes she was cheeky, speaking back and refusing to do extra work demanded by M. Fortier. Fortier was determined to give her a lesson; when she refused to make 100 more cigars, Fortier seized her, intending to put her over his knee and spank her. But Georgina fell to the factory floor; Fortier pinned her there and beat her with a cigar mould. When reporting the incident to the Royal Commission on Capital and Labour in 1888, neither Georgina nor Fortier seemed particularly perturbed. Georgina had left Fortier's at the end of her apprenticeship but had returned some time later and appeared quite docile; Fortier had not had to touch her again. Fortier, in fact, considered it his duty to correct the young people entrusted to his "care" by their parents.[3] And others shared his sense of duty: the Recorder of Montreal believed young factory workers probably received the same treatment at home; moreover it was certainly better to have young people safely in factories, no matter what the treatment, than to see them running the streets. The Commissioners may well have agreed, for their concern with Georgina was less the physical abuse of the young woman than the moral decency of "a man placing a girl of eighteen in that position."[4] In their investigations, the Commissioners would find other evidence to shake their sense of moral propriety but this was the only case of physical abuse to be found among the one hundred and two female witnesses before the Royal Commission on Capital and Labour.

There is, however, other information that can be discovered about women workers in the 1880s from that Royal Commission. One can, for example, hear the voices of some of Canada's industrial women recounting the kind of work they did, describing their working and living conditions and voicing their complaints. One can also glean the views of male workers and male employers on the question of female labour. And finally one can decipher, by the very questions asked, the attitudes of the male Commissioners towards Canada's industrial women. In the pages that follow these three areas will be explored.

Needless to say, the Royal Commission on Capital and Labour was not an enquiry into the nature of female labour in the 1880s. Female labour was only one of a multitude of subjects that the Commissioners were to investigate. Indeed, aside from the one hundred and two women witnesses before the Commission, only another two hundred and eighteen spokesmen offered any information or opinions on the subject of female labour. The remaining witnesses (close to 1800 people testified during the year and a half of hearings in cities and towns in Ontario, Quebec, New Brunswick and Nova Scotia) spoke of everything from factory laws to wages, from apprenticeships to rents, from arbitration to immigration and from convict labour to strikes.[5] The enquiry was in short an investigation of all aspects of that great nineteenth-century worry: Labour and its relation to Capital. Women were only a small part of such an enquiry.

The enquiry itself was also politically inspired, and, in spite of early efforts to obtain female suffrage and even some early successes in terms of the municipal franchise, women really had very little to do with politics in the 1880s[6] and even less so, it would seem, with labour politics.[7] But because of some labour agitation in the 1880s — including radical papers, political candidates and attempts to create national trade union centrals — the aging Prime Minister, John A. Macdonald, decided to establish the enquiry. Macdonald was also feeling pressure from the two central provinces. Both Ontario and Quebec, in the mid-1880s, passed factory legislation regulating hours and ages for working people. The Prime Minister had never shown the same keen interest in factory legislation; he was still counting on his political reputation as a friend of labour established back in 1872 when he accorded trade unions in Canada some legal status. However, he was not anxious to have the provinces establish an undisputed claim for sovereign jurisdiction in the area. In many ways, therefore, the Commission was as much a political manoeuvre as a labour enquiry. And, of course, women's place in that kind of activity was virtually non-existent. As an added incentive for the establishment of the Royal Commission, Macdonald had the unsettled economic conditions of the mid-1880s. The Prime Minister was anxious to show that his National Policy of 1879 had been and could continue to be beneficial to the Canadian economy and to the Canadian working class. The Commissioners in fact took this part of their undertaking very seriously; their reports credited the industrialization of the country to the National Policy.

But again, none of that had much to do with women. Hence the muffled quality of their voices: no one really wanted to hear from them. As witnesses before the Commission they constituted only one-fortieth of the Ontario witnesses, one-tenth of the Quebec witnesses, one-twentieth of the New Brunswick witnesses and one-thirtieth of the Nova Scotia witnesses. To understand the muffling that those figures reveal, one need only contrast them with the census figures for 1891. In the category "manufactures and mechanical industries," working women made up almost one-fifth of the labour force in Ontario, Quebec and New Brunswick and slightly more than one-fifth in Nova Scotia.[8] Another illustration of this muted quality is the anonymity of so many of the women witnesses. Forty-three of the one hundred and two voices had no name at all. And the women were decidedly more reticent than their male counterparts: in all seventy-three people chose to testify anonymously; only thirty of the close to 1700 male witnesses wished to hide their names.

Given the purpose of the Commission and the muffling of the women witnesses, it is surprising that much at all can be gleaned about Canada's industrial women. But historians of women are becoming used to squeezing every drop of information from every kind of source and this particular source can be subjected to the same treatment. The women themselves give description; the men, attitudes.

From the one hundred and two voices there emerges clearly the type of work these women undertook. Textile workers in cotton mills constituted the largest group overall and for each of the four provinces except Ontario. Other kinds of textile workers made up the next largest group: women in woollen and knitting factories. Then there were women in shoe-making factories, in match factories, in tobacco industries and in printing offices, where the women did the folding and stitching, not the typesetting. And finally there was an odd assortment of milliners, dressmakers, rope makers and paper bag makers. One portend of the future appeared before the Commission — a telephone operator; and one caricature-before-her-time appeared in the form of a WCTU executive member who had no answers at all for the Commissioner's probing questions.

Behind the hundred and two lurked even more women workers. When male employers commented upon female labour they often told the Commissioners how many "hands" they employed. In this way they revealed another, much larger group of women — some 5000 — not merely muffled but entirely voiceless and shadowy as well. Still their occupations are clear. In descending numerical order they were tobacco workers, cotton mill operatives, shoemakers, clothing makers, match makers and woollen mill workers. The occupations are similar to those of the one hundred and two; only the order is somewhat different. But how representative were these one hundred and two voices or these 5000 shadowy "hands"? Compared once again with the "manufactures and mechanical industries" category of the census of 1891 (where the majority of women in the labour force did not in fact appear; that majority was rather in the service and professional categories as servants and teachers), the occupational structure of the women is quite different. From the census, the occupations, in descending numerical order were dressmakers, seamstresses, tailoresses, milliners, cotton mill operatives, mill workers, boot and shoe workers and woollen mill operatives.[9] Even adding all the mill workers together would only move them to third place in the list of industrial occupations. But such a ranking might, however, put them in first place in terms of factory workers, since many dressmakers and seamstresses would work in their own home, in private homes, in very small establishments or as "outside workers" for retail clothing shops. And it was, after all, the factory workers that most interested the Royal Commissioners. By that very fact, factory workers would be more likely to hear of the existence of the Commission; hence they turned up in relatively larger numbers than their sisters in other occupations.

Nonetheless, one hundred and two voices remain a very small sample of the 57,283 women who worked in manufactures and mechanical industries in 1891.[10] And as the list of occupations given above indicates, their work was almost as limited as their numbers. But still some generalizations can be made, both about women workers and about Canada's nascent factory system. All those textile workers merely represented a transfer from home to factory of the traditional female skills and tasks. For the women, the role would be familiar; only the surroundings and perhaps the pace would differ. But the shoe workers tell us something else. They were a direct result of the factory system with its logic of breaking down attained skills into simple, repetitive and mechanical tasks. Where once the shoe trade required long apprenticeships and highly skilled men, now the factory-made shoes simply required highly attentive women to watch the machines. Women were, of course, cheaper. And finally, the matchmakers and the printing employees represented the flourishing of light industry in certain parts of Canada. Light industries required vast numbers of unskilled and therefore cheap labour. All of the industries were, in fact, welcomed by the women involved; in a society where domestic service or school teaching were the only independent economic paths women could take, the factory system opened new areas of paid employment.

The hundred and two voices also provide a glimpse of the working conditions of Canada's industrial women. The hours of work appeared to vary from west to east, with the women witnesses from Ontario working a nine-hour day, those in Quebec a ten-hour day and those in the Maritimes an eleven-hour day. Such a variation would obviously produce the Commissioners' findings of an average ten-hour day in the factories of eastern Canada,[11] but it does not reveal much more. More can be gleaned from the women's remarks about their wages. As perhaps might be expected, the wages varied with the age of the woman and her skill. For example, a fourteen year old folding in a printing plant earned $2.00 per week; a twenty year old in a cotton factory earned $4.00 per week; a middle-aged expert dressmaker earned $7.00 per week and a middle-aged forewoman in a tannery earned $10.00 per week.[12] But there were catches in those salaries. The women (as did most factory men at the time) earned their wages by piecework; they were paid by the number of items they produced, not by the day or by the week. But in order to make the items and in order to make enough of them to earn a "living wage,"[13] the workers had to be provided with the material for their work. If there was no material provided, they might hang around the factory all day waiting for non-existent work. The result would be a slimmer pay packet at the end of the week. Nor could the women count on those wages for the entire year. At a time of over-production, a factory simply stopped its machines, closed its doors and turned its workers out. Then, too, many occupations were of a seasonal nature: printing, dressmaking and millinery followed demand and fashion which determined thereby that women would not have year-round work. And women's wages were consistently lower than those paid to male workers. A final catch in the wage rates of women (and of men too) was the number of fines exacted for defective work or unseemly behaviour. A snag in a piece of cloth, a defective shoe sole, a late arrival, a chat, a giggle, a pincurl fabricated with paper from the factory "closet" would bring the foreman's ire and financial exaction.[14] For the most part women appear to have accepted without complaint this "muffling" of their behaviour.

Perhaps the women were used to similar curtailments of their activities at home. Although very few of the hundred and two talk at all about their living conditions, those who do admit that they could not afford to board out. The $2.00 per week demanded by private homemakers or a higher amount demanded by boarding houses or institutions[15] would put independent living beyond the reach of all but the most skilled of women workers. They lived at home, dependent upon their families to house and feed them, just as the families were dependent on the income that the young women could bring home. Where ages were mentioned at all, the women appeared to be between sixteen and twenty-four and many of them had been working since they were twelve or fourteen. It would seem then that a working class family required the wages of its youngsters and that, from about the age of twelve, a girl would be expected to contribute to the family income. Employers could count on this kind of interdependency; they were assured of a constant supply of willing workers and, because of those workers' living arrangements, they could also pay them low wages.[16]

Although the one hundred and two women were relatively open and forthright when describing their work and their working and living conditions, when the time came to voice complaints, their voices fell silent. The women were very reticent, even with the sympathetic probing of some of the Commissioners. Only when women gave their testimony anonymously would they dare to utter a word of complaint. In effect, only when they muffled their own voices, would they speak out. And they spoke of badly ventilated workrooms: they were either too hot, or too cold, or too dusty; "We have all got frightful colds; it is not good for the health, I assure you." They complained of extra time added to the work day without any financial compensation. They argued that they did not receive enough pay for the work they did. One woman even carried a personal feud into the hearing of the Commissioners: she claimed she worked much harder than the previous witness but she received the same pay. Other women complained that, on leaving a job, they did not receive the pay owing to them. Still others had to have the tiniest of complaints put into their mouths by the Commissioners:

Q. Wouldn't a half-day holiday on Saturday be a boon?
A. Yes.
Q. Do you think that you would not wish for anything more?
A. I think we would wish for a great many more things that we do not get.[17]

Where the women were willing to identify themselves, either their remarks were of a different nature or they themselves were different. For example, two factory workers in Ontario freely gave their names but when the time came to voice complaints, they stated that everything was fine in their factory. Another young factory worker and her mother gladly furnished their names, but the younger woman, it turned out, had been dismissed from her job: indeed the two complained that the daughter had lost her job because of testimony she had given at a court investigation of a workman's injuries. She had refused to be silenced but she had paid for that refusal. And finally there were the skilled dressmaker and milliner, employers of other women. They too were quite willing to give their names and to use the occasion to voice their complaints about the shoddy workers they were obliged to hire. The school system, they contended, simply had not prepared young girls for needlework jobs. Moreover, the girls were more interested in getting married than in being trained for a steady job.[18] Thus complaints from women workers only reached the ears of the Commissioners in indirect ways. Only those women who were removed from the immediate work at hand, by anonymity, by dismissal or by status would dare say anything critical. Even Georgina Loiselle did not complain about the treatment she had received at the hands of cigar manufacturer Fortier. But then Fortier was present during her testimony. It can only be concluded that the women were afraid and so muffled their own voices.

From the hundred and two themselves, there is little more to be heard. Fortunately the Commissioners pursued the question of female labour with both male workers and male employers. Again one must remember that the enquiry was not primarily about female labour; indeed the question was by no means the major concern of either the Commissioners or the male witnesses. Only 218 witnesses out of the 1800 spoke of female labour at all. Often there was a one word or at most a one sentence reply to a question about female labour and a quick passing on to a totally different subject. For example, one male witness all in one breath agreed that women teachers should receive the same salary for the same work as men teachers and then launched into a lengthy discussion of the drainage and sewers in London, Ontario.[19] In spite of these handicaps to a clear picture of industrial women in the 1880s, there are a number of things that can be wrenched from the comments, first of the male workers, and then of the male employers.

Men factory workers were decidedly ambiguous about the question of female labour. They had, it would seem, not yet come to terms with it. Where, for example, one cigar worker readily admitted that women could do the same work as well as men and that, therefore, they should receive the same wages, others, in printing, tailoring and cigar making, would justify the lower salaries paid to women by the contention that the women did an inferior job. Still other men, working in dry goods or tailoring establishments, recognized that the lower salaries paid to women encouraged employers to hire them rather than men; these men were fully aware that the wage difference was a means both of cutting into job opportunities for men and of depressing their wage rates. But the men had no ready solution to the vexing problem; they voiced only their personal concern. Other workers pointed out that there was a sexual division of labour in many factories: men and women worked at different tasks. There could be, therefore, neither comparison nor competition between the two and the women were paid less.[20] In short the factory system itself was another highly effective means of muting the voices of such women.

Some of the male workers were more direct. They believed, for example, that young girls should not be working in the large mills because there they would hear "immoral words" and thus become immoral. And they suggested that women, if they were working in factories, should leave their workplace at a different time from the men. In that way they would not hear the "bad words" uttered as the hands left the factories.[21] In both these cases the male workers voiced an opinion that was much more pronounced among the Commissioners: morally corruptible women had to be protected from the ill effects of words. Perhaps this moral concern on the part of the male workers was one way of covering their bewilderment at the economic competition they were suddenly facing from women factory workers. Certainly it suggested an effective way of controlling the women. But other male workers were even more blunt: one simply need not listen to the women. There was no need, remarked one man, to pay any attention to women factory workers complaining about dust in a work-room, because they were always "grumbling about something or other all the time."[22] The men warned the Commissioners thereby that they should not take the few complaints they heard from women workers too seriously. Short of muffling them directly by removing them from the factories, the men should do so indirectly, simply by not listening.

In fact, there were almost as many opinions about female labour as there were workingmen witnesses. This very diversity of opinion suggests that the male factory workers were unsure of just what female labour meant to them. As household heads they knew perfectly well that the wife's or daughter's wages were necessary to the family's survival. As union men they also recognized the necessity of equal pay for equal work.[23] As members of the working class they had always known that women worked. And yet . . . whether their backgrounds were rural or urban, these men also knew that women's work was different from theirs. Now the existence of factories implied — although did not always ensure — that women's work could be the same as men's, might even be better and usually was cheaper. Female labour did not augur well for men. Their uneasiness about it rings through their testimony.

Male employers, however, were quite direct and forthright. None of the worries of the male workers appeared. The employers liked female labour because it was "more profitable to us or we would not employ them."[24] And yet that very profitability was based on certain expectations about the nature of women workers. The employers expected the women to be docile, clean, quick, cheap and sober.[25] As long as women maintained those characteristics, traits which rendered them superior to male employees, they would be sure of jobs. The employers had very effective means of ensuring that women workers did maintain those qualities. Should the women protest any of their working conditions, should they, in effect, cease to be docile, clean, quick, cheap or sober, they could be "muffled" very easily. There was always another group of women with the appropriate behaviour ready to replace the protesters. This tactic worked well in the Stormont Cotton Mills in Cornwall when striking women, protesting the foreman's demand that they be quiet and orderly during the dinner hour, returned docilely to work under threat of being replaced.[26] And, as happened in another case, the employer simply moved his factory away from the offending women.[27] Muffling could take many forms, all equally effective.

Employers expressed still other expectations of women workers. They fully expected their female employees to be temporary workers;[28] the women would work a few years before marriage and then would vanish, to be replaced by another group of young women. This continual turnover not only enabled the employers to keep the wages of women low but also permitted them to dub the women unreliable, uninterested in learning a trade or in applying themselves seriously to it. That characterization, while perhaps applicable to the women, effectively concealed the fact that the women's positions were steady, unchanging and profitable. The employers reaped the benefits but justified them by muffling the women in terms of male expectations. Sometimes too the employers justified those benefits by claiming a paternal interest in their women workers. Fortier believed he was replacing Georgina Loiselle's dead father when he admonished her physically for disobedience.[29] And a master baker believed that the women working in his new, modern bakery would be better wives and mothers for their experience.[30] Women workers were so beneficial to male employers that the employers had to believe that they too were of benefit to the workers.

Finally, the employers counted on the women being less skilled than men. Such an expectation enabled the employers to justify the lower wages they paid their female hands. Some employers even enforced this particular characteristic of their women employees. Certain factories maintained a strict sexual division of labour, with the women assigned to the least skilled tasks. Other workshops maintained a sexual division of wages by which, for example, a male tailor would be paid by the week and a woman tailor by the piece.[31] The piecework rate ensured that the woman would work constantly and quickly, in order to produce enough garments to fill a pay packet. She may have succeeded in that task but the comment from the employer was that the man's work was finer. She could not win; nor was she intended to.

Male employers were quite clear in expressing, and often in enforcing, their economic interest in a certain type of female labour. Noticeably absent from their calculations was the moral interest which some workingmen had shown. Where that moral interest found full expression was in the Commissioners themselves. Just what that moral concern meant is, however, another matter. The workers' interest in protecting the morality of their female co-workers probably reflected their uneasiness at the prospect of economic competition from women. But obviously the middle class Commissioners had no such worries. Were they vaguely aware that the factory system was undermining their sense of family and of propriety? Were they afraid? Was something "catching" going on in the factories?[32] Or were the Commissioners simply revealing their middle class notions of the time: that women were both the guardians of morality and the most easily corruptible and that the poor were poor because of some flaw, usually a moral one, in their character? What then of poor working women? They truly were a scandal.

Certainly the Commissioners were not interested in the women as workers. Even when women constituted the majority in a given factory, the Commissioners' questions concerned the male employees.[33] And when the women witnesses were factory hands, their voices were effectively muffled by perfunctory questioning. The Commissioners asked about hours of work, about wages, about language and about closets. And that was all. But if the women witnesses happened to be employers of women, they had free rein to express their opinions on a wide variety of subjects, notably one dear perhaps to the hearts of the wives of the Commissioners: why young girls were unwilling to go into domestic service.[34] Women as workers were not the primary concern of the Commissioners.

Instead they searched diligently for what they most expected from working class women — scandal. Assuming that immoral behaviour was a necessary consequence of the mingling of the sexes in the factories, the Commissioners painstakingly hunted down every instance of immorality. They found it, they thought, in the language women heard. Immorality, it seems, was some kind of disease spread through language and particularly catching for women. Women should not therefore hear, much less use, violent language. But the working women obviously had a different set of values. While one Commissioner fretted over the kind of language a certain woman might hear in her factory, the witness in question took it all very casually. She must have shrugged as she replied offhandedly that the language was not violent — "just cursing; that is all."[35]

Undeterred, the Commissioners continued to track down instances of, or occasions for, immorality. They found them, they thought, in the "conveniences" that the working people had to use. Hence their recurring question: were there separate "closets" for the male and female workers? Here, immorality, at least in the minds of the Commissioners, seems to have something to do with toilets. The state of factory toilets amounted to a virtual obsession. "Did you ever see the men try to get into the females' closets when the females were in there?" "What is the height of the water closets separating the men from the women?"[36] Etc. etc. The concern probably reveals more about the strange inner workings of middle class Victorian minds than it does about the state of working conditions in Canadian factories but any investigation of that will have to await the flowering of psycho-history in this country. Certainly the Commissioners did find a sufficient number of "combined conveniences" to cluck about. But what the connection was with the morality of women workers remains unexplained.

Still they pressed on. How, they wanted to know, did the foremen and the factory owners behave toward the female employees? Was their behaviour "gentlemanly."[37] The lower orders were, it seems, expected to misbehave and the men in particular were expected to take advantage of women in subordinate economic positions. The Commissioners' self-appointed role of moral watchdog for the factory women may have been truly a part of their own gentlemanly protective impulse or it may have been an unwitting revelation of middle class behaviour. In the Canada of the 1880s there were far more women working as domestic servants than as factory workers and the domestics were far more susceptible to male (and middle class) aggressions. Indeed, studies of the period indicate that most prostitutes began their careers as servants.[38] The Commissioners may thus have revealed more of their own class attitudes to women than of the class reality of factory women. In any case, just as for their other questions, they were never able to find sufficient evidence to support their worries. There was only M. Fortier smacking Georgina while she lay on the factory floor.

And yet the Commissioners would not give up. They persisted in enquiring about the presence of "persons not married, in such a condition as they ought not to have been in" — a round-about Victorian way of looking for unwed mothers. And when they finally did discover a few such women, they referred to them as "the guilty party."[39] Only one of the Commissioners indicated any economic awareness of the problem when he asked whether a witness believed that low wages drove women into prostitution. But even that searching question was to be deflected, this time by the solidly middle class witness. Mayor Howland of Toronto restored the questioning to its proper level by remarking icily: "A good woman will die first."[40]

Finally the Commissioners were able to find one factory in Montreal that did confirm many of their preconceptions. At the St Anne's Cotton Factory they discovered men and women throwing water at each other over the partition in the closets; "pretty free" conduct on the part of men and women workers, "tough acts" by the manager and superintendent, and "young unmarried persons . . . in such a state that it was not fitting they should associate with others."[41] But even in this case, the workers were not willing to have the Commissioners confirm their preconceived notions. One of the women witnesses complained to the Commission that the local press had exaggerated the "goings-on" at the mill.[42]

Perhaps the Commissioners took the complaint to heart. Or perhaps they convinced themselves by their own scrupulous investigation. Certainly they left no stone unturned in their quest for misbehaviour. But in the end, when they made their reports, they had to conclude — albeit somewhat reluctantly one suspects — that there were no signs of "serious immorality" in Canadian factories. Indeed, in a grand gesture, they even conceded that the moral character of Canadian working women was "as high as that of other classes."[43] No one had asked them to inquire into the moral state of Canadian women but they had done so anyway and in the process had managed to muffle not only the women themselves but also the crucial economic and social questions raised by the factory system and by women's place in it. Given their moral concern they could not help reiterating the notion that women constituted a helpless class, that they needed both moral and physical protection from the dangers of the work world. In that, of course, the Commissioners were no different from their contemporaries who were passing factory legislation and demanding female factory inspectors. Protecting women from the world was a common concern in the 1880s.

The four groups of people discussed above seem to have been living in four different worlds. Working women, working men, male employers and male Commissioners constituted so many voices speaking in the dark. The women tried to speak of the reality of their working days but they did so in muffled tones. The working men hid their confusion about female labour in a flurry of contradictory opinions. The male employers spoke clearly: women were an economic asset in a factory as long as they fulfilled certain requirements. And the male Commissioners deliberately confused the entire question of female labour by treating it as synonymous with morality. The only characteristic that the four groups had in common was the muffling itself. And that muffling was omnipresent in the women's anonymity, in the male workers' ambiguity, in the employers' economic interest and in the Commissioners' moral interest. Perhaps one has here an aspect of "female culture,"[44] the silence that is both imposed upon and accepted by women. That silence may be both cause and consequence of the economic dependency of women in the family and in the factory. Certainly the injunction to be silent accompanied young women as they eagerly sought the variety of jobs the factory system offered. The trick for the historian remains however: how to crack that silence.

Notes

1. The Canadian Royal Commission on the Relations between Capital and Labour, named in December 1886, had been drawn up by the Justice Minister J.S. Thompson. To do so he studied similar enquiries in Pennsylvania, Connecticut, New Jersey and Kansas. PAC, Macdonald Papers, Thompson to Macdonald, 2 Sept. 1886. The Commission reported in 1889 with a single volume containing a majority and a minority report and five volumes of testimony.

2. See for example PAC, Macdonald Papers, T. Stewart to Macdonald, 21 Sept. 1887; A.T. Freed to Macdonald, 22 Sept. 1886; A.H. Blackeby to Macdonald, 26 Jan. 1887. Blackeby, the secretary of the Commission wanted to receive a salary before the Commission had begun its work, not for himself but to assist the local Conservative candidate, Cowan, in his campaign!

3. *Report of the Royal Commission on the Relations between Capital and Labour* (hereafter cited as RCCL), Quebec testimony, 91–2; 125–6.

4. Ibid., 126.

5. For a complete list of the subjects of interest to the Commission, most of which were also of interest to the trade union movement at the time, see RCCL, *Report*, 5–6.

6. See Catherine Cleverdon, *The Woman Suffrage Movement in Canada* (Toronto, 1974), 19–26, 105–111 and Carol Bacchi, "Liberation Deferred: the Ideas of the English Canadian Suffragists, 1877–1918" (Ph.D. thesis, McGill University, 1976), ch. 2.

7. One of the many aims of the Knights of Labour was equal pay for equal work but not many women have shown up in Knights of Labour Assemblies. The radical *Palladium of Labour* insisted on female suffrage as part of its Labour Reform platform for the Ontario election of 1886 (*PL*, 7 Dec. 1886) and it had the occasional article from a working woman but the *Palladium* was far from being a mass paper. The Trades and Labour Congress also endorsed the suffrage at its convention in 1886 but the trade unions, based as they were on skilled trades, also had few women members. See Jean Scott, *Conditions of Female Labour* (Toronto, 1892), 27.

8. Calculated from *Census of Canada*, 1891, vol. II, 152–5, 158–60, 164–7, 175–9.

	Women	Men	Total	% Women
Ontario	30,757	128,074	158,831	19.4
Quebec	17,792	75,414	93,206	19.1
New Brunswick	3,648	15,059	18,707	19.5
Nova Scotia	5,086	17,425	22,511	22.6
Total	57,283	235,792	293,255	19.5

For some reason the Quebec women witnesses seem to have been less easily muffled than their sisters in the other provinces!

9. Ibid., Dressmakers: 22,054; seamstresses: 10,083; tailoresses: 7,731; milliners: 3,141; cotton mill operatives: 2,954; mill operatives: 1,811; boot and shoe workers: 1,720; woollen mill operatives: 1,671. For purposes of comparison, there were 73,652 domestic sevants and 14,787 teachers recorded in the same census.

10. As in note 8 above. The total is only for the four provinces visited by the Royal Commission.

11. RCCL, *Report*, 37, 99, 135–95.

12. RCCL, Ontario evidence, 1163; Quebec evidence, 484; Ontario evidence, 347; Quebec evidence, 1311.

13. Somehow more significant than the "Living Profit" that businessmen in the same period have tried to make us believe was their just dessert. M.B. Bliss, *A Living Profit* (Toronto, 1974). As Terry Copp makes clear in his *Anatomy of Poverty* (Toronto, 1974), no one, except the poor themselves, worried too much about their inability to earn a living wage.

14. RCCL, Quebec evidence, 482, 987, 1146, 1147, 273.

15. Ibid., Ontario evidence, 358: Quebec evidence, 989, 1147, 1284, 818–19, 1350–51: New Brunswick evidence, 192, 196, 146; Nova Scotia evidence, 201, 203.

16. One workman, a weaver in charge of a woollen factory in Sherbrooke, believed however that those who boarded worked harder, since they had to earn more in order to pay their keep. Ibid., Quebec evidence, 1192. The piece-rate would then be an incentive.

17. RCCL, Quebec evidence, 984, 988, 1145, 1148, 1120, 1296–97, 1294, 1282–83, 1284–85; Ontario evidence, 1173.

18. Ibid., Ontario evidence, 1086, 1087: Quebec evidence, 639–40, 641: Ontario evidence, 358, 347, 348.

19. Ibid., Ontario evidence, 662.

20. Ibid., 919; Quebec evidence, 356; Ontario evidence, 810; Ontario evidence, 41, 48, 627; New Brunswick evidence, 73, 74, 211; Quebec evidence, 1072; Ontario evidence, 350; Nova Scotia evidence, 73.

21. Ibid., Ontario evidence, 665; Quebec evidence, 320.

22. Ibid., Nova Scotia evidence, 210.

23. Printers' unions insisted upon equal pay: they had however few female members. Ibid., Ontario evidence, 44, 48, 108, 596.

24. Ibid., Ontario evidence, 617.

25. Ibid., 621.

26. Ibid., 1074–5.

27. Ibid., 288.

28. Ibid., Ontario evidence, 289; New Brunswick evidence, 4.

29. Ibid., Quebec evidence, 126.

30. Ibid., 598.

31. Ibid., Ontario evidence, 693, 628, 1164; Quebec evidence, 854; New Brunswick evidence, 117, 339.

32. This sense of something dubious spreading from the lower orders to infect those above is something that Ned Shorter has turned on its head to posit a revolution in romance and sentiment spreading with industrialization from the working to the middle class. Edward Shorter, *The Making of the Modern Family* (New York, 1976). The book has been subjected to severe, and convincing, criticism in part on the grounds that the author has used middle class evidence to reveal peasant and working class reality. E.g. Joan Scott's review in *Signs* 2, 3 (Spring 1977): 692–96. I hope I have avoided that particular trap in this discussion. There certainly is no denying the uneasiness the middle class Commissioners felt in the face of female labour but whether that uneasiness was based on any working class female reality is quite another question.

33. E.g. RCCL, Quebec evidence, 1157.

34. E.g. ibid., Ontario evidence, 358–59; 1009. The question of the declining number of domestic servants bothered all middle class reformers throughout the last third of the nineteenth century and first quarter of the twentieth. See National Council of Women, *Yearbooks* and G. Leslie, "Domestic Service in Canada 1880–1920," in *Women at Work: Ontario, 1850–1930*, edited by Janice Acton, Penny Goldsmith, and Bonnie Shepard (Toronto, 1974), 71–117.

35. RCCL, Ontario evidence, 1162.

36. Ibid., Ontario evidence, 1079; Quebec evidence, 476.

37. Ibid., New Brunswick evidence, 193.

38. L. Rotenberg, "The Wayward Worker: Toronto's Prostitute at the Turn of the Century," in *Women at Work*, edited by J. Acton *et al.*, 33–63.

39. RCCL, Quebec evidence, 476, 483.

40. Ibid., Ontario evidence, 168. A.T. Freed was a curious Commissioner.

41. Ibid., Quebec evidence, 481.

42. Ibid., 485.

43. Ibid., *Report* I: 9; II: 79. Historians have begun to spill a lot of ink over the fact that the Commissioners divided themselves and produced two reports. See B. Ostry, "Conservatives, Liberals, and Labour in the 1880s," *Canadian Journal of Economics and Political Science* XXVII, 2 (May 1961):150–53; G. Kealey, Introduction to his one volume edited version of the Royal Commission, *Canada Investigates Industrialism* (Toronto, 1973); F. Harvey, "Une enquête ouvrière au XIXᵉ siècle: la Commission du travail, 1886–1889," *Revue d'histoire de l'Amérique française* 30, 1 (juin 1976):35–53, and G. Vallières, "La Commission royale sur les relations du travail avec le capital au Canada 1886–89" (M.A. thesis, University of Ottawa, 1973). The two reports are in fact quite similar although there does seem to be slightly more sympathy for the workers displayed in the second report whose signators were more closely connected with workers' associations. But on the question of female labour, the two reports differ only in wording.

44. Berit Äs, "On Female Culture," *Acta Sociologica* 18, 2–3: 142–61.

FARM WOMEN ON THE CANADIAN PRAIRIE FRONTIER: THE HELPMATE IMAGE†

SARA BROOKS SUNDBERG

As the prairie women who tell their stories in Sara Brooks Sundberg's article indicate, early twentieth-century farm women in stable and compatible marriages may have enjoyed mastering the wide range of skills involved in women's farm work and may have felt themselves to be real partners with their husbands. Certainly their work was basic to the survival of the family enterprise. Not only did they do the gardening, cooking, cleaning, sewing, childbearing and rearing, which were essential to the reproduction of farm labour, but they also produced goods and services for sale or barter. Farm women were invariably responsible for the dairy and the poultry; working from their homes they served as postmistresses, laundresses, — seamstresses, babysitters, and keepers of rooming houses. In such ways they helped subsidize the cash crop for which their husbands were largely responsible. These crops, usually wheat on the prairies, were vulnerable to weather conditions and market forces; without some dependable additional farm product or service from the wife, a farm family could fall helplessly into debt if drought or low prices cut into their earnings from staple production.

However, because the farm's long-term profitability was deemed to be based on the cash crop, most capital expenditures went to make that part of farm work more productive. New barns or up-to-date sowing and reaping machines were given a higher priority than a better sewing machine or new churns and the milk house that would have made the farm woman's sewing or dairying more efficient. Eventually, highly capitalized poultry and dairy farms and cheese factories, many times more productive than the wife's part-time efforts on the family farm, eliminated the local markets for her products. Adjusting, the farm wife continued providing services for pay, but increasingly did so not as entrepreneur, but as employee of the local hospital, school board, or business.* The aim was — and is — the same, however: to subsidize the primary family enterprise, the farm.

In addition to the market forces that have served in the twentieth century to make the production for which farm women were responsible more marginal to the overall operations of the farm, the legal system as well has not worked to their benefit. Because of homesteading provisions, almost all the agricultural land in western Canada was legally owned by men in the early years of this century. Women's traditional dower rights of one-third of their husband's estates had been suspended in the West in the late 1880s, and compensatory legislation was not passed until well into the second decade of the twentieth century. Until that time, in the case of marriage breakdown or widowhood, a farm woman, despite her clear economic contributions, could be left with nothing. As late as 1974, Irene Murdoch, an Alberta farm wife seeking a divorce, was refused a share by the Supreme Court of Canada of the property accumulated during her twenty-five year marriage. The Murdoch case made evident to Canadian women the necessity of having their vital contributions to the family economy recognized in law.

†Carol Fairbanks and Sara Brooks Sundberg, *Farm Women on the Prairie Frontier: A Sourcebook for Canada and the United States* (Metuchen, N.J.: The Scarecrow Press, 1983), 71–90.

* See Marjorie Griffin Cohen, "The Decline of Women in Canadian Dairying," *Histoire sociale/Social History* 18 (November 1984): 307–34; and Giselle Ireland, *The Farmer Takes a Wife* (Chesley, Ont., Concerned Farm Women, 1983), ch. 6.

> "Poor girl!" say the kind friends. "She went West and married a farmer" —
> and forthwith a picture of the farmer's wife rises up before their eyes; the
> poor, faded woman . . . hair the color of last year's grass, and teeth gone in
> front.[1]

In the case of farm life on the grassland frontiers of western Canada there is
little argument that life was difficult for women. Nevertheless, women were
part of the earliest efforts to establish agricultural settlements on the prairie
and plains of the western interior of Canada. What were the experiences of
these women, and how did they respond to pioneer life in the grasslands?

Previous attempts to answer these questions have not revealed women's
experiences in all their variety. Instead what has emerged are images that obscure
differences between individual women's experiences. Responding to these images,
this study examines, from the perspective of women themselves, one image of
pioneer farm women on the Canadian prairies — that of pioneer farm women as
helpmates.

In her analysis of the helpmate image for frontiers women in the United
States, Beverly Stoeltje writes, "the primary defining feature of [helpmates]
was their ability to fulfill their duties which enabled their men to succeed,
and to handle crises with competence and without complaint."[2] Carl Dawson
and Eva R. Younge, in *Pioneering in the Prairie Provinces: The Social Side of the
Settlement Process*, express this image when they use this description to depict
the experiences of pioneer farm women in Canada:

> As for the pioneer woman, what shall we say? When her man was at home
> she stood shoulder to shoulder with him in the conduct of the day's affairs.
> When he was absent . . . she cared for the family, she looked after the
> stock, she took upon her lone shoulders burdens which were none too
> light for husband and wife to bear.[3]

Because a pioneer woman's experiences were tied to the needs of her husband
and family she, as June Sochen explains in her study of frontier women, "is not
the prime mover in her life. She does not determine her own individual destiny."[4]
This image is taken to its gloomy extreme in the following interpretation of
prairie women's lives:

> A prairie woman's life was defined by the needs of her family. When her
> children left, the habit of working remained. Tasks which once were
> necessary for survival now had no point, yet they had become so much a
> part of her that only death could bring release.[5]

Another dimension of the image of pioneer women as helpmates is the notion
that farm work for pioneer women was drudgery. A recent study of Canadian
prairie women describes farm life for pioneer women in dreary terms:

> For the typical pioneer woman, life was a hectic chorus of mend, weed,
> pump, chop, churn, bake and scrub. If she had children — and families
> tended to be large in those days — they added their giggles and howls.[6]

The monotony of pioneer life was intensified by the isolation of the prairie
frontier. Women stoically endured these hardships because, as prairie pioneer
Nellie McClung explained, they were just too busy to complain.[7]

But Nellie McClung also observed "that people love to generalize; to fit cases to their theory, they love to find . . . farmers' wives shabby, discouraged and sad."[8] Women's writing challenge these images and generalizations. Autobiographies, letters, journals, and reminiscences recount the experiences of women as wives, mothers, daughters, and single women on the frontier. They are some of the sources used in this essay. These women are not representative of pioneer farm woman as a whole. Instead they are a small group of women who had the ability and the inclination to record their experiences and attitudes. In some cases women wrote contemporary accounts, in others they relied upon memory. Regardless of these distinctions and limitations, women's writings still clearly reveal a rich variety of experiences which are useful in examining images of pioneer farm women in the grasslands.

Most Canadian pioneer women came to the grasslands in one of two migrations. The first wave began about 1870 and lasted until the late 1890s. Prior to 1870 the grasslands were part of Rupert's Land, a broad expanse of territory controlled by the Hudson's Bay Company. Its boundaries lay between the Red River in the east and the Rocky Mountains in the west. In 1870, the Canadian government acquired Rupert's Land from the Hudson's Bay Company and the grassland began to be recognized for its agricultural potential. Settlers from various parts of Ontario, the United States, and Europe trickled into the grasslands.

By the late 1890s, a second, larger migration began. Promising free homesteads and assisted passages, the Canadian government and the Canadian Pacific Railway launched vigorous advertising campaigns to encourage agricultural settlement within the grasslands. Partially as a result of these campaigns, significant numbers of settlers from the United States, Great Britain, the Balkans, the Ukraine, and Russia immigrated to the grasslands of Canada. The rapid influx of settlers during this second migration lasted until about World War I. The pioneer experiences of most women cited in this study fall between 1870 and 1914.

The beginnings of the first migration to Canada coincided with the passage of Homestead legislation in 1872, which provided settlers with 160 acres of land for a ten dollar fee, providing they plowed the land, built a shelter, and lived on the property for six months out of a year for three years. The lure of cheap land, the chance for economic independence, captured the imaginations of women as well as men. Sarah Roberts, an early twentieth-century Alberta pioneer, remembered that land was a major factor influencing her family's decision to move from Illinois to Canada, "We had lived for years in Illinois where land is priced at one hundred dollars per acre. No doubt the thought of receiving 480 acres 'free' made more of an appeal to us than was justified."[9] It is important to note that Sarah Roberts included herself as part of the decision-making process to move west. Her participation in this process is contrary to the notion that women did not affect decisions concerning their futures and the futures of their families.

In fact, women were sometimes the first to recognize the opportunities inherent in western land. In 1880 Letitia McCurdy Mooney persuaded her husband that the future of their children depended upon their opportunity to acquire fertile land. Letitia's daughter, Nellie Mooney McClung, recalled her mother's persuasive argument to move west:

"We'll have to go some place, John," she said one night to my father. "There's nothing here for our three boys. What can we do with one-hundred-and-fifty stony acres? The boys will be hiredmen all their lives, or clerks in a store. That's not good enough!"

Father was fearful! There were Indians to consider, not only Indians, but mosquitoes. He had seen on the Ottawa what mosquitoes could do to horses; and to people too. No! It was better to leave well enough alone.[10]

Clara Goodwin, another late nineteenth-century Manitoba pioneer, remembered "my mother had visited Winnipeg the year before and was very much taken with the West. I remember quite distinctly her saying to my father, 'Richard, you MUST go to that country! That's the place to live!'"[11]

Sometimes it was not just the economic opportunities that persuaded women to suggest moving their families to the West. Letters from friends and family exerted a strong influence. Lulu Beatrice Wilken recalled that her mother was persuaded to go west to Saskatchewan by her brother Edward:

So he wrote to her to try to persuade Father to move his family West and to take up land also.

I am sure that it did not take long to convince Father of the advantages to be obtained in such a move, and, in the spring of 1891, Mother took her three small children and joined her brother.[12]

For Muriel Parsloe it was not enticements from family members, but a sense of adventure that caused her to initiate her family's move to Swan Lake, Manitoba. After reading an advertisement for western Canadian land she said, "We've tried Australia, let's take a trip to Canada and see how we get on there."[13]

A more conventional reason brought Kathleen Strange to the grasslands. It was because of their doctor's recommendation that Kathleen Strange and her husband purchased a farm in the remote area of Fenn, Alberta, in 1920. The active outdoor life on a farm in the west was their doctor's prescription for an injury received by Kathleen's husband in World War I.[14]

Unmarried women also came to farms in the grasslands. Western farmland offered these women a means for achieving economic independence. Land was not "free" for these women. Women could not obtain "free" homesteads unless they were the sole support for their families. Qualified women took advantage of this opportunity. A women's column in a 1914 issue of the Grain Grower's Guide carried this appeal:

Dear Miss Beynon: I am writing to ask for a great favor for a very deserving widow with children. She wants to homestead and has not the wherewithal to look about. . . . [P]erhaps some of the kind sisters know of one suitable for mixed farming. . . .
Intending Homesteader[15]

A notable example of a successful woman homesteader during this period is Georgina Binnie-Clark. For a period of about five years between 1909 and 1914, Binnie-Clark owned and operated her own wheat farm in the Qu'Appelle Valley in Saskatchewan. In her book *Wheat and Woman*, Binnie-Clark detailed her farming experiences and argued the case for farming as a means of achieving economic independence for women.[16]

Unmarried women came to farms in the grasslands for other purposes as well. In 1886 the Canadian Pacific Railway issued a questionnaire asking women about their lives in the Northwest Territories. One of the questions read, "Can hard-working honest girls easily obtain situations at good wages on farms or [in] households in the North-West? . . ." A concise reply came from Mrs. T.D. Elliott in Alexandria. She answers, "1. Good girls can get plenty of good places at good wages then marry good young men with good farms."[17] Opportunities for women in farm homes as domestics or home-helps promised gains for women in other ways besides wages. The shortage of females on the frontier was a prominent theme in appeals for female immigrants to the west. This theme was evident in the *MacLeod Gazette* of May 15, 1896:

> "Do you know" remarked W.D. Scott to a Toronto newspaper reporter, "one of the greatest needs in the North West at the present time? It is women, simply women. Married men with their wives are contented enough out there, but single men on farms are apt to get lonely. If girls could only be persuaded to go out there they would be sure of good situations, and I tell you it would not be long before they would get married."[18]

Educated middle-class women from the British Isles were prime targets for these appeals. At the turn-of-the-century the British Isles found itself saddled with an oversupply of single, middle-class women unable to find suitable jobs. Employment and marriage opportunities in the Canadian West offered relief to these women. In her book *West-Nor'-West*, published in 1890, Jessie Saxby, herself a middle-class British widow, expressed this concern:

> In Britain one of the most urgent social difficulties is what to do with our surplus women — how to provide for them, how to find remunerative employment for them. In Canada one of the most urgent social difficulties is how to persuade women to come there. . . . In Quebec, in Winnipeg, in Regina, everywhere, I was told the same thing. "Oh, if respectable women from the old country would come out West!"[19]

To assure the successful adaptation of British emigrant gentlewomen to the West, emigration societies and training schools were established to provide information about the west and to instruct women in necessary domestic skills.

Women did not always have a choice of whether to stay in their present circumstances or to take a chance in a new land. Edna Jaques' family migrated from Ontario to Moose Jaw, Saskatchewan, in 1902. She remembered her father announcing they would leave for Moose Jaw:

> His name was Robert Jaques. He came to visit dad one day in January 1902. They were in the parlor talking and laughing together. . . .
> Suddenly the folding doors between the two rooms opened and dad stood in the doorway (I can see him yet) and loudly announced to my mother, "We're leaving Collingwood." Taking a long breath he said, "We're going homesteading in the Northwest Territories. . . ."
> My mother fainted.[20]

Nevertheless, after the initial shock some women adapted to the idea, as did Jessie Raber's mother. Jessie Raber remembered that even though it was her father's idea to take up a homestead near Lacombe, Alberta, in 1895, her mother soon recognized the economic and social advantages of the move.

> Mother said perhaps she had been selfish in not being anxious to move to a farm in Canada before, for she knew that a growing family did need plenty of room. The milk, fresh eggs and the wonderful vegetables one could grow in Canada: for she did want us all to grow up into strong and healthy men and women, with good educations.[21]

Other women remained unconvinced of the advantages of a westward move. Clara Middleton "had no urge to go adventuring," but went along because "Homer was bent on it [and] that was enough for me."[22] Laura Salverson simply resigned herself to the inevitable, "And now George had the grand vision of the independent life of a landowner. . . . There was nothing to be done about it, except to let the disease run a swift unhindered course."[23]

Without the satisfaction that comes from participation in an important decision and without the confidence that comes from belief in the promise of a new land, women's journeys to Canada could be painful experiences. Maria Adamowska's family emigrated from the Ukraine to Alberta in 1899. She recalled her mother's sad experience:

> Mother, on the other hand, was tenderhearted. Of all the trials that had been her lot in life, this one was the most bitter. Whenever father had mentioned going to Canada, she started to cry. And she cried all the way on the train and missed seeing the lovely sights in God's good world.[24]

The experience of this unhappy emigrant woman fits one aspect of the helpmate image. That is, in this instance, Maria Adamowska's mother did not determine her own future. However, clearly this is not true for all women on the frontier. Women came to the grassland frontiers for themselves, as well as for others, and when they did come for others, they were energetic, as well as reluctant, pioneers.

Whatever their reasons for coming to the grasslands, women worked when they arrived. As prairie homesteader Georgina Binnie-Clark observed "On a prairie settlement the women work . . . I owe one debt to my life on the prairie and that is a fair appreciation of my own sex."[25] For married women, the home was the hub of pioneer farm women's work. In her study of frontier women's work, Susan Armitage identifies two categories of household work. The first category, household maintenance, involves routine activities, such as cooking and cleaning.[26] The lack of mechanical aids made their chores time consuming. The experience of Laura Salverson's mother, an Icelandic immigrant, illustrated this fact, "Mama was forever busy. She had a passion for keeping things scoured and scrubbed. . . . When you carried water from a pump half a block away or melted snow after the winter set in, all this washing and cleaning consumed a lot of time."[27] In another example, Kathleen Strange remembered a dreaded chore, wash day:

> Washing! What a job that always was. Usually it took me the entire day. In summer I washed outside; in winter, down in the basement. The boiling, sudsy water had to be carried in pails from the stove to wherever my tubs were set. More than once I burned myself severely, spilling water on unprotected hands and legs.[28]

Nevertheless, some women found satisfaction in these routine chores. Edna Jaques recalled the "glow" on her mother's face as the wash emerged "whiter than white."[29] Lulu Beatrice Wilken remembered the pride her mother felt in the polished appearance of the floor in their sod shack. Years of washing with hot sudsy water made it smooth and white.[30]

It was not just the lack of conveniences that made chores time consuming. It was also the number of people requiring women's care. Because children were potential laborers, large families were an asset. Women often had several children to tend, in addition to housekeeping chores. Jessie Raber, daughter of immigrant parents who homesteaded in Alberta during the early 1900s, remarked on her mother's experience, "Mother often wished she could bundle us all off to school or somewhere. Just think, seven [children] under her feet all day and every day. Such patience she must have had."[31]

The number of people in a household was enlarged in other ways as well. Hospitality was an integral part of frontier life and an important social custom. Saskatchewan pioneer Harriet Neville remembered "No stranger was ever refused meals or shelter night or day at our home."[32] Sometimes women turned this custom to profit by taking boarders and earning a wage.

It should be noted here that daughters, like their mothers, worked on the family farm. Often they assumed their mother's chores, thereby reducing their mother's overall workload. For example, as a teenager, Jessie Raber assumed responsibility for much of the cooking and for care of the younger children.[33] In some cases daughters' chores as surrogate mothers came at an early age. Because both her parents worked outside the home, Veronica Kokotailo, even though she was only five years old at the time, took care of the younger children![34] Daughters also worked as field hands. Nellie McClung recalled overseeing the cattle rather than going to school.[35]

Daughters contributed to the family's economic well-being in other ways. In some cases they worked as home-helps, a term applied to domestic help, to earn wages to assist their parents. Ukrainian immigrant Anna Farion remembered her work as a home-help. "My work was harder than the year before as there were four children, and four or five hired men to look after. But I stuck it out, as I wanted to help my parents as much as I could."[36] In another way Anna's experience illustrates the hardships some immigrant girls and women experienced. Earning only a few dollars a month, Anna requested a raise. Her employer "brushed me off with the rejoinder that she had trained me for the job and, besides, she had paid Kolessar $5.00 for me. Her words hurt me deeply. Evidently, I had been sold. . . ."[37]

Not all immigrant girls and women working as home-helps encountered discriminatory treatment of this kind. In an effort to evaluate employment opportunities for British women, Elizabeth Keith Morris travelled throughout western Canada during the early part of the twentieth century. She considered the position of home-help suitable employment for capable British women:

> The position of home help is a safe, cheap and sure way of earning capital to start in other work, of learning Canadian methods and requirements, and of feeling one's feet in a new country; but the work is hard and heavy including washing, ironing, baking, scrubbing, . . . therefore, only to be undertaken by the robust.[38]

The second category of frontier women's work was household sustenance. Armitage defines household sustenance as "work which contributed directly to family economy by making cash expenditure unnecessary."[39] Farm women were manufacturers in their own homes. Harriet Neville used skins to make "hoods, mittens, muffs and necks" as well as spinning wool to make clothing, bed mattresses and quilts.[40] The daily entries of Mrs. Seward St. John revealed she made butter and raised chickens to use in trade for other goods.[41] Lulu Wilken remembered "Soap making is an art. . . . The fat and lye water had to be boiled to the right stage, and the proper proportions of water and grease maintained or they would separate and it became a failure."[42] Mrs. Emma Phair remembered that her mother manufactured the fuel necessary for their cooking stove. "She knew just how many twists of straw it took to heat the oven for baking. . . . It took one hundred and twenty five twists to heat the oven; four bags altogether to heat the oven and bake the bread."[43]

Women's contributions to sustenance reached beyond the domestic sphere. They worked as field hands. Late nineteenth-century homesteader Harriet Neville drove the oxen while her husband pitched hay.[44] Another Saskatchewan pioneer, Mrs. Edward Watson, noted that she and her children built their sod barn, [45] and Sarah Roberts helped to brand cattle.[46] Some women, like Georgina Binnie-Clark preferred outdoor work. She wrote:

> I worked hard through June at the stoning, and started to harrow . . . From the beginning I was perfectly happy working on the land, only I wished it was someone else's turn to get those tiresome three meals a day.[47]

Sarah Roberts, on the other hand, said of her branding job: "I stayed with my job until it was done, and I am glad that I never had to do it again. I think that it is not a woman's work except that it is everyone's work to do the thing he needs to do."[48] Veronica Kokotailo's mother must have agreed. For two weeks she worked for a neighbor plastering his barn. Her payment was a pail of potatoes.[49]

Aside from their responsibilities as homemakers, home manufacturers, field hands, and wage earners, women performed other important functions. They were nurses and doctors for their families and neighbors. In a letter written to her grandmother from her family's Saskatchewan homestead, Maryanne Caswell described picking herbs for medicinal purposes.[50] Ukrainian immigrant Maria Adamowska remembered, "As I was reaping with a sickle, I cut my finger. The gash was so deep that the finger dangled, just barely held on by the skin. Mother managed to splice it somehow, and the wound healed."[51] Even in the prairie town a woman's medical skills were relied upon. As late as 1930, Fredelle Maynard, a young resident of the town of Birch Hills, Saskatchewan, recalled that a doctor's responsibilities were limited to declaring quarantine and delivering babies.[52] In more isolated areas women acted as midwives, even if they were inexperienced. Clara Middleton described such an experience:

> We got home about midnight and at one o'clock came Mr. Barnes. His wife was in labour, and would I come? I protested that I wouldn't be any good, that I knew nothing. . . . No; his wife wanted me.
>
> "It's up to you," said my husband, but I knew by his tone that he had no doubts. I could almost hear him thinking, "You're a woman and you're needed."[53]

The thoughts of Clara's husband are a fitting description of women's work on the prairie. Women performed whatever work was needed. Regardless of training or experience women were expected to be self-reliant. Sometimes the responsibilities of self-reliance could soften women's adjustment to the isolation of the frontier. For example, Clara Middleton remembered that women acted as morticians as well as doctors. The ritual of preparing a body for burial provided women the opportunity to support and comfort one another.[54] In another example, Harriet Neville, finding herself isolated from nearby schools during the winter of 1884–1885, ordered textbooks from Toronto and kept regular school hours for her children. Of this experience she said, "One thing these things did for me. I never had a moment to be lonely to feel the lack of neighbors. I slept well and did not dream so much about old friends."[55]

Nevertheless, the challenge of self-reliance proved too great for some women. On their way to their homestead in Manitoba, Nellie McClung remembered encountering a family returning from the prairie. The wife, dressed in a silk dress and flimsy shoes, was sobbing. She tearfully explained, "She hated the country . . . it was only fit for Indians and squaws. . . ." In an effort to comfort the woman, Nellie's mother suggested that perhaps the woman would be more comfortable travelling in simple clothes. The roads were muddy, sturdy shoes and gingham dresses were more practical. The woman did not sew, her mother had always done her sewing. "Mother's zeal began to flag, 'Take her back,' she said to Willard, 'she's not the type that makes a pioneer.' "[56]

The confining nature of women's work was a different source of discontent for women. Peace River pioneer Ida Scharf Hopkins articulated this frustration:

> Much as the woman becomes completely involved in the homestead life many of the challenges become repetitive. . . .
> We women were never unhappy, but sometimes life was a bit dull. There was so little variety in the day-by-day routine. So much necessary work to be done there was little time or energy left for anything else. We had to keep the homefires burning.[57]

But women did appreciate their vigorous lives on the frontier prairie. Saskatchewan pioneer Alice Rendell illustrated this when she wrote to a friend in 1904:

> I would never advise anyone to come out here who is the least afraid of work. They are better off at home. There is plenty of room to breathe in this country and if the work is hard the freedom, which is the indispensable attribute of life here, makes one far less susceptible to physical fatigue. . . . Here one feels that each week's work is a step onward whilst in the old country oftentimes a year's toil brought nothing but disappointment and additional anxiety.[58]

Kathleen Strange, like Alice Rendell, appreciated freedom. For Kathleen, pioneer life offered a new opportunity to work as a full partner with her husband. She missed this partnership in her later, less rigorous role of a city wife:

> My own life, on the other hand, is almost completely changed. And, most important of all, I am deprived of one particularly vital thing. On the farm I was a *real* partner with my husband, sharing with him in almost every detail of his daily work. Now his work is carried on in a downtown office, with professional help. There is little I can do to assist him.[59]

Prairie farm women like Kathleen Strange were indeed partners with their husbands, not only because they shared in their husbands' day-to-day work, but also because of their own day-to-day responsibilities. Farm women's roles as homemakers, home manufacturers, field hands, wage earners, doctors, morticians, and teachers meant that women made substantial contributions to the business of farming. These contributions receive inadequate recognition when interpreted from the perspective of women as helpmates. Viewed as ancillary to the work of farm men, our conception of prairie farm women's work loses equality within the economic structure of the farm, an equality which is justified given women's roles as providers of valuable goods and services.

In a similar way the diversity of prairie farm women's experiences is lost when they are assigned the blanket role of helpmate. Women in this study reveal that it is a mistake to assume that all women on farms were wives and mothers. Single women were farmers in their own right, and they worked on farms as home-helps or domestics. Women's experiences also reveal that contrary to the image of women as obedient helpmates, some women did affect the decision-making process which led to their pioneer experiences in the grasslands. Some women actively participated in the decision-making process, others made the decision on their own.

Women's experiences differed in other important ways as well. Although women's responsibilities on the farm meant hard work, prairie women did not unanimously agree that their work on the farm was drudgery. The notion of universal drudgery, more than any other aspect of the help-mate image, deprives women of any possibility of joy or fulfillment in the process of pioneering. Prairie women's experiences reveal that although some women found their chores monotonous and confining, others felt obvious pride in their accomplishments. Some even found their responsibilities to be useful buffers between themselves and the loneliness of the frontier. Others appreciated the freedom and opportunity resulting from their work. As Kathleen Strange perceptively observed, "Drudgery! That is a word with many connotations. What is drudgery to one person may not be drudgery at all to another."[60]

The image of the stoic, hardworking helpmate not only homogenizes prairie women's experiences, it leaves some experiences out altogether. What about the women who could not cope with frontier life on the prairie? What factors made the difference between success and failure? We lose part of the story of women who stayed, when we ignore those who left.

The experiences of women in this study raise more questions than they provide answers. Yet the diversity of experiences revealed in women's writings admonishes us to look more closely at our images of pioneer farm women on the Canadian prairie.

Notes

1. Nellie McClung, *In Times Like These* (1915; reprint ed. Toronto: University of Toronto Press, 1972), 109.

2. Beverly Stoeltje, " 'A Helpmate for Man Indeed': The Image of the Frontier Woman," *Journal of American Folklore* 88 (January–March 1975): 32.

3. Gerald Willoughby, *Retracing the Old Trail* (Saskatoon, 1933) quoted in C. Dawson and E.R. Younge, *Pioneering in the Prairie Provinces: The Social Side of the Settlement Process*, Canadian Frontiers of Settlement Series, vol. 8 (Toronto: Macmillan of Canada, 1934), 19.

4. June Sochen, "Frontier Women: A Model for All Women?" *South Dakota History* 7, 1 (1976), 36.

5. The Corrective Collective, *Never Done: Three Centuries of Women's Work in Canada* (Toronto: Canadian Women's Educational Press, 1974), 54.

6. Linda Rasmussen, et al., *A Harvest Yet to Reap: A History of Prairie Women* (Toronto: The Women's Press, 1976), 42.

7. Ibid., 42–43.

8. McClung, *In Times Like These*, 109.

9. Sarah Ellen Roberts, *Alberta Homestead: Chronicle of a Pioneer Family*, edited by Lathrope E. Roberts (Austin: University of Texas Press, 1971), 4.

10. Nellie McClung, *Clearing in the West* (New York: Fleming H. Revell Company, 1936), 32.

11. Audrey Peterkin and Margaret Shaw, *Mrs. Doctor: Reminiscences of Manitoba Doctors' Wives* (Winnipeg: The Prairie Publishing Company, 1976), 2.

12. Lulu Beatrice Wilken, "Homesteading in Saskatchewan," *Canada West Magazine* 7 (Spring 1977), 27.

13. Muriel Jardine Parsloe, *A Parson's Daughter* (London: Faber and Faber, 1935), 220.

14. Kathleen Strange, *With the West in Her Eyes* (Toronto: George J. McLeod, Ltd., 1937), 8.

15. "Sunshine," *The Grain Grower's Guide*, 11 March 1914, 20.

16. Georgina Binnie-Clark, *Wheat and Women* (1914; reprint ed. Toronto: University of Toronto Press, 1979).

17. Canadian Pacific Railway, *What Women Say of the Canadian Northwest* (n.p. 1886), 32.

18. *MacLeod Gazette*, 15 May 1896, quoted in Rasmussen, *A Harvest Yet to Reap*, 14.

19. Jessie M.E. Saxby, *West-Nor'-West* (London: James Nisbet and Company, 1890), 100.

20. Edna Jaques, *Uphill All the Way: The Autobiography of Edna Jaques* (Saskatoon, Sask.: Western Producer Prairie Books, 1977), 14.

21. Jessie Browne Raber, *Pioneering in Alberta* (New York: Exposition Press, 1951), 10.

22. Clara and J.E. Middleton, *Green Fields Afar* (Toronto: Ryerson Press, 1947), 12.

23. Laura Salverson, *Confessions of an Immigrant's Daughter* (London: Faber and Faber, 1939), 480.

24. Maria Adamowska, "Beginnings in Canada," in *Land of Pain; Land of Promise: First Person Accounts by Ukrainian Pioneers 1891–1914*, translated by Harry Piniuta (Saskatoon, Sask. Western Producer Prairie Books, 1978), 54.

25. Georgina Binnie-Clark, *A Summer on the Canadian Prairie* (London: Edward Arnold, 1910), 278.

26. Susan Armitage, "Household Work and Childrearing on the Frontier: The Oral History Record," *Sociology and Social Research* 63, 3: 649.

27. Salverson, *Confessions*, 37.

28. Strange, *With the West in Her Eyes*, 220.

29. Jaques, *Uphill All the Way*, 105.

30. Wilken, "Homesteading," 28.

31. Raber, *Pioneering*, 67.

32. Harriet Johnson Neville, "Pioneering in the North-West Territories," edited by Harriet Purdy and David Gagan, *Canada: An Historical Magazine* 2 (June 1975), 42.

33. Raber, *Pioneering*, 136–137, 140–141.

34. Anne B. Woywitka, "A Roumanian Pioneer," *Alberta History* 21, 4 (1973): 22–23.

35. McClung, *Clearing in the West*, 116.

36. Anna Farion, "Homestead Girlhood," in *Land of Pain; Land of Promise*, 92.

37. Ibid., 91.

38. Elizabeth Keith Morris, *An Englishwoman in the Canadian West* (London: Simpkin Marshall, 1913), 188.

39. Armitage, "Household Work and Childrearing," 469.

40. Neville, "Pioneering in the North West Territories", 48–51.

41. Seward T. St. John, "Mrs. St. John's Diary," *Saskatchewan History* 2 (Autumn 1949): 25, 29.

42. Wilken, "Homesteading", 29.

43. Isabel M. Reekie, *Along the Old Melita Trail* (Saskatoon, Sask.: Modern Press, 1965), 49.

44. Neville, "Pioneering in the North West Territories", 20.

45. Mrs. Edward Watson, "Reminiscences of Mrs. Edward Watson," *Saskatchewan History* 5 (Spring 1952), 67.

46. Roberts, *Alberta Homestead*, 226.

47. Binnie-Clark, *Wheat and Woman*, 151.

48. Roberts, *Alberta Homestead*, 226.

49. Woywitka, "A Roumanian Pioneer", 22.

50. Maryanne Caswell, *Pioneer Girl* (McGraw-Hill, 1964), 10th letter.

51. Adamowska, "Beginnings in Canada", 67.

52. Fredelle Bruser Maynard, *Raisins and Almonds* (Toronto: Doubleday Canada, 1972), 16.

53. Middleton, *Green Fields Afar*, 48.

54. Ibid., 51.

55. Neville, "Pioneering in the North West Territories", 30.

56. McClung, *Clearing in the West*, 58.

57. Ida Scharf Hopkins, *To the Peace River Country and On* (Richmond, B.C., 1973), 118–119.

58. Alice Rendell, "Letters from a Barr Colonist," *Alberta Historical Review* (Winter 1963): 24–25.

59. Strange, *With the West in Her Eyes*, 292.

60. Ibid., 276.

WOMEN, WORK AND THE OFFICE: THE FEMINIZATION OF CLERICAL OCCUPATIONS IN CANADA, 1901-1931†

GRAHAM S. LOWE

Men and women in nineteenth-century Canada did different sorts of work for pay, even in cases where physical strength was not involved. Work was, and is, a critical reflection and reinforcement of gender identity. Working at a job that the culture and time define as female has been one way to maintain a sense of being a woman, both in the eyes of the individual and in the eyes of others. This sexual division of labour has served important economic functions as well. Increasingly in the nineteenth century there came to be two kinds of jobs: those requiring a stable work force, skilled and experienced with expensive machinery; and those demanding less skill (or what was conveniently defined as less skill) and possibly involving relatively inexpensive equipment utilized by low-paid, easily-trained employees who could be hired and fired readily. Rather than all potential workers being drawn from one pool, there were, and are, several pools, with women, young people, ethnic minorities, and immigrants used to fill the lower-skilled positions. Taking advantage of women's limited employment choices, employers hired women, at wages lower than those they would have had to pay their brothers, to do routine, simplified tasks in new areas of endeavour or in areas transformed by the burgeoning economy. A slowly-increasing number of jobs became female occupations, paying the employee barely enough to support herself, and thereby making the jobs of little interest to men, who, for their part, were anxious to exclude women from their own employments. Sex segregation permeated virtually every aspect of the marketplace by the end of the nineteenth century and is still the rule rather than the exception today.

Originally a form of apprenticeship for men seeking managerial positions, clerical work was gradually transformed through a variety of means to make it acceptable only to women rather than to men; that is, it became feminized. In this article Graham Lowe suggests that we cannot understand the administrative revolution that occurred in major Canadian offices during the early years of this century unless we know the role that women played by flocking to new office jobs. He argues that the availability of low-priced female labour was essential to the transition "from small-scale entrepreneurial capitalism to modern corporate capitalism." Women's participation permitted the expansion of that part of the economy creating white-collar jobs, which in turn pulled in ever more female clerical workers. One hundred years ago women were an exception in Canadian offices. Now they form an overwhelming percentage of all clerical workers, and one out of every three Canadian women in the labour force does some kind of clerical work.

†*Canadian Journal of Sociology* 5, 4 (1980): 361–79. This is a revised version of a paper presented to the Political Economy Section of the Canadian Political Science Association Annual Meetings, June 1979, Saskatoon, Saskatchewan. I would like to thank Dennis Magill, Noah Meltz, Lorna Marsden, Rosalind Sydie, as well as three anonymous *Canadian Journal of Sociology* reviewers, for helpful comments on an earlier draft. I would also like to acknowledge the Canada Council's financial support of the research.

The spectacular growth of white-collar occupations in Canada since the turn of the century has fundamentally altered the nature of the labor force. One of the most striking features of the burgeoning white-collar sector has been the shift in the sex ratio of many jobs accompanying the rise in female labor force participation rates. Nowhere has this feminization trend been more pronounced than in clerical occupations. At the turn of the century the office was largely a male preserve. Yet by 1971, 30.5 percent of the entire female labor force was engaged in clerical work. And with about 70 percent of all clerical jobs held by women, the contemporary office is the prototypical female job ghetto.[1] Much can be learned about the emergence and maintenance of female job ghettos by examining how the feminization of clerical work occurred.

The purpose of this paper is to analyze how women came to predominate numerically in the office. A main theme of the paper is that the feminization process was central to the administrative revolution which occurred in major Canadian offices during the first three decades of the twentieth century. The administrative revolution accompanied, and indeed facilitated, the transition from small-scale entrepreneurial capitalism to modern corporate capitalism.[2] The hallmark of this revolution was the rise of large, centralized office bureaucracies and the growing importance of administration in regulating economic activity.[3] The nature of clerical work was dramatically altered: clerical ranks expanded tremendously between 1901 and 1931; the relative socio-economic position of the clerk was eroded;[4] and office organization and the clerical labor process were rationalized.

The feminization process is fundamental to all of these changes. For example, the influx of women into the office largely accounted for the growth of clerical occupations. This in turn undermined the socio-economic position of the clerical group, as women were paid less than men. And scientifically-oriented managers, seeking greater administrative efficiency and more direct control over the office, created a new stratum of routine clerical jobs into which women were chan-nelled. Thus, by the start of the depression, the old-style male bookkeeper had been replaced by an army of subordinate female clerks. As any observer of the contemporary office is quick to recognize, the legacy of this feminization process is still vital.

Four major questions will guide our analysis. First, how did clerical jobs come to be defined as "women's work?" Second, what factors motivated employers to shift their source of labor supply in this manner? Third, to what extent do the characteristics of female clerks (relatively low wages, low skill levels, lack of opportunities, powerlessness, lower aspirations and tenuous attachment to the labor force) reflect the nature of the jobs into which they have traditionally been channelled? And fourth, did women *displace* men in existing clerical jobs or *replace* them in qualitatively different kinds of work? . . .

The Feminization of Clerical Work: Historical Trends

The entry of women into the office can be traced back to the closing decades of the nineteenth century. In the post-Confederation period women were usually relegated to servile domestic chores. In 1868, for example, the federal civil service employed only one woman, a housekeeper.[5] This situation began to change, and by 1885 there were twenty female clerks working in the federal government.[6] Yet many of today's major offices were slow to hire women. Sun Life Assurance Company in Montreal, for example, did not appoint its first female clerk until 1894.[7] Attitudes towards the employment of women in offices were becoming more tolerant. Jean Scott was thus able to observe in 1889 that "women seem as fitted for (office) work as men, and have proved as competent where the work was not too severe."[8]

The small number of women found in Canadian offices prior to 1900 reflected generally low female labor force participation rates. The 1891 Dominion Census, the earliest to break down occupational data by sex, shows that 11.4 percent of the female population over the age of ten were gainfully employed, comprising only 12.6 percent of the entire labor force.[9] After the turn of the century, however, powerful new economic forces began restructuring the division of labor in industry. By the end of the First World War, the foundation for a modern industrial capitalist economy had been laid.[10] A number of other factors — the development of the modern joint stock corporation and the public bureaucracy; changing attitudes towards the employment of women; labor shortages during World War I; and the growing importance of more efficient forms of administration — combined with industrialization to shape the pattern of clerical feminization.

TABLE 1

Total labor force, clerical workers and female clerical workers, Canada, 1891–1971 *

	Total labour force	Total clerical	Clerical workers as a percentage of total labor force	Female clerical	Females as a percentage of total clerical	Female clerks as a percentage of total female labor force
1891	1,659,335	33,017	2.0	4,710	14.3	2.3
1901	1,782,832	57,231	3.2	12,660	22.1	5.3
1911	2,723,634	103,543	3.8	33,723	32.6	9.1
1921	3,164,348	216,691	6.8	90,577	41.8	18.5
1931	3,917,612	260,674	6.7	117,637	45.1	17.7
1941	4,195,951	303,655	7.2	152,216	50.1	18.3
1951	5,214,913	563,083	10.8	319,183	56.7	27.4
1961	6,342,289	818,912	12.9	503,660	61.5	28.6
1971	8,626,930	1,310,910	15.2	903,395	68.9	30.5

SOURCES: Canada D.B.S. Census Branch, *Occupational Trends in Canada, 1891–1931* (Ottawa, 1939), table 5; Meltz, *Manpower in Canada* (Ottawa: Queen's Printer, 1969), section 1, tables A-1, A-2, and A-3; 1971 Census of Canada, volume 3, part 2, table 2.
* Data adjusted to 1951 Census occupation classification

Tables 1 and 2 indicate that women made significant advances in clerical employment after 1901. There were relatively few clerks in the labor force in 1891, the vast majority being male (table 1). The number of female clerks increased from 4,710 to 12,660 between 1891 and 1901. While this represents a relative growth rate of 168.8 percent (table 2), almost ten times that for the total female labor force, the female share of clerical jobs only increased from 14.3 percent to 22.1 percent (table 1). But this marked the emergence of a trend which, by 1971, had resulted in the concentration of 30.5 percent of all female workers in clerical occupations (table 1).

The segregation of women into specific industries and occupations has remained surprisingly stable since 1900.[11] This is especially true in the case of clerical work. From 1901 to 1971, the share of clerical jobs held by females jumped from 22.1 percent to 68.9 percent. Segregation was even more pronounced within particular office jobs. In stenography and typing, for example, the "female" label became firmly affixed as the proportion of jobs held by women increased from 80 percent to 95 percent between 1901 and 1931.[12] Furthermore, changes in the industrial concentration of clerical employment between 1911 and 1931 set the course of future developments.[13] By 1931, manufacturing, finance and trade each accounted for over 20 percent of all female clerical employment.[14] These industries were at the forefront of corporate capitalism and their development required the rapid expansion of administration.

TABLE 2

Percentage increases, female labor force and female clerical workers, Canada, 1891–1971 *

	Female labor force	Female clerical workers
1891–1901	17.7	168.8
1901–1911	53.3	166.4
1911–1921	34.0	168.6
1921–1931	36.0	29.9
1931–1941	27.1	29.4
1941–1951	39.7	109.7
1951–1961	51.3	57.8
1961–1971	68.2	79.4

SOURCES: Canada D.B.S., Census Branch, *Occupational Trends in Canada, 1891–1931* (Ottawa, 1939), table 5; Meltz, *Manpower in Canada* (Ottawa: Queen's Printer, 1969), section 1, tables A-1, A-2, and A-3; 1971 Census of Canada, volume 3, part 2, table 2.
* Based on data adjusted to 1951 Census occupation classification.

The growth of administration is evident in table 2. From 1891 to 1921, the inter-censal decade growth rate for female clerks exceeded 166 percent, far outstripping increases in the total female labor force. In other words, clerical feminization originated during the 1890s and accelerated dramatically between 1901 and 1921. Indeed, the 1911–21 decade was pivotal to the development of the modern office, containing the greatest surge in clerical employment of the century. Clerical growth tapered off somewhat during the 1920s, but changes in the nature of clerical work make this a decisive period for the creation of a female job ghetto in the office. Women were well on their way to predominating in the office by 1931, holding 45.1 percent of all clerical jobs (table 1). . . .

We have traced the institutionalization of women as the major source of labor for modern clerical work. This underscores a central theme of the paper: that the entry of women into the office coincided with the proliferation of many new fragmented, routine jobs in the lower reaches of administrative hierarchies. Truncated employment opportunities for women and deeply engrained sex-based wage differentials resulted. We thus find that in 1901, female clerks earned 53 percent of the average male clerical salary, inching up only slightly to 58 percent by 1971.[15]

The working conditions faced by female clerks have created a vicious circle. Low wages tend to produce the kind of work patterns — high turnover, short-term labor force attachment and low aspirations — which reinforce employers' discriminatory attitudes and trap women in a relatively small number of female-dominated jobs. . . .

A Structural Explanation of Clerical Feminization: Selected Historical Evidence

In this section of the paper, we will document how major structural changes in office organization and the clerical labor process underlay the shift in demand from male to female clerical workers. Three case studies will be presented. The first will focus on the rise of a female labor market for bank clerks during the First World War. The second examines the clustering of female clerks in the lowest strata of the federal civil service. And the third outlines the mechanization of clerical work in major offices, arguing that this aspect of work rationalization was fundamental to the feminization process. All three cases highlight the connection between the administrative revolution and changing occupational characteristics. The emphasis will be on how the dynamics of labor market segmentation[16] and sex labelling[17] were borne out in the office.

Before considering the historical evidence, a brief outline of the structural basis of clerical feminization is in order. The rise of corporate capitalism in Canada after 1900 precipitated a revolution in the means of administration. Two trends converged, transforming the nature of clerical work. First, the flood of paperwork generated by the expanding economy required growing numbers of clerks. Second, managers came to rely on the office as the nerve centre of administration. As organizations expanded, managers replaced traditional, unsystematic methods of administration with "scientific" programs founded on the rational concepts of efficiency in organizational operations and control over the labor process. By the end of the First World War, these trends had greatly magnified the scope and complexity of office procedures. But the burgeoning layers of administration became a source of inefficiency, threatening to undermine the managerial powers vested in the office. This sparked a surge of rationalization in major Canadian offices, particularly during the twenties. By the end of the decade, the typical large central office exhibited certain factory-like features. Work had become fragmented and standardized; hierarchy and regimentation prevailed.

Task specialization was fundamental to this revolution in the means of administration. As the burden of office work increased, managers found that clerks performing simple tasks in rapid succession were cheaper to employ, produced more and were more easily regulated. The new jobs created in this manner lacked the skill components found in the craft-like work of the bookkeeper. Consequently, they were unattractive to middle class male clerks expecting upward mobility and comfortable salaries. Employers were pragmatic enough to recognize the clear advantages of women's higher average education, traditionally lower pay and greater availability for menial tasks. A permanent secondary labor market of female clerks thus developed. Its emergence was buttressed by a number of socio-economic factors, such as the rise of mass public education, male labor shortages during the First World War, the gradual loosening of social norms regarding women's employment, and the fact that female wages were generally better in offices than in domestic or sales work. In short, a hallmark of the modern office is the replacement of the general male bookkeeper by an army of female workers. As women flooded into these subordinate positions which employers had defined as "female," they became entrenched as the modern clerical corp.

The Impact of World War I on Women in Banking

Severe labor force disruptions during both world wars directly influenced the sex ratio of many occupations. It has been argued that far from transforming the economic role of Canadian women, World War I merely accelerated an earlier trend by creating a temporary influx of women into the world of men's work.[18] This generalization underestimates how the war precipitated lasting shifts in the balance of the sexes in the office.[19] The more enduring effects of the war on clerical occupations resulted from the development of shortages of male clerks at a time when major structural readjustments were occurring in the office. The fact that the war coincided with the administrative revolution helped to break down traditional barriers to female employment in some industries.[20] In banking, for example, the war was instrumental in establishing women as the most economical source of labor for routine clerical jobs.

Banks traditionally considered the ideal clerk to be a young "gentleman" from a solid middle class background. When there was an under-supply of Canadians of this description, the banks recruited in Britain. But acute shortages of male bank clerks during the war forced a reconsideration of staffing policies. We find, for instance, that the proportion of female clerks in the Bank of Nova Scotia's Ontario region rocketed from 8.5 percent in 1911 to 40.7 percent in 1916.[21] The war had shattered old restrictions, and even with postwar readjustments women still held over 30 percent of these positions in 1931.

Women were a rarity in turn-of-the-century banks. One of the largest banks in the Dominion employed only five women in 1901.[22] A major stumbling block was that bankers considered women unable to create the public confidence necessary for a successful branch operation. One branch manager, when faced with his first female employee in 1901, "discussed with the head office in all seriousness the advisability of having a screen — a good high one, too — placed around her to shut her off completely from the observation of the public."[23]

Prior to the war, women tended to fill jobs requiring no public contact, such as stenographic and secretarial positions and menial head office jobs. One bank, for example, employed 350 female stenographers and 273 female general clerks in 1916. These jobs were mainly at head office; only seven women held teller positions in branches. As the war escalated, bank officials had little choice but to deploy females to the branches as vacancies created by enlisting male clerks[24] combined with the general expansion of banking to precipitate a labor supply crisis. A female employee described the resulting diffusion of women throughout the bank's clerical hierarchies in these terms:

> The posts open to women in a bank are, of course, both stenographic and clerical, and on the former it is unnecessary to touch. In the head offices until quite recently the proportion of clerical openings was small, but it is rapidly increasing and affording, as the business of each bank expands, opportunities in the way of special openings calling for special ability. In addition to the ordinary run of clerical positions, women have been employed for the past few years in the branches of at least some of our leading banks in collection departments and on the ledgers; yes, on the ledgers. . . . Since the outbreak of the war, women have been filling positions both as clerks and as heads of departments which were formerly held by men. . . . In fact, the only two posts which are not at present occupied by women in a greater or lesser proportion are those of accountant and manager.[25]

Bank management reluctantly adjusted to the realities of the wartime labor market. In 1916, the Bank of Nova Scotia officially directed its branch managers to replace enlisted male clerks with women. Recognizing that the scarcity of male clerks would likely continue; bankers considered the possibility of placing women into previously male dominated jobs: "we might just as well realize at once that the services of young women will have to be utilized for ledgerkeepers, and at the smaller branches for tellers, so that attention should be paid to their training with this kind of service in mind."[26] While a good number of branch managers were unwaivering in their conviction that the male clerk was indispensible for business,[27] some were acknowledging the merits of female clerks. But this was tempered by the assumption that after the war most would return to the higher callings of homemaking and motherhood.

The economic necessities of the war clashed with the traditional social norms governing female conduct. Women were thus confronted with a dilemma. Many of the newly recruited female clerks proclaimed their intention to remain employed "not merely as the assistants of men but as their equals in service and remuneration."[28] Yet numerous other women demurred in the face of this challenge, thereby fulfilling the prophecy that "with the return of peace scores of girls will joyfully lay down their pens and return to their homes."[29]

The immediate postwar boom carried wartime feminization into the twenties. The *Monetary Times*[30] reported that "Canadian banks are busier than ever before, and by their policy of opening many new branches at the present time they are able to absorb their returning employees and still retain some of the temporary (female) help." The expansion of bank hierarchies channelled numerous former male clerks into supervisory positions. The recession in the early twenties resulted in many branch closures, curbing the hiring of women for a time. But when the economy picked up later in the decade, banks actively recruited women into their lower clerical ranks.

Changes in the clerical labor process, especially in large branches and head offices, tended to make the banks' time-tested recruitment and training procedures obsolete. Curiously, some bankers considered male juniors cheaper to hire than women. The *Monetary Times*[31] offered this explanation:

> Women do not cultivate "mobility" which is such a characteristic part of
> Canadian banking. Again, they are not suitable for very small branches,
> where the employees act to a certain degree as protectors. Moreover, they
> do not respond to opportunities for promotion as readily as men, who are
> in the business as a life work. They have not so large a capacity for work as
> the average male, and consequently more clerks are necessary.

In other words, men were an investment, contributing considerably more to
the bank in the long run by working their way up to responsible positions.

Even before the war, however, growing task specialization had increased the
number of routine clerical jobs at the expense of the general clerkships which
served as the training ground for aspiring males. As the banks modernized their
administrative structures, there arose a "good deal of discontent among the
younger men who . . . enter the banking service at low salaries with the
expectation of rising to more responsible and highly paid positions."[32] In sum,
the wartime labor crisis exacerbated organizational changes in the banks to
bring about a demand shift in the lower clerical echelons.

In order for women to become a permanent labor source by the end of the
1920s, the banks' occupational structure had to be segmented along sex lines.
It was this segmentation which facilitated the creation of a secondary female
labor market. At the root of occupational and wage discrimination in the office
was the nineteenth century attitude that while women were handicapped in
pursuing "male" occupations because of inherent disadvantages, they nevertheless possessed certain qualities useful in a limited range of subordinate jobs.
Scott explains:

> Woman has manifestly been designed by nature as a complement, not as a
> substitute for man. If society has put her under certain political
> disabilities, her creator has put her under certain physical disabilities. Even
> independently of the curse of Eve, the average women cannot calculate on
> her ability to work continuously with as well-grounded confidence as the
> average man, while in bodily strength she cannot compare with him. On
> the other hand, she excels him in delicacy of touch, in lightness of step, in
> softness of voice.[33]

Because their natural calling was thought to be in the home, women were
relegated to part-time, temporary employment. Strong social sanctions prohibited the employment of married women.[34] Women tended to internalize
these prevailing norms, making it that much easier for employers to build
sex-based inequities into the division of labor. A vicious circle developed. Tasks
defined as suitable for women were typically monotonous and unrewarding.
This helped to turn the assumptions underlying occupational discrimination
— the female's tentative labor force attachment, her primary vocation of
homemaker and mother, her lower aspirations — into self-fulfilling prophecies,
manifested in a lack of job interest and high quit rates. The way women reacted
to their relatively disadvantaged working conditions provided employers with
supporting evidence for the negative stereotypes which justified their recruitment
into routine jobs.[35]

Labor market segmentation and job sex labelling in the federal civil service

The treatment of women in the federal civil service is a classic example of the use of legislation and formal hiring policies to severely restrict female employment opportunities. Beginning in the late nineteenth century, the flow of women into the lower ranks of the Ottawa "inside service" steadily mounted. The relatively high government salaries and the introduction of merit-based entrance examinations in 1908 attracted many women into the swelling bureaucracy. This leads Archibald[36] to conclude that the "generally low labor force participation rates of women in the early part of this century were more a result of restricted opportunities than a female lack of interest in working." Women initially entered the civil service in response to a general demand for clerical labor. But the Civil Service Commission resorted to rules, regulations and legislation to segment the supply of clerical workers into male and female groups, confining the demand for female labor to menial jobs in the lowest reaches of the clerical hierarchy.

The inequality of opportunity built into the civil service bureaucracy early in the century helped create a cheap female labor pool.[37] But other factors also contributed to the discrimination against women in the service. Closer examination of employment practices reveals direct links between the processes of segmentation and sex labelling, traditional attitudes regarding woman's role and the growth and rationalization of government offices.

By 1891, women had been accepted as a permanent part of the service and were considered as efficient as male clerks.[38] Their numbers steadily increased, and in 1908, 700 of the 3,000 inside jobs were occupied by women.[39] The Civil Service Commission, however, reacted with alarm, predicting administrative chaos were the trend to continue. The Commission was even more concerned that the preponderance of women in the lower echelons of the service would eliminate these positions as a training ground for male officials. The Commission's solution was simple: restrict women to certain routine clerical jobs. In 1910 it limited appointments in the first and second division to men, leaving only the third division open to women. And blatant sex labelling was used to prevent women from monopolizing the third division:

> In the first place, there is certain work incidental to clerical duties, as in the handling of large registers, carrying of files and books up and down ladders, etc., which on physical grounds is not suitable for women. There are other positions in which, from time to time, the clerk may be called upon to travel considerable distances from Ottawa, alone or in the capacity as secretary or assistant. For obvious reasons, male clerks are required in positions involving such duties.[40]

The new rules forced women who passed the qualifying exam for the second division to take a position in the third. Temporary clerks had to pass typing or stenography tests, skills rare among males. Occupational segmentation was furthered by allowing department heads to label jobs "male" or "female."

Women therefore became stenographers and typists; men became general clerks.[41] These measures had the desired effect. Yet the Commission did not consider the problem solved until the 1918 Civil Service Act limited job competitions on the basis of sex and a 1921 ruling barred most women from permanent posts.[42]

It is significant that during the same period the civil service job classification system was being overhauled by a team of Chicago efficiency experts.[43] The "scientific" reforms increased the specialization and standardization of clerical procedures. The administrative division of labor advanced, adding to the pool of female jobs a growing array of routine tasks. Inequalities in the opportunity structure were becoming more rigid. Even though they constituted a stable supply of clerical workers, the status of the female civil servant can be best described as marginal. This sometimes had rather severe ramifications. For example, when the job market was tight, women were considered to have less right to employment than men.[44] In sum, the experience of the female civil service clerk supports Oppenheimer's contention that the effects of sex labelling are self-perpetuating.[45] Early discriminatory policies have thus left an indelible mark on the present occupational structure of the federal civil service.[46]

The Female Office Machine Operator

Mechanization had a disintegrating effect on traditional clerical occupations. It simplified tasks, reduced skill levels, standardized procedures and intensified the pace of work and the level of supervision. The women who now operate modern office machines are considered the most "proletarianized" sector of the white-collar work force.[47] Mechanized clerical jobs were a byproduct of the progressive rationalization of the office. Women did not displace men, for a female label was always attached to this kind of work. Because office mechanization is so closely interconnected with feminization, it provides clear evidence of how structural changes in the office underlay the shifting ratio of clerical jobs.

Stenography became the first female office occupation for a unique combination of reasons. Because of the arduous nature of the work, the special training required and the lack of obvious social or economic advantages, male clerks did not find stenography very attractive. Young women were being trained in typing in the early 1880s, at least a decade before the typewriter was modified into a practical office appliance. Typewriters thus helped create a new subgroup outside the male-dominated, mainstream clerical occupations. By 1900, any remaining doubts about women's ability to operate the new office machines had been supplanted. Prevailing social norms sanctioned these developments, provided women did not pose a competitive threat to the male clerk.

> A woman is to be preferred for the secretarial position for she is not averse to doing minor tasks, work involving the handling of petty details, which would irk and irritate ambitious young men, who usually feel that the work they are doing is of no importance if it can performed by some person with a lower salary. Most such men are also anxious to get ahead and to be promoted from position to position, and consequently if there is much work of a detail (*sic*) character to be done, and they are expected to perform it, they will not remain satisfied and will probably seek a position elsewhere.[48]

Stenography presents somewhat of a paradox in terms of the position of women in the office. On one hand, we have shown that women were shunted into the bottom layers of administrative structures. Yet on the other hand, mechanization afforded considerable socio-economic status and craft-like work to a select group of female clerks. Early stenographers closely approximated the ideal of craft work, as is evident in the range of their skills and their greater mastery and control over the work process. These conditions were significantly better than those in other clerical jobs, so much so that stenographers became career-oriented and tended to develop a strong occupational identification. This accounts for their longer years of service and greater earning potential. Consequently, we find that from 1911 to 1926 stenographers were the highest paid group of either sex in the Bank of Nova Scotia, with starting wages consistently higher than those for general clerks.[49]

The privileged position of the stenographer was undermined, however, by the advance of rationalization. By the start of the First World War, the two central elements of the job, dictation and typing, were being separated. The introduction of dictation machines facilitated the organization of central typing pools. Furthermore, there was a great surge of women into the occupation in search of high wages and steady employment.[50] In 1915, Toronto had twenty-eight business schools turning out stenographers and typists.[51] The market became glutted. Unemployment among stenographers reached 25 percent in Toronto that year[52] and only the most experienced operators could command top wages.

Management viewed the typing pool as more efficient, cheaper and easier to control than individual stenographers scattered throughout the office. Typing pools combined technical and organizational changes, giving rise to the "office-machine age"[53] which has culminated in the "word processing systems" and "administrative support centres" of today. By the mid-twenties, many large Canadian offices had central typing pools.[54] These paper-generating assembly lines obtained optimal efficiency from typewriters by keeping them in continuous use. Employees viewed the pool concept with suspicion. One insurance company reported that:

> Most stenographers who had seen or heard of transcribing machines were very much prejudiced against them, and the belief was almost generally entertained that the machine would ultimately force all stenographers to abandon their careers in favour of the much lower priced transcribing machine operators. . . . There was also a natural prejudice . . . against working in a Stenographic Department as compared with the more intimate contacts surrounding positions where they were required to take the work of only one or two dictators.[55]

Without downplaying the impact of the typewriter on the feminization process, it is accurate to say that the Hollerith machine fully launched the mechanical transformation of the clerical work process. The Hollerith punch card system was the most dramatic innovation in office technology prior to computers. International Business Machines was the main supplier, and by the early 1930s it had 105 major Canadian offices among its Hollerith customers.[56] The job title of "office machine operator" first appeared in the 1921 Census, signalling that a minor revolution in office technology was well underway.

The impact of the Hollerith machine was heightened by increasing bureaucratization and the introduction of scientific office management during the twenties. The women operators no doubt found that the machines tended to fragment and deskill work. As Shepard puts it, such devices "greatly accelerated the trend toward functional specialization. Many more special purpose machine-operating jobs evolved, placing employees filling these jobs in a relationship to technology similar to the mass-production factory worker. Work in these jobs is repetitive, mechanically paced, and minutely sub-divided."[57] In short, the female office machine operator had become a standard feature of the large bureaucratic office by the late 1920s. These women constituted what in Marxist terms might be called the "machine minders" of the modern office.

Conclusion

This paper has attempted to develop a new perspective on the feminization process. . . . We have been able to trace the origins of a secondary female clerical labor market back to transformations in the means of administration. The historical evidence presented supports Meissner's contention that "the structure of functional distinctions and social inequalities becomes visible in job assignments, wage differences, and job classifications."[58] The evolution of modern administration during the first three decades of this century in Canada created a new stratum of clerical jobs. As the number of these routine jobs grew, they became increasingly rationalized. Employers shifted their demand for clerks from men to women mainly because the requirements of the new administrative tasks were inconsistent with the established occupational characteristics of male clerks. Feminization was not simply a case of women displacing men. Rather, women became an administrative underclass because the division of labor had advanced to the point where male clerks were unsuited and unwilling, for a variety of social and economic reasons, to perform the new menial tasks. Segmentation resulted; men became office managers and technical or professional personnel and women occupied the subordinate clerical jobs.

The paper raises a number of issues worthy of further investigation, but two in particular stand out. The first has to do with the relationship between sex segregation in clerical jobs and the hierarchical organization of the office.[59] Specifically, how has the concentration of women workers in the lower reaches of administration helped maintain the hierarchical arrangement of control in the modern office? The second question links the workplace to the larger society. We have argued that in order to understand labor market processes, it is imperative to examine the social relations of production in the office. But to what extent are the social relations of office work reflected in the class structure? Davies[60] claims that lower level clerks form an integral part of the working class. Certainly our research suggests that office working conditions became "proletarianized" during the administrative revolution, at least to the extent that they became more factory-like. But does this mean that the women recruited into clerical jobs comprise a segment of the working class? Both of these questions present intriguing theoretical possibilities and will hopefully spark future research.

Let us conclude with a comment on the present situation. Clerical occupations now contain the greatest concentration of women in the labor force. The thrust of sex labelling and segmentation, when combined with the progressive rationalization of the office, have increasingly locked women into subordinate clerical jobs. Presumably, attitudes towards women's position in society have liberalized considerably since the 1920s. But sex-based inequalities and discrimination are so deeply embedded in the structure of the contemporary office that only the utmost tenacity on the part of women's groups and unions holds prospects for greater equality.

Notes

1. Hugh Armstrong and Pat Armstrong, *The Double Ghetto: Canadian Women and their Segregated Work* (Toronto: McClelland and Stewart, 1978); Harry Braverman, *Labor and Monopoly Capital: The Degradation of Work in the Twentieth Century* (New York: Monthly Review Press, 1974); Rosebeth Moss Kanter, *Men and Women of the Corporation* (New York: Basic Books, 1977); Graham S. Lowe, "The Administrative Revolution: the Growth of Clerical Occupations and the Development of the Modern Office in Canada, 1911–1931" (unpublished Ph.D. dissertation, University of Toronto, 1979). See table 1 for exact figures. It should be noted that clerical employment data from the censuses used in this paper are reclassified to conform with the 1951 census definition of clerk. This allows for accurate inter-censal comparisons. However, these adjustments mean that employment data in tables 1 and 2 for 1971 are slightly below those found in the actual census.

2. The concepts of corporate capitalism and entrepreneurial capitalism have been drawn from Wallace Clement, *The Canadian Corporate Elite* (Toronto: McClelland and Stewart, 1975), 71–80.

3. Braverman, *Labor and Monopoly Capital*; C. Wright Mills, *White Collar: the American Middle Classes* (New York: Oxford University Press, 1956); David Lockwood, *The Blackcoated Worker* (London: Allen and Unwin, 1966); Lowe, "The Administrative Revolution."

4. Between 1901 and 1921, the average clerical salary rose from 116 to 125 percent of the average wage for the total Canadian labor force. Yet after 1921, clerical earnings entered a steady decline, cutting below the labor force average in 1951. In 1971, the average clerical salary was only 77 percent of the labor force average (Lowe, "The Administrative Revolution," 224). Research by Lockwood (*The Blackcoated Worker*) in Britain and Burns (Robert K. Burns, "The Comparative Economic Position of Manual and White-Collar Employees," *Journal of Business* 27 (1954): 257–67) and Braverman (*Labor and Monopoly Capital*) in the United States also documents how the explosion of white-collar occupations since the turn of the century has been accompanied by a relative decline in clerical wages.

5. Robert M. Dawson, *The Civil Service of Canada* (London: Oxford University Press, 1929), 190.

6. J.L. Payne, "The Civil Servant," *University Magazine* 6 (1907), 511. In 1881, the Civil Service Commissioners argued that if more female clerks were hired, "it would be necessary that they should be placed in rooms by themselves, and that they should be under the immediate supervision of a person of their own sex, but we doubt very much if sufficient work of similar character can be found in any one Department to furnish occupation for any considerable number of female clerks, and it would certainly be inadvisable to place them in small numbers throughout the Departments" (Canada, *First Report of the Civil Service Commission* (1881), 26).

7. Sun Life Assurance Company, *Sunshine* (November 1911), 142.

8. Jean Thompson Scott, "The Conditions of Female Labour in Ontario" *Studies in Political Science*, series III, edited by W.J. Ashely (Toronto: University of Toronto Press, 1889), 24.

9. Canada, Dominion Bureau of Statistics, *Occupational Trends in Canada, 1891–1931*, Special bulletin (Ottawa: D.B.S., 1939), 4.

10. O.J. Firestone, "Canada's Economic Development, 1867–1952," (paper prepared for the Third

Conference of the International Association for Research in Income and Wealth, Castelgandolfo, Italy, 1953), 152.

11. Armstrong and Armstrong, *The Double Ghetto*, 20.

12. In 1971, 96.8 percent of all stenographers and typists were women (Canada, 1971 Census, vol. III, part 2, table 2).

13. Lowe, "The Administrative Revolution," 187.

14. Ibid., 189. Over the 1901–31 decades, women increased their share of clerical jobs in manufacturing from 16.5 percent to 40.7 percent; 22.7 percent to 52.9 percent in trade; 0.8 percent to 49.6 percent in finance; and 5.5 percent to 37.6 percent in government (Lowe, "The Administrative Revolution," 184). For an interesting discussion of the impact of changing industrial structure on female employment, see Joachim Singelmann and Marta Tienda, "Changes in Industry Structure and Female Employment in Latin America, 1950–1970," *Sociology and Social Research* 63 (1979): 745–69.

15. Lowe, "The Administrative Revolution," 223. This is consistent with the broad labor force trend. In 1971 the average income for women doing paid work was about half that of men (Hugh Armstrong and Pat Armstrong, "The Segregated Participation of Women in the Canadian Labor Force, 1941–71," *Canadian Review of Sociology and Anthropology* 12 (1975), 371). Yet within the female labor force, clerks were quite well off. For example, a 1921 survey (Canada Year Book (1928), 779) indicated that female office clerks earned more than twenty-two other female occupations. Only telegraph operators in Montreal and tailoresses, teachers, as well as telegraph operators in Toronto earned more. In 1901, female clerks earned 45 percent more than the average female wage. This fluctuated over the next several decades, rising to a high of 49 percent in 1941. This advantage gradually diminished, with female clerks only making 6 percent more than the female labor force average by 1971 (Lowe, "The Administrative Revolution," 224).

16. The term labor market segmentation refers to the fragmentation of labor power into jobs requiring diverse amounts of skill, stability, and supervision, and hence to the division of the work force into distinct pools from which these various jobs are filled. Men and women (in company with males from ethnic and racial minorities) tend to be segregated into separate, noncompetitive labor markets. (For further explanation of segmentation theory, see David M. Gordon, *Theories of Poverty and Underemployment: Orthodox, Radical, and Dual Labor Market Perspectives* (Lexington, Mass.: D.C. Heath, 1972); Richard C. Edwards, Michael Reich, and David M. Gordon, eds., *Labor Market Segmentation* (Lexington, Mass,: D.C. Heath, 1975); Marcia Freedman, *Labor Markets: Segments and Shelters* (Montclair, N.J.: Allanheld, Osmun, 1976). For a fuller explanation of segmentation theory and sex labelling (note 17), see the original article.

17. Sex labelling is a process by which employers tailor the labor supply for work they offer. By manipulating the demand characteristics of a job — such as skill and educational requirements, working conditions, and salary levels — employers are determining, in fact, whether they will have male or female employees. Thus, job requirements such as physical exertion, geographic mobility, or an unbroken career path are barriers to women. On the other hand, stereotypes of women as more manually dextrous and patient, but less effective at supervision than men, and as secondary wage earners, channel women into jobs at the lower end of the occupational spectrum. These stereotypes furnish the rationale for discrimination against women in terms of remuneration and opportunities for upward mobility.

18. Ceta Ramkhalawansingh, "Women During the Great War" in *Women at Work: Ontario 1850–1930*, edited by Janice Acton, Penny Goldsmith, and Bonnie Shepard (Toronto: Women's Educational Press, 1974), 261.

19. The tremendous expansion of the clercial sector during the war decade further segmented the labor market. For example, clerical jobs increased their share of the total female work force from 9.1 percent in 1911 to 18.5 percent in 1921. Fully 50.2 percent of the growth in office occupations over the decade was accounted for by women flooding into offices. In fact, 69,165 more clerical jobs were created during the 1911–21 decade than during the twenties. This works out to approximately four times more women entering the office.

20. The impact of the war on clerical employment opportunities for women was not even across all industries. In Montreal, for example, munitions plants hired women clerks to help administer war production as well as regular business (Enid M. Price, "Changes in the Industrial Occupations of Women

in the Environment of Montreal During the Period of the War, 1914–1918" (unpublished MA thesis, McGill University, 1919), 26). On the other hand, Montreal's post offices employed mainly female clerks in 1914 and the war brought about little change (ibid., 60). Similarly, in the Manufacturers Life Assurance Company, the war merely tilted the balance in favor of women, something that would have happened anyway (Lowe, "The Administrative Revolution").

21. Lowe, "The Administrative Revolution," 204.

22. *Journal of the Canadian Banker's Association*, July 1916, 316.

23. Ibid.

24. By early 1919, a total of 9,069 male bank clerks had enlisted in Canada (Lowe, "The Administrative Revolution," 284).

25. *Journal of the Canadian Banker's Association*, July 1916, 314–15.

26. "Circular No. 1,699 from the General Manager, 6 April 1916," Bank of Nova Scotia Archives, Toronto.

27. When conscription was imposed, the banks lobbied the government to exempt their male clerks, arguing that these employees possessed special qualifications and performed a vital role in the economy (*Monetary Times*, 29 March 1918, 22).

28. *Journal of the Canadian Banker's Association*, July 1917, 316–17.

29. *Monetary Times*, 8 August 1919, 10.

30. Ibid.

31. Ibid., 20 May 1927, 11.

32. *Journal of the Canadian Banker's Association*, January 1911, 11.

33. Scott, "Conditions of Female Labor in Ontario," 25.

34. In the early twentieth century, approximately 90 percent of women in the Canadian labor force were single. Mary Vipond, "The Images of Women in Mass Circulation Magazines in the 1920s" in *The Neglected Majority*, edited by Susan Mann Trofimenkoff and Alison Prentice (Toronto: McClelland and Stewart, 1977), 117.

35. Ironically, women who entered the labor force typically were somewhat better educated than men. This was an added bonus for employers, but how was the discrepancy between occupational status and education rationalized? Part of the answer is found in the ideology surrounding woman's social role. The "cult of domesticity" required that women, as the transmitters of culture to children, should have an adequate base of knowledge from which to work (W. Elliot Brownlee and Mary M. Brownlee, *Women in the American Economy* (New Haven: Yale University Press, 1976), 18). The growing number of women who entered the clerical labor market had to balance the contradictory demands of the world of work with those of home and family. Encouraged to gain specialized clerical skills by enrolling in one of the plethora of business colleges, yet all the while knowing her destiny was in the home, the young woman of the 1920s faced a basic quandry (see Vipond, "Images of Women," 120).

36. Kathleen Archibald, *Sex and the Public Service* (Ottawa: Queen's Printer, 1970), 16.

37. J.E. Hodgetts, W. McCloskey, R. Whitaker, and V.S. Wilson, *The Biography of an Institution: The Civil Service Commission of Canada, 1908–1967* (Montreal: McGill-Queen's University Press, 1972), 483.

38. Dawson, *Civil Service of Canada*, 191.

39. Hodgetts et al., *Biography of an Institution*, 483.

40. Canada, *Civil Service Commission Annual Report*, 1910, 17.

41. Archibald, *Sex and the Public Service*, 14.

42. Ibid., 16. The 1921 regulation made exceptions for married women who were self-supporting or if other suitable candidates could not be found. Married women in the service were forced to resign and reapply as temporary workers at the minimum salary.

43. Lowe, "The Administrative Revolution," 312–18.

44. Hodgetts et al., *Biography of an Institution*, 487.

45. Valerie K. Oppenheimer, *The Female Labor Force in the United States* (Berkeley: Institute of International Studies, University of California, 1970).

46. Archibald, *Sex and the Public Service*, 19.

47. *Work in America*. Report of a Special Task Force to the U.S. Secretary of Health, Education and Welfare prepared by the W.E. Upjohn Institute for Employment Research (Cambridge, Mass.: M.I.T.

Press, 1973), 38; James W. Rinehart, *The Tyranny of Work* (Don Mills, Ont.: Longman Canada, 1975), 92; Evelyn N. Glenn and Roslyn L. Feldberg, "Degraded and Deskilled: the Proletarianization of Clerical Work," *Social Problems* 25 (1977): 52–64.

48. William H. Leffingwell, *Office Management, Principles and Practice* (Chicago: A.W. Shaw, 1925), 621.

49. Lowe, "The Administrative Revolution," 231.

50. *Labour Gazette*, 1913, passim.

51. Ontario, *Report of the Ontario Commission on Unemployment* (Toronto: A.T. Wilgress, 1916), 182. Another contributing factor on the supply side was the attempt by typewriter companies to regulate the labor market for stenographers and typists through employment agencies (ibid.). The business schools and private employment agencies helped create a huge secondary labor pool of semi-skilled women, which employers drew on to fill routine typing jobs.

52. *Labour Gazette*, February 1915, 924.

53. Mills, *White Collar*, 195.

54. Lowe, "The Administrative Revolution," 363–67.

55. Life Office Management Association, *Proceedings of Annual Conferences*, 1926, 82.

56. Lowe, "The Administrative Revolution," 377–78.

57. Jon M. Shepard, *Automation and Alienation: A Study of Office and Factory Workers* (Cambridge, Mass.: M.I.T. Press, 1971), 63.

58. Martin Meissner, "Sexual Division of Labour and Inequalities: Labour and Leisure," in *Women in Canada*, edited by Marylee Stephenson, 2nd ed. (Don Mills, Ont.: General Publishing, 1977), 162.

59. Mary Stevenson, "Women's Wages and Job Segregation" in *Labor Market Segmentation*, edited by Richard Edwards et al. (Lexington, Mass.: D.C. Heath, 1975), 251, 253.

60. Margery Davies, "Women's Place is at the Typewriter: the Feminization of the Clerical Labor Force" in *Labor Market Segmentation*.

FEMINISM, NATIONALISM, AND THE CLERICAL DEFENSIVE†

SUSAN MANN TROFIMENKOFF

The role of women and the family frequently lies at the heart of what Canadians have believed to be the ideal society. The allocation of power and authority differentially among family members, most obviously between women and men, provides an influential model for order and hierarchy within the state itself. Fears about community viability, whether national, religious, or racial, focus almost invariably on female shortcomings and the threat of new female initiatives. Unruly women call into question a whole set of deeply felt assumptions about the proper relationship between the sexes, families, and the community at large.

At the turn of the century, French-Canadian lay and clerical élites, faced with the encroachment of Anglo-American influences and the ravages of urban industrial growth, forged a conservative nationalism, which, as Trofimenkoff suggests in this chapter from The Dream of Nation, *required women's rededication to home and hearth. Feminists, even those who shared many of the same concerns about social breakdown and disorder, were accused of disloyalty to the historic destiny of their race. Even the most circumspect of maternal feminism could not counteract this overriding suspicion. The relationship between feminism and nationalism is complex, as an earlier article by Trofimenkoff so well demonstrates.* Almost inevitably in both French and English Canada feminists and nationalists have articulated a related set of concerns. Both have identified an appropriately-constituted family as crucial to the survival or improvement of the community. The exact form to be assumed by the ideal community remains a critical question for both. However, feminism's proclivity for cross-cultural sympathies, as with the ties between the* Fédération nationale St. Jean Baptiste *and the National Council of Women of Canada and similar links among English and French groups in the 1970s and 1980s, raises a fundamental question of priorities, that remains, to some degree at least, unsettled. One suspects that the logic of feminism is indeed finally antithetical to the demands of nationalism, as the experience of women in fascist countries confirms.*

In the early 1900s, the social repercussions of industrialization dawned upon three distinct groups among Quebec's elite: feminists, nationalists, and clerics. Similar conditions in the 1880s had raised scarcely a murmur; now they produced a veritable chorus of concern. The difference appears to have been one of quantity rather than quality. The sheer number of industrial workers, the physical expansion of cities and towns, the commercial boom of metropolitan Montreal could no longer be ignored. Quebec was obviously shedding its nineteenth century agricultural skin and the process seems to have been more difficult for certain elite groups who had been urban dwellers for generations than for the rural emigrants. Feminists, nationalists, and clerics, all went about their self-imposed task of protecting the family from urban ills with varying methods and prescriptions, sometimes in co-operation and sometimes in conflict with

†Susan Mann Trofimenkoff, *The Dream of Nation* (Toronto: Gage, 1983), 184–199.

*"Nationalism, Feminism & Canadian Intellectual History," *Canadian Literature* 83 (Winter 1979): 7–19.

each other. Right up to the First World War when nationalists and clerics ganged up on the feminists to remind them of their rightful place in society, the three performed an intricate dance to the tune of their individual interests and their mutual sympathies.

Of the three, feminism was the newest on the Quebec scene. It was both a result of and a commentary upon the social turbulence of the time. The presence of so many women and children in the industrial work place upset many notions of social propriety. How could one maintain a strict demarcation of the species by sex, function, and location in the burgeoning factories of town and city? How could one ensure proper family formation when so many young women appeared to be discovering new ways of earning a living? By the end of the nineteenth century, they appeared in increasing numbers as salesclerks in shops, particularly in the new-fangled department stores, and in offices where they were so closely associated with the typewriter that they actually acquired the same name. Even so the notion of separate spheres may have continued to plague them as female clerical workers took over and at the same time devalued the young male occupation of clerk. The same thing had long since happened in the elementary teaching profession and by the late nineteenth century some young school-mistresses even dared to insist upon greater training either in normal schools or universities. Some English Protestant women went so far as to demand access to professional careers as nurses, doctors, professors, or lawyers, but their demands were seldom echoed by French Canadian women for whom the avenues to most professions were closed.

Newspapers and the women's associations informed the public of the many social changes involving women. By the end of the nineteenth century almost every large city daily had a female journalist contributing a regular column or editing an entire woman's page. One paper in the 1890s, *Le Coin du feu*, edited by Joséphine Marchand Dandurand, was intended solely for women. Most of the female journalists hid their identity, as if their work was somehow inappropriate. The women's pages themselves, by their segregation from the rest of the paper, indicated the force of the ideology of separate spheres; however, interspersed among the patterns and the novels, the recipes and the advice columns were discussions of feminism and of the women's movement in English Canada, the United States, France, and Great Britain. Higher education and votes for women were in the air and also in the press. Moreover, many of the journalists were members of, or close sympathizers with, the National Council of Women, a Canadian federation of women's organizations dating from 1893. There they discussed and passed on to their readers issues such as women's work, education, health, duties, and even, on occasion, women's rights. National and international meetings of women's organizations and the participation of individual French Canadian women at such gatherings as the Chicago World's Fair in 1893 or the Paris Exposition in 1900 brought reports to the Quebec press of the ever-increasing murmurings of women throughout the western world. It took only the burst of nationalism that accompanied the opening decade of the twentieth century to have French Canadian women form a feminist organization of their own.

Nationalism followed a similar path in the early twentieth century. Older than feminism, at least in Quebec, it was even more isolated and individualistic until the turn of the century. It had provided the language of revolutionary rhetoric in the 1830s and of the politics of survival in the 1840s, but it took varying forms thereafter. In the 1860s it could be discerned among both the proponents and opponents of Confederation; some clerics even attempted to hitch it to an ultramontane star. It gained a martyr in Louis Riel and the occasional journalist used it to predict a particular future for French Canada. But always it remained a thin thread of intellectual flirtation, a source for set speeches expected of orators at annual Saint Jean Baptiste festivities. Like feminism, it required an international climate of opinion to turn it into an organized, semi-political force. In the early twentieth century, the optimism of economic progress and the pessimism of imperial entanglements gave birth to a new form of Quebec nationalism, more public, more vociferous, more self-assured, and more critical than before.

The clerics were the oldest of the three elite groups troubled by the social scene of the early twentieth century. They were also the most experienced, used to adept manoeuvres to acquire and maintain a privileged position in Quebec society. In the early nineteenth century, religion had been insufficient to guarantee their social pre-eminence; they added education and then social work, filling a vacuum left by an indifferent state. Some of the bolder among them had even claimed a virtual clerical right of veto over all secular activities, including those of the state. But if the ultramontanes eventually retreated into largely intellectual corners, the church itself had no intention of giving up its acquired rights or status. It certainly had the bargaining skill and the political finesse to make its point. For example, the bishops apparently came to an agreement with Laurier over his compromise solution to the Manitoba school question: they would tone down their criticism if he would ensure that Quebec's Liberal government abandoned its intention to establish a ministry of education. Now, in the opening years of the twentieth century, the clerics were not about to give ground, in education or social concern, to feminist or nationalist upstarts. Or so they thought.

The three groups actually had much in common. They all saw themselves as guardians of the social order although each sometimes wondered about the other. The implications of feminism in particular concerned both clerics and nationalists, and the feminists spent a lot of time reassuring them. The nationalists meanwhile fancied themselves as the advance guard, ever attentive to the least sign of danger to the nation. They all suspected that most of the dangers centred around the family and they all claimed a public right to protect it. The feminists thought that as women they had a special insight. Who could know more about housing, infant mortality, parks, schooling, or the cost of living than mothers? They thereby attached their own desire for a recognized place in public life to their maternal concern for the everyday problems of families. The clerics on the other hand believed that they, as upholders of morality, had the most to offer families surrounded by promiscuity and licentiousness in large anonymous cities. The nationalists in turn thought that they had the most lessons to teach to the family. And yet few of the protectors knew the object of their attention at first hand. Class, education, and social status made them elites, removed from the households of Montreal's or Quebec's "city below the hill." Together they approached their self-appointed task with a decided air of *noblesse oblige*.

All three shared a dedication to the preservation of the family. They all believed that the family provided the foundation for religion and morality; they all regarded the state as an enlarged family. None of them could conceive of a social organization without the family at its centre. And each of them repeated the nationalist argument that the French Canadian family had some peculiar essence that rendered it inherently superior to English-speaking neighbours down the street or across the continent. That of course was just where the difficulty lay. Industrialization in Montreal did not really look very different from that in Chicago or Toronto or London or Paris: the same slums, the same illnesses, the same unemployment. In the large cities of North America, the family's private problems, hung out with the wash for all to see, were culturally and linguistically indistinguishable. Only by responding to those problems in a particular way could the distinctions be maintained. And thus feminists, nationalists, and clerics alike developed their own institutional responses to the social and familial ills they observed. Sometimes they collaborated willingly, working together in the same associations; sometimes they were reluctant companions and only the force of circumstances or the magnitude of the task forced them to collaborate. Just as often they were competitors: the educational interests of both the feminists and the nationalists worried the clerics; the feminist implication of sexual equality disturbed cleric and nationalist alike; while the clerical assumption of social righteousness troubled both feminists and nationalists. Their complex three-step through the opening years of the twentieth century did, however, succeed in alleviating some of the social ills of the time and also in giving a distinctive colour to the Quebec scene.

In 1907 the women's committee of the Montreal Saint Jean Baptiste Society formally constituted a new organization, the *Fédération nationale Saint-Jean-Baptiste*. Modelled on the National Council of Women, the *Fédération* was to be a co-ordinating body for the innumerable women's associations and clubs that proliferated throughout Quebec in the 1890s and 1900s. If women spoke with one strong, organized voice instead of whispering in a thousand tongues, they might have some public impact. Moreover, the *Fédération* could provide a secure public platform for opinions that might otherwise be discounted as individual idiosyncracies. The family connections of the founders certainly helped: Marie Lacoste Gérin-Lajoie and Carolina Dessaulles Béique came from and married into impeccable upper class, wealthy, and political families. Their interest in education and charitable work was part of what was expected of young women of their class, although it was also assumed that they would undertake such tasks in conjunction with the church. But they were already pulling against that stricture when Béique established a secular domestic science school in Montreal in 1907 and sent two of the instructors off to France for training. Gérin-Lajoie's sister, Justine Lacoste Beaubien, did the same by founding Montreal's Ste. Justine hospital for sick children the same year. Gérin-Lajoie herself had tugged at male prerogatives by her unusual interest in law. To occupy herself after a convent education and before marriage, she dipped into her father's law library and was shocked to discover the legal status of women in Quebec as mere adjuncts of their husbands with no personal, financial, or civil autonomy. She even considered turning down a marriage proposal in order to spend her life improving the conditions of women. But the proposer, a liberally minded grandson of Etienne Parent, persuaded her of his sympathies for such activities as long as she did not neglect her wifely duties. Gérin-Lajoie eventually wrote a legal handbook, the *Traité de droit usuel* in 1902, all the while keeping an eye on small children. Her legal expertise benefited both the National Council of Women with whose local council in Montreal she was closely involved and the fledgling *Fédération nationale Saint-Jean-Baptiste* whose first steps she guided.

The initial handicap of the new organization was the stigma of feminism. A term of ridicule throughout most of the western world, much like "women's lib" in the 1970s, feminism was particularly odious to many French Canadians. Anything that risked taking women out of their proper sphere was frowned upon as both a social and national peril. The women of the early twentieth century seeking socially useful roles beyond the family and outside the church appeared to be calling into question the very bases of French Canadian society. No wonder the early feminists trod warily. In 1901 Joséphine Marchand Dandurand defined feminism so broadly as to include everything that women did, even giving it a moral tinge with which she expected no one to disagree: feminism required of well-to-do women some action to help alleviate social distress. She deliberately avoided any criticism of the ideology of separate spheres that confined middle and upper class women to inactivity or mere social whirls. And although she approved of higher education for women, she justified it by the improved wives and mothers (of sons) that it would produce. As for votes for women, Dandurand thought them unnecessary. Women could exercise their civic spirit sufficiently by doing good deeds and influencing their husbands to vote wisely. Dandurand's careful skating around the danger signals of feminism is a clear indication that like the Liberals and even the Knights of Labour before them, early feminists had to find a niche in hostile terrain and camouflage themselves to maintain it.

The feminism in the new *Fédération* was, according to Carolina Dessaulles Béique, feminism of a particular kind. Rather than revolutionary feminism, a European or North American variety that pulled women away from their homes and their proper roles, the *Fédération nationale Saint-Jean-Baptiste* harboured Christian feminism which anchored women in their rightful duties and obligations towards others. Marie Lacoste Gérin-Lajoie was more specific but just as circumspect: the new organization was to be a centre for Christian women to aid themselves and to advance their own moral development, vocations as wives, duties as mothers, and their philanthrophic or religious works. Both women, thoroughly familiar, one suspects, with the history of the *Institut canadien*, sought and secured the sanction of the bishop of Montreal for their new organization. The bishop, Monseigneur Paul Bruchési, himself offered a definition of feminism as the "zeal of woman for all those noble causes in the sphere to which Providence has assigned her." He even gave some examples: temperance, the education of children, domestic hygiene, fashions, and the problems of young working girls in factories. Through them all, he expected the laywomen to support the existing activity of religious communities.

On the whole, the undertakings of the *Fédération* were well within the prescribed norms. The largest number of affiliated associations were in fact charitable groups controlled by nuns. Whether this raised internal difficulties or whether the nuns were actually feminists in disguise is an open question. Certainly the larger, secular *Fédération* was able to do fund raising for its membership on a scale that its religiously run affiliates could not manage. Within the *Fédération* the next largest group was made up of professional associations, some of the early and tentative alliances of women engaged in similar occupations. Associations of domestic servants, store employees, teachers, business women, and factory employees each found a place and support in the umbrella organization. The associations appear to have been as much social and cultural clubs as mutual benefit societies for particular kinds of workers. Middle class women worked through the *Fédération* organizing classes in commercial, technical, and household science subjects, delivering literary lectures, or sponsoring musical *soirées* in the various associations. For the factory employees they established a sickness fund, employment bureaus, boarding houses, and even country homes where working girls could go for inexpensive holidays. If their concerns were as much moral as economic, they were little different from those of feminist doers of good deeds in other North American cities. They also probably served to open a number of middle class eyes to the extent of urban poverty, although as late as 1913, journalist Henriette Dessaulles St. Jacques, writing under her pseudonym Fadette, commented benignly in *Le Devoir*: "Dear readers, you wouldn't even believe such ugliness existed." Quite removed from any ugliness was the third and smallest group of affiliates to the *Fédération*: cultural associations varying from book clubs and literary societies to musical and artistic guilds.

The *Fédération* sanctioned all the groups, created a network among them, and offered its annual meeting as an educational seminar for them. In 1909 for example members discussed the problems of alcoholism, infant mortality, popular education, housing for workers, and the implementation of homemaking courses in the schools. By 1914 the *Fédération* was particularly pleased with its public endeavours: it claimed the credit for the doubling of women teachers' pensions, the naming of a female factory inspector (actually it was the National Council of Women that had convinced the Quebec government to name two such inspectors in 1898), better lighting in factories, chairs for women clerks in stores, a reduction in the number of taverns, and the improvement in infant feeding by the establishment of pure milk depots which also offered courses in domestic hygiene and child care. The ubiquitous classes in domestic science, in both English and French, were designed to improve the lamentable state of knowledge about diet and housekeeping and, just perhaps, to improve the quantity and quality of young women available for domestic service in the spacious homes of Sherbrooke Street.

In those homes were other young women frittering away their time in pointless inactivity. The daughters of a number of the women associated with the

Fédération nationale Saint-Jean-Baptiste needed more education if they were to continue their mothers' public tasks. A convent education might provide a good secondary education, although some women were dubious even about that, but it was virtually a dead end. As indeed it was intended to be: only those young ladies obliged to earn their living were directed to the teacher training sections of the Ursuline convent in Quebec City or the *Congrégation de Notre-Dame* in Montreal. Young women without such an obligation were sent home at age seventeen or eighteen to prepare for marriage. Since access to universities was via the classical colleges and no such college existed for girls, the path to higher education was effectively blocked. In 1900 Laval University did consent to permit women to join the public audience for some of its faculty lectures in rhetoric or literature, but they were not to register for a degree, nor were any academic exercises required of them. There was no question of permitting them access, even as auditors, to the professional faculties of law and medicine. At the same time then that the *Fédération* was supporting domestic science training it was also urging the opening of a classical college for young women.

A combination of daring and discretion created the *Ecole d'enseignement supérieur pour les filles* in Montreal in 1908. Female journalists in the 1890s had demanded such an institution; the feminists of the 1900s exercised the pressure of their class and wealth upon certain sympathetic ears in the *Congrégation de Notre-Dame* to achieve it. Even the dubious bishop overcame his reluctance when he discovered that two other women journalists intended to establish a secular *lycée* on the French model. If young ladies really had to have higher education, and Monseigneur Bruchési was not at all convinced, they should at least acquire it within the proper religious framework. But it was all to be very discreet. The new *Ecole*, run by the nuns of *Notre-Dame*, was not even to have the title of college, something which it would only acquire in 1926 when it became the *Collège* Marguerite Bourgeoys. And it was expected to be self-supporting, student fees and the religious community providing the sole financing; neither church nor state intended to sanction this temerity of women. Laval did provide accreditation and the students took the same examinations as in the men's colleges, but the university also sent along its vice-rector to stress to staff and students alike the limitations placed upon the young female students. They might follow the same program as their brothers, but they were not to think that their futures would in any way be altered: they were to be submissive and graceful wives, not doctors, lawyers, accountants, or pharmacists. The *Ecole* dutifully added piano recitals, poetry readings, and afternoon teas to its heavy academic program. It also hid its chagrin at seeing no public announcement from Laval of the scholastic achievement of one of its first students. Marie Gérin-Lajoie, the daughter of one of the school's promoters, placed first among all the classical college students of the province. By then the school had also organized study circles to initiate young women students into the intellectual and practical aspects of contemporary social problems. In the 1920s some of the graduates joined Marie Gérin-Lajoie in forming the *Institut de Notre-Dame-du-Bon-Conseil* to provide a religious framework for their social work; others remained in secular life and exercised their activism through the *Fédération nationale Saint-Jean-Baptiste*.

The connection between schooling and social questions was not lost upon the nationalists either. Unlike the feminists, however, they tended to approach the question in a more intellectual manner. For them it was not just particular groups of people who needed practical or academic training, but rather an entire society that required an approach to learning that stressed secular, scientific, commercial, and industrial education. One expression of this point of view can be found in Errol Bouchette's series of writings in the 1900s: *Emparons-nous de l'industrie, Etudes sociale et économique sur le Canada*, and *L'indépendance économique du Canada français*. Fascinated by the economic development promised and delivered early in the new century, Bouchette was concerned that French Canadians play a prominent role in it. To do so they had to destroy an old myth of their being unfit for commerce and business, and they had to become aware of the effect of the new industrial order in Europe and the United States, so that Canada could extract the benefits and avoid the problems.

Such undertakings required education, training, and appropriate legislation. Bouchette was not at all convinced that the graduates of classical colleges had the necessary stuff to face the economic challenge of the new century; rather he suspected that many of the colleges perpetuated the notion of French Canadian commercial ineptitude. He rejected the idea of national characteristics and argued that knowledge could overcome all problems. But that knowledge had to be planned, organized, and integrated into the economy. Drawing on contemporary reports of industrial education in Europe, Bouchette suggested that government and employers co-operate in designing specific programs for schools and factories in order to increase the technical competence of industrial workers. The result would be not only a more skilled labour force but also a solidarity of interest between employers and employees. Education would thus guarantee social peace. The university too, while maintaining a theoretical approach, could play its part by expanding more into the pure and social sciences. Montreal's polytechnical school, a rather moribund institution established in the late 1870s, should attract students aggressively; it ought to house a bureau of scientific and industrial research as a source of information for the state's economic planning. The elementary school system should also be remodelled along French lines with the senior levels preparing youngsters for practical occupations in the work place and the lower levels at least attacking the shameful problem of illiteracy which, according to Bouchette, was greater in Quebec than in any other Canadian province. And the entire education system should be free, co-ordinated and directed by the state.

Bouchette justified his ideas on nationalist grounds. Without decent education, young people were bored, handicapped, and discouraged; their subsequent poverty forced them to emigrate to the United States. There at least they proved their industrial competence. But still they were lost to Canada. In a revealing analogy Bouchette argued that education protected industry the way an army protected a frontier or a parliament a constitution. Education, in short, was not only the key to industrial progress but also to national survival. The three were indissociable. By championing industry, French Canadians would be continuing the mission of their forefathers. Unlike other North Americans who came to the new land in search of subsistence or conquest or religious freedom, French

Canadians arrived with civilization in their pockets and it behooved them to be at the head of economic progress in North America. To fail in such a noble goal would be unpatriotic; to undertake it meant working for the salvation of an entire people. Such a blatantly nationalist argument also had a twist to it, peculiar to the optimism of the early twentieth century. Bouchette insisted that French and English co-operate in the industrial endeavours of the new century. Together the two people could create a distinctive North American community.

Bouchette's views were shared by his contemporaries in the *Ligue nationaliste*. Like the feminists, they were aware of international currents of opinion and they took many of their social cues from the American progressives. Like them, and indeed like most of their contemporaries, the nationalists were fascinated by the economic progress so visible in the early years of the twentieth century. But they were vaguely uneasy about the possible consequences. They wondered about the fitness of politicians to guide the state; they queried the moral rectitude and actual behaviour of the upper classes who were supposed to be models for society; they worried about the apathetic public spirit of their contemporaries; and they found the materialism that accompanied prosperity somewhat distasteful. They were not at all sure that a distinctive French and Catholic society could survive in the face of all that.

The *Ligue* itself, established in 1903, was still quite young when two nationalists engaged in a rather peripheral debate over its political orientations. Jules-Paul Tardivel, never a member of the *Ligue*, and Henri Bourassa, its inspirer, revealed that differences of opinion could divide nationalists as much as mutual sympathies joined them. Tardivel took the *Ligue* members, mostly from Montreal, to task for their Canadian as opposed to French Canadian nationalism. He published the program of the *Ligue* in *La Vérité* but complained that its desire for provincial autonomy within Confederation did not go far enough. French Canadians should be clearly defined as a distinct nationality in Confederation with their own patriotic aspirations, their own ideals, rights, and duties. Tardivel had once argued that the historical effort to preserve the language, institutions, and nationality of French Canada made no sense unless an independent nation was the eventual outcome. Now, with that same end in sight, Tardivel argued that the effort demanded the preservation of French Canadians themselves by means of agriculture, colonization, an end to infant mortality, and the creation of barriers against Protestant, Anglo-Saxon, and American infiltration.

Without denying any of the contemporary social or ideological evils that threatened French Canada, Henri Bourassa defended the new *Ligue*. He was not ready to admit that Quebec alone constituted French Canada. Nor was he convinced that Confederation was an impossibility. Rather, by strengthening French Canadian minorities beyond Quebec, the position of Quebec itself in Confederation would be strengthened. Bourassa shared Tardivel's passion for Catholicism, but he also justified the *Ligue*'s very toned down expression of it. Montreal was not at all the same city as Quebec; young people were already exposed to every conceivable idea through the popular press and the younger nationalists were not particularly religious at all. Far better to praise them for undertaking social and political action for the betterment of Canada than to condemn them for some ideological lapse. For Bourassa and the *Ligue*, the imperial question and the social question were of far more significance.

In bringing social issues to public attention, the nationalists of whatever political persuasion emphasized the powers and obligations of the Quebec government. In that, they went beyond both feminists and clerics who were content to see social problems remain the prerogative of concerned individuals, albeit increasingly organized ones. The nationalists were suspicious of the growing number of mergers among large firms in the province; the benefits were surely not accruing to French Canadians. Nor did they approve of the co-operation, open or veiled, between the state and large-scale business concerns. Instead of providing generous subsidies to such firms, the state should become a shareholder in them. That way it would have some voice in the economic exploitation of the province. As it was, the government appeared almost anxious to give away land and forest, rivers and mines, even throwing in a railway or two, to private companies for very small fees. And its activity was trumpeted by the newspapers, in the pay of one or other of the political parties, as the normal course of events. The consequence, argued the nationalists, was that French Canadians exercised little control over their economic resources. The government could not even offer colonization as an escape for urban workers locked into soulless industries because it had abdicated its control of lands, and hence any possibility of rational development, to large and mostly foreign companies. Moreover the government shared the hostility of industrial firms to any legislative or even trade union protection for workers. The nationalists of the early twentieth century feared the outcome: the political minority that the nineteenth century had made of French Canada was about to become an economic minority as well.

Some of the nationalist criticism actually struck a responsive chord in the government. Henri Bourassa's stint in the provincial legislature from 1908 to 1912 may even have helped. Although he was in opposition and an independent at that, he had an increasing public following and he was a formidable debater. Whatever his influence, by 1910 the province was leasing rather than selling water, forest, and mining rights; it was prohibiting the export of pulpwood cut from its lands; it was tentatively approving minimal labour legislation; and it was preparing to assist settlers heading into Abitibi. It was even scrutinizing and adapting some aspects of the educational system. Night schools and technical schools appeared in urban centres; agricultural classes were added to the program of rural schools. A graduate commercial school, the *Hautes Etudes commerciales*, began in 1907 with government backing to offer classical college graduates an alternative to the still too tempting literary, legal, and medical faculties of the university. The government also gave its guarded approval to a federal royal commission investigating industrial education between 1910 and 1913 on the condition that there be no question of the province's retaining exclusive control.

The increasing interest of feminists, nationalists, and even the state in education was sure to raise clerical suspicions. Much of the clerics' claim to social prestige was based on their educational activities. As long as education was primarily a matter of elementary instruction for the masses and elite schooling for the select few, church and state were able to agree on clerical administration in return for low costs. But the new century's accent on more advanced and more practical training prodded the state into action. The new technical and commercial schools, for example, were not placed under clerical control. The priests argued in vain that they had been teaching a commercial program in sixteen of the province's twenty-one classical colleges for years, but they could not stop the growing secular interest in education. Many of them in fact considered it part of the times. If the church were not to be totally discarded in an urban world of industrial disrespect for religious holidays, of bars being more numerous than churches, of alienation between priest and people, it would have to react. If no one else was going to defend the church's rightful place in the new industrial order, the church would have to do so itself.

Although launched to protect the clergy's places of power in society, the clerical defensive had a positive connotation — and name — in the early twentieth century. "Catholic action," similar in many respects to the social gospel movement within certain Protestant churches, lent a moral tone to all manner of practical undertakings by clerics all over the world. Supporters of Catholic action assumed that the social question that so agitated feminists and nationalists was above all a religious and moral question and hence required clerical intervention. In the French Canadian context they added the national question to the equation and again came up with necessary social action by priests.

The priests were certainly everywhere to be seen, organizing and encouraging numerous forms of Catholic action. At Laval in 1902 they fostered the *Société du parler français* to protect the French language from the corruption of a technical, urban environment. In the classical colleges in 1904 they grouped pious young men into the *Association catholique de la jeunesse canadienne-française*, a province-wide network of study circles and discussion groups to plan domestic and public Catholic action. After 1906 individual priests lent their local support to the fledgling *caisses populaires*, savings and credit institutions that were to be French Canada's alone. In 1907 the Quebec diocese gave its support to a newspaper appropriately titled *L'Action sociale* and just as appropriately retitled eight years later, *L'Action catholique*. In 1910 still other priests arranged to have the Catholic spotlight of the world on Montreal at the international eucharistic congress where nationalist speaker Henri Bourassa publicly rebuked a visiting bishop from Britain for his association of Catholicism and the English language in North America. To ensure that at least college students if not foreign bishops knew their history, the priests introduced the teaching of Canadian history into the curriculum. Among the teachers scrambling to prepare courses without textbooks was *abbé* Lionel Groulx, then teaching at Valleyfield but shortly, at the instigation of Henri Bourassa, to take up the first chair in Canadian history at Laval University's Montreal campus. Within a few years he, and not Bourassa, was the undisputed *chef* of a new generation of religiously oriented nationalists. In the meantime priests had also shaped that generation through the *Ecole sociale populaire*, begun in 1911 to publicize the Catholic response to social problems. And the clerics clearly established their linking of language and nationalism when Laval hosted a huge *Congrès de la langue française* in 1912, attracting delegates from all over North America. The priests were literally everywhere.

They even tried their hand at more specifically economic activities. Both bishops and local clergy, notably those outside the large metropolitan centres, were enthusiastic promoters of business enterprises and road and railway schemes. Depending on their location, they would advocate a cheese factory or a pulp mill, a foundary or a brickyard and harangue investors to initiate them. In small centres they acted as intermediaries between industrialists and the local population. In Quebec City the archbishop arbitrated a labour dispute between shoe manufacturers and some four thousand workers in 1900. The result of Monseigneur Nazaire Bégin's intervention was a clear statement by the church of the workers' right to join unions.

The type of union which the clergy advocated was, however, another matter. Few of the clergy were content with existing unions. They either saw them as unnecessary restraints on individual workers or as flags marking an unacceptable division of society into warring classes. Most of the unions crossed over ethnic and religious lines and frightened the clergy with the spectre of loss of faith. Moreover, the majority of them were affiliates of international unions and thus brought American norms to Quebec. Even the early national unions, most of which were in Quebec but were expelled from the Trades and Labour Congress of Canada in 1902 precisely because of their lack of international affiliation, were suspect. Although they favoured conciliation and even harmony between employers and employees and thus ought to have found favour with the clergy, their very presence testified to the rivalry and hostility among workers that clerics found so abhorrent. Besides, neither national nor international unions would tolerate clerical intervention in their affairs. And yet their numbers were growing. Unless the church could stake a claim to a presence within the union movement, vast numbers of French Canadians would exercise social relations quite divorced from religion. The church was quick to point out the evil consequence; it was more circumspect about the possible threat to the clerical position in Quebec.

The claim not only to clerical presence but to clerical leadership in unions came out of Chicoutimi in 1907. *Abbé* Eugène Lapointe was determined to organize the forestry and industrial workers of the region, but he wanted neither a company union in the pocket of employers nor an industrial or trade union directed by organizers from elsewhere. Rather he hoped to organize the workers on a confessional basis and to have the social doctrine of the church inspire his *Fédération ouvrière de Chicoutimi*. His union would teach respect for the rights of workers instead of class warfare and its interests would be broader than mere material benefits for its members. The workers, however, needed a lot of convincing. Lapointe had to overcome their scepticism not only about his union with its obligatory chaplain, temperance, Sunday observance, and retreats but also about his friendship with the major employer of the region, Alfred Dubuc. Gradually he won his point so that by 1912 a larger formation emerged from the forest lands of the Saguenay-Lac St. Jean, the *Fédération ouvrière mutuelle du nord*. Thereafter the movement grew as new unions were initiated by priests, or former national unions in Hull, Trois-Rivières, Sherbrooke, or St. Hyacinthe became Catholic ones. They never equalled the international unions in size or number, but they did grow sufficiently through the years of the First World War to form the *Confédération des travailleurs catholiques du Canada* (CTCC) in 1921. From then until their secularization as the *Confédération des syndicats nationaux* in 1960, priests continued to play an active role in one strain of the union movement in Quebec.

Of the three groups initiating social action in Quebec in the early years of the twentieth century, the clerics had the upper hand. Their longer past and more formal position in Quebec society undoubtedly guaranteed that. But an unofficial alliance between male clerics and nationalists against the feminists may also have helped. No formal grouping linked the two, but they often found themselves on the same critical side of the social or political fence. They collaborated on newspapers and in nationalist and Catholic action groups. Occasionally, in fact, they were the same people. But in spite of all the good deeds they willingly credited to certain groups of women, they were uneasy with the very concept of feminism. Unlike the women, they had the resources, in pulpit, press, and platform, to make their views known.

Sometimes the women themselves provided the occasion for expressions of male hostility. In 1913 while all the world watched British feminists battling with police and engaging in hunger strikes in prison in order to gain political equality by means of the vote, French Canadian feminists invited priest Louis Lalande to address the *Fédération nationale Saint-Jean-Baptiste*. The topic was the very one that had inaugurated the *Fédération*: the two kinds of feminism. Fearful lest Canadian women be attracted toward the worst kind and start demanding political rights themselves, Lalande denounced it for its shrill bitterness, as violent and brutal as the men it purported to despise; it could only lead to unnatural demands, the defiance of authority, and ultimately the break-up of the home. In contrast, Lalande pointed to the good works, particularly the moral protection of young workers, accomplished in the name of religion and feminine dignity and in the acceptance of authority and natural inequalities. The constrast could hardly have been more pointed. But if the members of the *Fédération*, well aware that the National Council of Women had openly espoused votes for women in 1910, had any misgivings about Lalande's portrayal, they kept them to themselves.

Nor did the *Fédération* ever respond publicly to Henri Bourassa's virulent attack on feminism in *Le Devoir* that same spring of 1913. According to Bourassa, the ultra-Catholic editor of the nationalist Montreal daily, feminism was a foreign import, another Protestant infection, bound to poison the French Canadian family and through it French Canadian civilization. Women in fact were the guardians of all that made for French Canadian cultural superiority in North America: they held the key to the survival of religion, morality, education, and the family. If they stopped behaving in the prescribed manner, if they ceased to embody all the ideal characteristics not only of French Canada but of humanity itself, they would bring down the social order in ruin about their heads. Drawing on religion and logic, biology and politics, propriety and ridicule, Bourassa lashed feminism with a vehemence that indicated more the febrile state of his imagination than the reality of Canadian feminism.

That reality was actually much closer to the ideal image of women that nationalists and clerics concocted for their own convenience. Canadian feminists, French and English alike, accepted the notion of separate spheres; they acknowledged, as eternally given, the social distinctions that stemmed from sexual distinctions; they agreed that they had a particular mission in life to be cultured, morally uplifting, soothing, and healing. Bourassa had only to read the columns of his own female correspondent, Fadette, in *Le Devoir* or even those of Colette (Edouardine Lesage) in the rival *La Presse* where an entire front page was given over in 1913 to depict the three types of women in the public eye. Dominating the page and contrasted both with the moderate suffragette, mistaken in her desire for the vote but permitted nonetheless to express her views, and with the violent suffragette, a fury who had discarded all her femininity, was the real woman, devoted solely to her maternal mission, the ornament of her family, the object of everyone's adoration. French Canada, *La Presse* was relieved to note, had only the last kind of woman. The feminists thought so too. When they took on public tasks beyond the home, they did so to protect the home. They were merely enlarging their maternal sphere for the benefit of society. If their entrance into the public arena of education and social welfare was in fact a criticism of the extent of the industrial mess men had created or of the efficacy of religious institutions to cope with it or even of the stifling role that the ideology of separate spheres thrust upon them, few of them said so. The clerics' and the nationalists' ability to spot danger where in fact none existed deprived Quebec women of the right to vote in provincial elections until the 1940s. In the second decade of the twentieth century it was easy enough to direct women into knitting socks and bundling bandages for soldiers overseas while the nationalists and the clerics, harbouring more ambiguous views about the First World War, fought the "Prussians" next door.

THE 1907 BELL TELEPHONE STRIKE: ORGANIZING WOMEN WORKERS†

JOAN SANGSTER

By the late nineteenth century women were eager applicants for every kind of respectable position that might release them from the restrictions of domestic employments. Companies such as Bell were just as enthusiastic about the advantages of acquiring a clean, well-spoken, and responsible workforce, on the cheap. The unreserved nature of this mutual attraction broke down quickly enough when female workers were continually pressed for higher levels of productivity without any concomitant recognition of their right to earn a living wage. The 1907 telephone operators' strike showed, as Joan Sangster illustrates, the limits of tolerance among even the non-unionized labour force. It proved a telling lesson as well for the communications pioneer which thereafter, and in line with many other up-to-date employers such as the Timothy Eaton Company and B.C. Telephone, invoked an evolving set of modern management practices to promote employee loyalty and forestall effective unionization. That lesson had to be repeated a number of times, as the job action by B.C. operators in the Vancouver General Strike of 1919 suggested. Women's willingness to accept terms less advantageous than men's was carefully nurtured by canny employers and encouraged, probably unconsciously, by the reluctance of male unionists to defend women on the same basis as themselves. Where companies failed to win over their employees, and unions intervened, as in the garment and cotton industries in the 1930s and 1940s, for example, female workers under leaders like Madeleine Parent of the United Textile Workers of America continued traditions of militancy. Many more women, however, influenced by the coincidence of labour management practices and sex role socialization, retreated from direct, on-the-job confrontations, to find their satisfactions in marriage and children. Working conditions in the home might be better and bosses were at least less numerous.*

In February of 1907 a dramatic strike of women workers took place in Toronto when over 400 operators walked off their jobs with Bell Telephone. For days, the dispute between Bell and the "hello girls" captured front page headlines in the Toronto newspapers. The determination and militancy of the "pretty young girls in their tailor mades"[1] in the face of Bell's intransigence created great public interest and aroused considerable sympathy. The threat of a crippled phone service raised the issue of strikes in monopoly controlled public utilities, an issue fresh in the public mind after a violent street railway strike in Hamilton only a few months earlier. As in Hamilton, public sympathy clearly lay with the strikers, since the monopoly controlled utility was highly unpopular with the local citizenry.

The Bell strike was seen as an event of great importance by government and business leaders. Rodophe Lemieux, the federal Minister of Labour, publicly

†*Labour/Le Travailleur* III (1978): 109–130. The author would like to thank Irving Abella and Ian Radforth for their valuable comments and criticisms of this paper.

*See Elaine Bernard, "Last Back: Folklore and the Telephone Operators in the 1919 Vancouver General Strike," in *Not Just Pin Money*, edited by Barbara K. Latham and Roberta J. Pazdro (Victoria: Camosun College, 1984).

pointed to the Bell Commission as a testing ground for the Industrial Disputes Investigation Act, legislation which provided for a cooling off period and public investigation in utilities strikes. Privately, he declared that the Bell strike "marked the turning point of our future legislation."[2] The Company also saw the strike as an event of some significance. Bell later claimed that the strike "brought an important new step in our labour relations thinking."[3] The operators' firm resistance to Bell's wage cutbacks and efficiency drive fostered the company's increasing awareness of the need for more refined scientific management and stimulated the introduction of consultation and welfare measures designed to enhance employee loyalty and diffuse unionization attempts.

As well as providing some insight into the mind of government and business, the strike furnishes an excellent picture of the working conditions, problems and attitudes of women telephone workers. Unfortunately, the strike did not mark a significant achievement for the operators because they failed to obtain their wage demands, failed to gain significant changes in their working conditions, and failed to form a union. Nonetheless, the strike was characterized by a militance and solidarity which contradicted the contemporary dictums about women's passivity and revealed the possibilities of protest against their exploitation.

By the turn of the century, operating had become a totally "female" occupation at Bell Telephone. After an experiment with women labour on both day and nights shifts in 1888, the Bell had decided to switch from boy to women operators. Boys were found to lack tact and patience; unlike women, they were seldom polite and submissive to irate or rude subscribers but "matched insult for insult."[4] Furthermore, Bell said, boys were "hard to discipline"[5] and were not as conscientious and patient as women. Taking these qualities into account, as well as the important consideration that "the prevailing wage rates for women were lower,"[6] Bell hired only female operators by 1900.

Bell demanded that their operators be physically fit in order to tackle the exacting work at the switchboard. Applicants had to be tall enough to reach the top wires, had to prove good hearing and eyesight, and could not wear eyeglasses or have a consumptive cough. Supervisors were instructed not to issue an application unless satisfied that the person was in "good health and physically well qualified."[7] An applicant was also requested to produce references, one from her clergyman, stating that she was "of good moral character and industrious habits . . . a person of truth and integrity, with intelligence, temperament and manners fit to be an operator."[8] With such qualifications Bell hoped to attract a "better class" of woman worker than was found in industrial employment. Early recruitment attempts stressed the occupation's white collar characteristics: the clean work place, "steadiness, possibility of advancement, shorter hours than factory work, and seclusion from the public."[9] The job specifications probably did result in a "better class" of employee. One early operator explained that she came to the Bell "while I was waiting for an appointment as a school teacher", while another commented that she became an operator because "few lines of work were open to women and these were not appealing, such as sales clerks."[10] Note was carefully taken of the "enunciation, education and penmanship"[11] of all applicants. This undoubtedly eliminated many immigrants and women with no formal education.

The Royal Commission revealed, however, that the operators' working conditions did not necessarily reflect their position as a "better class" of wage earner. In fact, the operator's shift work, close supervision, and ties to machinery made her job resemble blue collar, rather than white collar, work.[12] The operator's task was extremely exhausting for great mental concentration, accuracy and speed were essential. Each woman looked after 80 to 100 lines, with 6,041 possible connections and placed about 300 calls an hour. Backless stools and a high switchboard, which some women could reach only by jumping up on the stool rungs, made the operators' work physically uncomfortable and tiring. If her own calls lagged, a worker was not allowed to relax, but had to help the operator next to her. In order to create a "business-like" atmosphere, the rules were strict: the women were instructed to line up five minutes before their shift entered the operating room, and when seated, had to "sit up straight, with no talking or smiling."[13] Supervisors who paced behind the operators inspecting their work were told to "nag and hurry the girls."[14]

Other strains were added to the operator's rapidly paced work, such as the risk of physical injury and the knowledge that a monitor might be secretly listening in to check one's performance. Operators complained to the Commission that heavy headgear could produce painful sores and that women sometimes fainted and occasionally became hysterical from the pressure of rapid work. Maude Orton, a supervisor and leader in the strike, claimed that women sometimes were pushed to nervous breakdowns, and that she was compelled to take nerve medicine. "I never knew what nerves meant until I started to work at the Bell,"[15] she commented. The most dangerous work was on the long distance lines, where operators sometimes received severe electrical shocks, which could send them into convulsions and lay them off work for weeks.

For such demanding work, the women received a starting salary of $18 a month, which after three years service was increased to $25. Although this wage compared favourably with the hourly rate of many female factory workers, it fell below the monthly wage of the more skilled woman worker in industry, who could earn about $30 a month (and of course, it fell far below the male, skilled wage rate of $40–$60 a month).[16] The immediate issue precipitating the 1907 strike, however, was not inadequate wages: the issue was an increase in hours. On 27 January, the Manager of the Toronto Central Exchange, K.J. Dunstan, informed the operators that, as of 1 February, their five hour day would be lengthened to eight hours, and their salaries increased. Introduced originally in 1903, when noisy construction work made an eight hour day at the switchboard impossible, the five hour day was continued on as an experiment and then was "permanently" adopted in 1905 since management believed it to be a more efficient use of womanpower.

In late 1906, however, Dunstan became worried about the efficiency of the five hour day. At the same time, the company decided to standardize the operators' hours of work in Toronto and Montreal, which still had an eight hour day. In this period the policy of Bell Telephone President Charles Sise was to "eliminate all Bell's remaining competitors; to above all, give a better quality of service while keeping rates as low as possible."[17] Also at this time, American scientific management practices were adopted by some firms in Canada.[18] With the aims of increasing efficiency and raising productivity, programs such as cost and time studies, bonus systems, and job standardization were introduced into industrial establishments. Bell Canada, especially with its close branch-plant relationship to American Telephone and Telegraph, was influenced by these currents of thought. In late 1906, two expert engineers from AT&T were called in to make comparative studies of the Montreal and Toronto operating systems. In true scientific management style, the engineers performed stopwatch tests on the operators' responses, examined the quality of their answers, and from these calculated the speed and quality of operating.

Their reports agreed that the eight hour system more efficiently used labour power, but their findings were not a conclusive indictment of the five hour system, for one report called for "further investigation" and the other stressed the different personalities of the Office Managers in influencing the speed of operating.[19] Nevertheless, a decision was made to introduce an eight hour day in Toronto when a new exchange was completed in the summer. In January of 1907, however, Dunstan urged an immediate changeover because he knew that the self-supporting operators were becoming increasingly angry about their low wages. It was essential to raise the wages, he informed Sise, "and advisable that the increase in hours and wages coincide."[20]

Dunstan argued that the changes were necessitated by Bell's inability to secure operators, "for our rates were too low and to attract more women we had to increase wages, therefore we had to increase hours."[21] He also contended that the change was made for the sake of the operators' health. "It is the pace that kills",[22] he later told the Commission. The Company's primary motive, however, was to reduce the "uneconomical" overtime being paid and to give increased service while keeping labour costs down. Company correspondence brought before the Commission revealed that the new schedule was designed to "ensure the increase in wages would not equal that of hours and the cost per 1,000 calls should thus be lessened."[23]

The operators quickly realized that wages would not increase in relation to hours worked since the new schedule meant a reduction from approximately 21¢ to 16¢ an hour. For those operators who were entirely self supporting, the salary changes were particularly disastrous. These women had previously worked extra five-hour shifts in order to pay for their board and clothing. Under the new system, such overtime would be impossible: their income would be drastically reduced. A small group of women, composed of supervisors and the more experienced operators, began to organize a protest against the new hours. With the help of Jimmy Simpson, a Toronto printer, and well known activist in trade union and socialist circles, they formed the Telephone Operators, Supervisors and Monitors Association, and they engaged a lawyer, J. Walter Curry, to help them draft a petition of protest. Curry, a former crown attorney with strong Liberal connections, was active in the public ownership league formed in Toronto in February of 1907. He donated his services to the operators free of charge, eager to aid in the fight against the Bell monopoly, and with the help of W.F. Maclean, editor of the Toronto *World*, started a public strike fund for the women.

Bell refused to meet with Curry or with the group of protestors whom Dunstan dubbed "a few firebrands and agitators stirring up trouble."[24] On 29 January, 400 operators met at the Labour Temple to discuss their predicament. We have had grievances before, declared one operator, but never such good organization to back us up: "while it is the extension of hours we complain principally about now, it's the money too."[25] Faced by intransigent Company officials who were unwilling to discuss the issue, the meeting voted to plan a strike. This vote had immediate results. Fearing disruption of telephone service, Mayor Coatsworth wired the federal government for assistance. Mackenzie King, then Deputy Minister of Labour, hurried to Toronto, hoping to display his talents as a mediator. Bell, however, resolutely refused such "outside interference", and secretly made plans to bring in strikebreakers. Bell's head office in Montreal encouraged Dunstan's firm approach. Company President Charles Sise advised Dunstan to be "resolute . . . act with absolute firmness in rejecting consultation or compromise."[26] Not surprisingly, it was Bell that precipitated the crisis. On 31 January, the Company demanded that operators either sign an acceptance of the new schedule or resign. The operators had no choice but to walk out; in a sense the confrontation was a lock-out, not a strike.

That night, the women met again at the Labour Temple. The meeting, said the *Star*, "was militant and enthusiastic."[27] The women made an impressive show of solidarity and sisterhood. Strikers who lived at home contributed money for those independent women who had to make rent payments. Supervisors, monitors and operators, all with different rank and salaries, joined together to protest the Company's actions. Despite their higher salaries and positions of authority, the supervisors seemed to feel considerable concern for the operators' working conditions; perhaps these more experienced workers felt protective towards the younger women. The strikers were addressed by J. Lightbound, from the Internal Brotherhood of Electrical Workers (IBEW), who suggested that they affiliate with the union. The feeling of the strikers, reported the press, was strongly in favour of the idea.

Public sympathy bolstered the strikers' enthusiasm. Bell's monopoly made the Company unpopular with Toronto citizens, who objected to the lack of competition and the arbitrary methods of fixing rates.[28] Shortly after the women had walked out, a crowd gathered at the Central Exchange and cheered on the strikers, while snowballing scabs entering the building and hooting at Dunstan when he came out to address the crowd. The Company also had to ask for police protection for its strikebreakers, who were brought from Bell exchanges in Peterborough, Kingston, Ottawa and Montreal. (The Montreal operators were promised an expense-paid trip and were given a $20 honorarium when they returned home.) The first day of the strike, the scabs were taunted by the picketers at the Exchange door. "I hope you die of nervous prostration,"[29] shouted one irate striker. Some of the Montreal strikebreakers had to be removed from their hotel when bellboys objected to their presence; other scabs complained of harassment over the telephone as they worked.

All the Toronto daily papers were sympathetic to the operators. A *Globe* editorial heartily endorsed the strike, criticizing Bell's selfish and inhumane treatment of its women workers. The Company, however, was not censured for its use of strikebreakers, but rather for its neglect of the operators' health and mental well-being. In the York County Council a unanimous resolution was passed condemning Bell for its neglect of its employees' health; the Company was described as "inhuman, a menace to business . . . and should not be tolerated in a free Canada."[30] On Sunday, 3 February, Reverend J.E. Starr, a local Methodist minister, held a church service for the strikers. His sermon, taken from St. Paul's words "I entreat thee also yoke fellow, help those women", condemned Bell's "tyranny over the weaker sex" and called for a more humane employment system which would not "strain women beyond their capacity and impair the interests of the unborn."[31]

Yet, despite such public sympathy, the strikers gained no ground. Moralistic sermons and editorials were not backed up with laws compelling Bell to negotiate with the strikers, nor were the women even unionized. The only real weapon the women had in the dispute was the withdrawal of their labour power and that weapon had been quickly muffled by the use of strikebreakers. The Bell management was determined to avoid setting the precedent of discussing and negotiating working conditions with their employees: they were adamantly opposed to any semblance of collective bargaining. Charles Sise had made his ideological opposition to unions clear during a dispute with Hamilton linemen in 1900. In 1907 that opposition remained. Sise informed the Montreal press of his firm intention to lock out the women: "so far as we are concerned, the strike is over. The Company has all the new operators it requires."[32] Dunstan echoed this opinion, telling the Toronto newspapers that he might consider "on an individual basis only, any operator who wished to return to work on the eight hour schedule."[33]

The Company did make some attempt to counter its unfavourable public image. In his interviews with the press, Dunstan stressed three arguments. First, he emphasized that the Company's most important concern was its obligation to the community, justifying the use of strikebreakers by professing that Bell was interested only in continuing its service to the public. Secondly, Dunstan tried to prove that the strike was led by a few agitators and troublemakers, while the "majority would welcome the change and return to work."[34] Lastly, he claimed that compared to other women wage earners, operators were well off, and he pointed to the various "comforts" of the Toronto Exchange, such as restrooms and lockers, which were not found in most industrial establishments.[35] Bell's public relations efforts, however, did not include an offer to negotiate with the strikers. At a meeting on 31 January, the strikers had voted to accept an arbitrated settlement, believing that their cause was just. But Bell refused arbitration because the Company anticipated that an arbitration board would rule against them.

Faced with this deadlock, Mackenzie King adopted a new tactic, advising the operators to request a public enquiry from the Minister of Labour. The operators were persuaded by their male advisors to return to work and accept the eight hour day until the Commission made its recommendations. Although hesitant to end the strike with no concrete gains, the strike committee decided to place their hopes for redress in an inquiry. The operators' male advisors encouraged them to view the Commission with optimism. "I believe you will win", assured Curry, "for you have the public and the newspapers behind you."[36] The operators, reported one newspaper, were "jubilant, for they felt victory would emerge from the Commission"; enthusiastic cheering erupted when Simpson called for "No victory to the Company."[37]

The Commission, however, was clearly not a solution to the operators' plight for the Company later refused to be bound by its recommendations. The strikers had now suffered a dangerous set back; they returned to work on the Company's conditions, with no promise of negotiations on the issue of wages and working conditions. It is possible that King and Curry hoped public pressure would reverse Bell's decision and force concessions. On the other hand, there is abundant evidence that King's main aim in persuading the women to return to work was simply to bring peace and diffuse the conflict. There was quiet recognition by some trade unionists that the tactic of striking before unionization had been disastrous and that the strike was being crushed by the use of strikebreakers.[38] It is possible, therefore, that the women's advisors, foreseeing defeat, believed that the operators should regain their jobs as soon as possible. "They have fooled us," one disappointed operator realized, "we thought they couldn't get along for an hour without us, but they can."[39]

On 4 February, the operators returned to the Exchange to offer themselves for re-employment. President Sise had informed Dunstan in a letter that "under no conditions should we take back an operator. Our strong point will be to show our utter independence of the disaffected operators."[40] Yet, in a few days about 150 women were taken back, and after two weeks of Commission hearings, the Company announced it would make a concession and rehire all its former employees at their former salaries.

The Royal Commissioners were Mackenzie King and Judge John Winchester, a York county judge of Liberal persuasion, with a record of sympathy on labour issues.[41] The sessions were well attended and thoroughly covered by the press. The operators, many of them still unemployed, were present in large numbers, and every newspaper commented on "the beauty show adorning the courtroom."[42] Reporters described the attractive array of millinery and dress at the enquiry, always distinguishing between the operators and the "men carrying on the serious business of the strike."[43] Some of the women, however, did manage to rise above their Dresden doll image: the committee of operators who initiated the strike advised their lawyer, Curry, throughout the proceedings, while other operators found themselves threatened with eviction from the courtroom when they interrupted Dunstan's testimony with loud protests.

The Commission hearings concentrated on five main issues: the change in hours, the causes of the strike, the nature of the operators' work, medical opinion about the operators' workload, and lastly, the "listening board" issue which had come to light during the strike.

Bell's public image plummeted even further during the hearings. It was soon made clear that the Company had made its changes in hours for commercial and business reasons only, despite previous assertions to the contrary. Also, Dunstan had claimed before the Commission that Bell's new schedule would decrease the work load of each woman, but the evidence proved otherwise. All those operators who had been re-employed under the eight hour schedule testified that there was no reduction in load: "the promised relief hasn't come; we are working just as hard."[44] The hearings further embarrassed Bell by revealing that the Company had recently considered abolishing the workers' two week paid vacation and that officials were aware that the operators' wages were inadequate. At first, Dunstan implied that many women came to Bell simply to earn "pin money", or that they spent their wages unwisely: "some women," declared Dunstan, "come to us just to earn a fur coat or something like that and leave to get married after two or three years."[45] But boarding house rates were presented and self-supporting operators testified that without overtime they could not survive. Rent and food prices had escalated far beyond the reach of independent operators working only a five hour day. The $18 a month received by a starting operator was quickly eaten up by board costs of about $12–14 and food costs of at least $4; overtime was necessary even to obtain the other essentials such as clothing, car fare and laundry.[46] After these presentations, Dunstan conceded that for the 30-40% of the operators who were self supporting, their normal wages were inadequate. Bell was also forced to admit to the arbitrary manner in which it had informed its employees of its intentions at the time of the schedule changes. Curry skillfully emphasized this testimony, trying to portray Bell as a monstrously rich and ruthless exploiter, a monopoly mercilessly grinding down its employees. He demanded to know why wages were not influenced by Bell's ever-rising profits. Horrified, Bell's Chief Office Manager, Frank Maw, replied that wages most certainly should not rise with profits: "after all, you pay the market price for your goods."[47]

The Commissioners were especially concerned with the mental and physical hazards of telephone work. Testimony showed that operating was so rapidly paced and pressured that it resulted in unusually high nervous strain and mental exhaustion. Supervisors testified that they were told to pressure the operators to quicken their pace: "I know that the girls are worked to the limit, but we are told to drive them."[48] Dunstan claimed that the five hour day allowed many women to moonlight at jobs, such as housekeeping, while Maw argued that women came to work "already exhausted"[49] from roller skating, one of the operators' favourite pastimes. The strike leaders, however, vehemently denied these claims. After a day's work at the Bell, said Maude Orton, women could not moonlight anywhere: "they are only fit for bed."[50] The pressure of work, Miss Dixon continued, "doesn't allow young girls to enjoy themselves as they should, at roller skating or anything else."[51] Evidence also revealed that women often had to work extra relief periods for which they were never paid; extracting this free overtime labour was regular Company policy. The most disturbing testimony, however, came from the long distance operators who had suffered electrical shocks. One operator told the hearing that she was not informed about shocks when she took the job and in such an accident had lost the use of her left ear. Another woman who had suffered a severe shock and convulsion informed the Commission that she was still too terrified to return to work.

The Commission subpoenaed twenty-six Toronto doctors in order to obtain an objective view of the operators' conditions of work. All the medical experts agreed that the task of operating put exceptional strain on a woman's sense of hearing, sight and speech, and that the result was "exhaustion, more mental and nervous than physical."[52] A consensus of medical opinion (with the exception of the Company doctor) rejected the eight hour day. Most doctors suggested a five, six or seven hour day with assured periods of relief. One helpful doctor observed that the weaker sex should not engage in such work at all: choosing between a five and eight hour day, he said, was like deciding "between slaying a man with a gun or a club."[53] The testimony of these medical experts reflected prevailing medical and social views of woman as the "weaker" sex. Young women, it was emphasized, were extremely susceptible to nervous and emotional disorders; "we are laying the basis of our future insane asylums with operating,"[54] warned one doctor. Many doctors concurred with King's suggestion that women deserved the special protection of the state on matters regarding health and sanitary conditions in their place of work. One doctor added that it should definitely be medical experts who decided for the working woman: "they must be protected from themselves. . . . [T]he girls are not the best judges of how much work they should do."[55]

One other issue was investigated by the Commission. When the strike first began, some operators had mentioned the existence of a listening board which could be used secretly to intercept a subscriber's conversation. Despite Bell's assurances that the listening board was only used to investigate technical problems, the press and public were not satisfied. For a time the striking operators were all but forgotten by the press which denounced Bell for the irresponsible and arrogant use of its monopoly. "The public had been repaid for the inconvenience of the strike," said the Globe, "by gaining the important knowledge of listening boards. . . . [T]he opportunity for misuse is there."[56] Despite such fears, however, the hearings did not reveal that the opportunity had been taken. The newspapers' concentration on the listening board issue revealed how easily the operators could be forgotten. Many editorials and letters to the editor pointed to the strike as one more reason for nationalization of telephones and telegraphs. While disgust was expressed about the mistreatment of the operators, these proponents of public ownership were eager to use any argument, including threats to privacy and Bell's high rates, in order to buttress their case for public ownership.

On 18 February, the Commission came to an abrupt end. The Company's lawyers put forward a compromise solution which Curry and the operators accepted. A new schedule was proposed in which the operators were to work seven hours, spread over a nine hour day. Extensive relief was to be given, with no consecutive period of work extending over two hours. Wages were to be those proposed under the eight hour schedule, and a promise of no compulsory overtime was given. The operators were dubious about the offer, but decided in its favour after a conference with Curry and King. The women expressed fears that the load would not be reduced and announced that the "seven hour day was less injurious, but there was still too much strain."[57] Curry and King undoubtedly knew that the proposal favoured Bell, but at the same time believed that it was as much as Bell would surrender. It must have been clear that the Company was largely unmoved by the condemning testimony of the hearings and by adverse public feeling. Bell officials realized that it was unlikely that special legislation would be introduced to enact such a short (five hour) working day. They also knew that adverse public opinion would fade and that as a powerful monopoly, the Company could withstand a great deal of adverse public feeling anyway. A letter sent to King almost two months after the settlement made it only too clear that the operators were the losers. Curry informed King that:

> I learn from the young ladies that matters are not much improved from what they were before, that the only improvements are in the surroundings, not in the work itself.[58]

The seven hour schedule had not lessened the work load and had only reduced the amount of the wage cutback. The "compromise" agreement did little to solve the dilemma of the self-supporting operator. How was she now to pay for board and clothing when her wages still did not approximate her former five hours plus overtime salary?

Throughout the strike and the hearings Bell maintained a consistent attitude towards its women workers. First, the Company insisted on complete control of its own labour policy: it was unwilling to give its employees any role in determining their working conditions and it abhorred government intervention. Secondly, Bell made extensive use of the largely unorganized, highly fluid female working force as a form of cheap labour and excused its low wages with the argument that women were not breadwinners, but were only working for "pin money" while awaiting marriage. This was the practice of many business concerns, but Bell's case seems particularly reprehensible, for as a stable company with rising profits and dividends, Bell clearly did not need to make wage cutbacks. Thirdly, Bell's claims that their employees' health was an absolute priority was pure rhetoric. Instead of establishing a work load compatible with the women's health, Bell sought to push them "almost to the breaking point."[59] The Commission's Report concluded that "one looks in vain for any reference which would indicate that the health or well being of the operators was a matter of any consideration."[60]

In a 1963 report on Bell's labour policy prepared for the Company, G. Parsons concluded that some important lessons had been learned from the 1907 dispute. The Company had decided that, as a monopoly, Bell was subject to closer scrutiny and thus must be more aware of "good grievances:"[61] if ignored, these grievances would be likely to gain a public hearing and would perhaps attract government intervention. In the pre-war period in the United States, Bell increasingly sought employee loyalty by developing employee associations which were to give some feeling of consultation and negotiation, by pioneering an employee benefit plan, and by making offices more pleasant workplaces (supplying lounges and cafeterias).[62] In Canada similar consultation and welfare programs were gradually introduced. After the strike, for instance, the Company decided that attempts would be made to "foster better communications"[63] with their employees, keeping them more closely informed of the Company's plans and making some pretence of consultation. Secondly, the office surroundings were improved; in the Main Exchange a matron was hired to bring the operators tea and coffee. A few months after the strike, Sise decided to supply a free medical examination for every operator. He privately informed the Hamilton Manager that such examinations "may be desirable to save us trouble and expense inasmuch as we will avoid the training of useless operators who might be discharged because of unfitness."[64] Five years later, Bell introduced a Health Benefit Plan to aid its employees in time of illness. These welfare measures were part of the broader scientific management program to increase efficiency and consolidate management control. By playing the benevolent paternalist, the Company aimed to minimize dissatisfaction over wages, raise the prestige of the occupation, and discourage unionization. The 1907 strike was one impetus to the development of this welfare capitalist approach.

The strike not only acted as a mirror for Bell's labour policy; it also revealed Mackenzie King's approach to labour relations. King's view of women workers, of the governmental role in labour disputes, and his hopes for the Industrial Disputes Investigation Act were all exhibited in the hearings and the Commission Report. King's perceptions of the operators reflect a Victorian image of woman. As one of the latest commentators on King's personal "woman problem" has stated:

> the image of woman in Christian society has revolved around the contrasting conceptions of Eve the Temptress and the Virgin Mary. . . . [A]t no time was this paradox more actue than in the Victorian age from whence King came.[65]

King believed it was essential that a woman's maternal role be protected, not just for her own good but for the good of society as well. Thus, in the Report he worried about the results of the nervous strain of operating upon a woman's future role: "the effects moreover upon posterity occasioned by the undermining or weakening [of] the female constitution cannot receive too serious consideration."[66] Women, however, could also be seen as Eves. In the hearings King interrogated Bell rigorously about its treatment of self-supporting operators: his concern was that the Company's wage rates were inadequate to supply board in a "decent" home and thus women would be forced to turn to prostitution. It was King's first concern which predominated in his Report. He expressed both privately and publicly his horror with the Company's disregard for women's health. In his diary he wrote:

> the more I go into the evidence the more astounded I am at the revelations it unfolds. The image is constantly before me of some hideous octopus feeding upon the life blood of young women and girls.[67]

King's paternalism was revealed throughout the hearings and Report. Because women workers were weak and "easily led," he later remarked, "to seek to protect this class is noble and worthy to the highest degree."[68] As woman's nature is particularly sensitive to physical and mental strain, he warned, her industrial working conditions must be regulated by medical experts and the benevolent state.

This view reflected a broader social attitude towards female labour often expressed by middle class reformers. Doctors testifying before the Commission shared King's concern for future mothers. Their greatest fear was that nervous strain would disqualify a woman from motherhood: "they [the operators] turned out badly in their domestic relations, they break down nervously and have nervous children; it is a loss to the community."[69] The press also criticized Bell primarily for its disregard for women's health; the use of strikebreakers, the payment of low wages, and the need for unionization were not considered the important issues. It was the moral, rather than economic, question of woman labour which was emphasized. As Alice Klein and Wayne Roberts have suggested, the impetus for middle class reformers often came from fears that the femininity of woman workers was endangered by their working conditions.[70]

In order to ensure protection for women workers, King advocated cautious government intervention in industrial disputes. Later in *Industry and Humanity*, he claimed to be particularly concerned with public utilities where an absolute or quasi-monopoly existed. In such situations, he said, "there exists an insistence on the part of the public of a due regard for the welfare of employees."[71] It is also clear, however, that King did not see the government's role as the primary or controlling factor in labour-capital relations: the government would intervene to legislate protective guidelines only if all other reform attempts failed. In the Bell Report, King cited the need for protective legislation for women but he also pointed out the difficulty in securing it: "it is difficult to see wherein it is possible for the State to effectively regulate the speed of operating."[72] He concluded that the real hope for change lay in another area, namely a more enlightened attitude on the part of the Company. This attitude was to be the outcome of an impartial investigation, the pressure of public opinion, and the Company's own desire for efficiency.

King used the Bell dispute in his arguments for his Industrial Disputes Investigation Act (IDIA) which was presented for second reading in Parliament during the Commission hearings. Both King and Lemieux tried to use the Bell dispute as a public testing ground for the IDIA principle and both cited it as an example for the success of that principle. The IDIA provided for a public investigation of all labour disputes in public utilities and a thirty day prohibition of strikes or lockouts during the investigation. Although neither labour nor capital was legally obliged to accept the investigator's findings, King argued that the "pressure of public enquiry would force concessions and a settlement."[73] After the IDIA was presented for its second reading on 13 February, Lemieux informed King that:

> I am very anxious to succeed re the telephone enquiry. . . . By all means settle the telephone strike *cum summia laude* [sic]. It marks the turning point of our future legislation.[74]

In the Commons Lemieux argued that the Bell Commission provided an excellent example of an impartial commission and public pressure bringing compromise to a labour conflict. "Due to the thorough scientific enquiry of the Commission", said Lemieux, "the Company has already compromised on its earlier policy, and agreed to re-hire its former operators."[75] King used similar arguments to support the IDIA after the Bell inquiry was over. He maintained that a neutral inquiry and public opinion had been instrumental in bringing a settlement to the dispute. Writing to a Member of Parliament, King said,

> Take the case of the telephone girls in Toronto. What power had those girls, unorganized and unassisted, with no means of keeping up a strike. . . . When public opinion was brought to bear on the situation for the first time there was an approach to an equality between the parties.[76]

It is true that the investigation helped to end the dispute. The public hearings had brought some minor concessions from Bell for the Company agreed to reduce the amount of wage cutbacks and rehire all the strikers. (It is hard to imagine, however, that Bell could have continued indefinitely with out-of-town strikebreakers.) If peace was King's major objective, then perhaps the IDIA principle could be termed a "success". In his diary, King did optimistically claim that he thought the Report would "mean a gain for workingmen and women."[77] Yet, it is clear that his most important goal was immediate peace and not the kind of settlement the women received. Throughout the Report, King pointed to Bell's insensitivity and to public opinion and to "its motives of business cupidity above all else."[78] How then could King have hoped for the Company's enlightenment and reform? The contradiction between King's condemnation of Bell's greed and inhumanity and his hopes for its reform seems incredible.

Furthermore, King never replied to Curry's statement that the operators' working conditions had not improved; his willingness to ignore this letter seriously questions his expressed concern for the plight of the working woman. His delay in publishing the Report also makes his concern for the operators suspect. In early April the operators and Curry pleaded with King to move as quickly as possible. "I had hoped", wrote Curry "to have attempted to get legislation here before the rising of the House [on 20 April]. It would seem to be almost impossible now to accomplish that purpose."[79] King replied that there was some "advantage in delaying the report a little for it has given the Company a chance to show what it can do."[80] The only advantage was to Bell, for when the Report appeared six months after the strike, public interest had waned and over half the operators had left the Company.

The Bell dispute did not prove the value to labour of the IDIA principle, but rather its dangers. The operators placed their hopes in redress through public investigation; yet, Bell had been powerful enough to maintain wage cutbacks and arduous working conditions despite adverse public feeling. Public investigation, sympathetic editorials, and church sermons did not help the operators secure their demands. Better organization and an effective strike might have.

The issue of unionization was not central to the 1907 strike. After the strike had commenced the operators passed two resolutions favouring an arrangement of affiliation with the International Brotherhood of Electrical Workers (IBEW), yet these plans did not materialize. The operators waited until 1918 when another major attempt to organize into the IBEW was initiated.[81] The failure to sustain a union after the strike in 1907 was the result of three factors: the hostility of Bell, the disinterest of the IBEW and other male labour leaders, and the particular problems encountered by the workers because they were women.

Bell's policy with regard to trade unions was clearly stated by Sise in 1900: "we have never recognized these unions in any way nor would we oblige ourselves to employ only union men."[82] This attitude remained firm in the 1907 dispute. Bell refused to re-hire any of the strike leaders or picketers after the strike was over on 4 February. Even after the "amnesty" for strikers which the Company announced on 13 February, women connected with the IBEW were asked to leave the union or resign from their jobs. Such anti-union victimization was obviously a major factor in discouraging unionization. The Company's movement towards welfare capitalism and its attempts to "kill unionization with kindness" may have also successfully sidetracked the organization of the operators.

At the 4 February meeting of the operators a male labour leader admitted to a *Mail and Empire* reporter that "it was the general consensus of opinion that the girls have been beaten. . . . It is too bad the way they were led into their present position by men without a stake in the contest."[83] Because the women were not unionized before going on strike, he said, the Company had every advantage and the strikers no hope of sustaining a campaign of organization. It is questionable, however, how eager the IBEW was to organize the women. The IBEW had recently asserted its jurisdiction over telephone operators but the union was showing little interest in organizing them. The IBEW had developed a strong tradition of inequality; in the U.S., for instance, the few operators' locals existing before World War I were denied full autonomy and were given only half their voting rights. The Brotherhood, its historians agree, was convinced that women made "bad" union members; it believed operators could not build permanent unions as "women were flighty and came to the union only when in trouble, then dropped out."[84] Behind these convictions lay other fears. The electricians claimed that unskilled operators might make foolish decisions on craft matters which they did not understand. There was also strong apprehension about "petticoat rule":[85] the large number of operators, it was feared, would come to control the union. It is also possible that there was indifference to the operators simply because they did not threaten the earning power of other IBEW members. For all these reasons, the union Executive most often refused requests to lend any aid to the organization of telephone operators. Such hostility was probably an important factor in the failure of the Toronto IBEW to sustain a campaign of organization.

The IBEW's hesitancy to organize women workers reflected a broader view of woman labour held by many trade unionists at this time. At the 1907 Trades and Labour Congress convention, the issue of unionizing the operators was not discussed, although a resolution was passed calling for protective legislation for women telephone workers. One of the TLC's expressed aims at this time was "to abolish . . . female labour in all branches of industrial life."[86] The views of many craft unionists were dominated by their belief that woman's role was primarily a maternal and domestic one. Apprehension about female strikebreaking and undercutting wages fostered and buttressed rationalizations about woman's role as wife and mother. "The general consequence of [American Federation of Labor] union attitudes toward women", concludes Alice Kessler-Harris, "was to isolate them from the male work force."[87]

This thesis also seems relevant to the Canadian labour scene, as illustrated in the Ontario labour press. In the *Industrial Banner*, a London labour paper published by the Labour Educational Association, the telephone strike was not discussed. Some clues to the failure of male trade unionists to accept the need to unionize women workers are provided in the *Banner*, and in two earlier Toronto labour papers, the *Toiler* and *Tribune*.[88] Male craft unionists were concerned with protection and equality for women workers: decent working conditions and equal wages were always upheld as worthy aims.[89] But it was woman's contribution to the home, rather than her status as a worker, which was most often stressed in the labour press. In fact, concern that woman's wage labour would destroy the family was very strong.[90] Woman's contribution to the union movement, it was often maintained, could be made through her role as wife, mother and manager of the family budget: she was to support the union label campaign and educate the family to union ideals.[91] In the eyes of male trade unionists women were hardly delicate and decorative appendages to be shunted to the sidelines of the class struggle, but their stay in the workforce was not a desirable thing, and was to be temporary, only an interlude before marriage and maternity. Thus, it was understandable that although some labour leaders momentarily encouraged the operators to organize, they were hesitant to follow up with the necessary further support. Their rather ambivalent attitude — of sometimes supporting female workers' rights, but usually emphasizing the home as woman's vocation — in fact discouraged the unionization of women. Stressing the maternal image, male trade unionists isolated women from the mainstream of the trade union movement and buttressed the employers' excuses for women's lower wages.

Reinforcing the hostility of Bell and the ambivalence of organized labour, were the situations and the attitudes of the operators themselves. The great majority of operators were single women, about 17 to 24 years old, who stayed less than three years with Bell. Most women left to marry, although some were promoted to clerical jobs in Bell, went on to other operating jobs, or returned home to aid their mothers. Occasionally, women were forced temporarily to bolster family finances due to sickness or unemployment and when family circumstances no longer required extra aid, they gladly quit. This great fluidity of female labour obviously militated against successful unionization. By the time King's Report was published in September 1907, half of the operators employed at the time of the strike had left, including the former President and Secretary of the Telephone Operators Association. With personnel in perpetual motion, it was difficult to sustain educational and organizational work needed for effective unionization.

Despite the rapid turnover of operators, the physical setting of the telephone Exchange did aid worker solidarity and organization. As Wayne Roberts has pointed out, many women workers at this time were concentrated in trades such as garment making and domestic service, which were highly decentralized and divided the workers from one another. Operating, however, did not present such communication barriers; in fact, the militancy and solidarity of the Bell workers were in part a result of a physical setting conducive to organization. On the other hand, Bell women were not protected by craft skills or effective organization. Thus, strikebreakers from outside the city or inside the Exchange could easily replace the Toronto operators. The technology of the switchboard allowed continued service, if only with half the usual work force. Naturally, the nature of the Bell monopoly also worked against the women for, despite reduced service, Bell faced no loss of customers.

Another factor which may have handicapped effective unionization was the prevailing conception of woman's domestic and maternal vocation. Women workers like the Bell operators undoubtedly perceived their problems quite differently from the middle-class reformers who feared for the "working girl of delicate moral and physical viability, her womanliness endangered."[92] In the 1907 strike, the immediate issues of wages and hours, not their endangered maternity, were the concerns of the operators. Yet, while working women may not have assumed the decorative role imposed upon many Victorian middle-class women, or perceived wage labour as threatening to their femininity, they probably did accept the Victorian sentimentalization of the home and family.[93]

During this period women's columns in the *Tribune* and *Toiler* show some of the same ambivalence towards female labour as did male trade unionists. In the *Tribune*, May Darwin's column for women called for women's social freedom, equal pay, and the unionization of female workers. Yet, later in the *Tribune*, as well as in the *Toiler*, the women's section was concerned with personal improvement and domestic issues, or, "recipes and fashions". Even feminist May Darwin stressed that women's contribution to the labour movement could best be made by buying union label goods, supporting her trade unionist husband, and educating her young to union ideas.[94] Such activities may have aided the development of women's trade union and working-class consciousness, but they still defined women's contribution in family-centred terms. This suggests that for many women workers such as the Bell operators, the family ideal was of considerable importance (although admittedly the working class conception of the family may have differed considerably from the prevailing middle class one). For the many Bell operators who "left to marry" such social values could not have aided the difficult process of unionization. The operators were part of a rapidly changing group of young women workers, who constituted a small minority of the female population: "they were isolated politically and socially . . . from their elder sisters, all of whom had returned to the home on marriage."[95] Their brief experience in the workforce preceding marriage "meant that they were deprived of a continuity of experience that might have allowed them to come to grips with the political economy of their experience."[96] The idealization of women's maternal and domestic roles must have dulled the development of a truly feminist working-class consciousness which recognized women's special oppression as workers. The tendency to define women in terms of husband, children and home obscured a reality where women were also individual workers, sometimes breadwinners, needing adequate wages, job security, and unionization just like male workers.

The prevailing views on woman's maternal and domestic role were not, of course, the sole or primary causes for the operators' defeat in 1907. The Bell operators were severely handicapped by factors which impeded successful strikes and unionization for many male workers at this time. Most importantly, they were unskilled and lacked union protection; thus, their protest was easily and severely damaged by the importation of strikebreakers. Their cause was also injured when they were strongly encouraged to accept the bad tactic of abandoning their walkout and returning to work on the Company's terms, placing their hopes in a Royal Commission. The Commission was a dead end. Despite King's strong criticism of Bell, he could hide behind the qualification that labour legislation was primarily a provincial jurisdiction. The Report came too late for such legislation, which probably would have been difficult to obtain anyway. Six months after the strike, public concern had waned and the workforce at Bell had drastically changed; half the operators employed in September had not even experienced the strike. Unfortunately for the operators, the 1907 dispute came after the peak of public feeling for public ownership of telephones in Toronto: the Laurier government had already made clear its opposition to nationalization.[97] Thus, as a testing ground for the IDIA, the strike had revealed the dangers of this legislation to labour's interests, dangers which later provoked calls for the IDIA's repeal. The "mythical neutrality"[98] of King's IDIA was revealed in full: the main advantage of the principle of public investigation went to the Company.

For Bell, the strike was not without lessons. The Company's attempt to streamline its service and to increase efficiency, while reducing wages, had not been accomplished without a major labour conflict. Bell had learned the necessity of refining its techniques of scientific management, of tempering its management control with negotiation and welfare measures designed to increase employee loyalty, to enhance the occupation's prestige, and to diffuse the desire to unionize. Bell's combination of benevolent paternalism and blatant victimization of union members was effective in delaying unionization for many years.

Faced with the hostility of the Company, the ambivalence of organized labour, and the difficult realities of their working situation it is not surprising that the Bell operators did not make impressive gains. Despite these barriers, the operators effectively formed a strike committee, lobbied for change within the Company, then carried through a strike with impressive solidarity. "No surrender to the Company" was the enthusiastic and unanimous watchword of the strikers. The militancy of their protest contradicted the idea of passive femininity and indicated the potential for women workers' opposition to their economic exploitation.

Notes

1. *Toronto World*, 8 February 1907.
2. King Papers, A. Lemieux to W.L. Mackenzie King, 15 February 1907.
3. G. Parsons, "A History of Labour Relations in Bell", unpublished manuscript, 1963, Bell Canada Historical Collection, (hereafter BCHC).
4. Boy Operators file, BCHC.
5. Ibid.
6. Early Operators file, BCHC.
7. Circular to Supervisors re Hiring, Early Operators file, BCHC.
8. Ibid.
9. Newspaper clipping, Early Opertors file, BCHC.
10. Early Operators file, BCHC.
11. Circular to Supervisors, BCHC.
12. See John Schacht, "Toward Industrial Unionism: Bell Telephone Workers and Company Unions, 1919-1937", *Labor History* 16 (Winter 1975), 10.
13. *Toronto Star*, 11 February 1907.
14. Ibid.
15. Ibid., 12 February 1907.
16. Bureau of Labour Report, Ontario *Sessional Papers*, No. 30, 1907, 100-113, 150-167. For example, the weekly wage of a female typographer was about $12, boot and shoe worker $8, and furrier $7. In the same occupations male wages would be about $14, $14, and $15 respectively.
17. R.C. Fetherstonaugh, *Charles Fleetford Sise* (Montreal, 1944), 180.
18. See Craig Heron and Bryan D. Palmer, "Through the Prism of the Strike: Industrial Conflict in Southern Ontario, 1901-14", *Canadian Historical Review* LVIII (December 1977). Heron and Palmer see the 1907 strike as an outcome of a managerial drive for efficiency, but this was only one factor behind the operators' protest. Other complaints, such as wage cutbacks, were crucial to the strike.
19. *Report of the Royal Commission on a Dispute respecting terms of Employment between Bell Telephone Company of Canada and Operators at Toronto* (Ottawa, 1907), 13-14. (hereafter, *Report*).
20. Ibid., 15.
21. Dunstan in *Report*, 28.
22. Ibid., 63.
23. Ibid., 33.
24. *Toronto Star*, 30 January 1907.
25. Ibid.
26. G. Parsons, "A History of Labour Relations in Bell", BCHC.
27. *Toronto Star*, 1 February 1907.
28. See Canada, House of Commons, *Select Committee on Telephone Systems* (Ottawa, 1905), 1, 701-7.
29. *Toronto News*, 1 February 1907.
30. *Globe* (Toronto), 2 February 1907.
31. *Toronto Star*, 4 February 1907.
32. Ibid., 31 January 1907.
33. Ibid., 2 February 1907.
34. Ibid., 1 February 1907.
35. Ibid., 30 January 1907. Dunstan was later corrected by a striker who pointed out that the "comforts he speaks of are largely paid for out of our salaries." *Toronto Star*, 8 February 1907.
36. Ibid., 2 February 1907.
37. Ibid.
38. *Toronto News*, 9 February 1907; *Toronto Star*, 16 February 1907.
39. *Toronto News*, 1 February 1907.
40. Sise to Dunstan, Labour Trouble file, BCHC.
41. Winchester chaired the Royal Commission on employment of aliens on Canadian railways in 1904. He sided with the workers and made scathing criticisms of the C.P.R. See Donald Avery, "Canadian

Immigration Policy and the 'Foreign' Navy 1896–1914", Canadian Historical Association, *Historical Papers* (1972), 143.

42. *Toronto Star*, 5 February 1907.

43. *Mail and Empire*, (Toronto), 5 February 1907.

44. *Toronto Star*, 9 February 1907.

45. Ibid., 5 February 1907.

46. One independent operator estimated that one-third of her salary had to come from overtime work. Operators' board costs ranged from $2.50 to $3.50 a week. Food costs were estimated from dividing family budgets presented in the *Tribune*, 17 March 1906 and Department of Labour, *Board of Inquiry into the Costs of Living*, 1900–1915.

47. *Report*, 35.

48. *Mail and Empire*, 12 February 1907.

49. *Toronto Star*, 7 February 1907.

50. Ibid., 12 February 1907.

51. Ibid.

52. *Report*, 60.

53. *Toronto World*, 15 February 1907.

54. *Toronto Star*, 15 February 1907.

55. *Report*, 76.

56. *Globe*, 5 February 1907.

57. Ibid., 19 February 1907.

58. Curry to King, 3 April 1907, Strikes and Lockouts file, Department of Labour Records.

59. *Report*, 96.

60. Ibid.

61. G. Parsons, "A History of Labour Relations in Bell", BCHC.

62. John Schacht, "Towards Industrial Unionism: Bell Telephone Workers and Company Unions, 1919–37", 13.

63. G. Parsons, "A History of Labour Relations in Bell," BCHC.

64. Sise to Hamilton Manager, Early Operators file, BCHC.

65. R. Whitaker, "Mackenzie King in the Dominion of the Dead", *Canadian Forum* LV (February 1976), 9.

66. *Report*, 95.

67. King diary, 4 August 1907.

68. Canada, Parliament, Report of a Royal Commission into Cotton Factories, *Sessional Paper* no. 39 (1909), 11.

69. Canada, Parliament, Department of Labour, Report of the Deputy Minister, *Sessional Paper* no. 36 (1908), 129.

70. Alice Klein and Wayne Roberts, "Beseiged Innocence: The 'Problem' and Problems of Working Women, Toronto, 1896–1914", in *Women at Work* (Toronto, 1974), 212, 213, 226.

71. Canada, Parliament, Department of Labour, Report of the Deputy Minister, *Sessional Paper* no. 36, 121. See also W.L.M. King, *Industry and Humanity* (Toronto, 1973), 205–207.

72. *Report*, 98.

73. Canada, Department of Labour, *Annual Report*, 1908, 60.

74. King Papers, Lemieux to King, 15 February 1907.

75. Canada, House of Commons, *Debates*, 14 February 1907, 3009.

76. King papers, Memo re. Bill 36, undated, and M.P. Unnamed.

77. King diary, 11 September 1907.

78. *Report*, 96.

79. Curry to King, 3 April 1907, Strikes and Lockouts file, Department of Labour Records.

80. King to Curry, 4 April 1907, Strikes and Lockouts file, Department of Labour Records. Allan Studholme, Labour M.P.P. for Hamilton East, had suggested that a bill limiting the telephone operators to a five hour day be introduced into the provincial legislature. The bill was never introduced.

81. In August, 1918 the Toronto operators demanded a wage increase and organized into a local of the IBEW. After a Board of Arbitration sided with the operators, wage increases were given and Bell agreed to meet with operators from the union. After two years, however, the union's influence dwindled and in 1920

it was reported that "the union of telephone girls has decreased to two score" (*Globe*, 11 April 1920). The problems of 1907 reappeared: company hostility, disinterest of IBEW officers and lack of commitment by the operators. G. Parsons also notes that Company welfare measures made the International less attractive. By 1921 the union was replaced by a company union, the Telephone Operators Association.

82. Sise, quoted in G. Parsons, "A History of Labour Relations in Bell Telephone", BCHC.

83. *Mail and Empire*, 4 February 1907.

84. Jack Barbash, *Unions and Telephones: The Story of the Communication Workers of America* (New York, 1952), 3. See also M. Mulcarie, *The IBEW: A Study in Trade Union Structure and Function* (Washington, 1923), 131.

85. Jack Barbash, *Unions and Telephones*, 4.

86. Trades and Labour Congress of Canada, *Platform of Principles*, 1907.

87. Alice Kessler-Harris, "Where are the Organized Women Workers?", *Feminist Studies* 3 (Fall 1975), 98.

88. The *Toiler*, an organ of the Toronto District Labour Council, was published from 1902 to 1904. The *Tribune*, edited by J.H. Perry, was published from 1905 to 1906.

89. See *Industrial Banner*, July 1907; *Toiler*, 16 October 1903.

90. See *Toiler*, 16 May 1902; 1 July 1904.

91. See *Industrial Banner*, April 1908; January 1909.

92. Alice Klein and Wayne Roberts, "Beseiged Innocence: The 'Problem' and Problems of Working Women, Toronto, 1896–1914", 251.

93. For similar conclusions about British working class women see for example, Peter Stearns in *Suffer and be Still*, edited by Martha Vicinus (Bloomington, 1972), 112 and Dorothy Thompson, "Women in Nineteenth Century Radical Politics", *The Rights and Wrongs of Women*, edited by J. Mitchell and A. Oakley (London, 1976), 138.

94. *Tribune*, 11 November 1905.

95. Wayne Roberts, *Honest Womanhood: Feminism, Femininity and Class Consciousness Among Toronto Working Women 1893 to 1914* (Toronto, 1976), 11.

96. Ibid.

97. In 1905 agitation for more public control of telephones was appeased with the Parliamentary Select Committee to investigate telephone systems. After eight volumes of testimony, the Commission reported it was "impossible to come to any conclusions." William Mulock, who had voiced sympathy for public ownership, retired as Postmaster General and was replaced by Allan Aylesworth who had acted as counsel for Bell. The *World* and *The News* reported that Mulock had been driven out by Bell, which had already established close political relations with the Laurier cabinet. Sise had been reassured during the Committee's hearings that the government had no intention of public ownership. See J.E. Williams, "Labor Relations in the Telephone Industry: A Comparison of the Private and Public Segments" (unpublished Ph.D. Thesis, University of Wisconsin, 1961), 83–85.

98. R. Whitaker, "Mackenzie King in the Dominion of the Dead," 153.

"HELPING THE POORER SISTERS": THE WOMEN OF THE JOST MISSION, HALIFAX, 1905–1945†

CHRISTINA SIMMONS

Women helping women has been a persistent feature of Canadian life. Until the emergence of the welfare state in the twentieth century most assistance was religious in inspiration and character. In the nineteenth century, Catholic, Protestant, and Jewish women initiated a wide range of institutions to succour the unfortunate of their sex. While the Catholic Church reaped substantial advantages from its teaching, nursing, and social work sisterhoods, other religions were able to harness female energies in lay initiatives such as Halifax's Jost Mission. Motivated by a complex mixture of religious charity, noblesse oblige, and empathetic sisterhood, middle-class women gradually developed and staffed a range of social services for the female poor and their families. Significantly, as Christina Simmons observes, they did not interpret their mandate to include direct intervention in the labour market, as with the setting of wage rates. To this degree at least the separation of private and public spheres and the allocation of responsibility by gender for each were acknowledged. Recipients recognized the value of the services, especially day care, but seemed, at least from Simmons' sample, to have retained a strong sense of dignity and pride. Such self-possession would have been much more difficult to maintain in the Poor Law institutions (publicly rather than privately funded like the Jost Mission) that continued to exist in Atlantic Canada throughout the period under discussion. Nova Scotia's tardy adoption in the 1930s of provincially-run mothers' allowances for the needy also promised some preservation of respectability but the principle of women helping women continued to find wide appeal right up to the present with the appearance across the country of transition houses for battered women, initiated and maintained by female workers. The maternal feminism of an earlier day has largely given way to more modern feminist forms but a good part of the inspiration — a strong sense of sisterhood — remains the same.

In late 19th century Halifax a substantial church-like structure shared space with brothels and a Salvation Army Corps on Brunswick Street, just below the Citadel and the famous Clock Tower. Founded in 1868 by Halifax businessman and Methodist Edward Jost to serve the city's poor, the Jost Mission in the early 20th century became an important centre of activity for Halifax women. The Mission established a placement service for charworkers, a day nursery for the workers' children, and clubs and educational programmes for working-class mothers and adolescents. The Mission served as a meeting-ground for women from several phases of "women's sphere": the Mission's services were intended primarily for the working-class mothers of the city's North End, and they were coordinated by trained religious workers employed by the Mission and by unpaid women volunteers from the city's Methodist churches.[1]

Each of these groups of women had a place in the Mission's hierarchy and brought to their role a particular experience informed by social class and gender. Working-class women, pushed into the labour force by their husbands' death,

†*Acadiensis* XIV, 1 (Autumn 1984): 3–27.

disability, desertion, or unemployment, went out from the Mission by day to clean the homes of middle-class families. The deaconesses, lay matrons, and teachers, who administered the Mission's activities, were among the more advantaged female paid workers, early representatives of the many women who would enter social work as the century progressed. The churchwomen who managed the Mission acted in one of the only public roles available to them — charitable work — and in so doing they reaffirmed the bonds of female friendship and the Christian concern of the well-to-do for the poor. Within the limits of a vision of Christian sisterhood and of women's essential domestic and maternal identity, between 1905 and the mid-1940s the programmes of the Jost Mission evolved primarily in response to the participation of working-class women in the labour force and to the middle-class women's commitment to helping their "poorer sisters".[2]

The services for women and children at the Jost Mission succeeded earlier evangelical activity. The original inscription on the building read: "And He said unto His servant, Go out into the highways and hedges and compel them to come in". Under the interdenominational leadership of the Young Men's Christian Association from 1868 to 1878, and subsequently under Methodist direction, the Jost Mission had operated as a city mission. Revivals and worship meetings, Sunday Schools, and sewing classes for women and girls were established. However, the Mission was closed in the 1890s while Jost's will was being settled. The estate's legal problems were finally resolved in 1904, and by spring 1905 a graduate of the Toronto Deaconess Training School had arrived at the Mission.[3]

The two deaconesses assigned to the Mission and the nearby Brunswick Street Methodist Church cooperated in beginning programmes which were almost exclusively directed toward women and children. They instituted "kitchen garden" (domestic science) and sewing classes for little girls, "fresh air" work with the girls at a cottage on the shore, and charitable visiting in the neighbourhood of the Mission.[4] In 1910 the Mission began a day nursery for the children of wage-earning mothers and by 1913 was operating an employment bureau to place women in domestic work. Other activities included a kindergarten, mothers' meetings, a sewing class, Sunday afternoon and evening religious meetings, and clubs for adolescent girls. The matron provided emergency relief to needy families from a store of food and clothing contributed by Methodist churches. These activities constituted the bulk of the Mission work until the 1940s.[5]

Halifax, the commercial centre for the Maritime region and a major port, was experiencing a limited economic boom during the first decade of this century, when the Jost Mission was being reopened. Investment in manufacturing grew, traffic through the port increased, and the rate of population growth increased. Unfortunately, after the First World War, manufacturing declined, and a period of depression began in the 1920s and lasted until the next world war.[6] Poverty and the unemployment of working-class men left many working-class mothers in need of the services offered by the Mission.

In its daily operations the Jost Mission was a women's institution. Except for the religious services, which ended after the 1910s, programmes at the Mission were directed toward women or children, and the staff and immediate managers were all female. This pattern, which grew out of the separation of male and female spheres in 19th-century life, characterized much of both charity and social reform work in Canada and the United States.[7] A group of male trustees held formal control over the Jost bequest but exercised little direction over daily affairs. The trustees were a group of four (later five) men, who administered the investments, paid the salaries of workers at the Mission, and oversaw major repairs and alterations of the building such as those which were made in 1917 to accommodate more children in the nursery.[8] The Woman's Committee (also informally called the Ladies' Committee and later simply the Jost Mission Committee) was established in 1915. Its purpose was to raise funds by keeping the cause "constantly before the churches", but the women also took over management of routine finances formerly handled by the deaconess in charge. Through appeals to the various Methodist churches and through classic female fundraising events like pantry sales, garden parties, and musical teas, these women raised the remainder of the budget (for food, materials, heating, and clothing and linens for the nursery). Barrels of apples, quilts, jars of preserves, baby clothes, and cash donations poured in from churches and individuals around Nova Scotia. The majority of donors, especially of in-kind contributions, were women.[9] In 1923 the trustees began to pay a regular amount of the investment income directly to the Woman's Committee, and the Committee took over payment of salaries as well.[10] The Committee met monthly to hear the matron's report and plan its own work. Meetings began with Scripture and the Lord's Prayer. Each month members were delegated to make weekly visits to the nursery. Female rituals such as sending flowers to the sick and condolences to the bereaved among the Committee members and Christmas and wedding gifts to employees were regularly noted in their minutes. Christian sisterhood meant showing friendship and concern among themselves and the staff as well as "helping the poorer sisters."[11]

The trustees and members of the Woman's Committee were financially comfortable but do not appear to have been part of Halifax's wealthiest class. The trustees whose names are known, serving in 1918 and 1927, comprised the owner of an insurance company, a chartered accountant, the presidents of a dental supply company and a lumber contracting firm, and the proprietor of a downtown restaurant. Three of them were married to women on the Woman's Committee. After Presbyterians and Methodists joined to form the United Church in 1925, the trustees began regularly to include a clergyman appointed by the Conference.[12]

The members of the Woman's Committee were active churchwomen of secure middle-class backgrounds. The great majority were married. More than half of the 21 members in 1916 were the wives or daughters of accountants or proprietors of businesses. Other husbands included a minister, the president of the Technical College, a city official, and a skilled artisan at the dockyard. By 1927 more Committee women were married to professional men — a dentist, a lawyer, a minister, and three engineers — but businessmen still predominated. In this year the Committee, expanded by the addition of formerly Presbyterian churches, did include the wives of a few lower-status men — a locksmith, a streetcar operator, and a police sergeant. One Committee member, an unmarried woman, was employed as a postal clerk, and at least one married member worked with her husband in the family business. Women who served as officers for five years or more between 1915 and 1940 and whose influence was probably greatest, were all married to men in business, insurance, or accounting. They also belonged to the Methodist churches in the oldest and most prosperous residential areas of the city. The Committee and its leaders were composed of the wives and mothers of Halifax's comfortable business class.[13]

As married women, the Jost Mission Committee members could not act with complete independence, but no evidence suggests that either trustees or husbands controlled the women directly. The Committee consulted formally with the trustees primarily over major expenditures on the building. The relative autonomy of the women in managing the Mission, their large role in raising operating expenses, and the cultural background of separate male and female spheres meant that women controlled the Mission. Its programmes and atmosphere reflected the ideas of the churchwomen and the staff as they encountered the women of the neighbourhood.[14]

Directors of the Mission's daily operations were the deaconesses or matrons, who lived in the building, and the kindergarten teachers or other assistants, all single or widowed women. One or two deaconesses were in charge of the Mission until 1920, when a Salvation Army nurse became the matron. Two widows, one of unknown education and one a former teacher, followed the nurse in the position; the second worked from 1924 until her death in 1940, when a deaconess replaced her. The deaconesses cared for the children directly in the 1910s, led clubs and classes, and dealt with the domestic workers. By 1920 the matron was supervising young nursery "maids" hired to watch the children.[15] She also kept daily accounts, distributed relief, did public speaking to raise money, and mediated between the Committee and lesser employees. The Committee asked the matron in 1931 to attend their meetings throughout rather than merely to present a report.[16] This action suggests the growing importance of the employee in this position.

The history of the Deaconess Society shows the background of some of the women who filled this managerial position at the Mission. Founding the Order of Deaconesses in 1894 was a hesitant step toward giving women professional roles in the Methodist Church. It also reflected jealousy of the Roman Catholic Church, which "has won its victories in America far more by its white-capped sisters than its black-cassocked priests", explained an article on "The Secret of the Success of the Deaconess Movement" at the turn of the century. The "secret" was that "The world wants mothering". Deaconesses wore a dark navy-blue uniform and bonnet with white tie which set them apart in appearance like nuns and Salvationists. Until 1917 they received maintenance only from the institutions employing them. At that time they became salaried, after a period of conflict between advocates of traditional feminine self-sacrifice and proponents of women's right to be paid for their work. Some deaconesses were trained nurses and others performed religious work; all were supposed to combine traditional female religious commitment with modern, social scientific method. The deaconesses assigned to the Jost Mission worked in several recognized specializations: settlement and industrial work, which aimed to bolster domestic skills among immigrants or rural Canadians new to the city; nursing, which involved both active care and educating people in the "laws of health"; and kindergarten work.[17]

Deaconesses, matrons, and teachers at the Mission were well-educated, self-supporting women for whom the work at the Mission constituted a career. Two deaconesses, Amy Sherwood and Mabel Newsome, were high school graduates, and two others, Bertha Shier and Leone Winter, had partially completed high school. Elda Caldwell, the kindergarten teacher from 1915 to 1925, came from a comfortable Halifax family. She left the Mission to become superintendent of the women's department of a government bureau and remained single into the 1930s. E. Bryon, the Salvation Army nurse who was matron from 1920 to 1923, could well have been from a working-class background as many of her sect were, but as a nurse she had a good education and a strong occupational identity. Lillian A. White, a widow and once a schoolteacher, returned from Saskatchewan to her native Nova Scotia to work at the Mission in 1924. She thought of herself as a committed worker in the field as well as a dedicated Christian. She attended with pleasure and reported to the Committee on two meetings of the National Conference of Day Nurseries in New York City in 1929 and 1931. The salary levels of the women in these positions reflected their identity as professionals. Bryon's remuneration was raised to $50 per month in January of 1921 (in addition to room and board). Caldwell, who did not live at the Mission, received $60 per month as kindergarten teacher and assistant to Bryon.[18]

The nursery maids and the cook, local working-class women, constituted the lower echelon of Mission workers. One maid, Mary Carr, came from a nearby Catholic family. Her father did manual labour for the city, and her mother worked as a dressmaker but occasionally served at fancy teas in the homes of the wealthy. When Carr's mother worked out, she placed her children in the Mission nursery. Carr was in grade eight when her mother took her out of school and sent her to work at the Mission about 1921. Carr's co-worker was a 16-year-old "Salvation Army girl" from Newfoundland with a brother "on the boats". These young women shared a "spotlessly clean" room at the Mission. Each day they "pottied" and put nursery clothing on 18 to 25 or more children, changed babies, prepared formula, gave bottles, served lunch to older children, and washed dishes. They washed diapers and clothes daily and scrubbed down the entire nursery weekly. They were allowed time off every other evening, one afternoon a week, and Saturday afternoon through Sunday every third week. Carr received $20 per month by the winter of 1924, and her friend, as "head girl", was paid $25 per month in 1925. This work was harder than caring for one child in a wealthy home, recalled Carr, yet easier than her later married life as the mother of eight.[19]

The women who used the nursery and employment service came from the surrounding area, a mixed business, industrial, and residential neighbourhood which included clothing, candy, cigar, boot and shoe, and paper box factories, a bakery, a brewery, and the city market.[20] Women found some factory work there, but domestic and personal service remained by far the largest category of female work in the city throughout the period under consideration. Although domestic service was a common occupation, it was unpopular especially when living-in was required. Since at least the 1880s, single women in Canada had been refusing service whenever other work was available. Discrimination and domestic responsibilities, however, confined married women primarily to domestic work, in the form of charwork (day work) up to the Second World War. In Halifax, the proportion of women employed in domestic and personal service remained higher than the national averages but was declining more rapidly. Between 1911 and 1941 this category dropped from 47 to 37 per cent of the female workforce in the city (compared to 37 and 34 per cent nationally). Halifax offered increasing numbers of teaching, nursing, sales, and clerical positions for single women during these years, and the relatively few married women in the paid labour force found plentiful if ill-paid domestic jobs in the city's middle- and upper-class homes. Nationally, wages ranged from an average of $7.75 per week employed in 1931 to $8.45 in 1941. Many women, of course, worked neither six days per week nor throughout the year.[21] Ellen Blackwood, a Jost Mission domestic worker who placed her children in the nursery, reported earning $2 to $2.25 per day in 1937, plus carfare and frequent donations of used clothing.[22]

Many of the charworkers were widowed, deserted, or married to unemployed men. Susan Smith, for example, had been left with three children in 1916 when her husband, an Army man, deserted her. Ellen Blackwood, born in a Nova Scotia outport, immigrated to Halifax in 1929 when she was single and pregnant. The man she lived with and later married was unemployed for much of the 1930s, but for some time she earned good money serving noon and evening meals to sailors and dockworkers in her modest downtown dwelling. When her third child followed 11 months after the second in 1934, she could no longer manage the cooking. Whether earning wages or not, her husband did not assist her in the business, and in desperation she turned to the Jost Mission to get day work. Lack of education was one of this long-suffering woman's greatest regrets because, as she recalled: "I couldn't choose anything. There was only the one thing left for me, and that was the hard work, like cleaning".[23]

The Woman's Committee, the matrons and teachers, and the working-class women and children of the neighbourhood together shaped the life of the Jost Mission. The churchwomen and the professional workers held obvious authority in planning Mission programmes. Yet the needs and realities of working-class lives limited and directed what the managers did. The Mission managers' commitment to Christian sisterhood, the charworkers' need for employment, and the children's demand for care, centred the Mission's work increasingly on the needs of wage-earning mothers.

Despite a reputation for social and political conservatism, Halifax participated in the currents of reform and radicalism which affected the nation as a whole. The Methodist Conference of Nova Scotia accepted the collectivist ideas of the social gospel and participated in the Social Service Council which was formed in 1909. The Halifax Board of Trade supported an "uplift" campaign in 1911 in which reforms like public housing and child welfare were discussed. Two socialist parties flourished briefly in the city in the pre-war years. Female activists supported suffrage and took new public roles in volunteer work during the First World War.[24] The Halifax Welfare Bureau, begun in 1916 to promote cooperation among social welfare agencies, churches, and institutions, exemplified the change "from the old idea of charity to philanthropy . . . to the thing we call 'social justice' ".[25] The work of the Jost Mission was influenced by some of these ideas but remained essentially within the tradition of 19th-century women's Christian charity.

The outlook of the Woman's Committee approximated what historians have variously called social, domestic, or maternal feminist.[26] Unlike women who sought equality for women as a natural right, maternal feminists attempted to extend the boundaries of women's public roles on the basis of their differences from men. They often did so through campaigns for pure milk, playgrounds, and better housing, intended to assist working-class mothers and children, and through reforms such as temperance, which were attacks on a male culture seen as harmful to women.[27] They did not challenge women's identity as mothers, or women's primary responsibility for domestic labour and child care, but they often addressed the conditions of women's work in the home and attempted to increase respect for what women did. The women of the Jost Mission Committee were not creating new roles for women. Most were married; few were employed; they appear to have done no political lobbying (though they supported temperance); and the church had been a sphere of public work for women for decades. They shared the social mothering roles of maternal feminists, however, and like them also, sought to ameliorate the conditions of poor women and children. Committee members' sympathy for the charworkers seems to have been rooted in the churchwomen's own material situation as married women and mothers, and the programmes they offered were intended to help women carry out their family responsibilities. Girls' classes and clubs, the nursery, the employment bureau, and the mothers' meetings affirmed the value of women's unpaid domestic work at the same time that they helped some mothers obtain paid domestic jobs. The Mission workers did not address the conditions of the paid work itself.

The first deaconesses, assisted by "lady workers from the churches", carried on evangelical work. Missionary calls to people's homes initially served as advertising for Bible classes, worship services, and other programmes. Deaconess Bertha Shier in 1904 saw conversion as an antidote to pauperism. Although affirmation of the Christian life remained central to all the Mission's work, the emphasis on revivals and conversion had ended by 1918. Training receptive young children became the dominant form of religious outreach. Mission workers hoped families who received material aid could then "send their children regularly and respectably clad to Sunday School."[28]

Domestic education for young girls became an early emphasis in the Mission's classes and clubs and reflected the influence of the movement for domestic science. Courses in domestic science were beginning in schools and colleges as an effort to upgrade the status of women's domestic labour by giving its skills the legitimacy of science. While this movement was distinct from proposals for schools for domestic servants, some potential employers may have hoped that the Mission's kitchen garden classes would produce better servants. Reported one deaconess: "How to lay a table, how to serve food, and how to clear away and wash dishes" were skills taught little girls, who at the annual Nova Scotia Exhibition in 1905 demonstrated their agility before an admiring audience, many of whom were said to be "victims of slovenly and careless servants". No further references to servants appeared, however, and after the early 1920s no instruction in cooking or cleaning took place.

In the early years deaconesses took groups of girls for a week each to a cottage at the shore in the summer. They spent most of their time playing and swimming but also practised housekeeping skills. Such activities expressed a vision that good health and domestic skills benefited the working-class family. A good homemaker would keep the family together and set standards for home life. The deaconess wrote in 1905 that "the environments of these children are such that the lessons cannot be practised at home in their entirety, but the principles . . . will influence even the poorest surroundings".[29] Clubs for young girls, which began in 1918, offered time for sewing, knitting, reading, and socializing. Sewing and knitting not only prepared girls to fulfill future maternal responsibilities but also allowed them to make for themselves stylish clothes too expensive for them to buy ready-made. In the 1930s girls in the club made several garments for themselves each winter. This domestic orientation was common to the culture and female education as a whole.[30]

Between 1920 and 1925 the Mission offered a club for workers at the Moir's candy factory, one block from the Mission. It, too, illustrated the domestic orientation of the Mission. The club began as a series of Friday noon meetings with speakers and musical soloists, and expanded to include a class on home nursing one evening per week. Later the club sponsored noon-time hymn-sings, religious meetings, sleigh rides, and festive suppers for up to 80 young women. YWCA and Salvation Army workers also cooperated in these activities with club director Elda Caldwell. The club ended in 1925 when the factory owner refused for unknown reasons to allow the programme to continue. The Moir's club combined support for Protestant religious culture, recreation, and instruction in skills for wives and mothers. The Mission workers gave no evidence of supporting unionization or demands for better wages.[31] The owner's opposition may suggest, however, that even social ties among the workers could be threatening.

The nursery, a service to both wage-earning mothers and their children, began in 1910 at the instigation of the Golden Rule Society of Fort Massey Presbyterian Church, a group led by May Sexton. Sexton had graduated from the Massachusetts Institute of Technology and was married to F.H. Sexton, president of the new provincial technical college. A member of the Local Council of Women, May Sexton advocated technical education for women to improve their marginal position in the labour force. The Council supported her but was rebuffed by the provincial legislature when the women lobbied for an industrial school for women. Few politicians were ready to support proposals which assumed that women were serious or permanent paid workers. However, the nursery provided a more acceptable kind of assistance to female wage-earners who were mothers. A report in the Wesleyan asserted: "So many babies are left at home with improper food and care. We know from what mothers have told us . . . how worried they are through the day . . .".[32] When the Woman's Committee of the Jost Mission was formed in 1915, Sexton served on it briefly.

The Mission nursery provided extensive and flexible childcare. It was open to children from the age of three months and there was a charge of 10 cents per day or "by arrangement". By 1913 the Mission was also providing lunches and afterschool care for older children. The annual total of childcare-days rose from about 2,000 in 1915 to about 9,000 in 1925. In 1912–13 the deaconess and her assistant cared for 22 children per day. The building was renovated and expanded in 1917 to make space for more children. In 1923 the number arriving daily sometimes reached 60, and the matron and Committee set a limit of 40 because the two nursery maids could manage no more. The Committee hoped for more space and workers to accommodate all who needed the service, but the nursery continued to take 30 to 40 per day, plus nearly as many school children, until the late 1930s. Many children paid reduced or no fees for the nursery. The service was sometimes closed for one or two weeks due to epidemics of measles and other diseases, but it usually remained open throughout the year. The numbers of children fluctuated regularly according to the cycle of domestic work; September through December and April through June (spring cleaning) were the busiest times.[33]

The children's daily routine reflected the goals of the Mission — training in manners, familiarity with Protestant ritual, cleanliness, and proper food, rest, and play. In 1916 the deaconess began receiving babies at 8:15 a.m. All the children under three were bathed and dressed in clothes belonging to the Mission. Older children played in a yard outside with a sandbox when the weather was good. Dinner (lunch) included soup and pudding, bread and molasses, milk and water or cocoa. Naps followed. For the three- to five-year-olds an hour or two of kindergarten filled part of the afternoon. Mary Carr recalled that the Mission was very clean and well-stocked with food and baby clothes. The workers were not allowed to strike the children. However, staff to child ratios between 1:10 and 1:20 meant they could rarely lavish individual attention on the children. A custodial function predominated outside of the kindergarten. The babies were restricted to high chairs while they were awake.[34]

The Mission provided special events such as summer picnics in the country and the Public Gardens as well as camping (in the 1910s and again in the 1930s). Wealthy patrons offered automobile rides in the warm season. Christmas parties with a tree and a Santa to distribute gifts for about 150 children took place regularly. Mrs. White so missed her "graduates" that in 1935 a second Christmas party was started for school-age children who came to the nursery as babies. From 70 to 100 children also partook of a chicken or turkey dinner every Christmas. The special events particularly expressed the churchwomen's tender feelings for the children, whom they often referred to as "little ones" or "kiddies".

The Committee and the Mission workers hoped to instill Christian values and orderly behaviour in the children. The deaconess noted in 1913 that the children "come to us sometimes so uncontrolled, so unaccustomed to regular habits of living. But after being here a little while they are quite glad to stay." Religion and mental development were combined in the kindergarten. There she was teaching the children "to pray to Jesus, to sing His praise, and to have all their life brightened because every faculty is stimulated by use". The Woman's Committee may have had views closer to the communal orientation of the social gospel. They referred to their efforts in 1918 as "settlement or community work". The formally religious content of nursery routine seems to have declined after

1920 when deaconesses were no longer employed as matrons. Raising "the standard of Canadian citizenship" was a goal in 1925. Despite the secular phraseology, as late as 1930 the Committee and matron were still concerned about getting children to Sunday School. Churchgoing and citizenship were closely related.[35]

Increasingly, nursery workers stressed physical well-being, through medical care, food, rest, and fresh air, as the basis of spiritual welfare, an emphasis of the social gospel in ideas about child welfare.[36] The nursery employed a trained nurse between 1915 and 1923 and subsequently co-operated with nurses at the city's Massachusetts Health Centre, established with relief funds from Massachusetts after the Explosion in 1917. The Centre at one point informed the Mission that the children needed more milk, and the Committee set up a Milk Fund. In addition, the nursery and the mothers' programmes both provided instruction on diet and "habits of health and hygiene" such as toothbrushing. The summer picnics and drives combined recreation and exposure to the healthful country air.

The nursery served as an arena for missionary effort. The neediness of the children provided well-to-do Christians with "opportunities for service" as they sought to fulfill their sense of Christian obligation.[37] Picnics at the shore, lavish holiday celebrations, and the programmes for health, education, and moral training were all attempts to assert a universal Protestant community where good will extended beyond class divisions. Scientific standards of hygiene and education reflected the influence of the social gospel and modern social welfare.

In caring for the children, the nursery also served the needs of the mothers who were responsible for them. The nursery, the employment bureau, and the mothers' meetings formed the heart of the Jost Missions' programme for adult women. Committee women offered charity to both wage-earning and non-wage-earning mothers, but they believed it was best for mothers to stay at home with their children. As late as 1927 the committee asserted: "Our problem, is not to fill the Nursery with children, but to aid and teach the Mother, so she may be able to care for her own children at home".[38] They hoped women's need for assistance would be temporary. By 1940, however, the emphasis of Mission work had shifted toward the wage workers, whose need to earn cash grew even more urgent during the depressed 1920s and 1930s. Although state provision for social welfare grew during the 1930s and mothers' allowances began in Nova Scotia in 1930, the levels of support were very low and qualifying was difficult. The Mission reported constantly increasing numbers of women seeking wage work during the 1930s.[39]

The employment bureau may have begun as early as 1906; it was definitely operating by 1913. Through the 1910s the number of women placed grew steadily. Days of work per year jumped from 218 in 1912–13 to 2,633 for 1915. The bureau was distributing charworkers for more than 6,000 days of work by 1925. The actual number of women being employed is unclear, but in 1940, a busy year, 75 women were on the active file.[40] The bureau operated to bring together potential employers and the women who were judged in greatest need. Employers phoned the Mission the night before they wanted workers. Each morning the women who wanted work gathered at the Mission, left the children, received assignments, and went out to work between 8:00 and 9:00. Often employers asked for particular individuals, and regular weekly arrangements were set up. The women worked until about 4:30 or 5:00, usually returning by 5:30 to pick up the children.[41]

Toward the working-class mothers the Mission Committee and staff showed both sympathy as women and the judgmental eye of social superiors. Because women's right to work in their own homes when mothering children was assumed, men who deserted, neglected, or abused their wives were considered villains. The deaconess in 1913 echoed the sisterly concern of the female temperance movement: "In almost every home the demon of drink has entered, and the father (and sometimes the mother) is his slave. To those homes where the wife has been forced to struggle for actual food for herself and her little ones the mission has been of very real help".[42] In stressing that most of the mothers were sole breadwinners, the churchwomen conveyed their respect for women trying to survive without male support. Married women's vulnerability in their dependence on men was familiar to Committee women as well. In the context of the Protestant emphasis on self-sufficiency, mothers, usually expected to be financially dependent, appeared especially worthy when they were struggling to support themselves.[43]

Yet the privileged position of the givers of aid allowed them to impose their values on the recipients. The expectation that mothers should be at home meant that only the most desperate circumstances warranted giving them outside employment, and the deaconess or matron called at women's homes to determine who was neediest and distributed jobs to those she judged most deserving. The goal reported by deaconess Leone Winter in 1916 — "to encourage habits of thrift among parents" — suggests the basis for judging the worthy. Pure charity remained suspect. Stated the Committee in 1929: the employment bureau was to help the women "help themselves".[44]

The Committee's benevolence was limited, too, because they were serving the needs of middle- and upper-class Haligonians who wanted domestic workers. The rapid increase in placements of women during the 1910s showed the considerable demand. Although the Woman's Committee seriously considered eliminating the employment bureau in 1930, possibly because the service was duplicated elsewhere, they did not do so. The Mission workers also imposed standards of work-discipline. The deaconess in 1916, for example, tried to get the women to work by 9 a.m.: "the lesson we must oft repeat is the necessity of being honest with their employers' time and being punctual". Mrs. White complained to the Committee in 1925 about "her problems in placing women who were not capable of giving a good day's work, yet who came day after day and thought they were unfairly treated". Most importantly, the Mission does not appear to have set wages. The Mission staff and benefactors supported women by providing childcare, clothing, and emergency relief and medical care. Addressing charworkers' need for better wages, however, would have challenged both women's prevailing identity as non-wage-earners and the conception that domestic labour itself stood essentially apart from the world of the market.[45]

Mothers' meetings were the most prominent of the Mission's social programmes and were initially directed toward mothers at home. In the 1910s the meetings included religious talks and sewing lessons. Scripture reading and prayer, readings, music, and a minister's address on motherhood were all mentioned in Mission reports. On Wednesdays, the deaconess and one of the Committee ladies taught sewing with materials donated or provided at cost by the Mission. The meetings, attended in 1921 by an average of 22 women, ended with a "bountiful tea" provided by the Committee members on an alternating basis. Annual summer picnics, one for participants in the mothers' meetings and one for the employment bureau women, supplemented the winter gatherings. In 1924 and 1925 dieticians and nurses from the Health Centre gave "practical talks" and demonstrations on topics such as stew-making. The advice on food and the physical care of children disseminated modern notions of child care (which middle-class women would have read in books and magazines) and complemented the medical supervision of the nursery tots. In November 1924 newspaperwoman E.M. Murray, a participant in the suffrage campaign and a member of WCTU, spoke to the group. A woman missionary back from India spoke in 1929 and "showed to our mothers some of whose lives are hard and uninteresting that there are others in far parts of the world whose lot in life has even less of happiness than theirs".[46] These meetings reflected Protestant values and maternal feminist ideas. Most presentations were intended to upgrade and rationalize mothers' work in the home.

In 1928 the Committee asserted the importance of the employed mothers by beginning a "Working Mothers' Club" in which 20 to 25 women met on Monday nights. The distinction between employed and home-bound mothers disappeared at this point, for this was then the only mothers' club, and a single annual mothers' picnic was held for all "Jost Mission mothers". Soloists and readers, games, and refreshments furnished by the various churches, attracted local women. Pastors of the various United Churches and the ladies of the Committee graced the club with their presence, and all joined in singing and devotions. The ladies must have worn themselves out in the winter of 1928-29, for they changed from weekly to monthly meetings the following year. Institution of a special Christmas dinner for the nursery mothers in 1930 was further evidence of the growing attention paid to this group.

The meetings for mothers, like the events for children, demonstrated Christian charity and a vision of community that crossed class lines. The Committee believed that the mothers' meetings, for instance, were for many of the mothers the "only entertainment or social gathering ever attended" and the picnics "to many the only holiday of the year". These activities provided further opportunities for Christian service and for positive contact between social classes, as when a businessman took time to drive the mothers out along the shore in his automobile. The social events were among the more visible of the Mission's good deeds: "We would not have the public think that we regard these mothers as machines and so on a wonderful summer's day we took forty-five of them and one hundred of the children to Dartmouth".[47] Despite the continued assumption that mothers ought to be at home, the change of emphasis after 1928 from all mothers to "working mothers" suggests a recognition of many women's ongoing need for paid work.

The working-class women and children at whom the Mission programmes were aimed made good use of the services but participated in limited ways in the

Protestant community envisioned by Mission workers. The nursery served a basic need well. Blackwood commented that the nursery was a "godsend" for her when she used it in 1937 and 1938: "what would I have done with those children only for the Mission and Mrs. White. She was such a wonderful person, you know. The children couldn't help but like her . . . she was the mother type". The kindergarten gave the oldest child a bit of education — "her ABCs and her one, two, threes" — and the clothes, shoes, and overcoats were of considerable help. Blackwood's children enjoyed the Mission: "You know, you'd go in there with them in the morning, and it was the same as if they were going home, you know, they were right eager to get there". Her stepson, Ed Taylor, one of the school children who received lunch and spent half-days at the Mission, recalled the regular rests, good food, and the swings, sandbox, and supervised play in the yard. The food, cleanliness, and sense that no child was neglected impressed him: "I can't think of anything bad that happened at that Jost Mission. There was always a friendly . . . a nice feeling. Like today, even, when I get talking about it, I still have a nice feeling". (This was in contrast to his feelings about St. Paul's Anglican Church, for example, where he often got hot breakfasts but where he resented being made to sit in the balcony for Sunday service. There he felt "outside" because of his shabby appearance.) Enjoyment of the food at the Mission was especially vivid in Taylor's memory of the late 1930s when meals at home were meagre. Betty Smith, a nursery child from about 1918 to 1920, had been impressed with the food as well as the games and songs led by the kindergarten teacher.[48] The nursery exemplified the sort of childcare available in Canada at that time — mostly custodial but increasingly concerned with education and moral training and influenced in the 1920s by new standards of medical care, food, rest, and exercise. The Mission nursery seems to have provided reliable care of a good quality for the times, a service essential to employed mothers.

Working-class mothers who used the nursery and employment service also experienced middle-class intrusion in their lives. The domestics who were complaining of ill treatment in 1925 must have resisted employers' standards of "a good day's work". Employers routinely asked about Blackwood's family circumstances. Whether friendly or not, the question presumed a right to personal information that would not have been completely reciprocal. On the other hand, some women appreciated the interest shown them. Ellen Blackwood called matron Lillian White "very understanding", and Betty Smith reported that while the mothers waited for children to be dressed on winter afternoons, "the matron always had something nice to say to the women and asked them . . . how they were getting along".[49]

Smith and Blackwood frankly recognized their class status, wished for better, and judged employers and givers of charity alike according to moral standards based on working-class needs. Both women numbered themselves among "the poor", and both expressed a sense of entitlement to charity. They resented it if churches or charitable institutions charged anything, however nominal, for used clothing. Employers were appreciated if they paid on time, including extra for longer hours and carfare, and showed generosity and basic respect for the worker. Smith, who became a domestic worker herself in the 1930s, especially disliked wearing a uniform or eating in the kitchen. Good treatment, however, could not compensate for the hard work, low wages, and degraded status of domestic work as an occupation. Both women would have liked to work in sales. Blackwood worked on the cleaning staff of Simpson's department store in the 1940s and preferred the sociability and equality among the workers there to what she found in private homes.[50]

Women and girls attended the social clubs and sewing classes in substantial numbers and with enthusiasm. In 1921 an average attendance of 20 was reported for the girls' club. The Moir's workers came in large numbers, though they did not meet in the summers, when they preferred to eat lunch outside. The girls of the late 1930s Sewing and Reading Club were reported to "love Mrs. Rathkins", the volunteer leader. The neighbourhood women seem to have expected and genuinely enjoyed the mothers' meetings, especially the sewing classes and picnics. Attendance was high. The Committee reported that social events were "greatly enjoyed"; the summer outings rendered the mothers "deeply grateful for all that had been done for their comfort and pleasure". The Committee hoped for and tended to perceive a positive response, but the attendance figures and persistence of the clubs suggest that the programmes were successful. The poverty and domestic responsibilities of working-class women, especially married women, limited their leisure severely, and probably made the Jost Mission events attractive. A mothers' meeting offered women a chance to sit quietly, sing, talk with other women, and partake of "a substantial lunch [small late-evening meal]".[51]

It is not surprising that sewing classes were well attended, since sewing was a much-desired skill among Nova Scotia women. Evening classes in dressmaking were also well-subscribed during this period. Women in a quilting class in 1920 and 1921 asserted themselves by asking to sew garments as well as quilts; clothes may have been more useful. (By then quilting was less economically necessary since factory-made blankets were cheaply available.) When the class ended, the women presented the deaconess with two plants as a token of their appreciation. Women's economic contribution to the household in unwaged labour was still substantial at this time, and sewing exemplified this. Ellen Blackwood regretted having had little time to attend the classes: "it would have been helpful if you had of been able to 'tend it up, you know, because there was lots of things you could learn; lots of things that you could make over, you know, if you could attend the classes. It would have been wonderful".[52]

Finally, the religious appeal of the Mission's programmes attracted some women, but a distinct social distance remained between them and the middle-class churchwomen. Religious rituals such as praying and singing hymns included Protestant women in a religious community that was of value to them. Blackwood had gone to the Baptist church in her home town and would have liked to go to church more often in Halifax had her family duties not been so heavy. The minister of the Brunswick Street United Church, near the Mission, came to her home and invited her to church. "God was a poor man", he said, "Don't stay away from church because you're poor". She enjoyed church services as a time to be off her feet and to think about her life. She concluded that "what I was doing was all wrong by blaming somebody else for my troubles. . . . I was blaming the rich for taking . . . our opportunity away from us, which was all wrong. We didn't have an opportunity to take away. We had to work for our opportunity". She never spoke to anyone at the services except one of the church workers. Blackwood certainly remained a fighter despite her reflections: she summoned the courage in 1942 to divorce her alcoholic and abusive husband. Later she worked at two jobs to buy a car and was able to marry the sweetheart of her youth. Smith, on the other hand, criticized "church people" (though not the deaconesses) for insensitivity: "they would come on a Sunday morning wanting Mother to go to church . . . [and] used to find her washing and they'd say, well, why are you washing, my goodness, this is Sunday, this is the Sabbath. Well, Mother got cross one day and she said, well, she said, if you paid me, she said, to go to church I'd go for my day, you know, I could leave this go and send it to the laundry and pay for it that way but, she said, I've got to clean and wash and cook on Sunday, that's the only time I have". She wanted to attend church but could go only to evening services after chores were finished. These experiences turned Smith herself against organized religion.[53]

During the 1940s the Mission's focus shifted. During the Second World War more married women entered the paid work force. The Mission's employment bureau could not meet all the calls from private homes. Mothers were working instead in "office, factory, store, restaurant"; they also cleaned the troopships in Halifax harbour. During the war, according to the Annual Report of 1945, the nursery and the kindergarten had become "the most important part of our work". As the opportunities for women's work became more diverse and the federal government assumed greater responsibility for management of the labour market, the Mission's employment bureau closed.[54] The day nursery became the sole focus of the work. Continuing in operation to this day, the day nursery was perhaps the Mission's most important legacy to the women of Halifax.[55]

Years of devoted work gave the women of the Committee rewarding and significant if unpaid roles outside the home, while the "Jost Mission mothers" resorted to the Mission to aid in their struggle for survival and self-improvement. Although the Jost Mission Committee believed that mothers ought to work only in their own homes, they assisted working-class women to find employment and cared for their children. Like many other philanthropists and reformers of the early 20th century they did not envision women as serious or permanent wage-earners and did not help them improve their position in the paid work force. But as married women continued to seek employment, the managers of the Mission responded, expanding the nursery and turning their attention more toward the wage-earning women. Defining their role as a mothering one in the larger social sense, the Committee and matrons addressed what they saw as the needs of poor children and their mothers. The churchwomen's dedication to personal charity and cross-class contact may have sharpened their understanding of the "poorer sisters" even if it could not bridge the social gap between them.

Notes

1. I use the terms paid work, employment, wage-earning, and unpaid work, rather than work and nonwork, to avoid the implication that domestic or volunteer labour is not "work". The research for this

paper was done with the support of the Social Sciences and Humanities Research Council of Canada, 1981–1983. I wish to thank Susan Porter Benson, Mari Jo Buhle, Judith Fingard, Ernest Forbes, Frances Early, Riva Krut, Ian McKay, John D. Thomas, and the *Acadiensis* readers for their helpful comments on an earlier draft of the paper. I thank Margaret Campbell and Judith Fingard for sharing research which touched on the history of the Mission.

2. Primary sources for this study include the *Annual Reports* of the Toronto Deaconess Home and *Annual Reports* of the Deaconess Aid Society (after 1906 the Deaconess Society) of the Methodist Church, [*Deaconess Annual Reports*], Archives of the United Church of Canada, Toronto, and the *Annual Reports* of the Woman's Committee of the Jost Mission (from 1918 simply called the Jost Mission Committee), 1915–1945, [*JMAR*], and surviving Minutes of the Jost Mission Committee, October 1920 to November 1931, [*JMC Minutes*]. The trustees of the Jost Mission have voted to place the records in the Public Archives of Nova Scotia, but at present they remain in the hands of the trustees.

3. Margaret Campbell, "The Jost Mission," in "No Other Foundation", manuscript history of the Brunswick Street Church; *Deaconess Annual Report*, 1904–05, 21, and *Christian Guardian* (Toronto), 19 April 1905. *Deaconess Annual Reports*, 1894–1920, give information on the founding of the order and list annual appointments of deaconesses. Additional articles specifically on Halifax deaconesses (at Brunswick and Grafton Street Churches as well as at the Jost Mission) appeared in the *Christian Guardian*, 27 January 1904, 26 July, 1 November 1905, 9 July 1913, 8 March, 23 August 1916.

4. *Christian Guardian*, 9 July 1913. The matron during the 1940s was still providing relief to needy families: monthly report of the matron, deaconess Edna Pearson, March 1941, Jost Mission Records.

5. *Deaconess Annual Report*, 1906–07, 93. In 1906–07, the four Nova Scotia deaconesses (three in Halifax, one in Sydney) secured work for 23 persons. Figures increase in successive years but do not show at what institution(s). The first definitive account that the Jost Mission is running an employment service is in the *Christian Guardian*, 9 July 1913.

6. David A. Sutherland, "Halifax, 1815–1914: 'Colony to Colony' ", *Urban History Review* 1 (June 1975): 7–11; L.D. McCann, "Staples and the New Industrialism in the Growth of Post-Confederation Halifax", *Acadiensis* VIII, 2 (Spring 1979): 60–61, 66, 79.

7. D. Suzanne Cross, "The Neglected Majority: The Changing Role of Women in 19th Century Montreal", *Histoire sociale/Social History* 6 (1973): 215–16, and Linda Kealey, "Introduction", in *A Not Unreasonable Claim: Women and Reform in Canada, 1880s–1920s*, edited by Linda Kealey (Toronto, 1979), 2, and other essays in the volume. See also Nancy Cott, *The Bonds of Womanhood: 'Woman's Sphere' in New England, 1780–1835* (New Haven, 1977); Barbara Berg, *The Remembered Gate: Origins of American Feminism: The Woman and the City, 1800–1860* (New York, 1978), 220, 231; Susan Porter Benson, "Business Heads and Sympathizing Hearts: The Women of the Providence Employment Society, 1837–1858", *Journal of Social History* 12 (1978): 302–12; and John Cumbler, "The Politics of Charity: Gender and Class in Late 19th Century Policy", *Journal of Social History* 14 (1980): 98–111.

8. *JMAR*, 1917, 5–6. Alterations were almost completed when the Halifax Explosion occurred on 6 December 1917, when a munitions ship collided with another vessel in the harbour, producing an explosion which devastated two square miles of the city. The building was damaged but usable. Women from the Halifax Old Ladies Home were housed in the building for some time after the Explosion and the nursery and employment work were carried on from two cottages on the Commons provided by the Halifax Relief Commission for part of 1918.

9. *JMAR*, 1915, 5, 6, 8. Every *Annual Report* listed donors and their gifts.

10. JMC Minutes, January and April 1923.

11. JMC Minutes, passim; *JMAR*, 1915, 5; Interview with Janet Barkley [pseud.], daughter of a Committee member who served from 1920 through the Second World War, p. 8. I interviewed six people connected with the Mission: the woman cited above, a domestic worker who used the nursery and placement service, her son who attended the nursery, a woman who worked as a nursery maid, a woman who had attended the nursery as a child, whose mother was a domestic worker and who herself became a domestic worker, and a Committee member who served during and after the Second World War. All are white. I have changed all the names in this paper to protect their privacy. The tapes and transcripts (of all but the last named, who did not agree to taping) are available in the Sound Archive of the Public Archives of Nova Scotia, Halifax.

12. *Halifax City Directories*, 1915, 1927; David Sutherland, "The Personnel and Policies of the Halifax Board of Trade, 1890–1914" in *The Enterprising Canadians*, edited by Lewis R. Fischer and Eric W. Sager (St. John's, 1979), 205–29. I am indebted to David Sutherland for help in assessing the class background of the trustees and husbands of the Committee members.

13. Barkley's mother worked with her father in his business after the Explosion: Barkley Interview, 3. The officers of the Committee who served terms longer than five years belonged to the Grafton St. Church and Robie St. Church (later combined to form the United Methodist, then St. Andrew's United Church), the Brunswick St. Church, the Kaye St. Church (later Kaye-Grove, then United Memorial), and Fort Massey Church (formerly Presbyterian). St. Andrew's and Fort Massey served congregations from the wealthy South End, and the Brunswick St. and United Memorial served mixed-class neighbourhoods in the North End. The interview with Barkley made it clear that middle-class members of the United Memorial congregation tended to run the organizational life of the church though all classes attended worship services: p. 21. The members of the Committee who could not be clearly identified tended to offer the most possibility of being lower in social status. Sometimes their husbands' first names or initials were never given in Annual Reports. They also tended to be on the Committee for shorter periods of time than the prominent women. Those who were less well-off would have had less money for domestic help to free them for the Committee work.

14. Benson, "Business Heads", and Cumbler, "The Politics of Charity", suggest clearly how distinct the ideas and activity of male and female charity workers could be even when they came from the same class and were married to each other.

15. Maids may have been hired to care for children by 1918. The rebuilt and expanded Mission building had space for 40 children, too many for two deaconesses to care for and also carry on other activities: *JMAR*, 1918, 8.

16. JMC Minutes, September 1931.

17. "The Deaconess Society", United Church Ministry Personnel and Education leaflet, April 1976, United Church Archives; Deaconess *Annual Report*, 1900–01, 9, ibid., 1903–04, 21, ibid., 1906–07, viii, ibid., 1901–02, 13, ibid., 1902–03, 6–12. Deaconesses enjoyed one month of vacation per year and were moved from assignment to assignment every few years. A good common school education was initially required of applicants, but by 1914 the Training School preferred one or two years of high school. In addition to Bible study and personal spiritual development, the training included progressively more sociology, social gospel theology, and practical settlement house experience between 1910 and 1920. For a good explanation of the origins and development of the order and the change from maintenance to salaries, see John D. Thomas, "Servants of the Church: Canadian Methodist Deaconess Work, 1890–1926", *Canadian Historical Review* XLV, 3 (September 1984): 371–95.

18. I am grateful to John D. Thomas for information on the background of four of 14 deaconesses who worked at the Jost Mission. Caldwell taught kindergarten in 1918 at the Community House started by the Halifax Welfare Bureau after the Explosion: Halifax Welfare Bureau (formerly Bureau of Social Service), *Third Annual Report*, 1918–19, 27, Jost Mission Records. On Caldwell see *JMAR*, 1925, 4. The information on White comes from personal conversation with Janet Barkley and a memoir, "Lillian Agnes Burgess White", by her daughter Frances Lillian White Preston, September 1984, in possession of this author. The large number of single women officers in the Salvation Army suggests that it was a route to independence for a number of women in the early 20th century. Information on the Salvation Army comes from the regularly published *Disposition of Forces*, 1902–1950, which lists officers, and from interviews with three retired female Salvation Army officers, Public Archives of Nova Scotia. In 1923 a deaconess's salary would have been $65/month excluding board: JMC Minutes, April 1923. Veronica Strong-Boag gives average annual wages of various female occupations in "The Girl of the New Day: Canadian Working Women in the 1920s", *Labour/Le Travailleur* 4 (1979): 147, 149. On average, employed women's annual wages were one-half of men's in Halifax in 1920.

19. Interviews with Mary Carr [pseud.], 15 February 1982 and 15 March 1982, 17, 24–34, 42–44. This hierarchy of workers was typical of day nurseries at the time: see Patricia Vandebelt Schulz, "Day Care in Canada: 1850–1962", in *Good Day Care: Fighting for It, Getting It, Keeping It*, edited by Kathleen Gallagher Ross (Toronto, 1978), 142. Domestic service wages in Ontario in 1916 were $18–20/month plus room and board: Ceta Ramkhalawansingh, "Women during the Great War", in *Women at Work: Ontario, 1850–1930*, edited by Janice Acton, Penny Goldsmith, and Bonnie Shepard (Toronto, 1974), 278.

20. Betty Smith [pseud.], who attended the nursery around 1918 to 1920 while her mother did day work, told of friends in the 1930s working at Clayton's (clothing), Moir's (candy), and Ben's (bakery): Interview with Smith, 15 June 1983, 18–19. See also McCann, "Staples and the New Industrialism", 73, 77. All but two of the mothers who used the nursery in the early 1920s were married, according to Mary Carr. She recalled two single mothers who worked at Moir's and left their babies at the nursery: Carr Interview, 15 February 1982. After 1945 some unmarried and divorced mothers were applying to the nursery, but no information exists on the earlier period.

21. Charworkers contained by far the highest proportion of women workers aged 35 and over (hence, probably married) of any category of female work in the early 20th century. The number of recorded female charworkers in Halifax grew from 38 in 1911 to 109 in 1921 and 137 in 1931, dropping to 73 in 1941. Some women may have been included under the predominantly single "domestic servant" category. See the following volumes from the *Census of Canada*: 1911, Vol. VI, table VI, 326–67; 1921, vol. IV, p. xi, and table 5, 396–97; 1931, vol. VII, table 43, 277; 1941, vol. VII, table 9, 245–55. Other information on women's work and the decline of domestic service appears in Genevieve Leslie, "Domestic Service in Canada, 1880–1920", in *Women at Work*, edited by Acton et al., 74, 76, 86–90; Helen Lenskyj, "A 'Servant Problem' or a 'Servant-Mistress Problem'?: Domestic Service in Canada, 1890–1930", *Atlantis* 7 (Fall 1981) 3–11; David Katzman, *Seven Days a Week: Women and Domestic Service in Industrializing America* (Urbana, 1981), 44–94, 144–5; Wayne Roberts, *Honest Womanhood: Feminism, Femininity and Class Consciousness Among Toronto Working Women, 1893–1914* (Toronto, 1976), 14; Peter D. Lambly, "Toward A Living Wage: The Minimum-Wage Campaign for Women in Nova Scotia, 1920–1935" (Honours Essay, Dalhousie University, 1977), 26–7, 96; Ramkhalawansingh, "Women During the Great War", 263, 269, 280, 289–94; Strong-Boag, "Girl of the New Day", 132, 138–9. Married women constituted the following proportions of the female work force: 1921, 7.2 per cent; 1931, 10 per cent; 1941, 12.7 per cent.

22. Interview with Ellen Blackwood [pseud.], 21, 22 November 1982, 56.

23. Smith Interview, 25 May 1983, 2–3; *Presbyterian Witness*, 7 July 1917, 5; Blackwood Interview, 38–40, 45–48, 52–56, 6.

24. E.R. Forbes, "In Search of a Post-Confederation Maritime Historiography, 1900–1967", *Acadiensis* VIII, 1 (Autumn 1978): 3–21; "Prohibition and the Social Gospel in Nova Scotia", *Acadiensis* I, 1 (Autumn 1971): 14, 24; "Edith Archibald and the Feminist Movement in Halifax, Nova Scotia", unpublished manuscript 1983; David Sutherland, "Halifax, 1815–1914", 10, and "The Halifax Board of Trade", 214; David Frank and Nolan Reilly, "The Emergence of the Socialist Movement in the Maritimes, 1899–1916", *Labour/Le Travailleur* 4 (1979), 94.

25. Halifax Welfare Bureau, *Third Annual Report*, 1919, 7, 10.

26. William L. O'Neill, *Everyone Was Brave* (Chicago, 1969), x, 49–54; Daniel Scott Smith, "Family Limitation, Sexual Control, and Domestic Feminism in Victorian America", in *A Heritage of Her Own: Toward a Social History of American Women*, edited by Nancy Cott and Elizabeth Pleck (New York, 1979), 236, 239. See Kealey, "Introduction", *A Not Unreasonable Claim*, for a useful discussion of all three terms. For examples, see O'Neill, *Everyone Was Brave*, 77–106, Suzann Buckley, "Ladies or Midwives? Efforts to Reduce Infant and Maternal Mortality", in *A Not Unreasonable Claim*, 131–50, and Wendy Mitchinson, "The WCTU: 'For God, Home and Native Land': A Study in Nineteenth-Century Feminism", ibid., 155. The advantage of the maternal feminist perspective was that, at its best, it took seriously the social importance of domestic labour and childrearing and the needs of women and children whose subordination within an already subordinate class made their vulnerability extreme. The limits of this view were in its failure to confront the roots of female dependency in women's exclusive responsibility for children and inequality in the paid labour force as well as in its often class-bound vision of reform. Very few women during this period, even socialists, seemed able to make a critique of women's reproductive roles, perhaps because most women's lives were materially rooted in motherhood and so few alternatives were available. Linda Gordon has argued that in the late 19th and early 20th century women's sense of greatest dignity stemmed from their role as mothers, and their consciousness reflected the importance of the work of mothers. Certainly the WCTU's success in wooing "conservative" women to suffrage suggests how many women saw their domestic roles as the basis for their claims to wider social power. See Gordon, *Woman's Body, Woman's Right: A Social History of Birth Control in America* (New York,

1976), 133, and Paula Baker, "The Domestication of Politics: Women and American Political Society, 1780–1920", *American Historical Review* 89 (1984), 634–5, 637–8. See also Linda Kealey, "Canadian Socialism and the Woman Question, 1900–1914", *Labour/Le Travail* 13 (Spring 1984): 77–100. Women who did point to family roles as a source of female inequality included American feminists Charlotte Perkins Gilman and Crystal Eastman and Canadian Flora MacDonald Denison. Margaret Conrad comments helpfully on these issues in "The Re-Birth of Canada's Past: A Decade of Women's History", *Acadiensis* XII, 2 (Spring 1983): 147–50.

27. On temperance, see JMC Minutes, January 1931.

28. *Christian Guardian*, 27 January 1904, 9 July 1913. Deaconess *Annual Reports* list the number of calls made, and the *JMAR* make clear the shift in emphasis of the programmes by 1918.

29. *Christian Guardian*, 1 November 1905: Deaconess *Annual Report*, 1906–07, 94; Robert M. Stamp, "Teaching Girls their 'God Given Place in Life' ", *Atlantis* 2 (Spring 1977): 18–34; John G. Reid, "The Education of Women at Mount Allison, 1854–1914", *Acadiensis* XII, 2 (Spring 1983), 30. John Thomas did not find that training servants was a major motivation of deaconess work, and David Katzman notes that any domestic science programme suspected as training for servants drove students away: *Seven Days A Week*, 134–5, 244, 255. Strong-Boag says the 1919 Technical Education Act promoted "domestic service for poorer students" and "domestic careers for all": "Girl of the New Day", 135.

30. Stamp, "Teaching Girls", 25, 31–3; Barbara Ehrenreich and Deirdre English, *For Her Own Good: 150 Years of the Experts' Advice to Women* (New York, 1978), 171; *Christian Guardian*, 1 November 1905, *JMAR* 1918, 7; ibid., 1938, 5. Ages of the girls in clubs are never stated but seem likely to have been early adolescent. I am indebted to Janet Guildford for sharing chapter 3 of her M.A. thesis, "Technical Education in Nova Scotia, 1880–1930", Dalhousie University, 1984, and for the idea about the importance of fashion as a factor in the popularity of sewing.

31. JMC Minutes, December 1920 to September 1925. There are no hints as to Moir's reasons, but in January 1925 the work was reported to be "at a standstill".

32. Forbes, "Edith Archibald", 13–15; *The Wesleyan* (Halifax), 9 March 1910. Betty Smith reported just such an incident. Her mother left Smith's brother with a neighbour during the workday and one day returned to find him unattended: Smith Interview, 15 June 1983, 4.

33. *Christian Guardian*, 9 July 1913, 15, and 8 March 1916, 17. In 1931 the Committee discussed plans for extension of the space and for opening a section for sick and convalescent children of employed mothers, and Mrs. White asked for a third nursery maid. The same year a major fund drive paid for expensive renovations of the nursery quarters. The Convalescent Room with 24-hour care was opened in 1938. The operation of the Jost Mission nursery was similar to that described by Schulz in "Day Care in Canada". Records showed, however, that the Jost Mission nursery opened in 1920, not during the First World War, as Schulz states. Calculations made from Mission reports of children's fees collected suggest that many children did not pay full rates. In 1915, for example, for every two children who paid 10 cents a day, one came for free. It is unclear when black children were first admitted. The records do not mention race until 1944 when the Annual Report notes "colored and white" women at the Christmas dinner. Betty Smith recalled black children in the early 1920s, but Mary Carr did not. Ed Taylor [pseud.], Blackwood's stepson, said there were black children attending in the late 1930s: Taylor Interview, 3 May 1982, 8.

34. *Christian Guardian*, 8 March, 23 August 1916; Mary Carr Interview; 15 February 1982. An account of 1916 reported that 30 children were enrolled in the kindergarten not only from the nursery but also from the neighbourhood. Although the kindergarten was important, when resources became scarce in the late 1920s, a paid kindergarten worker was dropped. Over the Depression and Second World War years volunteers seem to have been used, but the records do not make this clear. The nursery clearly had priority.

35. *Christian Guardian*, 9 July 1913. In 1916 most of the children were Roman Catholic. The matron reported to the Committee in 1925, though, that only three families were Catholic. Mary Carr was Catholic. The importance of the religious training lies more in the assumption that Protestant culture is *the* public culture than in definite aims to convert Catholics. My thanks to Susan P. Benson for discussion on this point. The deaconesses may have tried to convert Catholics during the 1910s, but for the early 1920s Carr recalled only grace at meals and Smith remembered no hymns, only children's games and songs: Carr Interview, 15 March 1982, 35; Smith Interview, 25 May 1983, 14. A surviving nursery schedule for 1945 suggests grace before meals was the only religious ritual. Apart from rituals, however, Christian values surely

suffused teaching. Nationalism and Christian commitment had been closely linked in the vision of the Methodist church leaders during the First World War: J.M. Bliss, "The Methodist Church and World War II", *Canadian Historical Review* XLIX, 3 (September 1968): 213–33.

36. The Social Service Council of Canada, a social gospel organization to which the Methodist Church belonged, affirmed in 1913 the "right of children to birth, happiness, and mental and moral education" as well as freedom from exploitation in child labour: Methodist Board of Evangelism and Social Service, *Annual Report*, 1912–13, 11. See also Richard Allen, *The Social Passion: Religion and Social Reform in Canada, 1914–1928* (Toronto, 1971), 66.

37. *JMAR*, 1924, 4; ibid., 1915, 5, 6.

38. Ibid., 1927, 5. Early nurseries in 19th-century Montreal also had placement services: Cross, "Neglected Majority", 209.

39. Strong-Boag, " 'Wages for Housework': Mothers' Allowances and the Beginnings of Social Security in Canada", *Journal of Canadian Studies* 14 (Spring 1979), 27; James Struthers, "A Profession in Crisis: Charlotte Whitton and Canadian Social Work in the 1930s", *Canadian Historical Review* LXII (1981), 169. Blackwood received some relief during the 1930s but noted that it was never enough: Blackwood Interview, 61.

40. Deaconess *Annual Report*, 1906–07, 93; Deaconess *Annual Report*, 1913–14; *Christian Guardian*, 9 July 1913. Demand for charworkers from the Mission appeared to meet or exceed the supply of workers available throughout most of the period except in 1919 and 1920: *Christian Guardian*, 9 July 1913, *JMAR*, 1919, 1929, 1940, 1944, and JMC Minutes, November 1920 and May, December 1926.

41. *Christian Guardian*, 23 August 1916: Carr Interviews, 15 February 1982, and 15 March 1982, 30–1; Blackwood Interview, 54–6. The relative impersonality of the job placement service tempted two brothels on Morris St. to request day workers in the 1930s. The Mission matron was suspicious and asked the charworker, Ellen Blackwood, to leave if it were a "bad place". Blackwood stayed all day each time because she needed the money but reported what she saw to the matron: Blackwood Interview, 66–8. This occurred again in 1941: Deaconess Edna Pearson's monthly report, March 1941, Jost Mission Records.

42. *Christian Guardian*, 9 July 1913. See also Mitchinson, "The WCTU", 155.

43. *JMAR*, 1925, 1930, 1932, 1938. The *Annual Report*, 1941, for the first time mentions women working to supplement family income as well as sole breadwinners.

44. *Christian Guardian*, 8 March 1916; *JMAR*, 1929, 4–5. See JMC Minutes, November 1920 and *JMAR*, 1932, on distributing work to the neediest.

45. *Christian Guardian*, 8 March 1916; JMC Minutes, October 1925. In the *Annual Report*, 1919, 6 the committee noted an "improvement in the class of workers now being sent out". The Woman's Committee affiliated in 1922 with the Local Council of Women, which had been quite vocal on the "servant problem" in the 1910s and later opposed the minimum wage for female factory workers because it might reduce the supply of domestics: Lambly, "Toward a Living Wage", 60–65. The Committee never recorded any discussion of wages or any Council issue except temperance, but some of them (or prominent supporters) may have agreed with the Council's position. Blackwood did not know if the Mission set wages. She knew only that she took what employers gave: Blackwood Interview, 58. The Mission charged employers 50 cents per year for use of the service in 1915 but seems to have stopped charging by 1931 after several years of wrangling with recalcitrant employers who refused to pay the fee despite its charitable purpose. This exemplifies how employers could limit the benevolent aims of the Mission volunteers. One 19th-century example of women's charity, the Providence Employment Society, did set wages: Benson, "Business Heads", 303. My thanks to John Thomas for discussion on this point.

46. *Christian Guardian*, 9 July 1913, 8 March 1916; JMC Minutes, November 1924; *JMAR*, 1929, 4–5; Catherine L. Cleverdon, *The Woman Suffrage Movement in Canada* (Toronto, 1950, 1975), 157.

47. *JMAR*, 1923, 5; ibid., 1929, 4–5.

48. Blackwood Interview, 62, 63; Taylor Interview, 3 May 1982, 7–8, 11–12, 27–8. Betty Smith spoke very positively of the food and of matron Bryon, who was "strict but nice". Smith Interview, 25 May 1983, 13, 14, 19; 15 June 1983, 9–10, 43.

49. Strong-Boag, "Wages for Housework", 28; Blackwood Interview, 60, 109–10; Smith Interview, 15 June 1983, 10.

50. Blackwood Interview, 19–22, 58, 60–61, 93, 95, 96, 125–7; Smith Interview, 25 May 1983, 9–10, 23–25; 15 June 1983, 7, 10, 12, 18, 20–23, 25, 35, 42. Smith thinks domestic workers need to be unionized: 15 June 1983, 19.

51. *JMAR*, 1921, 5–6; ibid., 1923, 5; ibid., 1924, 6; ibid., 1938, 5; ibid., 1940, 6; JMC Minutes, May and June 1922, February and April 1923. Kathy Peiss explains that working-class culture and leisure as treated by recent historians have largely meant a public male culture associated with extrafamilial institutions such as taverns, lodges, and unions, in which women were absent or marginal because of sex segregation and women's family responsibilities: "Working Class Gender Relationships and Leisure in the United States, 1890–1920", paper presented at the Sixth Berkshire Conference on the History of Women, Smith College, 2 June 1984, 1–8.

52. Blackwood Interview, 129; Patricia Mainardi, *Quilts: The Great American Art* (San Pedro, Calif., 1978), 9, 12; Guildford, "Technical Education in Nova Scotia", chapter 3; M. Patricia Connelly and Martha MacDonald, "Women's Work: Domestic and Wage Labour in a Nova Scotia Community", *Studies in Political Economy* 10 (Winter 1983), 48.

53. Blackwood Interview, 133–4; Smith Interview, 15 June 1983, 44–5.

54. *JMAR*, 1944, 4–5; ibid., 1945, 4–5. On women's labour force participation, see Connelly and MacDonald, "Women's Work", 49. In Ontario and Quebec, where the Dominion-Provincial Wartime Day Nurseries Agreement had been in effect, women pressed for extension of government support after the war because they still needed the child care: Ruth Pierson, "Women's Emancipation and the Recruitment of Women into the Canadian Labour Force in World War II", *Historical Papers/Communications historiques* (1976), 160–1.

55. The nursery operated in the original location until 1976, when the Jost Mission building was destroyed in order to make way for the new Metro Centre. This fact was noted with outrage in all of the interviews conducted for this study. The Jost Mission nursery is now located at the Bethany United Church.

"EVER A CRUSADER": NELLIE McCLUNG, FIRST-WAVE FEMINIST †

VERONICA STRONG-BOAG

As it involved the public sphere, the suffrage movement, predictably, was the first subject concerning women on which historians focussed. The pioneering historians tended to see the suffragists as heroines, organizing lobbying campaigns and overcoming the prejudices of their day to win the vote. The next group of historians, however, either dismissed suffragism as a superficial reform based on an inadequate analysis of the economic and social order, or saw late nineteenth and early twentieth-century suffragists as middle-class reformers seeking the vote so as to impose social controls on immigrants and the working class. They pointed out that these first-wave feminists tended to see their maternal role as the justification for their empowerment, not questioning women's "natural" responsibility for home mainte-nance and childcare.

Veronica Strong-Boag's article represents a third stage of scholarship on this topic. She, along with other historians, perceives women's demand for the vote as potentially radical, offering as it did the unconventional prospect of women seeking a direct connection with the state rather than allowing male family members to act as mediators for them. Given their dependence on marriage for respectability and financial support, women sought to bring in the state on their own behalf to counterbalance the advantages that custom and law at that time gave to men in the marital relationship as well as in the public sphere. Their demands served as an indictment of patriarchal authority as it was exercised.

Strong-Boag maintains that much of the dynamism propelling the feminist movement of the late nineteenth and early twentieth centuries came from women's sense of urgency about disturbing changes in private life. Whether they chose to join the Woman's Christian Tem-perance Union or a suffrage association, or to agitate for improved working conditions for female factory operatives, activist women started from an awareness, sometimes personally experienced, of the vulnerability of women in both home and job. Like Nellie McClung, they may have seen their maternal responsibility for children and all living things as the motiva-ting force behind their reform zeal, but that did not make them respectful of male authority.

Contemporary feminists differ from first-wave feminists in many respects, including a belief that assignment of the maternal role to women serves more social than biological functions. Nevertheless, they depend upon equal divorce and guardianship, the right to con-trol their own earnings, and the vote, all achieved by the efforts of earlier feminists.

"Never retract, never explain, never apologize — get the thing done and let them howl." Such were the fighting words of Nellie Letitia Mooney McClung (1873–1951) who captured the imagination of her contemporaries and who in many ways embodied Canadian feminism in the first quarter of the twentieth century. Nellie McClung was an activist: a prominent crusader in the successful drives for female enfranchisement in Manitoba and Alberta, a nationally known feminist

†This article has not been previously published. My thanks to Anita Clair Fellman whose generous assistance and own considerable knowledge of the suffrage generation helped immeasurably with the writing of this article. I would also like to thank Barbara Tessman of Copp Clark Pitman for her thoughtful advice.

and social reformer, an MLA in Alberta. An unpaid contributor to a host of good causes, she belonged to the first generation of female volunteers to have its expertise officially acknowledged and rewarded. As a representative of her sex, she was invited to the Canadian War Conference of 1918, and to the World Ecumenical Conference in 1921. Fifteen years later she took her seat as the first female member of the Canadian Broadcasting Corporation's Board of Governors and, in 1938, as a Canadian delegate to the League of Nations. Working with the Canadian Women's Press Club and the Canadian Authors' Association, she also commanded attention as a strong exponent of cultural nationalism. Sixteen books and numerous articles made her one of Canada's best-known authors. Her fourth book, *In Times Like These* (1915), with its faith in women's power for good, survives as a classic formulation of the feminist position of her day. Indeed its potent mixture of wit, satire, good humour, and down-to-earth common sense is hard to match among popular appeals from first-wave feminists anywhere in the English-speaking world.[1]

Nellie McClung was born Nellie Letitia Mooney in 1873 in Grey County, Ontario, and in 1880 with her family joined the great rush to Manitoba's wheatfields. Her stance toward life would be forever marked by her Scots mother's strong sense of personal duty, by her Irish father's storytelling abilities, and by her family's commitment to the positive values of ruralism and hard work. During her lifetime Canada was experiencing major unheavals, to which McClung, like many of her contemporaries, responded both as a citizen and as a concerned woman. The largely unregulated growth of the commercial and industrial sectors exacerbated problems of labour relations and transformed the conditions for earning a livelihood. On the land the idealized family farm confronted new marketing and capitalization requirements that challenged its very survival. Rural emigration combined with immigration, increasingly from nations new to the Canadian ethnic mix, crowded the cities, creating a host of problems to which there were no easy answers.

These changes engulfed women as well as men. With the gradual but steady decline in importance of domestic production, many more women had to labour outside the home. The emergence of new employments in factories, offices, and shops offered both opportunities to aid shaky family finances and the prospect of independence from oppressive authority within the family. The ultimate attraction, of course, for young women seeking work, whether in the new occupations or in traditional domestic service, was a living wage. Yet their limited range of options and their marginally skilled status increased the vulnerability of such workers in a labour market that treated them as a readily exploitable resource.[2] Too often, uncertain and inadequate salaries had to be supplemented by family support and occasionally, by prostitution. Middle-class wives whose husbands earned enough to maintain the entire family did not have to face the same bleak prospects but they too were struggling to define their place in a modern community. As the economic order shifted in favour of white collar employments and heightened levels of consumption, many middle-class women sought to find in enhanced standards of childcare, housekeeping, and domestic management the authority and status that previously might have been theirs by virtue of their responsibilities for household production. The strain of such transformations was deepened by the instability of male income, subject to all the vicissitudes of a maturing capitalist labour market.[3] In response to such forces, relationships among kin inevitably began to shift as well.

Contemporaries were acutely conscious of distress within the confines of the patriarchal family. The consequences for women appeared most visibly in desertions, alcoholism, appropriation of female wages and property, and domestic violence. Yet solutions for women facing bad marriages were far from obvious. Not only did they face social opprobrium for their "failure" as wives, but when divorced or deserted they had little hope of getting a fair share of their husbands' estate or any reasonable support for the children of the marriage. Even their right to child custody in preference to a delinquent father could not be taken for granted. At the same time they and their daughters were routinely excluded from much of the training and schooling that gave entry to the better-paying craft and white-collar jobs and professions offering some prospect of independence. Confronted with the threats to their domestic position and with limited alternatives outside the household, many women became intensely conscious of their vulnerability and the need to do something about it.

Right from the beginning, the campaign to better the position of their sex was led by middle-class women. Their perspective and views on proper behaviour and standards infused the feminist movement, making it at times intolerant of ethnic and class diversity and often unwilling to confront profound inequities in capitalist society.[4] Imperfect as it was, however, their vision of a more equitable future challenged some fundamental structures in a society where male authority was largely unquestioned. Lacking their wealthier sisters' resources, working-class women concentrated instead on the demands of day-to-day survival. Occasionally, however, the intransigence of employers like Toronto's Bell Telephone Company in 1907 and the inspiration of radical arguments from organizations like the Knights of Labour and the Socialist Party of Canada recruited working-class women to feminism's standard.[5] Even then alliances with middle-class feminists remained problematic, involving, as they so frequently did, a choice between the loyalties of class and gender.

Women whose temperament and circumstances permitted a feminist analysis soon turned to political solutions. This was hardly surprising. The increasing complexity of the Canadian economy with markets, corporations, and elites taking on regional or national dimensions appeared to demand political solutions on a similar scale. More than ever before, citizens of the late nineteenth century looked to legislative means rather than custom or individual action to regulate the activities of many sectors, public and private, of Canadian life. This meant that those who wanted some say in changing the terms on which life was conducted had to have access to electoral bodies, municipal, provincial, or national, both as voters and as elected officials. The absence of such power had meant little when most people's lives went relatively untouched by governments. In the last half of the nineteenth century this situation was changing. The achievement of voting rights by the vast majority of males during the course of these decades also highlighted as never before women's special predicament and contributed to strengthening their sense of group identity.[6] As a result, soon after Confederation, women began to focus their energies on enfranchisement as the enabling means to correct the many abuses and injustices they saw around them.

Feminists demanded the vote on two grounds. The first was special interest. Women themselves, like virtually everyone in Canadian society, identified their sex with a maternal role. A re-invigorated motherhood, the natural occupation for virtually all women, could serve as a buttress against all the destabilizing elements in Canada. Just as the rich and the regions were to be represented and protected in the makeup of the Canadian Senate, women demanded that their distinctive concerns and needs be granted direct input into the legislative system. Vote in hand, they would be able to maximize their influence for good. Feminists also claimed the franchise on the basis of natural justice. Every human being, regardless of sex, had the right to participate in government to the fullest extent of his or her abilities. Women's suffrage was no more or less than the natural culmination of democracy.

The implications of this claim to rights beyond the domestic sphere were enormous. Female enfranchisement, in particular by challenging "the male monopoly on the public arena,"[7] and in making women's claim to full citizenship, called into question the appropriateness of women's subordinate position within the patriarchal family itself. With their demand for the vote, women were suggesting that they should have a direct relationship to the state as individuals rather than one mediated through their fathers or husbands. As voters women gained the potential to use the state to alter the balance of power between the sexes in the home and the world at large. Behind a political agenda that included demands for better married women's property acts, women's right to their own wages, equal guardianship of children and equal divorce, better paying jobs with improved working conditions, access to institutions of higher learning, and protection of women from alcohol abuse among men lay a powerful threat to male supremacy.

At first women were largely alone in their insistence on the vote and in their sense of their sex's urgent need for reforms. Their first assaults on an inequitable system brought few active male allies. In 1876 Dr. Emily Howard Stowe founded the first Canadian suffrage organization, the Toronto Women's Literary Club, but not until 1883 were its members sure enough of their ability to withstand the deeply ingrained misogyny of their society to "come out" as the Toronto Women's Suffrage Club.[8] By organizing parades and study groups, by flooding the Ontario legislature with suffrage petitions, this band of middle-class women established the pattern for other feminist campaigns across the country.[9]

Only in the 1890s did feminists begin to find general support from liberally-minded men and non-feminist women who rallied to them not so much because of any enthusiasm for women's rights but more out of a general interest in community betterment. The emergence of a major middle-class progressive movement in the last years of the nineteenth century created an environment in which the suffrage campaign could flourish, and forced reluctant governments to pay heed to their female citizens. Like the feminists who preceded them, the new reformers concentrated on transforming the state in order to bring its full weight against the abuses of private power, whether it be in unregulated industry, in an unmanageable urban environment, or in the nation's homes. In the course of their investigations they repeatedly encountered women's special plight. The identification of women as the particular victims of social disarray helped legitimize the older feminist analysis and cement a feminist-reform alliance. The acceptance of women as allies in public reform movements, and in public life generally, in this period was based more on the belief in women's higher morality than on any abstract notion of justice, but the latter rationale never completely disappeared from the feminist agenda. Nellie McClung represents that generation of women who were active in both the reform and the feminist communities. As such she was in the mainstream of turn-of-the-century feminism.

Canada's reform and feminist communities were close-knit. An intense network of friendships and alliances maintained energy and spurred enthusiasm. Winnipeg was one centre of reform agitation and women like Nellie McClung, Francis Beynon, and Cora Hind were enthusiastic apostles of a fairer world.[10] The crusades of such progressive women — temperance, urban renewal, social welfare, social purity, female suffrage — were undertaken while the Social Gospel of the Protestant churches was prompting the entire society to self-examination.[11] When Nellie McClung pitched in to help the Methodist minister, later leader of the Cooperative Commonwealth Federation, J.S. Woodsworth, in Winnipeg's All People's Mission, she embodied suffragists' links with a semi-evangelical, nation-wide crusade to purge Canadian society of its immoralities and make it a beacon to the rest of the world. Like many other feminists, McClung drew on a deep religious faith to help sustain her optimistic liberalism.

Women's special capacity for nurture was also central to McClung's feminism. In some ways not dissimilarly to anti-feminists such as Stephen Leacock, Andrew MacPhail, Goldwin Smith, and Henri Bourassa,[12] she regarded successful motherhood as the fulfillment of her sex. Like other feminists, however, she took the logic of women's particular nature further than conservatives could tolerate. Women must emerge from the home to use the state to protect their interests and thus serve and save humanity. McClung again parted company with conservatives in laying claim to the full inheritance of liberal democracy. Feminism was as she put it, the demand for "plain, common justice" or equal rights.[13] The distinction between maternal and egalitarian arguments was not always spelled out in McClung's thinking or in that of many of her contemporaries. For this hard-pressed generation, politics was a pragmatic exercise: the niceties of theory dissolved before the need to win supporters. Defenders of male prerogatives appreciated, however, that feminism, empowered by such beliefs, constituted a critical threat to patriarchal authority.

In the forays for equal rights the ebullient McClung was in her element. Well known as the author of the best seller *Sowing Seeds in Danny* (1908), and already active in the Woman's Christian Temperance Union, the thirty-eight year old gravitated towards progressive circles when her husband, a pharmacist turned insurance agent, was transferred to Winnipeg in 1911. By this time British and American feminists were making frequent lecture tours across the continent, and the visit of England's militant suffragette Sylvia Pankhurst to Winnipeg in 1912 strengthened McClung's long-felt resolve to do something for her sex.

That same year she joined the Winnipeg Political Equality League, an association acknowledged as "one of the most enterprising and successful suffrage organizations in the Dominion."[14] An outspoken critic of barriers to women's economic equality, the League had taken up the cause of female wage earners in the city. To demonstrate the urgent need for state supervision, McClung led Manitoba's Premier Rodmond Roblin through city sweatshops employing large numbers of women. His procrastination in acting on conditions hastened McClung's political quickening. Roblin's assertion that "nice women" did not want the franchise brought a characteristic retort from the woman who would be the most energetic stump speaker against him in the next election: "By nice women . . . you probably mean selfish women who have no more thought for the underprivileged, overworked women than a pussycat in a sunny window for the starving kitten in the street. Now in that sense I am not a nice woman for I do care."[15]

Rodmond Roblin's resistance to polite female instruction spurred the suffrage forces. Unfortunately for him McClung had dimensions unforeseen by the government apologist, the Winnipeg *Telegram*, when it dismissed her as a pesky mosquito. Showing better judgement, the provincial Liberals endorsed women's suffrage, thereby acquiring an outstanding campaigner. To publicize their case the Winnipeg suffragists presented "The Women's Parliament" in January 1914. This tactic, in which women replaced male legislators and men petitioned women for the vote, was an old feminist manoeuvre, previously employed in Toronto and Vancouver. Manitoba feminists had been rebuffed in another suffrage petition just before they restaged this farce in Winnipeg; the premier had suggested that female sensibilities would be offended by the sordidness of politics. Like many anti-suffrage arguments this stance was, at best, paradoxical. If women were inherently purer, as was implied, they might be the saviours rather than the victims of the electoral system. Nellie McClung had listened particularly intently to Premier Roblin. To the great entertainment of all she mimicked and mocked his presentation for three packed performances of the "The Women's Parliament." The implications of feminists' claim to public power were dramatically revealed as upsetting the "normal" order in which women petitioned and men stood in authority. One of Nellie's novels, *Purple Springs* (1921), which dramatizes the incident of "The Women's Parliament", leaves readers with little doubt that women's direct access to the state would better their situation and the nation's in general. During the provincial election of June 1914 McClung addressed at least a hundred meetings for the Liberals. The Conservative party retained power with a reduced majority, but it had not lost its nemesis: in the summer of 1915 McClung returned from her new home in Edmonton to help topple Roblin's scandal-ridden Tories.

In Edmonton she joined forces with another prominent feminist, Emily Murphy or "Janey Canuck" as her pen name identified her.[16] Murphy had been instrumental in the passage of the province's Married Women's Relief Act of 1910 assuring wives of certain, albeit limited, inheritance rights, and she remained in the forefront of the crusade to better women's legal position until her death in 1933. Her friendship provided Nellie with the basis of a feminist support network much like the one McClung had known in Winnipeg. The shift westward was all the more auspicious since the suffrage campaign in Alberta never met the same kind of bitter opposition it faced in Manitoba. The Liberal government was sympathetic to many reform causes and, as an ally of the most powerful organization in the province, the United Farmers of Alberta (UFA), McClung's reception by legislators was cordial.

Like many feminists and progressive reformers, including farm activists, McClung favoured ending the party system. Long years of obstruction from governments of all persuasions had made her cynical about the cronyism and favour-trading of political parties. Nevertheless, like most western feminists, McClung also opposed the creation of a purely Woman's Party.[17] Instead she envisioned a great body of independent, intelligent women who would judge political issues solely on the basis of the public interest. Standing virtuously above political strife, but holding the balance of political power, women would be decisive in shaping the policies of every party. Unlike many suffragists in central Canada, the heart of "separatist" politics, prairie activists like McClung were optimistic about the potential for influencing male politicians, especially those in the organized farm movement. This role depended heavily, however, on women maintaining their reputation for superior moral judgement. Without this they could easily become but one more interest group striving for political favours.

McClung's activities were not confined to the West. She was on call to feminist forces anywhere. If the movement had a national voice, it was hers. One observer wrote, "No Canadian woman has spoken to both parts of the Dominion as she has spoken. Women from Great Britain have come to Canada to advocate the cause of suffrage, but their words have not exactly fitted the case on this side of the water. The need was for the awakening of consciousness of reform from within, and not so much for advice from without."[18] McClung herself, however, was also intensely aware of feminism's international character. She frequently cited feminists in the United States and Great Britain. On her visits to these countries she shared in the friendships that made feminism broader than any national community. She also felt considerable sympathy for British militants like Emmeline Pankhurst, but she retained her faith in the efficacy of more peaceful tactics in the New World. Her comic sense, acerbic wit, and close relationships with other women armed her well for dealing with her Canadian opponents. Confident of mass support in her own region, she was never tempted for too long beyond the impulse to use her umbrella on the obdurate Roblin.

The First World War was important in broadening the appeal of woman suffrage. Manpower shortages highlighted the extent of female employment, making the image of the sheltered female still more obviously inapplicable to Canadian circumstances. The Union government, indebted for the support of the female relatives of military personnel after the Wartime Elections Act of 1917, and anxious to increase its popularity, was especially vulnerable to feminist demands. At the same time women's patriotic work gave governments a ready justification for reversing their position. Manitoba became the first full suffrage province in January 1916, closely followed by Alberta, Saskatchewan, and British Columbia in the same year. Ontario joined them in 1917 and by 1918 Nova Scotia and the Dominion government had espoused the widened franchise. New Brunswick's women had to wait for the provincial vote until 1919, Prince Edward Island's until 1922, and Quebec's until 1940.

While she campaigned for the franchise, McClung, the mother of a young son serving overseas, also worked for the Canadian Red Cross and the Patriotic Fund. Armistice and enfranchisement freed her to test the results of such labours. In 1921 she ran for the Alberta legislature as a Liberal, adopting that label more out of a sense of gratitude for the conferral of suffrage than any strong sense of partisanship. The entry of eight female candidates was a noteworthy feature of the campaign. They covered the political spectrum, including one Conservative, two United Farmers of Alberta members, one Independent, one Socialist, one Labour candidate, and two Liberals. One of the latter was Edmonton's Nellie McClung. Like the other women she campaigned for the retention of prohibition as one sure way of protecting women and their children from male abuse. Her defence of the Liberal record brought her success but elsewhere the tide ran strongly against the government. When the count was in the UFA held 29 seats, the Liberals 14, Labour 4, Independents 3, and Conservatives 1.[19]

Unlike Agnes Macphail, the federal parliamentarian elected from Grey County for the United Farmers of Ontario in 1921,[20] McClung was not the only successful woman candidate in Alberta. She was not even the most powerful. This title fell to Irene Marryat Parlby, the former president of the United Farm Women of Alberta (UFWA) who swept her rural constituency.[21] The results of the 1921 election set the character of McClung's five-year term in the provincial legislature. As a parliamentary novice she could not easily overcome the disadvantages facing herself and her party. Dispirited by their losses, the Liberals lost the initiative. The party's difficulties were all the greater when members like McClung insisted on their freedom to break party lines. She could be an uncomfortable colleague and her "best" friend in the Legislature was undoubtedly Irene Parlby. As Nellie was the first to admit: "I was not a good party woman . . . . I could not vote against some of the government measures which seemed to me right and proper, and I tried to persuade my fellow members that this was the right course to pursue. I believed that we were the executive of the people and should bring our best judgement to bear on every question, irrespective of party ties."[22]

McClung's role in the legislature can be quickly summed up. As an opposition member her opportunity to press for women's rights was limited. In 1922, for instance, Parlby introduced a bill for "An Act to Provide a Minimum Wage for Women" despite McClung's greater familiarity, although still limited, with the issue. In the same year, another prominent government member brought forth a bill for "An Act Respecting the Rights and Property of Married Women." A year later, Parlby ushered in a bill for "An Act for the Children of Unmarried Parents" and another UFAer produced a bill to amend the Mothers' Allowance Act. Not until April 1924 did McClung get a real opportunity to lead the House in the matter of women's rights. Then she moved, seconded by Parlby:

> That in the opinion of this House the Parliament of Canada should amend the divorce laws of this Dominion now in effect in the province of Alberta in such a way as to grant equal rights and privileges to husbands and wives, with respect to the causes or acts which entitle them to remedy by way of divorce.[23]

Nellie was a long-time supporter of equitable divorce laws, arguing in one of her inimitable comparisons: "Why are pencils equipped with erasers if not to correct mistakes?"[24] Here was a clear instance where women could use their new public power to rectify abuses in the private sphere.

Another intervention from McClung about the same time also recalled traditional feminist concerns. With the unanimous agreement of the House she moved that naturalization laws put the two sexes on an equal footing and no longer disenfranchise a British woman marrying an alien. Since these reforms were the prerogative of the federal govenment, both were forwarded to Prime Minister William Lyon Mackenzie King. In her reply to the Throne Speech in 1924, however, McClung identified an area of provincial jurisdiction. Urging the UFA to reform the Married Women's Property Act, she spoke forcefully of "the women of the country . . . looking to this legislature to do something to remove the last relic of barbarism which sullies our laws."[25] For all the symbolic significance of such initiatives, neither they nor those introduced by Parlby and the UFA matched the great hopes of the suffrage campaigners. Nellie discovered, as did other feminist office-holders, that women could not set the agenda in a public forum where they remained a tiny minority and where their training and traditions were at odds with the male majority.

The provincial defeat of prohibition heralded the crusader's political demise. Prospects for a dry Alberta were shattered in 1924 when the UFA, responding to pressure for relaxed laws, became a convert to the idea of government sale. McClung and the temperance cause failed to rally the voters. Nor could Nellie count on the support of an active feminist movement. Like the forces of prohibition, this too had declined steadily since 1921. A move to Calgary and a new constituency exacerbated her political difficulties. Whereas Edmonton had offered the advantages of a familiar and sympathetic reform milieu, Calgary's was not nearly so promising. Yet even there the 1925 election was close and for a time uncertain. Nellie blamed anti-temperance forces for her defeat but she also expressed some disillusionment with female voters, concluding:

> Some of us thought emancipated women would do this [regenerate the world]; we thought that their love of conservation, love of beauty, love of child welfare, would spur them on to finer things. But women hadn't the nerve; hadn't the courage. They were too afraid of being considered "queer" if they failed to fall in line with custom.[26]

Her loss could be interpreted as enfranchised women's failure to redeem the reform pledge that the feminists had made on their behalf. Certainly such betrayal was one way McClung explained the unfulfilled expectations of the 1920s.

Some years later Prime Minister King asked Nellie to take to the Calgary hustlings against R.B. Bennett but never again would she test voters' gratitude or idealism. Fortunately the activist's voice continued to be heard in other forums. In 1927 she joined her old Edmonton friend, now Magistrate Murphy, the Honourable Irene Parlby, the ex-MLA Louise McKinney, and a vice-president of the National Council of Women, Henrietta Edwards, in petitioning Parliament for an interpretation of the clause in the BNA Act dealing with senators. Although the question of eligibilty to the Senate was specifically at issue, the judgement had much wider implications. It would determine whether women were "persons" within the whole context of the British North America Act. The Supreme Court of Canada declared against them in 1928 but the case was carried before the Judicial Committee of the British Privy Council where, in October 1929, a favourable decision was received.[27] This victory really capped McClung's career as a feminist and, in a symbolic way, that of Canada's first wave of feminists as well. The decision asserted once again that women's right to equality in the public sphere was the cornerstone of any strategy for remedying injustice in private relationships. The continuing significance of such public rights was reaffirmed many years later in 1981 when a powerful feminist lobby secured Section 28 of the new Charter of Rights and Freedoms of Canada's Constitution. This read that "Notwithstanding anything in this Charter, the rights and freedoms referred to in it are guaranteed equally to male and female persons."[28] McClung would have understood the importance of that guarantee.

Nellie McClung's activism did not end in 1929. Church work, for instance, remained an important part of her life. Her old dreams of an invigorated and activist Christianity took root in the new United Church of Canada. Such hopes did not preclude feminist criticism. The absence of women ministers was the outstanding grievance. "There was," she reminded listeners, "no bar in reason or religion against the ordination of women." Obstacles were man-made since "no biological difference can hinder the soul's relationship to God."[29] McClung's active espousal of their cause helped United Church women gain the right to serve as ministers in 1936.[30]

Ecumenicalism was basic to many of her hopes for the Dominion; it was also a partial explanation for her internationalism between the wars. Blaming traditional and masculine diplomacy for the errors of World War I and its aftermath, she looked to the League of Nations for idealistic inspiration and practical guidance in preserving the peace. Despite her disillusionment with the initial results of women's enfranchisement, the western feminist maintained her faith that "it is easier for women to see to the heart of the peace issue than for men."[31] The prominence of women and their organizations in the Dominion's League of Nations Society, like the work of the Women's International League for Peace and Freedom, identified the post-war peace movement as one heir of feminist hopes. Here was an issue that attracted both the older generation of feminists like McClung and many of their successors as well.[32]

In the years after her electoral defeat McClung also remained in demand across the country as a well-established novelist and lecturer. Books such as *All We Like Sheep* (1926), *Flowers for the Living* (1931), *Leaves from Lantern Lane* (1936), and the two autobiographical volumes, *Clearing in the West* (1935) and *The Stream Runs Fast* (1945), reiterated her commitment to feminism and social reform and her hostility to apathy and corruption. Responding to critics who claimed that her "didactic enthusiasm" had "marred" her "art" she asserted:

> I hope I have been a crusader. . . . I have never worried about my art. I have written as clearly as I could, never idly or dishonestly, and if some of my stories are . . . sermons in disguise, my earnest hope is that the disguise did not obscure the sermon.[33]

Such sentiments did not lack sympathizers between the wars but feminism, while it frequently survived strongly as an individual creed, faltered as an organized movement. The loss of confidence in women's moral superiority, the victim of its failure to deliver on overly sanguine suffragist hopes and of the influence of Freudian-inspired psychology, undermined maternalism as a justification and explanation for public service. Female biology no longer implied so much special talents that were readily transferable to a broad range of employments within the community but a fundamental irrationality that was best expressed within the nursery and the bedroom. Yet for all its shortcomings, only the maternal ideology had the power to give women confidence in the wider applicability of their experience and to direct women's attention as a group beyond the home.

Feminism's inability to mount a sustained attack on male prerogatives in the public sphere after the suffrage campaign had serious repercussions. Rampant prejudies against women in education and employment were among many discouraging signs. One observer sounded the common note of despair when she surveyed the University of Toronto. Although the institution was ostensibly co-educational, "Practically, there seems to be a strong cross-current of prejudice which prevents free intercourse between men and women students."[34] Nor were universities the only offenders. The phrase "Girls No Longer Wanted"[35] seemed to keynote the postwar years. In the Great Depression of the 1930s married women found themselves hard-pressed to assert even their right to gainful employment.[36] Many feminists fought these trends but it was tempting for women to concentrate their energies and talents on the homefront where their place was unquestioned even when their rights were not always protected.

Nellie's success as an agitator and a politician depended in large part on the presence of a healthy, highly conscious and well-organized women's movement. Yet in the 1920s feminism could not mobilize its sympathizers under any single banner. Unable to capitalize on its proud traditions of pioneer work, its energies were dispersed throughout a multitude of causes and often lost. Individuals like McClung, Violet McNaughton of the *Prairie Producer*, Agnes Macphail, MP, Emily Carr, artist and author, Dorothy Steeves, politician, and Dorothy Livesay, writer and social worker, remained committed to feminist ideals but few could find a comfortable home in the postwar years, either as feminists or progressives.[37] All their courage could not make up for the absence of an organized feminist community to interpret and support their initiatives. Yet, in time, their vision of a world in which women both shared public power and experienced equality in private relationships would constitute an essential legacy for Canada's second wave of feminists.

Notes

1. Veronica Strong-Boag, Introduction to *In Times Like These* (Toronto and Buffalo: University of Toronto Press, 1972). For the use of the adjective "first-wave" see Carol Lee Bacchi, "First-Wave Feminism: History's Judgement" in *Australian Women: Feminist Perspectives*, edited by Norma Grieve and Patricia Grimshaw (Melbourne: Oxford University Press, 1981).

2. For a very useful discussion of the difficulties facing female workers see Margaret Hobbs, " 'Dead Horses' and 'Muffled Voices': Protective Legislation, Education and the Minimum Wage for Women in Ontario" (M.A. thesis, University of Toronto, 1985).

3. For one overview of this period see Ramsay Cook and R.C. Brown, *Canada, 1896-1921: A Nation Transformed* (Toronto: University of Toronto Press, 1974).

4. For a critical discussion of the class biases of the suffragists see Carol Lee Bacchi, *Liberation Deferred? The Ideas of the English-Canadian Suffragists, 1877-1918* (Toronto: University of Toronto Press, 1982).

5. Joan Sangster, "The 1907 Bell Telephone Strike: Organizing Women Workers," *Labour/Le Travailleur* 11 (1978): 109-30 and this volume, and Linda Kealey, "Canadian Socialism and the Woman Question, 1900-1914," *Labour/Le Travail* 13 (Spring 1984): 77-100.

6. See John Garner, *The Franchise and Politics in British North America* (Toronto: University of Toronto Press, 1969).

7. Ellen DuBois, "The Radicalism of the Woman Suffrage Movement: Notes Toward the Reconstruction of Nineteenth-Century Feminism", *Feminist Studies* 3, 1/2 (Fall 1975): 65. DuBois's reassessment has encouraged me to reconsider my earlier views of the Canadian suffrage campaign.

8. See Joanne Thompson, "The Influence of Dr. Emily Howard Stowe on the Woman Suffrage Movement in Canada," *Ontario History* 54, 4 (December 1962): 253-66.

9. The best treatment of the suffrage campaign in Canada remains Catherine Lyle Cleverdon, *The Woman Suffrage Movement in Canada*. Introduction by Ramsay Cook (Toronto: University of Toronto Press, 1970).

10. For a good introduction to Winnipeg's reform community at this time see Ramsay Cook, "Francis Marion Beynon and the Crisis of Christian Reformism" in *The West and the Nation*, edited by C. Berger and R. Cook (Toronto: McClelland and Stewart, 1976).

11. See Richard Allen, *The Social Passion, Religion and Social Reform in Canada 1914-1928* (Toronto: University of Toronto Press, 1971).

12. Unfortunately we are still waiting for an extended treatment of anti-feminism as an intellectual force in the period. The first steps in this direction are found in Susan Mann Trofimenkoff, "Henri Bourassa and 'the Woman Question' ", *Journal of Canadian Studies* 10, 4 (November 1975): 3-11. See also Stephen Leacock, *Essays and Literary Studies* (New York: John Lane, 1916); Andrew MacPhail, *Essays in Fallacy* (New York: Longmans, Green and Co., 1910), and Goldwin Smith, *Essays on the Questions of the Day* (New York: Macmillan, 1893).

13. McClung, *In Times Like These*, 59.

14. Cleverdon, *The Woman Suffrage Movement*, 55.

15. McClung, *The Stream Runs Fast* (Toronto: Thomas Allen, 1945), 109.

16. For an early biography of the powerful Murphy see Byrne Hope Sanders, *Emily Murphy, Crusader* (Toronto: Macmillan, 1945).

17. See Bacchi, *Liberation Deferred?*, 129-31 for an introduction to this fascinating difference of opinion.

18. Norman Lambert, " 'A Joan of the West,' " *Canadian Magazine* XLVI (January 1916), 266.

19. For a discussion focussing on McClung's career in the 1920s see Strong-Boag, "Canadian Feminism in the 1920s: the Case of Nellie L. McClung", *Journal of Canadian Studies* (Summer 1977): 58-68.

20. For an early biography of this important woman see Margaret Stewart and Doris French, *Ask No Quarter: A Biography of Agnes Macphail* (Toronto: Longmans, Green, 1959).

21. For an early biography see Barbara Villy Cormack, *Perennials and Politics: The Life Story of the Hon. Irene Parlby* (Sherwood Park, Alta: Professional Printing, 1968).

22. McClung, *The Stream Runs Fast*, 173.

23. Alberta, *Journals of the Legislative Assembly*, 1 April 1924, 100.

24. Margaret K. Zieman, "Nellie was a Lady Terror," *Maclean's*, 1 October 1953, 2.

25. Provincial Archives of British Columbia, Nellie L. McClung Papers, v. 25, folder 4, "Address Given by Nellie Letitia McClung in the Reply Debate January the Thirty First, 1924," 4.

26. McClung, *More Leaves from Lantern Lane* (Toronto, Thomas Allen, 1937), 19.

27. See Rudy G. Marchildon, "The 'Persons' Controversy: The Legal Aspects of the Fight for Women Senators", *Atlantis* 6 (Spring 1981): 99-113.

28. Penney Kome, "Anatomy of a Lobby", *Saturday Night* 8 (Jan. 1983): 9; see also Kome, *The Taking of 28* (Toronto: Women's Press, 1984).

29. McClung, *Edmonton Journal*, 30 January 1929.

30. See Mary E. Hallett, "Nellie McClung and the Fight for the Ordination of Women in the United Church of Canada," *Atlantis* 4 (Spring 1979): 2-16.

31. McClung, *Leaves from Lantern Lane* (Toronto: Thomas Allen: 1936), 134.

32. See Strong-Boag, "Peace-Making Women: Canada 1919-1939", *Women and Peace*, edited by Ruth Roach Pierson (London: Croom Helm, 1986).

33. McClung, *The Stream Runs Fast*, 69.

34. 'M.G.T.', "A Plea for Co-Education," *The Rebel* 4 (November 1919), 121.

35. F.C. Beckett, "Girls No Longer Wanted," *Canadian Home Journal* 18 (March 1922), 12, 25.

36. See, for instance, the case put on behalf of married women workers by Emily Murphy, "Matrimony and the Matter of Money", *Western Home Monthly*, April 1932, 12-13, 54, 58.

37. See, *inter alia*, Dorothy Livesay, *Right Hand Left Hand* (Erin, Ont.: Press Porcepic Ltd., 1977) and Susan Walsh, "The Peacock and the Guinea Hen: Political Profiles of Dorothy Gretchen Steeves and Grace MacInnis" in *Not Just Pin Money. Selected Essays on the History of Women's Work in British Columbia*, edited by Barbara K. Latham and Roberta J. Pazdro (Victoria: Camosun College, 1984).

A PIONEER WOMAN IN THE LABOUR MOVEMENT†

ANNE B. WOYWITKA

Immigrant women in Canada have histories made unique by the widely varied process of ethnic group adjustment to Canadian life. At the same time they share with Canadian women of divergent ethnic backgrounds but equivalent economic and social circumstances, experiences to which they have often responded in a similar manner. Anne Woywitka's description of the Ukrainian labour activist, wife, and mother, Teklia Chaban, compels us to look beyond the stereotype of the silently enduring Ukrainian prairie woman. Right from her decision to immigrate to Canada through her participation in efforts to unionize Alberta's coal mines, Teklia, like many Canadian women, actively sought to improve her own life and that of others in the community. Wives such as this, much like members of the largely Anglo-Saxon Ladies' Auxiliary of the International Woodworkers of America in Vancouver Island's logging industry in the 1940s,* were indispensable allies in their menfolk's efforts to organize. Not only on the picket line itself but with their ability to manage the household on much less money during strikes, women like Teklia gave the union greater cause to hope for victory. In the 1970s Sudbury's Inco women called on similar reserves of strength to join battle with an employer who threatened male livelihoods and family survival. Particularly in single industry towns such as Cardiff, Alberta and Sudbury, Ontario, work and family have been so intimately and self-evidently connected that although women could rarely accede to "men's" jobs they might understand the frustrations of the male worker only too well. The resulting awareness of the justice of the union cause drew Teklia and many other women out of the home to intervene directly in workplace politics. In the twentieth century such activists were a force to be reckoned with in any labour conflict.

Life in the Ukraine for Teklia Chaban (nee Hryciw) was one of unhappiness. Deprived of schooling by parents who considered education for a girl as unnecessary, Teklia spent her childhood years at the turn of the century pasturing her father's cows on the village green while her contemporaries attended school. As she grew older, and still smouldering with resentment, she took on fieldwork and household chores to make herself useful around the home. The drabness of her life was relieved only by an occasional evening out in the company of other young people when they met in song and dance. Though eligible young men were scarce, many having emigrated to Canada, her parents kept insisting it was time for her to marry and settle down.

An uncle who had emigrated to Canada several years earlier had kept in touch with the family and in his letters he said there were a number of young men working with him who were anxious to marry but were unable to do so because of the lack of girls. Why didn't his niece come and see for herself?

---

†*Alberta History* XXVI, 1 (Winter 1978): 10-16.

*Sara Diamond, "A Union Man's Wife: The Ladies' Auxiliary Movement in the IWA, The Lake Cowichan Experience," in *Not Just Pin Money*, edited by Barbara K. Latham and Roberta J. Pazdro (Victoria: Camosun College, 1984).

The more Teklia thought about it, the stronger became her desire to emigrate. She was a pretty 20-year-old woman, outgoing by nature and full of life. In 1914 when the rumblings of an impending war became more pronounced and young men were being conscripted, Teklia knew it was time to leave. She broached the subject to her parents but it took a lot of talking to convince them that she, indeed, had made up her mind. In the end, they agreed to pay her fare to Canada in lieu of a dowry and, bidding farewell to family and friends, she was on her way at last.

Arriving in Canada, Teklia went to her uncle's home near the coal mines at Cardiff, 15 miles north of Edmonton. Her surroundings, though strange were nonetheless exciting. For one thing, young men in search of wives were plentiful and Teklia found herself the centre of attraction. But the field soon narrowed when Teklia fell in love with Steve Chaban, a 27-year-old miner who was steadily employed. He owned his home which, though not much, had a roof and was big enough to include a stove, table, bench and bed. They were married in December of 1914.

Steve also owned a horse and light delivery wagon and when not working in the mine, he delivered coal and other goods to householders in Cardiff and surrounding points. At Teklia's insistence, he soon added a cow, some chickens and a couple of little pigs. Teklia revelled in her new role. She was mistress in her own home. She milked the cow and what milk she couldn't use, she sold to her neighbours. She tended the chickens and had eggs for her own table and a few to sell. Young, strong and ambitious, she was anxious to get ahead but when she decided to take in washing, she found her house too small. Steve then obligingly added a lean-to to please his wife, making their home seem almost spacious.

Throughout the long winter evenings, Steve set out to teach Teklia to read and write the Ukrainian language. Not being the most patient teacher, there followed some stormy sessions before Teklia mastered the basics of reading and writing. But once this was accomplished, she found that reading broadened her horizons in a way she had not dreamed of; among the Cardiff miners she discovered a lot of reading material, much of it radical in nature.

She learned that centuries of oppression extending from the Tartar invasions to the days of Austro-Hungarian, Polish overlords, had helped to spawn a breed of men whose thinking differed from that of the subservient peasant. Works by such authors as Ivan Franko and Taras Shevchenko struck out at the injustices of the landed gentry and of the church against the peasant.

In the Ukraine, in spite of strict foreign rule, *chytalnie* or reading halls had sprung up in many villages. Readings of foremost writers were conducted in these halls, then discussed, the more revolutionary works being done in secret. The movement was strengthened by drama groups acting out plays, using this subtle form to bring home a message to the people without outwardly antagonizing their rulers. Theatre kept the young people interested because of its challenge. Older people enjoyed it for its entertainment value. Free thinking was encouarged.

At the time of Teklia's arrival in Canada, there was nothing to fill the miners' time after work except chess, cards and drinking beer at the Cardiff hotel. To those who were more aware, it seemed an awful waste of human resources. Accordingly, at the instigation of Peter Kyforuk, a few people met in Gregory

Waliuk's home in 1915 for a session of choral singing. Teklia, having sung in choral groups in the old country, was a popular participant. She had a rich contralto voice that inspired the others to excel. From that first day on, many of the miners' evenings were filled with song and good will, instead of the drinking and brawling at the pub.

At this time, the Cardiff miners were as yet unorganized. The three mines employed a total of 100 men and operated under the jurisdiction of the Alberta Coal Commission. The miners received $3.25 for an eight-hour day, which was comparable to unionized mines at the time. To meet war-time demands for coal, the miners worked on a steady basis.

In 1916, Michael Knizewich arrived from Winnipeg to organize the Social Democratic Party (Ukrainian Branch). Practically everybody joined and arrangements were made to rent the space above the local pool hall for meeting purposes. Stanley Luchka, who had directed a choral drama group in the old country, offered his services to the cultural group of the newly-organized branch. Once again, Teklia Chaban came to the fore. She had a natural talent for the theatre and a highly retentive memory so it became a matter of course that she played the leading role whether it be drama or comedy. Rehearsals throughout the long winter nights kept the amateur actors busy.

The Cardiff Cultural Group held its first concert early in 1916. A few weeks later, it was followed by a play. The hall, packed to capacity each time, included local patrons as well as people from Fedorah and Edmonton. From then on, each new production was awaited eagerly.

Late in the spring of 1916, the cast of players was invited to present their play at Waugh. Travelling by wagon over muddy trails, the 30-mile trip took the better part of the day. Portions of the road were so bad that the travellers were forced to take off their shoes and hitch up their skirts or trousers in order to wade through the mud, while the driver tried to drive through with the lighter load.

The play was presented on a makeshift stage in a newly-built barn on the Checknita homestead. Again, disregarding the poor condition of rural roads, people came from miles around. It was an opportunity to meet one's friends, as well as to be entertained. The event was a highlight in an otherwise hum-drum existence of the over-worked homesteader and his wife. It provided a topic of conversation for months, thanks to the efforts of the Cardiff group.

The arrival of a baby daughter temporarily slowed Teklia's participation in the Cardiff cultural life. For a while, she was fully occupied with the care of the baby, the housework and the outside chores, which included a garden. But she found it hard to give up the stage entirely. At times when she could coax Steve to stay with the baby, she would still attend the evening choral rehearsals which she loved dearly.

Throughout the war years, 1914-18, Steve Chaban continued to work in the mine while, after work hours, he made deliveries with his team and wagon. They soon owned two horses and a colt, as well as two milk cows, and since neither of them was afraid of work, they gradually made headway.

When the war ground to a halt in 1918, it brought about considerable social and industrial unrest. During the war, most of the miners had fallen under the government classification of "enemy aliens" as the Ukraine at the time was under the subjugation of the Austro-Hungarian Empire. Such aliens were registered with the police and were assigned jobs vital to the war effort. Their movements were restricted and they required police permission to change jobs or locations. But as long as they kept on working and producing, they had nothing to fear.

However, by early 1919, the industrial climate began to change. Orders for coal slackened drastically and miners were reduced to part-time work. Veterans returning from overseas expected to find employment but because there wasn't enough work to go around, the miners felt their jobs were threatened. A union seemed to be the answer so upon the invitation of Cardiff miners, I. McDonald, organizer for the United Mine Workers of America, came to address a local meeting.

The mine owners, getting wind of what was happening, attempted to prevent the miners from joining the union. Since the majority of the men were not Canadian citizens, their employers asked the police to intervene, using deportation as a threat. They also approached Peter Kyforuk, a serious young man with considerable influence among the miners, and tried to bribe him with an offer of foreman's position. In return, he was to oppose the union. When he refused, police were set on his trail, forcing him to go into hiding. In spite of these tactics, the Cardiff miners signed up with the U.M.W.A. but discovered the union was ineffectual when the coal companies refused to recognize it as a bargaining agent. Then, on May 24, 1919, when thousands of organized Canadian workers walked out in a General Strike in support of the One Big Union, Cardiff miners joined in sympathy. The mine owners retaliated by closing down the mines.

When the General Strike ended in failure, industries shifted into gear again. In Cardiff, the mines re-opened but a number of strikers, including Steve Chaban, lost their jobs. The situation provided a hot-bed for later developments in Cardiff, ending in strike and violence in 1922. Along with other miners, Steve was later re-hired but it brought home to the young couple the seriousness of the situation. They were more convinced than ever about the necessity of a strong union.

During this period, a split in the ranks of the Social Democratic Party (Ukrainian Branch) caused a serious upheaval in the organization. Following on the heels of the October Revolution in Russia, the Ukraine broke away from the Austro-Hungarian Empire to become a member of the Union of Soviet Socialist Republics. In Canada, this alliance met with strong disapproval from that segment of S.D.P. who were waiting for an independent Ukraine. Other splinter groups believed there was no alternative against foreign aggression by a vulnerable country like Ukraine, and approved of its union with Soviet Russia. This latter group, supported by Steve and Teklia Chaban, broke away from the parent body to become members of the Ukrainian Labour Temple Association.

In Cardiff, the entire membership of the Social Democratic Party (Ukrainian Branch) swung to the left and the Chabans, as members of the U.L.T.A. (later the Ukrainain Labour Farmer Temple Association), played an active role, both in the cultural and political aspects of the organization. In 1922, with the formation of the Women's Branch of the Association, Teklia took on further responsibilities in the work of the group.

Although based on ideological lines, the first objective of the Women's Branch was to abolish illiteracy among its members. There were oral readings of the *Working Woman*, published in the U.S., to acquaint the members with problems facing the working woman and her husband. The role of the woman in the industrial world was stressed and the organization took a stand against social problems like drinking and gambling. It declared that women had basic rights like limiting the size of their families and should have a say in the way their children were raised. There were also discussions and debates to encourage public speakers from among their ranks.

For many women, it was a glimpse of a world extending beyond the church and the kitchen. Meeting two or three times a week, some of them met with opposition from their husbands who felt threatened by the role of the "new woman". But for the members, it was the dawning of a new era and they were reluctant to give it up.

Teklia continued her participation in the field of song, music, drama and meetings, and by her efforts encouraged others to do likewise. She was now the mother of two little girls, but still found time to carry on with duties, both at home and out of it.

By the early 1920s, work at the Cardiff mines had become sporadic. There was considerable unemployment in the country and those who worked did so under a cloud, never sure when they, too, might be thrown out of work at the company's whim. Though Cardiff miners were members of the U.M.W.A., the union still had not been recognized by the companies, so it could do little for them. At this stage, pay for Cardiff and Edmonton area miners lagged far behind that received by the Drumheller and Crowsnest miners where the union had been recognized. When winter orders for coal increased, discontent among the miners increased also.

On November 10, 1922, a statement appeared in the *Edmonton Journal*: "It has been a matter of common knowledge that organizers of the United Mine Workers of America have been active in this district." This activity culminated in a general meeting in Edmonton on November 12 where it was decided to start a drive for members in District 18, an area involving a total of 1,100 miners in the Edmonton, Beverly, Clover Bar and Cardiff districts and in several other smaller mines.

In Cardiff, 80 percent of the miners were already signed up and, being the most militant of the group, they were the first to take action in the Edmonton district. In a letter sent by the U.M.W.A. to the Cardiff mine operators, it was stated that unless the companies recognized the union, the miners would not return to work. The miners wanted recognition of their union and a wage scale comparable to mines in the Drumheller area.

The mine owners, in refusing the demand, claimed they had not received any complaints from their employees through regular company channels. They also stated flatly they would not listen to any demand made by Calgary-based officials of the U.M.W.A. who said they were out to promote discord among the miners. In response to the letter, the companies closed all three Cardiff mines.

In turn, a general walkout was called by the union for the entire Edmonton area, but the other mines were able to remain open, operating with skeleton crews and scab labour. By December 1, the *Edmonton Journal* was able to proclaim:

"General Strike of miners proved fizzle in Edmonton field. Outside of Cardiff every mine in district is turning out coal."

Three days later, when Bill Ryan, secretary-organizer for the U.M.W.A., was arrested at the Black Diamond mine, the operators hoped the stike would collapse and the mines would re-open for full operation. Instead, the strike snowballed when 1,000 miners in Drumheller had a temporary wildcat walkout in sympathy for the Edmonton miners.

Although the Edmonton mines remained open in spite of the strike, they continued to operate on a much smaller scale. To protect the strike breakers, the mine operators called on the city and provincial government for police support. The availability of scab labour was assured when police officers were placed throughout the mining district to see that there would be no "breach of peace".

As the winter of 1922-23 progressed and cold weather deepened, orders for coal increased but the output was insufficient to supply the demand. As a result, the Cardiff operators decided to open their mines but when they approached the strikers and asked them to go back to work, the strikers refused. The companies then ordered the miners to remove their shacks located on company land. Steve Chaban, who was affected by this order, bought a plot of land and made arrangements to transfer his house. Meanwhile, the U.M.W.A. hired a tractor to pull the shacks off company property.

When their turn came, Steve's home was halfway across the railroad tracks, when it split in two. Teklia, following on foot with her two children, watched in horror. At 20 below zero, where would they all find shelter? She was deeply upset by what happened and her resentment against the companies increased. Steve patched the house together as best he could, then went back to the picket line. By this time, it was common knowledge that the companies had recruited 40 men and billeted them in the Cardiff hotel in readiness for the push to re-open at least one mine.

In the meantime, James Murdock, Minister of Labour in Ottawa, declared the strike for a closed shop in District 18 unlawful. Rumours of foreign influence, though denied by the miners, led to talk of a federal investigation and threats of deportation against the foreign-born strikers. Refusing to be intimidated, the Cardiff strikers held steadfast. It had been pre-arranged among themselves that one of their men, a Frenchman who was a bugler, would sound the call to action when the time came to fend off any strike-breakers.

Early in the pre-dawn of December 18, the strident notes of the bugle woke the restless strikers. The message had come, via the grapevine, that the companies with their scab labour were ready to force their way into the Cardiff mine. Men and women scrambled into their clothes and rushed to their posts.

Teklia, having made arrangements beforehand for the care of her children when the time came, hurried out into the cold winter darkness to join scores of other women. Stationed on the right-of-way to the mine where it crossed the railroad tracks, the women girded themselves on the first line of defence against the onslaught which they knew would come. Armed with stout sticks, they felt their blood pressures rise with dread and fear of the unknown danger ahead. But what affected their men affected them also, and they knew what had to be done. A few hundred feet away, their men waited, prepared to defend the entrance to the mine.

The women talked very little and then, only in whispers. The cold and the silence deepened around them as they waited. Then out of the darkness, they could make out the dark mass of men marching towards them on silent feet. The initial encounter between the women and their opponents burst into a frenzy of yells, shouts and loud curses. Sticks and clubs swung on both sides. Women screamed, men swore and struck, and received blows in return. In the end, the strike breakers forced their way through the crowd of women and rushed towards the mine entrance with the women in hot pursuit.

Alerted by the wild commotion, the Cardiff miners were well prepared for the onslaught of police and strike breakers. They met their attackers head-on, trading blow for blow until blood ran freely. In the enuing melee, six people were seriously hurt, among them Constable Olson who later died in a hospital. Many others were left to nurse their bruised heads, injured limbs and swollen eyes. In the end, enough strike breakers succeeded in breaking through the cordon to enter the mine and start working. Later, increased police protection for the scab force enabled them to keep the mines operating.

Teklia Chaban was among those arrested following the confrontation between strikers and the mine operators. Charged with disturbing the peace, she was given a year's suspended sentence; a few others received short jail sentences.

During the next few weeks, the strike was marked by successes and failures. On December 22, two small mines, the Frontier and the Premier, both agreed to recognize the U.M.W.A. as bargaining agent for the miners, but none of the other operators in Edmonton and district followed suit. Then, on January 2, more than a hundred strikers were arrested after a fight while picketing the Standard mine. It was later claimed that the battle had been instigated by paid company agents, resulting in the mass arrests of strikers. The number behind bars left both police quarters in Edmonton and the jail in Fort Saskatchewan crowded to the limit.

As an active supporter of the strike, Steve Chaban went with a few other men to lend a hand to the Beverly strikers, just east of Edmonton. Feelings had been running high in the little hamlet after an incident where mine operator Starkey had fired a number of shots into the air from the safety of his car. Then emerging from the vehicle and surrounded by a ring of police, he had offered to take on anybody who wanted to fight. This was the type of intimidation which the strikers were finding hard to cope with. Steve was there on January 5 when another bloody encounter occurred at the Penn mine. The fight lasted for 15 minutes and resulted in six men and five women being arrested. Later, Judge Emily Murphy gave suspended sentences to Mrs. Carpuk, Syroid, Onyschuk and Wozny.

During the winter, the prolonged strike caused severe hardships among the strikers' families and a delegation of five women, headed by Miss Vuhay, was obliged to meet with Edmonton Mayor Duggan with a petition for welfare help.

Repercussions of the strike were felt throughout the province and there were rumours that the federal government was sending the R.C.M.P. to help the provincial police. The general feeling among the strikers was one of deep resentment against the injustice meted out to them by the combined efforts of the mine owners, Edmonton city council, the provincial and the federal governments. As a result, when the Federal Mine Inspector offered to investigate the causes of the strike, both parties declined.

At this point, the Alberta Federation of Labour had joined in the discussions and although the mine operators consented to meet with their committee of five on January 20, nothing came of it.

That same night, the hotel in Cardiff, which housed the 40 scab miners, burned down to the ground and, although arson was suspected, it was never proved. The men were lodged in a railway car for the duration of the remainder of the strike.

Late in February, a large number of accused picketers were put on trial. Eighty-three were given suspended sentences, 28 were fined $25 each and one man received a month in jail. A few days later, five more were given suspended sentences and six were each given three months in jail.

No sooner were the men released, than their families were taken off relief. Funds, never sufficient, were now non-existent. Striking families had to be fed and clothed and homes had to be kept warm. Conditions in the Chaban home were probably not as critical as in many others. They still had their own milk, butter, cheese, eggs, potatoes, and cabbage. But money for other essentials was scarce. Forced to contend with these adverse conditions, the strikers, one by one, began to drift back to work and the backbone of the strike was broken without the miners having achieved their objective.

After a while, Steve, too, went back to ask for work but he was turned down, probably because of the prominent role he had played in the strike. Together with several others who were not re-hired, Steve found work in the Sturgeon mine, four miles from Cardiff, and remained there until 1924, walking to and from work, regardless of the weather.

In the spring of 1924, Steve and Teklia sold their home and land and moved to Edmonton. This marked the end of their mining days. In Edmonton, Steve went to work for Swift Canadian Packers and through the sale of their home and through frugal perseverance, they managed to save enough money to buy a modest home in north-east Edmonton. While Steve worked, Teklia took care of home, children, garden, cow and chickens and also kept several boarders.

In spite of the setbacks suffered through their participation in the strikes in 1919 and 1922-23, they remained steadfast in their convictions. In Edmonton, they became members of the local U.L.F.T.A. where Teklia continued her cultural work walking three miles of railroad track each way in order to attend meetings and rehearsals.

In 1932, her active participation in the Hunger March in Edmonton brought a suspended sentence for Teklia, her second within ten years. Five years later, Steve was among the 147 men, less than half of the total employed at Swift's, to go on a sitdown strike in demand for a 5½ day week. Again Teklia went on the picket line where she suffered injury and again Steve lost his job and was not rehired.

During their early years, Steve and Teklia had always been active in support of the labour movement, but as they grew older they willingly let younger people take over where they had left off. They finally retired to live in their own home where they had time to enjoy their garden and to think of times long past. Somewhere along the way, perhaps they stopped to assess what they had been able to contribute to the well-being of the men and the women who followed after them.

VIVIAN DOWDING: BIRTH CONTROL ACTIVIST
1892–†

MARY F. BISHOP

Demography, the study of the characteristics of human populations, has been used as a first tool with which to illuminate the daily existence of people in the past and hence the lives of women, often more confined to the private sphere. The age at marriage, the size and make-up of a household, the number of children, and the age at death are all important data, allowing us to form a realistic notion of the prevalence of extended families, the frequency of widowhood, and the years women spent in childrearing.

Demographers tell us that Canada's birthrate has been dropping since 1871. Such a decline is interesting, especially since, as Mary Bishop reminds us, birth control was illegal in Canada from 1892 until 1968. At this point we must move beyond the externals of laws and statistics about birthrates to probe deeper. Knowing that the birthrate declined does not tell us how or why it declined. Clearly, unless there was some biological reason for decreased fertility, people must have found ways of circumventing the legal system's prohibition of birth control devices. Who wanted fewer children? Was it women or men, or were they in agreement? Some historians have maintained that nineteenth-century women, believing that they should have a greater say about the frequency of pregnancy and the number of children, struggled for control of marital sexuality. Certainly there exists enough popular lore on the subject to suggest that prevention of conception was a central concern of a female-based culture. Relatives and friends passed on remedies. In the nineteenth century, social and economic changes may also have made the prospect of a large family frightening. Birthrates seem to have declined first where there were shortages of good farmland for sons. Compulsory schooling and factory laws aimed at curbing excesses in child labour also turned children from an asset to a drain on family resources until a later age than in previous generations.

The technology for making adequate birth control devices was there; it was a question of making the devices available to those who were interested. Because of the long-term illegality of the subject, there are minimal records of the dissemination and use of contraceptives in Canada. Without oral histories, such as this one dealing with Vivian Dowding, we would underestimate the degree to which birth control devices were being employed even by the poor as early as the 1930s. Women in small town and rural British Columbia were not unusual in seeking help to reduce births. Women's pages of every newspaper, and female doctors in particular, were frequently used as resources. Whatever advice and concrete assistance they could offer supplemented women's own informal exchange of information.

The legal risks of birth control[1] promotion more than forty years ago never thwarted Vivian Dowding as she drove the back roads of British Columbia in her work for women's welfare. Employed as a field worker by the Parents' Information Bureau (PIB) of Kitchener, Ontario, and based in Kamloops, she brought this preventive health program to low-income women in the BC interior every summer from 1937 to 1944. At the same time, by correspondence, and

†*Not Just Pin Money. Selected Essays on the History of Women's Work in British Columbia*, edited by Barbara K. Latham and Roberta J. Pazdro (Victoria: Camosun College, 1984): 327–335.

without fee, she advised Reverend A.H. Tyrer of Toronto in the preparation of *Where Did WE Come From, Mother Dear?* This must have been the first factual "sex education" book for children ever published in Canada.[2] She returned to PIB work in the Vancouver area from 1956 to about 1965. Dowding's story is particularly interesting because of the background against which her activism developed, and because to her it was more than a job: her mission was to help other women end their fears of unwanted pregnancy. Although she knew the dangers of the work, she "enjoyed every minute of it."[3]

To understand the background of Dowding's motivation, one should know that, after World War I, the climate for birth control advocacy was full of contradictions. Birth control had been illegal since 1892. Section 207 of the Criminal Code of Canada stated that, unless an accused could prove that promotion or provision of birth control methods had not "corrupted morals" but was "for the public good", a conviction could bring two years in prison.[4] Also, the subject was taboo in "polite" conversation. Nevertheless, by abstinence, by contraception, by induced abortion, even infanticide, the crude birthrate of Canada had been declining since before the national census of 1871. Total fertility had shrunk from 6.8 children per married woman in 1871 to 2.6 children in 1937. Although prosperous couples had smaller families, high fertility among poor women remained.[5] For many of the latter, escape from debilitating annual pregnancies was a continuing quest. Those who had no knowledge of contraception, or whose attempts at contraception failed, often risked their lives through self-induced abortions or visits to illegal practitioners. Some women died.

The practice of contraception proceeded to discredit the 1892 law. The well-to-do could purchase commercially made contraceptives from "under the counter" of a friendly pharmacist, or they could obtain materials for homemade birth control methods through department store mail order catalogues. But not the poor. Because health and welfare services for low-income families were meagre or non-existent, many social reformers urged the use of birth control. Not only was a small family a right, but maternal and child health would benefit. Relatively effective methods of birth control did exist, they said, and governments should offer them free to all who wanted them.

From the 1920s, a few Western Canadian feminists like Violet McNaughton of the *Western Producer*, quietly told inquirers how to get help.[6] Nellie McClung and Judge Emily Murphy wrote in favour of the idea.[7] In the British Columbia Legislature in the 1930s, MLAs Dorothy Steeves and Laura Jamieson advocated provision of birth control information and services.[8] Members of some women's organizations, for example, the United Farm Women of Alberta in 1932, passed resolutions demanding such programs.[9] Unlike the fight for the vote, however, women did not mobilize large pressure groups to win the birth control "cause". Only a few small groups dared to try. Some health and welfare professionals and public officials privately supported the idea, but they used the 1892 law to justify their inaction.

Although some growth-oriented business, religious, and political interest groups were strongly opposed to birth control, one fearless exception was Dowding's employer, Canadian industrialist A.R. Kaufman, who manufactured rubber boots. This philanthropist believed that palliative measures were useless in meeting social needs. Therefore, early in 1930 he began to establish birth control services for the Kitchener unemployed. Being a cautious man, he obtained legal advice and through his factory nurse he sought the opinions of his own laid-off workers. Their response was positive. After experiments in service delivery, Kaufman settled on a closely controlled, cost-effective system of home-visiting followed by mailing safe, easy-to-use contraceptives. The non-profit program could meet demand and yet serve "the public good".

Kaufman continued his defiance of the 1892 law. By mid-1930s he had expanded the service by employing married women as nurse organizers and field workers in many parts of Canada. Unexpectedly, one of the Parents' Information Bureau staff, Dorothea Palmer,[10] who was charged with violation of Section 207 of the Criminal Code was arrested in an Ottawa suburb in 1936. After a lengthy trial, Kaufman's lawyers won a landmark defence based on "the public good". Records of the PIB program are incomplete,[11] and most of the employees have disappeared; however, Vivian Dowding's story describes the role of the field worker, and brings out its human interest aspects.

In a society changing its attitudes towards birth control, Dowding's motivation to work for the PIB lay also in her own experience with pregnancy and birth control, and her growing feminism. Before her marriage in Kamloops in 1913, her mother had instructed her in douching for prevention of conception. Planning to space her pregnancies, Dowding managed very well for the first three years with this method alone. When it failed, she had three sons in three years:

> I tell you, when I got pregnant the third time, I was just about ready to jump off a bridge. I was just in tears. My husband would take me to a picture show or something, and as soon as I came out of the picture show I would drip tears all the way home. . . . I didn't want another one so quickly.[12]

She and her husband used contraceptives to avoid another pregnancy. They had some success with foam tablets and she recalls nightly trips to the kitchen tap to check condoms for leaks. Faced with such uncertainty, she decided to learn all she could about contraception. Reading about Margaret Sanger's fight for birth control, Dowding developed a strong admiration for her courage.

She wrote to Sanger in New York for a copy of the "revised fourteenth edition" of *Family Limitation*, re-issued by Sanger's Clinical Research Bureau about 1930. Dowding treasured it for many years. The pamphlet contained information about contraceptives. It described the condom, the "pessary" or rubber womb cap, and several examples of diaphragms and cervical caps. Also, it told how to block the entrance to the cervix with a sea sponge or cotton tampon soaked in a spermicide. It gave recipes, too, for homemade, soluble, vaginal contraceptive suppositories. The pamphlet doubted the effectiveness of the "safe period", coitus interruptus (withdrawal), breast feeding, and the douche, but it did recommend douching "for cleanliness".[13] As time went on, the diaphragm became the most popular and, seemingly the most effective, method in North America.

Also, Dowding wrote to Reverend A.H. Tyrer, a retired Anglican clergyman in Toronto who, in the early 1930s, was becoming well known for his well-researched birth control information. Tyrer sent her his own leaflet. A lengthy correspondence followed, during which Tyrer sent Dowding drawings of human male and female reproductive organs, and a description of the physiology of human reproduction. Dowding also acquired a diaphragm for herself.[14]

By this time, since Kaufman and Tyrer were also collaborating, Tyrer recommended Dowding as a prospective PIB field worker in British Columbia. To help other women in this special way appealed to her feminism. Furthermore, the job was a unique combination of service and adventure. Because her husband had taught her how to drive their car, she agreed to work for the PIB in the BC Interior.

Dowding began her mission in the summer of 1937. She does not recall the number of women she visited during those seven years, but she worked for the PIB every summer until she and her husband moved to Vancouver in 1944. She would make calls from Kamloops east to Salmon Arm and Vernon, or north to Quesnel and Wells, near Barkerville. She might travel north to the lumber town of Giscome, north-east of Prince George. Another summer she might go west to Lytton, and the Bralorne mine, or east and south through the Okanagan Valley and Trail or to the Lower Fraser Valley. She was determined to deliver the program wherever there was demand.[15]

Although Kaufman had won the Palmer defence in Ontario there was always a chance that opponents of the Parents' Information Bureau in BC would challenge it in some way, and that Dowding, too, might be harassed. In those days, too, it took courage to drive alone over the narrow gravel highways in the province. It took more courage to negotiate the steep side roads and hair-raising switch-backs leading to logging and mining camps where she had heard wives were waiting for her help. She recalled one place where she had to drive across a deep gulch on two boards! In another place:

> You could only use the road at certain times because of the trucks coming down, and there were places where you couldn't pass, and it meant backing up. I only went over that road once, but if there was only one woman up there who needed me, I'd go again. They knew I had a feeling for them. One woman told me she even thought of setting fire to the house, and burning herself and the whole family — she was so beside herself.
>
> My work was to be with people that were low income. I wasn't to go house-to-house. I was to go to a doctor first, and tell him who I was, and why I was there. And I got a wonderful reception, most of the time.

Many doctors told her that they knew nothing about contraception, which was not taught in medical schools. When a few had learned anything about it, they had learned from each other. Although some doctors had sets of rubber rings to measure diaphragm size, their skills were uncertain. One woman told Dowding that she had been given a pessary so large that it had popped out of her vagina when she leaned over the baby buggy!

Doctors were not her only source of referrals; Dowding was expected to get them from local women. When she arrived in a new community where there was no obvious starting point, she would find the poorest looking neighbourhood and look for a clothesline covered with diapers. She would be welcomed, Dowding said, and referrals would be easy from that moment on. She said, "Everybody knew who had a baby; and they often discussed their birth control problems with each other."

Using Tyrer's drawings, Dowding would explain ovulation, fertilization, and contraceptive methods. She would tell them that two methods used together were more effective than one; for example, a condom with contraceptive jelly was a recommended combination. With each client, Dowding would fill out an application form for contraceptives. The necessary information included the number of children, living and dead; the woman's medical history, including her abortions; income, condition of the house, and religion. Her desired methods would be listed. If the client's doctor had fitted her for a diaphragm, its size and the doctor's signature were added. If the woman was illiterate, a friend could sign the request. Then, Dowding would send the application, with her own comments, to the PIB in Kitchener. As the PIB was always watching for enemies, the application would be scrutinized.

When the request was approved, a package of contraceptives would be mailed directly to the applicant. A leaflet describing all the methods and the locations of other sources of relevant information would be enclosed. The box would contain contraceptive jelly with an applicator, condoms, and/or foam powder to be used with a sponge or an absorbent cotton tampon. The first package was usually free. From that point on, the woman was expected to reorder. If she could afford a "donation" of two dollars she would enclose it. When she was unable to pay the charge, she explained her reasons, so that Kaufman could authorize free service.

The PIB paid Dowding. Her wage of two dollars per client, even in the Depression years, was enough to cover her travelling expenses and leave extra income for herself. On the road, the she would usually stay at a local hotel or, if necessary, at a client's house. Her first visits were in Salmon Arm. She recalled:

> I was absolutely amazed at the number there who were on relief.[16] Some were so poor I often bought food for them. They lived in hovels — in shacks and lean-tos they had built themselves. Some had to walk miles for their relief cheques. The men working in the relief camps for twenty cents a day were better off.[17] . . . I was always well received. A woman turned me down only once. That was in the Mission district . . . but she was really nice about it. The doctor there was the only [medical] exception, and he was very rude. I was in his office and he practically pushed me out. . . . The waiting room was full of people . . . and I was very embarrassed. He told me he wasn't interested in any way, shape or form, and that he was going to get the police to run me out of town. I went to the police myself, and told them the doctor was trying to put me out of town for talking birth control to mothers. They told me not to worry. It would be all right. So I went on just the same. . . . Every other doctor was cooperative — terrifically so.[18]

In Trail, Dowding found numerous clients, but when their PIB packages started coming in the mail, the postmaster held every one. She thinks he opened one, or perhaps one broke open. In any case, he believed the contents were illegal. When one of the women told Dowding that she had not received her box, Dowding recalled the following: "I went to the post office. When I looked through the wicket I could see them . . . so I wrote Mr. Kaufman . . . and they were out of there in no time."

In Chilliwack, the wife of a returned World War Two soldier was in very poor health from repeated pregnancies, yet her husband was demanding more babies so that she would receive more family allowances. Dowding said, "She was so frightened of another pregnancy that she sort of hung on to me. I was glad to help her".[19] Also, Kaufman was willing to finance voluntary sterilizations for poor women; Dowding arranged many such operations. Sometimes, however, she would fail. On one occasion a school teacher asked her to call on a young woman with several children who was living common law with an older man.

> I was told that the children would never get past grade two or three. So I went there and talk about flies!! I never saw the likes of it. . . . A smelly little baby in a crib, with flies all over it. Oh dear! I went to a store and bought a dozen of those fly things and told her to put them up. Then I persuaded that girl to have a sterilization. Because she wasn't married, I had to get her mother's consent. Then I told the doctor that Kaufman would pay $25.00 for the operation. He said he would have to take it up with the hospital board because there was no one to pay the hospital bill. I said, "Well, the hospital is going to have a baby every year, so who's going to pay for that?" The hospital gave in, and I got it all arranged, but that old man talked her out of it. Said he'd leave her if she had the operation. Oh dear! What a case!

Dowding's interest in birth control involved her in education beyond BC. Although she never met Tyrer in person, he consulted her by mail during the late 1930s about the content of *Where Did WE Come From, Mother Dear?* This forty-six page book assisted mothers who wanted to answer children's questions honestly. The opening chapter on fathers and mothers was followed by a discussion of babies and love, a description of love among the flowers, and finally sections on fish and birds. The book described human babies and conception and concluded, "Love is the greatest thing in the world!" Some of the illustrations were done by one of Dowding's sons, then a student at the University of Toronto. The foreword was written by Dr. Alan Brown, internationally known physician-in-chief at the Hospital for Sick Children, Toronto. Support for the booklet came from the National Committee for Mental Hygiene, from the eminent psychiatrist Dr. Brock Chisholm, and others.[20] Tyrer's debt to Dowding was acknowledged in his inscription of her copy: "With love and deep regard to my dear friend Vivian Dowding, to whom I owe more than I can ever repay for many suggestions, and still more for much inspiration in my later life work. Toronto, Ontario, March 12, 1940."[21]

A sixteen-page promotional leaflet, *Your Child Needs Your Help*, urged the use of *Where Did WE Come From*, also available in French, to assist children in understanding their sexuality. Parents were urged to explain wet dreams and menstruation to boys and girls before either event occurred. Emphasis was placed on informing children about venereal diseases and their consequences. Circumcision was not necessary, it continued, nor would masturbation cause insanity, as was commonly believed.[22]

As noted, Dowding returned to PIB work in the Vancouver area in 1956.[23] Starting in 1960, a new birth control association, the Society for Population Planning, was being formed in Vancouver so she was no longer alone in the advocacy field. According to its minutes, many of its first cases were referred to her and the PIB, but she was also a member of its executive committee in 1961 and 1962.[24] Before she retired in 1965, Dowding's support for birth control included voluntary sterilization for men.

By 1960, vasectomy was becoming very popular in British Columbia, but men had to travel to the United States for the procedure. When, early in 1963, Dr. Philip M. Alderman of North Vancouver added the operation to his general practice, Dowding asked him to accept her referrals. Alderman recalled:

> Mrs. Dowding and I seemed to be riding some kind of crest of interest in and popularity of vasectomy, and, within a year or two, she was referring dozens of patients to me each month. I was doing many more than I ever dreamed of, and everybody seemed pleased with what was going on.[25]

In her reminiscences, she stressed that she had been very happy in her work and would do it all again. She said, "I can hardly remember a town I wasn't in." Her sympathetic understanding of other women's fears "just seemed . . . to put some new spark of life in them".[26] Dowding remains a staunch supporter of the birth control movement, and of the principle of voluntary choice.

Notes

1. The term "birth control" was coined by Margaret Sanger and her friends in New York in 1914. It meant "pregnancy prevention," i.e., contraception, and did not include induced abortion.

2. A.H. Tyrer, *Where Did WE Come From, Mother Dear?* (Toronto: Marriage Welfare Bureau, 1939), *passim*. Private Collection.

3. Vivian Dowding, adapted from an interview and other conversations with the author from November 1, 1978, to March, 1984. See also Mary F. Bishop, "The Early Birth Controllers of BC," *BC Studies* (Spring 1984). All uncited quotations are from the above interviews and conversations.

4. Some forbidden activities included under "publishing obscene matter," Section 207 of the Criminal Code of Canada, as adopted in 1892, were manufacture, sale, or distribution of any obscene book or other printed matter, or any picture or model, or any indecent show, "any means of instruction or any medicine, drug, or article represented as a means of preventing conception or of causing abortion . . . or an advertisement of any means, instruction, medicine, drug, or article for restoring sexual virility or curing venereal diseases or diseases of the generative organs." *Journal of the House of Commons, Dominion of Canada*, Ottawa, 1890–1892, Reel 301. The phrase "preventing conception or" was not removed from the Criminal Code until 1969. See also Mary F. Bishop, "The Politics of Abortion . . . Revisited," *Atlantis* 9, 1 (Fall 1983): 106–117.

5. Jacques Henripin, *Trends and Factors of Fertility in Canada* (Ottawa: Statistics Canada, 1972), Catalogue C599–541/1972, Table 2.3: 30. See also T.R. Balakrishnam, G.E. Ebanks, and C.P. Grindstaff, "Total Fertility Rate, 1902–1971, and Fertility Cohorts born from 1874–1938, Canada", *Patterns of Fertility in Canada*, 1971 (Ottawa: Statistics Canada, December, 1979), Catalogue 99–759E, Chart 1.1: 31; Table

1.7: 39; p. 248. See also Neil Collishaw, *Fertility in Canada* (Ottawa: Statistics Canada, 1976), Catalogue 99–706, Bulletin 5:1–6, especially "Differential Fertility", 3.3; 3.4; 3.5; pp. 37–60, and "Summary and Conclusions": 61.

6. Violet McNaughton to Mrs. T.B. Wilson, Harris, Saskatchewan, 6 May 1922, 12 June 1923; McNaughton to A. Morgan, Aquadell, Saskatchewan, 15 May 1922. McNaughton Papers, Saskatchewan Archives Board.

7. For example, *Clearing in the West* (Toronto: Thomas Allen, 1935): 208, 335. "Janey Canuck," *The Vancouver Sun*, 27 August: 5; 3 September: 3; 10 September: 4; 17 September: 2; 24 September: 5; 1 October: 2, 1932.

8. Mary F. Bishop, "The Early Birth Controllers of BC".

9. *Birth Control Review*, March, 1932: 93.

10. Dorothea Palmer's married name is Ferguson.

11. Kaufman did not end the program until 1976. Whether he feared more lawsuits, or was merely following business practice, Kaufman stripped his files regularly. Although he was accused of manufacturing condoms, he only briefly manufactured average size diaphragms and foam powders. Author's unpublished research.

12. Vivian Dowding, see note 3.

13. Margaret Sanger, *Family Limitation*, 14th edition (1930). From the author's private collection.

14. Ibid. Dowding has described how, in 1933, a group of friends in Kamloops brought Laura Vaughan from her private clinic in Vancouver to Kamloops for a public meeting on the need for local services. They had rented another room where Vaughan fitted a number of women for diaphragms. Dowding acquired her own diaphragm at that time. See also Mary F. Bishop, "The Early Birth Controllers of BC".

15. See note 3.

16. Ibid.

17. Vivian Dowding, interview with Sara Diamond, Vancouver, 1978(?) Tape 2045 B, Simon Fraser University Library, Reserve.

18. See note 3.

19. Ibid.

20. Muriel Tyrer, Letters to Tyrer dated 30 December 1939, 28 January 1940, respectively. Private Collection.

21. See note 3.

22. *Your Child Needs Your Help* (Toronto: Marriage Welfare Bureau, n.d., probably 1940). Hugh Dobson Papers, Box 13, File 7, United Church Archives, Vancouver School of Theology, UBC, Vancouver BC.

23. Anna S. Weber, RN, Parent's Information Bureau, Kitchener, Ontario, to Vivian Dowding, 19 July 1956, given to author.

24. Planned Parenthood Association of BC (formerly Society for Population Planning), minutes 13 April, 30 October, 20 November, 1961; 25 April; 13 September, 1962.

25. Phillip M. Alderman, North Vancouver, interview with author, 25 June 1979.

26. See note 3.

"AN IDIOT'S FLOWERBED" — A STUDY OF CHARLOTTE WHITTON'S FEMINIST THOUGHT, 1941–50†

PATRICIA T. ROOKE AND R.L. SCHNELL

Charlotte Whitton (1896–1975) had two careers, each of which made her famous in her day. In her first she did much to professionalize social work and to reform child welfare practices in Canada. In her second she was the high-profile first woman mayor of Ottawa. There was an involuntary hiatus between these two pursuits during which Whitton rethought, as people often do in periods of crisis or transition, her assumptions about success, marriage, and individual effort. For most of Whitton's life feminism was something she lived, rather than spoke or wrote or agitated about. During that one, difficult decade, however, in figuring out what was going wrong in her life, Whitton brought to the surface and articulated many of the tensions implicit in the feminist lifestyle of women of her era.

Born at the end of the first generation of women to whom a career was available as an alternative to marriage, Whitton pondered the choices and decided for the expansive, public life of a career over the more private service and pleasures of marriage. Like others of her time, she firmly believed that she could not have both, that one way or another, women had to make a sacrifice. With a like-minded female companion, Whitton built a full and interesting life, largely among women. Her public experience in social welfare work, like her private life, contained many women, but it was conducted on the same terms as men's. Patricia T. Rooke and R.L. Schnell characterize it as "stern, competitive, plainspoken, ambitious and flamboyant." Her views of both spheres, private and public, were quite conventional. She accepted them as she found them, arguing mainly that women should have the opportunity to choose the male world if they wanted, and should be rewarded for whatever talent and energy they displayed. Although she voluntarily and pleasurably lived more completely than most women in a female culture, she did not feel she had much in common with the majority of married women.

Consequently when her successful social welfare career ended, Whitton was ill-prepared for a period of failure in the male world. She found it difficult to confront the biases of people who seemed predisposed to relegate her to the status of other women despite her renunciation of conventional female life. While Whitton became more sensitive than ever before to the difficulties of women's position in the public sphere, she was not ready to deal with the preoccupations that would face increasing numbers of women in the postwar years, namely, how to combine, whether out of necessity or choice, the two worlds of home and work. Both these worlds would need restructuring if women were to be comfortable in them. It was not until the modern feminist movement that Canadian women were ready to confront the separate spheres as inexorably intertwined.

†*International Journal of Women's Studies* 5, 1 (January–February 1982): 29–46. The authors acknowledge the S.S.H.R.C. and the University of Calgary Research Grants Office for assistance in support of the research on which this paper is based.

> I get all sorts of little piles, all hoarded up, of similar colours . . . looking like an idiot's flower bed — and then I start and lift them all in great pieces, into the pattern which I have had in my mind's eye. — Charlotte Whitton (1944)[1]

Charlotte Whitton's cheerfully casual observation as to how she solved jigsaw puzzles in contrast to more timid souls who picked out "the straight edges and filled out the frame" provides us with the *leitmotif* for our essay. Since historians tend also to see history as an unsolved jigsaw puzzle and hopefully arrange pieces into an "interpretation," the metaphor seems an appropriate way of looking at the complex pieces of this extraordinary woman's feminist thought.

Given Whitton's enormous significance, it is surprising that few Canadians know of her work in child welfare between 1920 and 1941. Although many of the older generation would assert her significance lies in the fact that between 1950 and 1964 she was the much publicized first woman major of Ottawa, most of the younger generation would not even know that. Yet Whitton did more to reform child welfare and to professionalize social work across the nation than any other Canadian. In no English-speaking province was her presence not felt.[2]

Moreover the authors are bold enough to claim that no woman in Canadian history exceeds this formidable and sometimes irascible social reformer in importance for a span of some 40 years. From 1920 when she began a singular career in the Canadian Welfare Council until her retirement in 1941, Whitton reached heady heights of national influence. Her contemporaries described her variously as "Canada's best known and most provocative woman" and "Canada's social work ambassador extraordinary."[3] The decade between 1941 and 1951 was a decade in which she articulated most clearly her feminist views as a lecturer, writer, and publicist, in an apprenticeship which prepared her for municipal politics.

The purpose of this paper is to examine, not her outstanding contributions to Canadian social work and child welfare, which have been discussed elsewhere, nor her well-known years in civic politics, but the decade between these two careers. These years could be seen initially as a hiatus in her life and certainly, in contemporary parlance, a period of "mid-life crisis" and "retooling." These were the years when she preached the feminism that she had lived. The paper is divided into three parts. Part one discusses the first piece of the jigsaw which was to direct her whole future in social work and her feminist views — her decision not to marry. Part two examines her mid-life crisis in terms of the objective reality she faced in her own career pattern, which in turn sharpened her awareness of feminist issues, and contrasts this period with her previous experiences. Part three examines some aspects of her feminist involvement and the views she expressed during this period.

The unmarried state has provided for women a viable alternative to the restrictions of precontraceptive marriage with its onerous demands of family and household. Nevertheless it was relatively infrequent that such a drastic course (for so it seems to the more timid) was deliberately and self-consciously made. Therefore when such a decision is recorded in the correspondence of an influential social reformer her subsequent public life takes on more meaning than perhaps it would otherwise. Charlotte Whitton's voluminous correspondence was carefully put aside by the woman herself so that future biographers might understand both the radical nature of her decision regarding marriage and the extent of her contribution to child welfare in English Canada.[4]

Whitton's youthful correspondence tells us much about her views of her own temperament, ambitions, and visions of society. Even before she entered Queen's University, a pattern had been forming in her mind's eye and its colours were bright by the time she graduated from this prestigious Canadian institution. Consequently, her friends had complete faith in the future of this energetic, brilliant, and capable young woman, assuming that she was made "of the stuff [of] women who accomplish things in their world," and that she would make "the world a better place . . . for having lived in it."[5]

However, Whitton anguished over the temptations of marriage and motherhood feeling dismayed at her desire for a career in social work, a field which offered scope for her social vision, her organizational genius, and the affective side of a generous and a passionate nature. She lamented the fact that "any sensibility of lurking incompleteness" always haunted her "to the point of sheer temper" and knew that marriage must interfere with her singlemindedness of purpose. She recognized her tendency to "dictate" and "dominate" and her lack of patience with others or tolerance for opposition, criticism, or even advice — characteristics which remained with her throughout her life. Yet the words of a mentor from her adolescent years persuaded her that she was indeed "capable of serving her time and generation in a large way."[6]

Whitton was the first paid worker for the Social Service Council of Canada in 1918 before moving on to the Canadian Council on Child Welfare (CCCW) in Ottawa two years later. At the time of her first job, a close friend of "the young cyclone" in a warm and humorous letter mentioned that Whitton's sense of service to society as well as her temperament and ideals meant that when she gave of herself — either in a career or in friendship — it had to be "all or not at all." "Yet," her friend continued, "that decision will involve sacrifice which will perhaps leave a place in your woman's heart forever unfulfilled." A year later this same friend observed that she could never picture Charlie as a "kitchen ornament or a fireside tabby cat" but she wondered whether Whitton's fears regarding the future and the seductions of marriage were needless or whether her ambitions might result in "a lonely middle age."[7]

In 1923 an ardent admirer from her Queen's days and whose courtship spanned ten years wrote to her about his jealousy not of a rival but of her "love of work" and her provincial success. He felt that he could not compete with the political and influential contacts she was already making as secretary to Mr. Lowe, Minister of Trade, while serving as honorary secretary to the CCCW. He had asked her two years before if she would ever again be able "to drop back into low gear" while regretfully noting that "it was by reasonable assumption" that she would become a "figure of prominence in a short time given the rate she was travelling." It is apparent that he could not see himself as part of the pattern of leadership rapidly unfolding nor could he keep abreast with the enthusiastic buzz of her letters always written "in everlasting haste."[8]

By the age of twenty-eight, Charlotte had made up her mind not to marry. She had withstood the stress of courtship from Bill King and had refused a proposal from another equally eligible admirer.[9] The first piece of the jigsaw was in place, making room for the next piece which would naturally fit in her full time career. This second piece, by far the most pivotal, was a twenty year love affair with child and social welfare. The pattern in her mind's eye was set into motion.

Whitton was fully cognizant of the choice that she had made as hers was a generation bereft of many of the liberating aspects available to present marriages and a generation which was sometimes brutally forced to face a single life (and frequently a celibate one) if women were to devote themselves fully to a career. Too often the choice was either/or — either marriage and motherhood or career and independence. Many of Whitton's generation faced their single futures with bleak hearts because the war had spoiled their chances but Whitton was not among the involuntarily unmarried. In a 1943 article, "Women and the Future of Family Life," she referred to the "shattered dreams" of women after the Great War and pointed out that she had chosen to go "proudly unwedded."[10] Instead Charlotte Whitton chose to share her companionship and domesticity for almost thirty years with her most intimate friend and career woman, Margaret Grier, who was the assistant secretary for the Anti-Tuberculosis Association and assistant to the Deputy Minister of Labour.

In a 1947 feminist address presented as the first lecture in the Susan B. Anthony Memorial series at the University of Rochester, Whitton observed that of the several classes of women over the centuries one historical alternative had existed "for the woman who remained in control of her own life or who attained . . . and found interesting, life and companionship, with others of the same sex."[11] Whitton's life testifies to the comfort she found in this alternative. For although several men in social work retained deep and abiding ties of collegiality and friendship with her, Whitton's most interesting and satisfying contacts were with women from all walks of life, and by some accounts, hers was a charmed circle of gracious and capable female associates in which one felt privileged to be included.

It seems, too, that her attractions to her own sex remained with her: if a friend from Queen's could write of "light days and magical evenings" spent in her company in 1916, some thirty years later, on the occasion of her fiftieth anniversary, another friend congratulated her with equal warmth on the celebration held at her's and Margaret's home in Ottawa. "There was no flaw — flowers so gay and beautiful and two hostesses blooming like the loveliest of them," she wrote.[12] Whitton's private life was a woman's world of affection, loyalty, generosity, hospitality, and gentility whereas her public life was stern, competitive, plainspoken, ambitious, and flamboyant.

It is noteworthy that Whitton's most vocal feminism coincided with a new consciousness in her middle years regarding her single status and the tenuous position she found herself in as a "free lance" woman publicist. This new and anomalous position sharpened her awareness of the socio-economic inequities between the sexes. From 1941 to 1950, after she had retired from the leadership of the Canadian Welfare Council and before she triumphantly captured the imagination of Ottawa's electorate, Whitton's statements on the status of women became increasingly more vigorous. She had, of course, spoken about woman's socially subordinate role in more general and muted ways previously, while at the same time exemplifying its opposite assumptions as an able and aggressive reformer.

During her leadership in child welfare she had asserted feminist views wherever these seemed necessary but generally her energies were taken up by the extraordinary events of her life and its never ending commitments. Royal commissions into social and child welfare, inquiries into delinquency and industrial training, investigations into relief and unemployment, surveys of child care and social agencies in all major cities and provinces, as well as hundreds of speeches, addresses, pamphlets, and campaigns for child welfare reforms — all of these were part of her everyday life. Representing Canada on several occasions before the League of Nations, receiving honorary degrees and a CBE, participating in international child labour conferences and often serving as key speaker before welfare committees in Canada and the United States — these were common enough activities in a life teeming with others. Without making it a "cause," Charlotte Whitton was nevertheless identified as an exemplar of inter-war years feminism. For example, in 1934, on being awarded the CBE, a sincere outburst of praise poured in from women's groups across the country, who undoubtedly saw the honour as due recognition of women's role in society. Congratulatory telegrams expressing pleasure from groups such as the National Council, the International Order Daughters of the Empire and the Canadian Women's Press Club, and individuals such as the Canadian author Marshall Saunders as well as American admirers such as Grace and Edith Abbott numbered into the hundreds.[13]

Whitton's awareness of feminist issues was, in some ways during her child welfare career, diverted by her own singular success. Although social work was generally acknowledged to be a "feminized" profession, as with teaching, males held the prestigious ministerial portfolios, official positions, and government posts. This was especially resented by Whitton when her own position as Director of the Council was taken over by Dr. George Davidson who had been director of social welfare in British Columbia.[14] In 1946, in a succinct address on sexual politics, "But He's a Man!", she drolly observed of social work that "the boys have discovered it now, especially its enlarging administrative and executive opportunities."[15]

Therefore a compelling reason for Whitton's quiet but active feminism during the social welfare years was her own personal success story. She saw her undisputed leadership and capabilities as statement enough of female talent. During her years in social work her relations with men had fallen into an atmosphere of mutual respect due to the common tasks facing the early generations of social workers who sought to professionalize the field. J. Howard Falk of the Vancouver Social Agencies and Robert E. Mills, director of the Toronto Children's Aid Society, immediately come to mind as men who were not merely colleagues but also close friends. Social work was an area where women's contribution thrived and where men and women worked side by side in close contact and cooperation. Moreover, as the acknowledged spokesperson for child and social welfare her relations with prominent male figures were cordial and she received no little deference from them for her organizational acumen and practical insights. Prime Minister R.B. Bennett, R.P. Vivian, Ontario Minister for Social Welfare, John Bracken, leader of the Progressive Conservative Party, F.C. Blair, Deputy Minister of Immigration, and Dr. E.W. Montgomery, Manitoba Minister for Health and Public Welfare, to name only a few, retained her services and heeded her advice. Virginia Woolf's words in *A Room of One's Own* are apropos at this juncture — that to a woman of earned status and earned income "men were no longer to her the opposing faction. She need not waste her time railing against them."[16]

While at the helm of the Council Whitton seemed impervious to the corrosive and pervasive onslaughts of the prevailing "ideology of inferiority." Indeed, in respect to women her professional success contradicted its basic assumptions. That her feminism was relatively unsung during these years was a consequence of both her achievements and the feminization of her particular profession. These two things neutralized her, for she was psychologically and politically committed to the Petrarchan view of *virtus et fama*, that is, that individual success could be ascribed to nothing less than one's own merits and efforts. Until 1941 nothing had persuaded Charlotte Whitton to think otherwise. It was, however, the personally devastating event of her retirement in 1941 that drastically altered this point of view. Whitton's retirement had been urged upon her and she fought it desperately. She could not imagine the Council or child welfare without her because she had been their luminary for almost twenty years.[17] Before her retirement Whitton had observed, without false modesty and not without much truth, that the Council revolved largely because it had "revolved around her."[18] The *Ottawa Citizen*, 5/5/1942, reported an address given in her honour by her successor George Davidson in which he noted that:

> The indelible records of her mind cannot be matched by any filing system left to the Council office. Charlotte Whitton was, and still remains the greatest single depository in this country of information on social work matters.

Despite their antagonisms and fundamental philosophical disagreements Davidson could have said no less.

The reasons for Whitton's retirement are complex and cannot be taken up in this essay. They included the alienation of Council staff because she found it difficult to delegate responsibilities, and the creation of a network of loyal colleagues across the country at the expense of others. Whitton was simultaneously admired and disliked with equal passion. Moreover, her politically conservative views, in both the social and party sense, no longer kept abreast with debates on social welfare that had resounded since the great depression and that were fired again by the agonies of the Second World War. Finally committed to the principles of subsidiarity, Whitton opposed the coming Welfare State and railed against the increasing incursions of the state into the lives of individuals with the erosion of citizen effort. Out of step with rapid industrialization patterns which caused major demographic dislocations and not in agreement with new assumptions about economic and social reorganization, she resisted these transformations which were occurring in the Council itself. Her leadership had become anachronistic. The Council, which she had led into social significance, moulded into a national organization, and seen grow from a token public agency to a significant aegis of welfare reforms, was to expand its functions in keeping with the philosophy of the welfare state without Whitton directing it.

Moreover, if the "boys" had gained the plush executive jobs, the emerging intellectual leaders were also men. Although Whitton had been engaged in organizing welfare structures for two decades with consummate skill, men such as Harry Cassidy and Leonard Marsh wrote the books on social welfare and acted as research advisors. She challenged their views on welfare organization with her own manifesto, *The Dawn of Ampler Life* (1943), which was dubbed the "Whitton Plan" for social security.[19] Whitton's document was partly the result of her annoyance that the Committee on Reconstruction, which issued a report on "Post War Problems of Women" with Marsh as research advisor, had entirely overlooked her expertise.[20] Her relations with Davidson, Marsh and Casidy were often vitriolic.[21]

Let us review the situation Whitton found herself in at the time of her reluctant retirement in 1941 at age forty-five years. She was unmarried and not from that class of women with independent means. She was unemployed. At forty-five she was middle aged and uncertain whether she could find a satisfactory replacement for her previous professional status. Her "free lance" work as journalist, publicist, and writer was not only precarious but it provided a minimal living for maximum effort.

Once again, words from Virginia Woolf's insightful feminist statement come to mind especially as Whitton herself was known to have used the analogy. Like the heroine in the book, Whitton found herself to have become "a bluestocking with an itch for scribbling" (and lecturing) merely "to put money in her purse."[22] "Gainful occupation" and "independent income" became the keywords to much of her future feminist thought; indeed, they became the necessary mortar to cement together the broken up pieces that the confused jigsaw of her life now seemed to be.

Without the support system of a predominantly female world of social workers and without the prestigious structure of the Council behind her, she faced a vastly altered and bewildering reality. For the first time in her life she came to a conscious understanding of those social forces that promiscuously wasted female energies and talents. For the first time that pervasive sexist suspicion toward co-operation between men and women in the work place was recognized and its principles totally rejected by Whitton. And last, but by no means least, she came to realize the anomalous status of the single woman divested of authority and without prestige in the average world of married solidarity and lack of interest in her kind.[23]

The bold pattern that had emerged during her child welfare career seemed to shift and move with alarming impermanency. The jigsaw was in disarray. The pieces no longer fitted comfortably although in her mind's eye that jigsaw was not yet nearly completed.

Both objectively and psychologically several things had happened. First, her previous network had protected her from the ordinary vulgar discourses on "spinsterhood" and her professional importance had proven it merely irrelevant. In fact, her single state had been beneficial by affording her an independence marriage could not. She had been able to travel freely and unencumbered across Canada and abroad on significant tasks and consequently enjoyed an exceedingly fertile and exciting life. Furthermore, having enjoyed prestige and position in a "feminized" profession, she had not before her resignation baldly confronted the realities of sexual politics in a male dominated socio-economic order which included the insidious prevalence of the ideology of inferiority, unequal pay for equal work, and the automatic exclusion of women from important posts. The words "men preferred" in advertisements for numerous classes of jobs outraged her.[24]

Second, Whitton found herself not only "competing" with men but also competing with married women who were joining the workforce in increasing numbers since their wartime work experience. At this time, these women seemed to militate against altering the existing economic order wherein men earned higher salaries as they saw theirs as only a "second income." This point is essential in understanding some of the subsequent ambiguities in her feminist thought.

Third, Whitton found herself dependent for her actual livelihood upon the very group of women of whom she had not formerly been part, that is, the middle class married matrons or the wealthy and independent women who met at their mid-week Gyro Club, Church group, Local Council of Women, at charity meetings or afternoon teas. Her lecture tours across Canada and the United States depended upon their goodwill, interest, and most importantly, honoraria. This economic dependence cannot have been other than a burden and an irritation. The receiving of a meagre fee plus expenses in remuneration for her services as a publicist could have been neither pleasant nor satisfying to a woman who had enjoyed esteem and unprecedented success. Her speeches and addresses are themselves telling. Those given to some lesser service groups are in florid rhetoric and are of forgettable mediocrity whereas the addresses to more prestigious groups such as the Canadian Women's Press Club, the Business and Professional Women's Associations, universities and social welfare meetings, were witty and erudite social criticisms. The anxieties and economic uncertainty involved in free lance writing, too, must have been psychologically debilitating although *Macleans*, *Chatelaine*, *Canadian Home Journal* and *Saturday Night* frequently published her articles.

Whitton also found herself economically dependent upon that very group of women for whom she had little sympathy — the volunteer charity worker. In the past she had agreed with the description that they represented the "apostolic succession of volunteers" and had unceasingly and remorselessly tried to place them under experts and qualified personnel during her campaigns to professionalize social work. Yet during this period, her very livelihood depended on their wishes. Once again, one recalls Virginia Woolf's exclamation — "What a change of temper a fixed income will bring about!" Did Woolf's other observations such as those about doing the work "one did not wish to do" but doing it "flattering and fawning" because "the stakes were too great to run risks" haunt Whitton?[25]

Did all this touring, lecturing, speechmaking, attending banquets and chit chatting at luncheons, become to Whitton "like a rust eating away at the bloom of Spring" while every "changing of a ten shilling note" meant that a little of that inevitable rust was "rubbed off"? Given her temperament and experience we can only suppose Whitton feared, and felt, the "rust" setting in each time she sipped tea and nibbled her *petite-fours*.

While the consciousness of a foreign inferiority and unfamiliar anonymity must have partially taken her breath away, Whitton needed very little time to get her second wind. The next years were frantic ones of recovering confidence in herself by engaging in harrowing lecture tours as a publicist and feminist speaker. These tours meant that she was living out of a suitcase and in hotel rooms for months at a time. In 1942 alone she lectured in California, and the Western States, as well as Victoria, Vancouver, Western Canada and Ontario. Her tours took her to bustling San Francisco and remote Parry Sound, to urban centres like Milwaukee and Cleveland and towns like Chilliwack or Prince Rupert.[26]

Where a more timid woman might have failed, Whitton's verve and resilience triumphed but not without careful social analysis and emotional distress. From 1941 to 1952 she relentlessly perservered in defending women's rights, investigated the inequities of women involved "in gainful occupation," criticized her church's (the Anglican) sexist structures, wrote numerous articles for magazines, papers, and journals and conducted scrupulous surveys into numerous aspects of women's problems. She was also commissioned to study Ontario's welfare services and the problems of female juvenile delinquency for brief periods during 1943 and 1944.[27]

Ten years is a long time in a life and this decade in Whitton's "mid-life," while as full and as frenzied as her years in child welfare, has a sense of desperation the previous years do not. A successful woman, accustomed to respect and authority, faced the possibility of a future as a "has-been" eking out a mediocre existence as a publicist and journalistic hack. These years, however, proved to be ones of consolidation that prepared Whitton for her second career. During this period Whitton addressed two feminist issues, that is, the problems of women in the work force and in politics, which she personally confronted.

In a pithy 1947 article for *Macleans*, "The Exploited Sex," Whitton wryly observed that "Eve got the drop on Adam and men have been getting back ever since. Practically any dumb-bell is paid more than a woman just because 'he's a man!' "[28] This comment, however, must be balanced with others she made with equal irony and point. For example, Whitton felt strongly about the trend of working women to shift the job of child rearing and housework onto someone else. Such sentiments fall harshly upon the ears of contemporary women although the following comment draws attention to a major flaw in present middle class feminist reality if not thought. In "Women: A Necessary Evil," an historical overview of attitudes towards women read before the Business and Professional Women of Montreal in 1950, she caustically noted:

> Yet the definite trend today is toward this type of woman whose career is the major motivating power of her life, who desires marriage as a satisfying attribute to her living, and accepts motherhood, incidental thereto,

providing it occurs not too frequently nor too inconveniently, and that most of the duties and responsibilities appertaining thereto can be assumed *by some other woman or women, of less essential value to the community.*

She forthrightly added that such women felt that they "must not be deprived of [their] own intellectual, social or technical contribution."[29] Elsewhere she referred to "the growing parasitism among upper and middle class women" who ignored "the piteous penury and overwork among the lower."[30]

Her concern for women of the lower socio-economic groups was paramount in the suverys she conducted on women "in gainful occupation."[31] Whitton divided working married women into two classes: those who, like single women, were compelled through economic necessity to work and those who worked for other than compelling economic reasons. While criticizing unequal wages for equal work, she pointed out that men were not the only rogues in perpetuating inequity but that the second class of woman seemed uninterested in that class which felt the injustice most because they needed the money more. In the case of the first class, she agreed with Grace Abbott's words before the International Labour Conference of 1935 that "many women work for the same reasons as men, because they must live." As a single woman Whitton was in no position to think otherwise.

Although she believed that a married woman's "instinctive natural preference is for home and family life," Whitton asserted that those who chose to work outside the home must be given rates better than the "subsistence levels eked out by small cash bonuses for children."[32] As a social and philosophical conservative, Whitton was suspicious of cash allowances which rewarded "reproduction" instead of "production," a point of view rarely shared with her social work peers. She often stood alone in the opinion that services and care (called "social utilities") should be given to mothers and families rather than baby bonuses.[33] The *Telegram*, 26/10/1943, reported her as saying that "cash grants of themselves, could not assure wiser or more nutritional provision for the urban child, nor affect greatly the feeding of the rural child." She viewed family allowances as "a tax upon the childless for the subsidy of the childbearing citizen."[34]

In addition to these views, Whitton protested the inequities of a taxation system not based on the principle of the earnings of households, *personnes soles.* She insisted that if tax advantages were given to married couples with dual incomes then (in absolute justice) they must also be given to two friends or two relatives (such as brother and sister) who kept joint households. Better that the policy be abandoned altogether and each income be separately taxed. As the law stood, the unweds were penalized by differentials in taxation between single and unmarried status as well as the inequalities in pay between single and married males in favour of the married.[35]

It was also in "Women: A Necessary Evil" that Whitton praised the fact that 23% of the gainfully employed were female, and that women "were taking over much of the work of the world," while at the same time she observed the deplorably low wages they received. In the same breath she charged that married working women "want marriage and a married woman's status . . . but are not prepared to pay the price of it."[36] She was dismayed at the growing tendency to subordinate wifehood and motherhood to jobs, or the prevalence of "short-changing" one or the other because of dual loyalties. "Rarely," she said, "could a woman serve the god of her home and the mammon of a full time job."[37]

It is when we juxtapose these 1950 observations with those in her 1947 lecture "Society and the Revolution in the Status of Women" that Whitton's ambivalence on the matter is apparent. Before the Susan B. Anthony Memorial Series audience at Rochester, she noted that many women wanted to continue with their careers after marriage and motherhood because

> It must be realized that they are not seeking escape from marriage and the home as much as searching [for] satisfying use for the talents and training they possess, escaping the sense of waste and frustration and futility that so breed unhappiness where there is idleness and underuse of endowment and skills.

She pointed out that mechanization increased the homemaker's sense of boredom and discontent and she identified women's groups as necessary to prevent the "rust" that would otherwise set in.[38]

How are we to understand these two divergent points of view, the first to the women at the University of Rochester and the second to the Business and Professional Women of Montreal, uttered within three years of each other? The more cynical explanation is that Whitton knew her audiences well and understood that the educated and feminist audience attending the Rochester lectures would not take kindly to her real views and was aware that the United States was far ahead of Canada in its numbers of married working women. In short, to have said otherwise would have been impolitic. She was very familiar with her Montreal audience having given key note addresses before them on other occasions. The audience was more likely to have been made up of single career women like herself and certainly many of her previous colleagues from social work belonged to regional business and professional associations.

Another view, however, makes the issue more complex than this suggestion without necessarily excluding the practical considerations of the first view. Whitton's real sympathies were with the opinions expressed in the Montreal statement. During her social work years she often had attributed the source of family life problems to working mothers. We postulate, therefore, that these two statements found in various forms elsewhere, are signs of her inner struggle with feminist issues and that she herself had not come to any final synthesis of conflicting beliefs and emotions. They can also be understood as expressions of an extreme ambivalence which came out of her own unmarried feminist stance.

Twenty years or so of active employment filled to the brim with "doing" rather than intellectualizing had given her little leisure to formulate a distinctive social theory on the role of married working women apart from what she always saw as their major role, that of mothers and homemakers. Her social work, dealing with intervention into family life and child care, was premised on the commonplace philosophy reflecting Christian values and conservative socio-economics that the family was the essential unit, not only for social stability, but no less for the perpetuation of western civilization itself.[39] For a radical shift of view to have occurred after years of implementing the opposite assumptions would be almost unthinkable. Moreover, Whitton did believe firmly that women were morally superior to men. For example, in "Women and the Future of Family Life" (1943), she congratulated her sex by saying that they

> by necessity of nature, as well as by the will of society, being under a more rigorous rule of virtue than men, [are] by reason thereof schooled to greater self discipline, and on the whole, moral balance.[40]

Women, therefore, had grave responsibilities as educators of their children and keepers of their households for the family unit was the bastion of "citizen, responsibility and character training" which the State could "provide or purchase in no other way."[41] An analysis of her social and child welfare policy and philosophy bears testimony to the depth of these beliefs.

Apart from her belief in the superiority of woman's moral nature and in the bourgeois family ideal, Whitton's ambivalence toward the married career woman was predicated on her single status and the choice she had felt constrained to make in her own life. Quite obviously she resented what she saw as a "bread buttered on both sides" attitude and her religious beliefs as well as her probable celibacy meant that her views on family planning remained rather nebulous and perhaps even repressed. It was difficult for her to comprehend that the "either/or" choice of precontraceptive marriage had radically altered after the war.

Because she had never enjoyed either the social status or the economic securities of a bourgeois marriage and motherhood, and because she was now living precariously without guaranteed income, Whitton felt little sympathy for those who, having chosen otherwise regarding marriage, complained of its tedium and disadvantages. She must have viewed their choice as timid just as she saw their eventual discontent as trivial. Yet theirs was an emerging feminist issue with perennial roots and Whitton had to wrestle with her fears, doubts, frustrations, and ambivalence as a single woman no longer in a professional position superior to most women and equal to many men.

A further aspect of Whitton's ambivalence can be seen in her views that most women, whether married or not, were "of the marrying mind." One assumes that she is referring here to the mentality that marriage is the prime aim of females, even for career women, and that few would choose the career over the marriage if the situation actually came to that. Moreover, perhaps she keenly felt during this time of uncertainty, middle age, and crisis, the not uncommon complacency, like-minded congratulation, and group identification that occurs among the married and which, all too unfortunately, expresses itself in a dismissal of the social importance of the unmarried. Whitton also protested that women of "the marrying mind" were in the end greater enemies of women than men, and that "husband's wives" were hostile to the working partnerships between non-related men and women which were increasing as more women entered the work force. Such "jealousy" she isolated as counterproductive to the lessening of sexual antagonism in the workplace for she recognized that it was essential that the workplace be purged of such attitudes before men and women could claim equal wages let alone equality as persons.[42]

This observation leads us to wonder if Whitton had encountered such wifely disdain during her social welfare years when she not only worked with men on an equal basis but when she had a superior position to many of them. Her feelings on the matter are strong enough to suggest that Whitton's rise in those years had met with sexist opposition from both males and females "of the marrying mind."

In addition to women in the workplace two other issues became part of the jigsaw of Whitton's feminist thought during this decade of crisis and retooling. These dealt with sexual discrimination in politics generally and party work particularly. In a lively 1945 election speech, she asserted that "the great reserve of electoral strength, not yet formed in its battalions" remaining in Canadian society was "the woman's vote." A year later she accalimed that, "We women are the new power. We are the untried power. We are the unused power that can go forward to changing this Era."[43]

Whitton rejected the idea of a Women's Party as doomed to failure because it was based on doubtful assumptions that artificially divided the sexes' mutual interests. She always protested the use of women and youths as "auxiliaries" to political parties and challenged women to boycott "special women's set-ups" by demanding nothing less than equal participation in the electoral processes. Fund raising ventures were necessary but the assumption that they were "women's work" was offensive. She found the suggestion that celebrated Canadian women should be given Senate representation equally offensive because she saw this august parliamentary body as pasture set aside for "the politically embarrassing, uncertain, outworn, or useless" and which saved the Party from "their unpredictability in the hustings," or served to "protect them against inclement weather, or just for value received." Her position was clear. Women must prove that they, too, were able "to serve and master the difficult apprenticeship and journeymen's processes of an elective system."[44] She unambiguously rejected paternalism, patronage, and any suggestion of "token womanhood" on political committees, platforms, or in legislative bodies where they remained political eunuchs.

After the papal pronouncement to the women of Italy in 1945 — "Tua res Agitur" (your destiny is upon you, women) Whitton used these words often to encourage women to act directly upon social and political structures. She obviously considered that if the Vatican could unequivocally assert women's right to equal pay and that they were bound to participate in the community as well as in the home then the case for the opposition was closed! Her views on women's involvement in politics were uncompromising as she felt that the logical arena for the majority of females to participate in (as most women were married and mothers) was in the local area. She noted that local politics was as bereft of female representation and effort as the broader political arena and that this was not universally a case of male oppression but also of female apathy. Local politics were available to woman "right where she is," Whitton stated before a St. Louis audience in 1946.[45] She pointed out that if marriage and motherhood need not interfere with work as educated women claimed then neither ought they be used as an excuse to avoid political input. Indeed, she saw political involvement as the perfect solution to the feelings of uselessness, parasitism, and underuse of their talents and endowments that such women expressed. Women's reluctance to contribute even to local politics meant that "democracy [was] made and controlled by others."

Quoting damning figures of women's representation in the market place, the economy, and in politics, Whitton reiterated in her Rochester lecture the words of Margaret Hickey, President of the National Federation of Business and Professional Women, that "Industry's courtship with women is over. Perhaps its intentions were never honourable." She pointed out that in 1943, 13.3% of women were gainfully occupied, exclusive of agricultural occupations, a 350% jump since the turn of the century with 25.5% of these being single women between 15 and 19 years. Yet their political and economic gains were disproportionate in comparison; indeed they seemed to be losing ground. It was as if the males in society were shrieking Cato's maxim, "As soon as they begin to be equal with us they will have the advantage."[46]

Whitton's political views were all the more poignant when one remembers her own party allegiance. She was a stalwart member of the Progressive Conservative party, which was almost always out of office. Had Whitton been a member of and an activist for the Liberal party without a doubt she would have gained a political appointment either by patronage or though election, given her reputation, energy, and stability. It must be noted too, that Whitton must have been fully aware of the fact that she belonged to the wrong party. It is to Whitton's credit, no matter what views one might hold regarding conservative political philosophy, that her loyalty was such that despite the seductions of "crossing the floor," she did not. Neither did she decline to assert her affiliations although she could have chosen opportunistic silence. Whitton flirted with the idea of political office at all levels frequently during her career and toyed with the idea of the possibility of a ministerial position in public welfare. Despite her work for various commissions and investigations, however, no such position was offered her and she felt that this was due to her gender.

Despairing of the Progressive Conservative party's policies on social welfare, British relations, and its incapacity to recognize women as equal, she never abandoned faith in the party's fundamental principles. In 1944 she declined the offer from the party's national director to take on the women's organization and activities in preparation for party candidature, as well as an offer for a constituency, on feminist grounds and because women were inevitably placed "in slaughter house ridings." Whitton agitatedly wrote to Winnipeg alderwoman Hilda Hesson in 1944 that she had urged the party "that our policy all hang together — manpower and war policy, empire relations, the position of women as other than bonused breeder, as an expanding resilient economy, not a subsidized baby crop." "Surely," she cried, describing the number of able women around, "we can foregather and light a light that need not go out!"[47] In this same year she also wrote to Ontario's Premier, Colonel George Drew, that she was beginning "to give up hope that there is any possibility of a woman like me — and there are others — finding much real opportunity of worthwhile service in the Conservative Party in the Dominion or even in the Province."[48]

During the decade of the 1940's Whitton was also contracted by the Anglican church to conduct a national survey on the role of women at the parish level. The survey results were oriented toward her major concern of women in "gainful occupation," an emphasis that the church authorities were far from pleased about. She noted that the church disregarded "the changed status of its women" and wasted their talents in auxiliary positions as did the political parties. The sole preparation for full church membership was through marriage, motherhood and homemaking. "In the Church of England," she complained. "it would take the twelve apostles (and the assured absence of St. Paul) to establish women as equals."[49] Women involved in church politics today would find that these sentiments still have a contemporary appeal.

The decade between Whitton's resignation from the CWC and her entry into civic politics represents several smaller pieces to the jigsaw of her social thought. Although these pieces consisted of surveys, commissions of inquiry, journalism and lecturing, none of these activities were as significant as her previous social welfare career nor as visible as her later public life. Nevertheless the decade with all its activities represents a necessary "moratorium" which prepared for her a new career with a new constituency. Before this occurred, however, two pieces remained to complete the pattern forming in her "mind's eye" in anticipation of this second career. These were easy fits and were placed quickly one after another.

One piece represents the events which took place in the province of Alberta in 1947–48 and which successfully publicized her again while restoring her reputation as a leader able to expose shameful child care conditions; the other piece consisted of the final move into civic politics in a remarkable campaign supported by the Ottawa Council of Women.[50] The Alberta publicity enhanced Whitton's image and the dramatic events surrounding her study of child care regained her previous national support and captured the imagination of Ottawa's electorate. The findings of a commission of inquiry into Alberta child welfare vindicated many of Whitton's own findings publicized from the 1947 study she had conducted under the auspices of an Edmonton chapter of the Imperial Order Daughters of the Empire. This report scandalized a country prepared to be skeptical of Alberta Social Credit aspirations. Moreover when she and two others were brought before the Alberta courts in 1948 "for conspiracy to publish defamatory libel" the national furor this aroused and the support she received from across the country were staggering.[51] The confrontation between the maverick from the Ottawa Valley and the Welfare Department of the "last best west" proved to be a political *tour de force* whose halo effect lasted into the Ottawa campaign. Thus in 1950, at age fifty-four, the last large piece of the jigsaw was fitted.

The previous decade had been a winter of her discontent during which Whitton could not have been certain that her former usefulness and esteem could ever be recaptured. It had been an economically precarious and psychologically corrosive period. During the first months of the Alberta trial her private domestic life had been shattered by the death of her companion and dearest friend, Margaret Grier, from which Charlotte took many years to recover emotionally.[52] The stressful public events surrounding the Alberta affair had dislocated her grief and had delayed the ritualistic expressions of bereavement and renewal immediately following the death.

Whitton did not succumb to the indulgences of self-pity during a decade that was objectively penurious and psychologically critical. Neither did she become paralyzed by a fear of uselessness or the dread of aging. Instead, these were the years in which she practised what she had preached by serving and mastering that apprenticeship into elected politics. Her motto during this period was "Tua res Agitur," because, as a highly individualized and independent woman herself, she believed firmly in the possibilities of other women controlling more aspects of their own lives. She exemplified this belief by quoting Shakespeare's words,

The fault, dear Brutus, is not in our stars
But in ourselves, that we are underlings.[53]

Whitton's life demonstrates again what we have always known, that significant historical actors do not usually, "pick out the straight edges and fill out the frame." They seize those opportunities ("all sorts of little piles") which make up the pattern intuitively formed in their "mind's eye." The events of Whitton's life, and her personal ambitions, were combined with an astute psychological capacity for transforming these events and ambitions from a personal into a social vision — one that was far from being an "idiot's flowerbed."

Notes

1. Whitton to Mrs. James Richardson, Winnipeg, 29 December 1944, Whitton Papers, Vol. 95, Public Archives of Canada (PAC) (hereafter cited as WP). We wish to thank Ms. Françoise Houle for processing and opening the Whitton Papers by request for the authors in 1979.

2. For aspects of her career, see Tamara Hareven, "An Ambiguous Alliance: Some Aspects of American Influences on Canadian Social Welfare," Social History 3 (April 1969): 82–98; James Struthers, "A Profession in Crisis: Charlotte Whitton and Canadian Social Work in the 1930's," Canadian Historical Review 62 (1981): 169–185; and obituary by Phillis Harrison, "In the Beginning was Charlotte," Canadian Welfare 51 (1975): 14–15. None of these authors had access to the Whitton Papers.

3. Gertrude Hall, "Contemporary Women: Social Welfare and Public Relations" (October–December 1947), WP/5, and The Memberscript (YWCA): 4, 26 (May 1942).

4. Detailed essays by the authors on Whitton's child and social welfare career include, "Child Welfare in English Canada, 1920–1948," Social Service Review 55 (Sept. 1981): 484–506; "Making the Way More Comfortable: Charlotte Whitton's Child Welfare Career 1920–48," The Journal of Canadian Studies XVII, 4 (Winter 1982–83): 33–45; "Charlotte Whitton and the 'Babies for Export' Controversy 1947–48," Alberta History 30 (Winter 1982): 11–16; and "Charlotte Whitton Meets the 'Last Best West': The Politics of Child Welfare in Alberta, 1929–1949," Prairie Forum (Fall 1981): 143–63.

5. Margaret MacLachlan to Charlotte Whitton (CW), 21 September 1913, 28 November 1915, 1 October 1918, WP/3.

6. CW to Esther, 28 February 1918, CW to Mo, 23 August 1918, WP/3.

7. Mo to CW, 20 May 1917, 5 May 1917, 29 May 1919, WP/3.

8. Bill King to CW, 29 December 1923, 18 December 1917, 18 December 1918, 10 December 1924, and 25 January 1925, WP/3.

9. Telegram and reply, 21 January 1924, WP/3.

10. "Women and the Future of Family Life," YWCA Monthly (Dec. 1943), 4.

11. "Society and the Revolution in the Status of Women," 15 February 1947, p. 12, WP/84. Allen F. Davis, American Heroine: The Life and Legend of Jane Addams (New York: Oxford University Press, 1973), 86–91, argues for the "romantic" and emotional sustenance the first generations of college women gave each other.

12. Wilhelmina Gordon to CW, 24 December 1916, WP/3, 5; and Marjorie Bradford to CW, 13 March 1946.

13. WP/4.

14. WP/18.

15. This became "The Exploited Sex," *Macleans Magazine*, 15 April 1947. She observed in 1945 that the social services were the "last preserve of patronage" in politics. Davidson, after being director of the CWC, rapidly became Deputy Minister of Health and Welfare by 1945 for the federal government. CW to Edith Abbott, 20 June 1945, WP/5.

16. Virginia Woolf, *A Room of One's Own* (London: The Hogarth Press, 1959), 139.

17. The psychological significance of this period has been discussed by the authors in an unpublished paper, "Charlotte Whitton: A Study in Ambition, Crisis and Resolution."

18. CW to George Davidson, Director of Social Welfare, B.C., 26 April 1939, WP/18.

19. Charlotte Whitton, *The Dawn of Ampler Life* (Toronto: Macmillan, 1943); "Now It's the Whitton Plan," *Saturday Night*, 16 October 1943; "The Second Mile," address to Montreal Welfare Federation, 3 October 1944; MS "Toward Changing Vistas of Human Welfare" (1942), WP/83; and "Some Fundamental Principles in Obtaining Security," *Tennessee Public Welfare Record* (Feb. 1944), 2–7. Whitton's social thought has been discussed by the authors in "Women as Social Reformers: Charlotte Whitton," a paper presented to the Fourth Biannual Conference on Social Policy, Carleton University, Ottawa, April, 1981. Her views on medical services as "a social utility" are another sign of her complexity because they were more radical than either Marsh or Cassidy, as Cassidy himself acknowledged. She was incensed at what she saw as "medical fascism" when the Montreal medical profession called her views "socialized medicine under another name." CW to Abbott, 20 June 1945, WP/5; and Cassidy to Prime Minister W.L. Mackenzie King, 10 December 1943, WP/4.

20. CW to Leonard Marsh, 2 February 1943, WP/4.

21. "The Co-ordination of Welfare Services" CWC submission to Rowell-Sirois Commission (April 1938), and correspondence between CW and Harry Cassidy (1938–41) especially files 179 and 183, Canadian Council of Social Development, Vol. 99 (CCSD/99), PAC; CW to Cassidy, School of Social Work, Toronto (1945), Cassidy to CW, 18 June 1945, CW to V.R. Smith, 13 June 1945, 15 June 1946, WP/5; and a criticism of Cassidy in the Montreal *Gazette*, 24 May 1945, WP/88.

22. Woolf, 97.

23. We believe that attitudes toward and problems of the "never married" are qualitatively different from those of the divorced and separated or the single parent phenomena that are receiving so much psycho-sociological discussion today. The "never married" class remains relatively unexamined in a prevailing ethos of heterosexual coupling. Attitudes towards them as "losers" have not radically altered with the divorce and separated being able to transcend this stigma having "made it" at least once in a society that urges its members into marital relationships.

24. "But He's a Man!" The civil service was even more blatant by stipulating "Males Only." Whitton pointed out that: "It is not democracy to permit the economically stronger . . . to exploit the economically weaker and less potently organized." Yet discrimination existed "on the basis of an inherited sex prejudice that we would not tolerate were it similarly applied on grounds of race, colour, nationality or religion." 17–18, 22, WP/98.

25. Woolf, 57.

26. WP/5.

27. "Report on Administration of Welfare Services in Ontario" (1943), Pts. 1 and 2 submitted to Hon. R.P. Vivian, 1/12/1943; correspondence between CW, Rita Farquaharson and Hon. George Dunbar; and "Summary of Findings and Recommendations . . .'" (1944), WP/30, 31.

28. Macleans, 15 April 1947, 9.

29. 19 October 1950 (emphasis added).

30. "Society and Revolution . . ." (1947), 19.

31. For example, "Women and the Future of Family Life," *World's YWCA Monthly* (Dec. 1943).

32. Alan Randal to CW, 4 April 1945, reply 4 April 1945, WP/83.

33. See *The Dawn of Ampler Life* (1943) for such views, as well as "Priorities in Child Care and Development," address to the Ontario School Trustees, 10 April 1944, WP/83; "Toward a New Era of Family Life," *Health Education Group Vancouver* 9, 2 (1943), 22; CW to Canon W.W. Judd, General Sec. of the Canadian Social Service Council, 4 April 1942, WP/22; and "Women and the Budget," *Ottawa Citizen*, 8 July 1946.

34. "Society and the Revolution . . . ," 24, and *Ottawa Citizen*, 8 July 1946.

35. "Society and the Revolution . . . ," 24, 27.

36. "Women: A Necessary Evil" (1950), 20.

37. *Ottawa Citizen*, 8 July 1946.

38. "Society and the Revolution . . . ," 21.

39. See the following addresses: "Rebuilding Canadian Home and Family Life," *Canadian Dietetics Association*, 11 June 1947, "Woman as Educator in Home, School and Nation," F.W.T.A.O., 26 August 1948, "Self Control and State Control," Provincial Council of Women, 3 November 1949, WP/84; and "Intelligent Maternity: Responsible Paternity," Cleveland Maternal Health Services Association, April 1945, WP/83. Also see MS. "Citizenship" (n.d.), WP/88; "Women the World Over," *The Quotarian* 24 (Oct. 1946) 2–3, 14, and 16; "The School in Continuing Society," *Canadian School Journal* (June 1949), 229–232, and "The Churchwoman in the National Life" (1945), WP/24.

40. Address to World Y.W.C.A. Conference on Post War Problems, Washington, D.C., 29–31 Oct. 1943, 4, WP/83.

41. Ibid., p. 15.

42. "Society and the Revolution . . . ," 24, 25, and "Women: A Necessary Evil," 19–20.

43. "Woman Holds the Balance of Power" (1945), WP/88, and "Women the World Over" (1946), 16.

44. "Woman Holds the Balance of Power."

45. These views are found in "Manarchy or Matriarchy?" address to the Quota International, St. Louis, 3 July 1946, WP/5. Also, Agnes McPhail to CW, 24 February 1945, discussing "Women and What's Wrong With Us," WP/14; "Women the World Over: Women Slow in Political Field," *Vancouver Sun*, 29 October 1942; "It's Time for the Woman Voter to Learn the Facts of Political Life," *Saturday Night*, 12 April 1947.

46. "Society and the Revolution."

47. CW to Hilda Hesson, 11 August 1944, WP/81.

48. CW to Colonel George Drew, 26 June 1945, WP/5. Other correspondence about her political motivations and interests are "Charlotte Whitton May Be Candidate in Next Election (and perhaps Minister of Social Welfare)," *Ottawa Citizen*, 7 December 1944; CW to Harry Willis, 29 July 1944; CW to John Bracken, 29 July 1944; and R.A. Bell to CW, 1 August 1944, WP/81.

49. Her feminist criticisms of the church are found in: "Memo on Problems Re Women and the Work of Women in the Church of England in Canada," 3 December 1948; "The Women of the Church" (1948); "Women in Industry: Tentative Agenda" and "Women Not Affiliated," in Anglican Advance surveys, WP/22. Also "Community Study for Community Service" CCSD/132; memo to Dean R.H. Waterman (1946), WP/24; "Women: A Necessary Evil," 18 and "Society and the Revolution," 16.

50. "The Needle and Thread Brigade is on the March," *Ottawa Journal*, 7 November 1950.

51. This event has been analysed by the authors in "Charlotte Whitton Meets 'The Last Best West' " and a shorter piece "Charlotte Whitton and The 'Babies for Export' Controversy, 1947–48." Sources for these are taken from WP/31–34 and "Premiers' Papers," Provincial Archives of Alberta.

52. Whitton's response to Grier's death has been examined in "Charlotte Whitton: Ambition, Crisis and Resolution."

53. Quoted in "Women Hold the Balance of Power."

IT'S GOOD, IT'S BAD: THE CONTRADICTIONS†

JULIE WHITE

As the Canadian economy changed in the eighteenth and nineteenth centuries from being largely agricultural subsistence to increasingly commercial, greater numbers of men undertook full-time wage work, leaving women in the old patterns doing occasional work for pay. Whereas previously most members of the family had worked only periodically to provide needed cash, beginning in the nineteenth century, it fell mainly to married women to augment, by part-time work, the more regular income brought in by husbands and older children. The clients of the Jost Mission as described by Simmons, and the farm wives depicted by Sundberg both exemplify the ways in which families in the past have required the part-time or sporadic wage work of married women in order to survive.

In fact, this work has been so taken for granted that it has become either invisible or trivialized, dismissed as pin money or ignored altogether. Only in recent years, largely due to the efforts of the modern feminist movement, has it been recognized as work worthy of study. This recognition is taking two forms. One is awareness of the "double day" put in by many wives and mothers who still provide most of the labour power in the home as well as forming an increasing proportion of the labour force. The second is the realization of the emergence of part-time employment as a major and expanding feature of the Canadian economy. In some industries part-time workers have become the norm.

As Julie White demonstrates in Women and Part-Time Work, *from which this chapter is taken, the phenomenon of part-time jobs cannot be understood without reference to gender. It is more than a matter of chance that the restructuring of the labour market in favour of greater part-time work has proceeded most quickly in industries such as trades and services that have a heavy concentration of women. Employers use part-time help to provide an element of flexibility in the labour force, serving to increase productivity at the lowest possible costs. Women's domestic responsibilities and the inadequacy of support services such as affordable, quality child care make them the largest and most vulnerable pool of workers for the part-time jobs being created. The consequences for women have not been entirely negative but, as White outlines elsewhere in her book, it is essential that the wages, benefits, and security of part-timers be guaranteed union and legislative protection. Without these guarantees part-time work will continue to contribute to the secondary status, ghettoization, and low pay of women.*

Willingly or not, women have been in the forefront of what may very well be a massive shift in labour patterns, a shift that may eventually engulf significant numbers of male as well as female wage-earners. The study of female experience in this instance may do much to enlighten us about the consequences of certain influential economic trends. Without a sensitivity to the implications of gender we would lose a major tool for understanding the nature and consequences of key developments within our society.

It would be difficult, perhaps, to find a subject more fraught with controversy than part-time work. It has been applauded as an ideal solution and denigrated as exploitation. Much of this disagreement has centred around the role of women since almost three-quarters of all part-time workers are women.[1]

†*Women and Part-Time Work* (Ottawa: Canadian Advisory Council on the Status of Women, 1983): 1–24.

In 1970, the Royal Commission on the Status of Women suggested that part-time work enabled women to combine work and family life and to maintain their skills in preparation for a return to full-time work. The report concluded:

> We also believe that part-time work will help women to achieve equality of opportunity in employment. Women who need or want to supplement their income should have a chance to do so, a chance many can only get by working part-time. Part-time work may also alleviate the feeling of alienation from society which some housewives suffer.[2]

More recent studies have echoed these arguments, particularly the argument that part-time work enables women to combine work with home and family responsibilities. From this perspective it has been argued that part-time work should be expanded, so that more women can benefit from its advantages. The Royal Commission recommended "that the federal government undertake a study of the feasibility of making greater use of part-time work in the Canadian economy."[3]

According to the proponents of part-time work, its advantages are not confined to women. One study has suggested that working part-time not only serves the needs of mothers with young children, but also helps students who need to finance their education, handicapped workers who need a reduced work week and older workers making a transition to full retirement. Moreover, part-time workers are said to enjoy "better mental health" and "higher job satisfaction through exercising choice of work arrangements."[4] Even more broadly, some researchers have argued that part-time work may be an important way of dealing with the current economic recession and the resulting high levels of employment. It has been suggested that the available work must be "spread over as many workers as possible" and that "forcible reduction of hours, and hence earnings" may become necessary.[5] Yet another advantage of part-time work has been suggested, the "reduction of claims on social assistance through increasing opportunities for employment."[6]

All of these acclaimed benefits of part-time work have been thoroughly attacked, and part-time work has been denounced as detrimental to workers in general and women in particular. When the Quebec government announced plans to expand part-time work, a coalition of major women's organizations and unions was formed to oppose it. The coalition's initial press release of December 1981, "200,000 Women Denounce the Trap of Part-time Work," began:

> Part-time work is just another means by which women are kept in job ghettos where they are badly paid, where chances of unionization are limited and where they are subjected to indecent work conditions. We refuse to accept the fact that the future of women workers is restrained within the framework of part-time work and we denounce its use.[7]

Some studies have suggested that part-time work only camouflages the real problems workers face. As such, part-time work is for mothers to whom day care is unavailable, for students with inadequate grants, for unemployed youth who cannot find full-time work and for older people and mothers on welfare whose incomes are inadequate.[8] The argument made here is not to expand part-time work as the solution to these problems, but to provide expanded day care services, reasonable student grants and adequate social security payments.

Nor is it accepted that part-time workers choose to work part-time. In fact, far from resolving the unemployment problem, part-time work is perceived as merely camouflaging the real extent of the crisis. Workers are driven involuntarily, it is argued, into part-time work. The result is underemployment, not increased employment opportunities.

> The hiring of part-time employees initiated by our employer is being presented as the "magic" possibility of being able to work whenever one chooses. What irony! When it is in fact the employer who has the possibility of organizing the work to suit themselves and certainly not in the best interests of the workers, for part-time work is merely a new disguised form of unemployment.[9]

Is part-time work the solution to the mother's double work day, or does it ensure her exploitation in the labour force as well as in the home? Does part-time work force women who need full-time jobs into underemployment and low pay, or are there many women who want part-time jobs and cannot get them? Perhaps part of the problem of part-time work is that those who are concerned with the issue have often felt obliged to take one side or the other. Either part-time work is exploitation, cheap labour and underemployment, and should be restricted, or it is the perfect solution to women's double work day and should be expanded.

In fact, such a choice between "good" and "bad" is not conducive to a proper understanding of the issues. There are such contradictions inherent in women's dual role of domestic labour and paid employment that what may be beneficial for one may be disadvantageous for the other. It is necessary to look at the issue of part-time work from an approach that recognizes both women's domestic responsibilities and the position of women in the labour force.

To this end, the discussion in this chapter looks first at what it means to be a woman with young children and the various pressures which make part-time work a practical compromise. Then the situation of part-time workers in the labour force is detailed and the evidence of their secondary status reviewed.

Being a Mother — the Social, Economic and Ideological Realities

The large majority of women experience being a mother, each woman having two children on average.[10] Because the role of mother is not only biologically but also socially and culturally determined, it is a crucial part of a woman's life. The fact is that in our society women not only give birth to children, they also bear almost the entire responsibility of their care. The tremendous impact of this primary social role upon the lives of women both at home and in the labour force has received increasing attention, but it has yet to be accorded the importance it deserves. It is not possible to understand the phenomenon of part-time work without grasping the social, economic and ideological realities of being a mother.

A woman with children experiences conflicting pressures as to whether she should work in the home or go out to work in the labour force. The discussion that follows considers the kinds of pressures experienced by mothers, including finances, day care, housework, paid work and ideology.

I Need the Money — Finances

It is not news that we live in a period of economic recession with high unemployment and high inflation and, recently, unpredictable interest and mortgage rates. To meet the increased cost of living and to deal with economic insecurity, even in order to live above the property line, a second income has become a necessity for many families. In 1980, there were 391,050 two-parent families living below the Statistics Canada poverty line, 7% of all two-parent families. However, if the wives' incomes are deducted, a further 214,240 of the families fall below the poverty line, raising the percentage of impoverished families to 12%.[11] In a recent study which interviewed 40 married women with pre-school children and full-time jobs, nearly all of the women worked either because "their households were in a economic crisis" or because economic disaster was anticipated in the future and it was important to build up a nest egg for the hard times.[12]

Since economic necessity is a major incentive for many women to work outside the home, it is not surprising that as husbands' incomes fall, women are proportionately more likely to find paid work outside the home. In 1980, in families where husbands' incomes were less than $5,000, 72% of wives worked in the labour force; 60% of wives were employed when husbands earned more than $30,000.[13]

Part-time women workers are in the labour force for the same reason as full-time women workers. A Saskatchewan study found that 63% of the part-time women workers surveyed gave finances as their reasons for working. Their responses are summarized in table 1. A small study of 97 women part-time workers in Manitoba also found that financial need was the most common reason given for working.[14]

TABLE 1

Main Reason for Working Part-Time

Main Reason for Working	Women Part-Time Workers	
	Number	Percent
One income inadequate	113	26
Finance education	94	21
Support family and for self	71	16
Prefer work out of home	104	23
Other	59	14
Total	441	100

SOURCE: Saskatchewan Department of Labour, Women's Division, Research Unit, "A Study of Part-Time Employment in Saskatchewan," September 1979, p. 25, table W8.

The need to add to family income is a major incentive for women seeking paid employment.. However, there are also economic disincentives, and the major one is the cost of day care.

Who Will Look After the Children? — Day Care

The cost of supervised day care (in day care centres or supervised family day care) varies from one region to another, but the average cost in 1982 has been estimated at $12 per day for full-time supervised care, that is, almost $3,200 per year.[15] At this price, the only families able to use supervised care are those with very low incomes who can obtain government subsidies and some high-income families who can afford the full fee.[16] The nature of the subsidy system is such that only the lowest income families can obtain financial help. In 1980 even a one-parent, one-child family earning just $10,000 per year before tax would have to pay a minimum of $240 to $360 annually in five provinces, from $720 to $1,000 in four provinces and a remarkable $1,800 in Newfoundland.[17] The vast majority of two-income families are excluded from the subsidy system and find supervised day care beyond their means.

While studies have found that parents prefer care in a day care centre for their children, cost and lack and space are often insurmountable barriers.[18] In fact, only 12% of pre-school-aged children with working mothers attend centres or supervised family day care.[19] The rest, the vast majority, are placed in unsupervised day care situations, usually with a woman who takes several children into her home for a fee. Such private babysitters are cheaper than supervised care, although the cost is still substantial. A 1978 Toronto study found that the charge for such private care was on average $1,104 per year, and this figure is now five years out of date.[20] Of course, all of the costs quoted here have been for just one child; for two the price would be doubled.

While the cost of day care is one concern, the issue of quality is another. For the 88% of children whose mothers are in the labour force and who are in unsupervised placements, the quality of care is unregulated and unpredictable. Although a minority of such arrangements are good, most have been found to be only adequate to very poor.[21] In the most recent survey, 281 private babysitters in Toronto were interviewed, of which 76 were relatives of the working parents.[22] The results were disquieting. Education and income levels of the caregivers were low, while health problems affected one-quarter. The vast majority of the sitters reported that the children in their care watched television on average more than two hours per day, and the survey found that one-third of the sitters did not offer an adequate program of trips and excursions. While 20% of the sitters were judged to be providing excellent care for the children, a further 20% were considered to be very poor. The majority were found to be adequate, but the comment on this 60% of private sitters was: "Like the prepackaged instant macaroni and cheese dinners that so many of the care-givers reported serving to their charges, their program seems to lack enrichment and variety."[23] Different studies have found anywhere from one-quarter to two-thirds of working parents less than satisfied with their child-care arrangements.[24]

The problems of child care do not cease during the early school years, and in some ways they worsen. School hours could hardly be organized more effectively to prohibit women from working, particularly in full-time work. School is likely to start at 9:00 a.m., finish at 3:30 p.m. and deny responsibility for the children during a one-hour lunch break at midday. Then, there are the school breaks at Christmas and Easter, the long summer vacations and several professional development days in between. In 1980, just 16,718 children of school age in Canada had supervised child care arrangements for the time outside school hours — less than 1% (0.68%) of children aged 6 to 16 years with mothers in the labour force.[25]

Part-time work may be sought because there is no day care at all, because it costs too much or because its quality is poor. For a mother in need of extra income, taking a job working two evenings and Saturdays in a supermarket, or cleaning offices at night, means that the father or older children can be at home to care for the youngest children. Family relationships may be disrupted, but the problems of day care cost and quality are avoided. Alternatively, a woman may work just four hours each day because the quality of care is low, and she justifies placing her child in less than satisfactory care by the fact that it is only a few hours each day. . . .

It is hard to exaggerate the problem of day care for women with young children. In fact, it has been suggested that if good, low-cost day care were readily available, the need for part-time work would be virtually eliminated. However, as the following discussions of housework, paid work and ideology reveal, the problem of day care is not the only disincentive to full-time work.

It Still Has to Be Done — Housework and Child Care

In our society, women have responsibility for housework. Once a woman is also a mother, the domestic work-load is not a question of how neat and tidy she is or whether she washes the kitchen floor every week, month or year. As a mother, a woman is confronted with the necessity of providing for her children and a long list of chores are unavoidable — shopping, cooking, washing up, clearing away dishes, tidying toys, collecting dirty clothes, changing bed linen and doing laundry. Young children must be fed, bathed, dressed and undressed, settled into bed and cared for in every way. Then there is housecleaning, including vacuuming, dusting, washing floors and windows, cleaning the oven and refrigerator, the sinks and the bathroom. The reality of the work that is done in the home is only just beginning to be recognized after too many years of silence and misunderstanding.

Two important Canadian studies have analysed the housework and paid work done by husbands and wives.[26] Three hundred forty couples in Vancouver and 1,051 couples in Halifax completed daily time budgets on how their time was spent, including very detailed breakdowns of household chores. The results from different ends of the country were remarkably similar. According to the studies, a housewife works a full-time week of 46 to 51 hours on household and child-care responsibilities, with 37 to 39 hours per week for leisure activities. This picture changes dramatically when she enters the labour force. Her overall work-load (now paid work and housework combined) increases by 11 to 17 hours per week, up to a 63-hour work week. Even with this long work week, the two jobs are maintained only with a radical reduction in housework. The number of hours of housework are reduced from between 46 and 51 to between 22 and 27 hours per week. While certain tasks are dropped and others done less frequently, the reduction in hours spent on housework may well mean that the tasks are compressed by a speed-up in the pace of work. Another major adjustment for housewives who enter the labour force is a reduction in their leisure time by 9 to 11 hours per week.

What happens to the husband when the wife enters the labour force after being a full-time housewife? The short but accurate answer is nothing. His hours of paid employment drop slightly by one or two hours per week, perhaps indicating a reduction in overtime. The amount of housework undertaken increases by only one or two hours, leaving the total hours for all work at the same 56 to 58 hours which prevailed when the wife was at home. Meanwhile, his leisure time varies only slightly, actually increasing by one half hour to two hours per week.

In sum, when a wife with children also works in the labour force, she works six or seven hours more per week than her husband, and has eight hours less leisure time than he does. As one of the studies concludes, "Despite the radical difference which a paid job makes in the working week of married women, their husbands' contribution to the regular necessities of the household remain small and virtually unchanged. . . ."[27]

The working lives of men and women are different, the difference being household responsibilities. One means of adjustment which mothers make, and most fathers do not have to consider, is part-time work. For many women it is a realistic response to otherwise intolerable working conditions. As one study noted.

> Women with children under five were unwilling to consider full-time work unless financial pressures were extreme. Those currently working part-time felt it would be difficult for them to cope with full-time work in addition to their domestic responsibilities. Women working full-time generally said that it was their financial situation which prevented them from working part-time.[28]

Part-time work has been viewed as an easy option, a free choice by women who can choose to dabble in the work force rather than be seriously committed. The reality for most mothers who work in low-paid, low-status part-time jobs while maintaining their families at home is very different. There follows a description of a regular work day by a part-time worker. It was considered typical by the researchers since there were so few differences in the work-loads of the women interviewed:

> I get up about quarter to five, make the children's lunches up, get the children up about half past six, get breakfast, do their hair and everything and then I go out to work about ten to seven. I get home at lunch-time, make the beds and do the housework. I just sort of make a drink of tea and a sandwich and I keep going while I'm eating because if I sit down I don't feel like working. I pick the children up from school, go swimming one night, then it's their tea time. I make the dinner, get the children to bed and that's it really. Most nights I'm either doing the garden or doing the ironing. I never really do sit down. I never watch much telly unless I get worn out sometimes. I can't sit down if I know something has to be done. I'd rather get stuck into it. I go to bed between ten and eleven, otherwise I can't get up for work.[29]

Paid Work for Women

Women in the paid work force are disproportionately ghettoized into low-paid, low-status jobs with little hope of advancement and a future which for many offers only more machines and more tedium.[30] Teaching and nursing are the only two occupations with higher pay and prestige that have been available to women. But most women are clerical workers in offices and banks, salespersons in food and department stores, service workers in hospitals, hotels and restaurants, and production workers in factories.[31] They are paid on average half of what men earn with a work status to match.[32] While such jobs are not devoid of interest, content or companionship, many have been gradually deskilled with the introduction of new technology, and now require less knowledge and more repetition.

In describing the paid jobs that most women do, one describes jobs which have all the characteristics required to produce high stress levels. Job dissatisfaction is a primary cause of work-related stress and is itself caused by underutilization of skills, lack of recognition and low status accorded to work, lack of control over work and the work environment, and by work which is paced by machines.[33] All of these criteria are common elements of the work many women perform, that is, support services accorded little status or control and often paced by machines. As a result, as one expert on work-related health has stated, "Stress is a major occupational health hazard for a majority of employed women."[34]

Mothers of young children add all their household responsibilities to their already stressful jobs, creating yet higher stress levels. It is interesting to note that, apart from job dissatisfaction, stress-inducing factors include excessive hours of work, responsibility for the welfare of others and juggling time schedules for multiple responsibilities.[35] A mother in the labour force is clearly subject to all these factors. She works a 63-hour week, is responsible for the welfare of her children and must balance the requirements of two jobs. She gets up early to feed and clothe her children so that she can get to work on time, does her family shopping in the lunch-time, and rushes away from work to pick up her children and make dinner, and she must remember that one child has a doctor's appointment the next day. Meeting both family and job commitments involves for women a delicate balance of arrangements, easily upset by anything from a temper tantrum at breakfast to chicken pox or an increase in day-care fees. Part-time work is one way to reduce the stress caused by the combined health hazards of a stressful job and responsibility for a family.

Parts of Me Wants to Stay Home — Ideology

It is now the case in this country that just over half (52%) of all women with children under 11 are in the labour force and 46% of women with pre-school-aged children work outside the home.[36] It is undoubtedly the case that mothers working outside the home have become an increasingly accepted part of Canadian life. However, it is also true that there remain strong ideological pressures upon women to stay at home to care for their young children, and 54% of women with pre-schoolers do so. A Saskatchewan survey of 1,708 parents found that about 30% felt that mothers should care for children under the age of 12.[37]

The controversy around whether or not mothers with young children should or should not work does not need to be considered here. The fact is that many women do decide to stay at home with their children during the early years. They want to care for their children because of the emotional attachment which makes child care unlike any other kind of work.

It is interesting that mothers are now almost evenly divided between those who do work in the labour force and those who do not. The situations reflects the ambivalence that many mothers face in making the decision whether or not to undertake paid work. Part-time work also reflects that ambivalence. It allows a mother to divide her time between working in the labour force and spending time with young children at home. While 52% of all mothers with children under 11 work outside the home, only 43% of those employed work full-time and full-year. The majority, 57%, work either part-year or part-time in the labour force.[38]

Summary

There is no doubt that a significant proportion of women workers want part-time work. Forty-three per cent of women part-time workers state that they do not want full-time work.[39] Of unemployed women, 20% say they are seeking part-time jobs.[40] More than one study has found that a proportion of full-time women workers are interested in part-time work.[41]

In this section an attempt has been made to outline the circumstances under which many women become part-time workers. It represents not so much the free choice of an ideal solution as a necessary compromise between conflicting pressures and a response to working conditions. Part-time work brings in extra income while avoiding some of the hardships of combining home and labour force responsibilities, and at the same time enables mothers to spend time with their young children. It is a realistic response by many women with young children to their current social, economic and ideological circumstances, circumstances that will change only very gradually. Women need part-time work and will need it for the foreseeable future. It is on this basis that the issue must be approached and the problems dealt with.

Part-Time Work Means Exploitation

There is no doubt that part-time workers are accorded a secondary status in the labour force, with jobs, pay and conditions to match. While some of the evidence to support this statement is scattered and derived from small studies, all of it points to the same sad conclusion.

Only Certain Jobs Are Part-Time Jobs — Ghettoization

Part-time work is confined to a limited number of industries and jobs, within which part-time workers occupy the lowest level positions and have few, if any, chances for training or promotion.

Three-quarters (74%) of all part-time workers are employed in just two industries, retail trade and community, business and personal services. Within the services they are disproportionately employed in personal services, hospitals and education. By comparison just 43% of full-time workers are employed in the retail trade and services industries.[42] The jobs that part-time workers do are equally confined to just a few occupations. Two-thirds (66%) of all part-time workers are service, clerical or sales workers, compared to 37% of full-time workers.[43] Not only is the range of work available to part-time workers very limited, but it is concentrated into areas which have traditionally been regarded as "women's work." That such jobs offer low pay and little status has been fully documented elsewhere.[44]

Moreover, within these occupations part-time workers are confined to the lowest level jobs with little chance of training or promotion. In the one study that has looked at the issue, training was offered less often to part-time than full-time workers. In this Hamilton study of 39 companies, while 82% of the companies provided training to full-time workers, only 60% did so for part-time workers.[45] Thirty per cent provided on-the-job training of one week or less to part-time workers, while 22% provided on-the-job training of more than one week. Only 10% of the companies provided any classroom training to part-time workers.[46]

In the same study, the lack of training was reflected in the fact that promotion opportunities were not available to part-time workers in 17 out of the 39 companies surveyed, and that 29 out of the 39 did not have any part-time workers in supervisory or management positions. Two-thirds of the companies stated that there was no possibility for part-time workers in supervisory or management positions. Two-thirds of the companies stated that there was no possibility for part-time workers to obtain such positions.[47] These findings are supported by other studies in which employers have clearly indicated that they do not consider part-time workers appropriate for any skilled, professional or management positions.[48] One company representative stated that part-time workers were useful in that they could be hired for the most tedious and monotonous jobs, jobs which would not be considered tolerable for full-time workers.[49] In fact, occupational data for Canada for 1981 shows that 1.8% of part-time workers occupied managerial or administrative jobs, compared to 9% of full-time workers.[50]

Part-Time Pay is Low Pay

Part-time workers earn less than full-time workers on an hourly basis. Table 2 gives the results of the Survey of 1981 work history by Statistics Canada, which provides the only national data available on the wages of full- and part-time workers. In every occupational category part-time workers receive lower hourly wages than do full-time workers. In the first three occupations listed in table 2, that is, services, clerical and sales jobs, are employed two-thirds of all part-time workers. In all three occupations, most part-time workers earn less than $5 an hour, while the majority of full-time workers earn more than this. For example, in services 70% of part-time workers are paid less than $5 an hour compared to only 46% of full-time workers. Looking at all occupations combined, almost half (49%) of all part-time jobs paid less than $5 an hour in 1981, compared to 21% of full-time jobs.

On the basis of a 40-hour week for 52 weeks per year, $5 an hour amounts to an annual income of $10,400. According to the Statistics Canada low-income lines for 1981, many two-person families and all three-person families would be living in poverty on such an income.[51] Almost 9% of part-time jobs paid less than $3 an hour ($6,240 per year), which would not maintain most single people above the poverty line. Part-time workers are both low paid and lower paid than full-time workers.

TABLE 2

Percentage of Jobs Held by Paid Workers by Full-Time/Part-Time, by Hourly Earnings and by Occupation, 1981

Occupation	Hourly earnings							
	Under $3		$3-4.99		$5-9.99		$10 and above	
	Full-time	Part-time	Full-time	Part-time	Full-time	Part-time	Full-time	Part-time
Services	9.2	12.3	36.5	57.8	42.8	24.7	11.4	5.1
Clerical	2.7	7.4	20.4	37.6	65.6	44.1	11.4	10.8
Sales	4.6	7.2	27.3	57.2	49.2	29.4	18.9	8.1
Managerial, admin., technical	2.4	4.0	6.7	13.4	39.4	43.3	51.5	39.2
Materials handling	2.0	9.7	19.2	38.4	52.8	40.3	26.0	11.6
Primary	11.1	24.7	22.8	37.1	43.0	25.7	23.2	12.5
Processing	2.0	6.8	15.5	35.2	53.8	42.3	28.6	15.7
Transportation	3.1	4.7	12.7	25.0	55.4	46.8	28.7	23.6
Construction	2.4	3.6	8.5	17.2	44.7	47.7	44.4	31.6
All occupations	3.7	8.7	17.7	40.1	49.9	35.9	28.7	15.3

SOURCE: Statistics Canada, Labour Force Activity Section, unpublished data from the special survey on work history, 1981.

The work history data is too general, and the occupational categories too large, to indicate why part-time workers are paid less than full-time. Many factors may be involved. Differences in age, qualifications and tenure of part-time and full-time workers, and differences in the type of part-time and full-time jobs available may all be important. A study in Ontario in 1975 surveyed in more detail the pay of full- and part-time workers within specific services industries, such as hotels and motels, restaurants and taverns, laundries and cleaners, and barber and beauty shops.[52] Looking at non-supervisory staff employed in the same industry, the study found that the 57,124 part-time workers earned $2.73 per hour on average, compared to $3.32 for full-time workers. Thus part-time workers were paid

82% of the full-time wage, earning 18% less than the full-time workers. Such findings are supported by studies from other countries, where part-time workers have been found to be much lower paid than full-time workers.[53]

Part-time workers receive lower pay partly because most are ghettoized into the lowest paid occupations, in hotels, restaurants, stores and offices. Within these low-paid sectors they are confined to the lowest level jobs, since training is rarely provided to part-time workers and higher level or management positions are not made available to them. The ghettoization of part-time workers into low-paid jobs is then compounded by the fact that often they are paid less per hour than full-time workers. In the Hamilton study mentioned above only 14% of the part-time workers received prorated pay, that is the same pay as full-time workers according to the hours worked.[54] Even where part-time workers are hired on at the same starting pay as full-time workers, that is often where they stay. Many are not eligible for the regular increments that are obtained by full-time workers.

Few and Far Between — Benefits for Part-Time Workers

The various benefits now found in many work places are important and substantial additions to the actual pay rate. A Statistics Canada survey in 1978 found that employee benefits averaged $33.97 for every $100 paid in basic wage rates.[55] Vacations, statutory holidays, pensions, health and life insurance, sick leave, maternity leave and various other benefits have become an expected part of the total pay package for many workers.

How do part-time workers fare in regard to such benefits? Two studies have been conducted in Canada that compare the benefits provided to full-time and part-time workers. In 1974, 304 work places in Saskatchewan were surveyed, covering 1,314 workers of which 375 were part-time.[56] On all the eight benefits reviewed, fewer part-time than full-time workers were covered. The results on the four most important benefits surveyed are reproduced in table 3.

The study concludes, "The survey results clearly indicate that benefits are not being extended to part-time employees on the same basis as they are to full-time employees."[57]

TABLE 3

Comparative Benefits for Full- and Part-Time Workers, Saskatchewan, 1974

Benefits	Percentage of workers covered	
	Full-time	Part-time
Sick leave	53.0	21.7
Accident and sickness policy	28.8	0.8
Life insurance plan	26.0	9.8
Comprehensive pension plan	36.4	13.0

SOURCE: Saskatchewan Department of Labour, Research and Planning Division, "A Comparative Study of the Provision of Selected Non-Wage Benefits to Part-Time and Full-Time Employees in Rural Saskatchewan, April-June 1974," October 1975.

The Hamilton study also compared fringe benefits for full-time and part-time workers. In this case, the coverage in general was higher, but again there was a considerable disparity between the coverage for full- and part-time workers. Of interest in this study is that intermittent, or casual, part-time work was considered separately and these workers generally received less coverage than regular part-time workers. The results on several of the major benefits surveyed are given in table 4.

TABLE 4

Comparative Benefits for Full- and Part-Time Workers, Hamilton, Ontario, 1978

Benefits	Percentage of companies with workers covered (%)		
	Full-time *N:39	Regular part-time N:36	Casual part-time N:19
Sick leave	87.2	44.4	21.1
Medical/hospital insurance	82.1	41.7	21.1
Disability insurance	59.0	13.9	0
Life insurance	76.9	25.0	15.8
Superannuation	48.7	16.7	10.5
Vacation pay	97.4	91.7	68.4
Statutory holidays	92.3	77.8	42.1
Maternity leave	87.2	52.8	36.8

*N = the number of companies in the sample.

SOURCE: Wendy Weeks, "The Extent and Nature of Part-Time Work in Hamilton, Survey Results of Selected Hamilton Businesses – 1978," Hamilton, September 1980, table 29.

It is clear that part-time workers, and especially casual part-time workers, are seriously disadvantaged by the lack of benefits regarded as basic by many full-time workers.

Inconvenienced, Overworked and Insecure — Conditions for Part-Time Workers

Many part-time workers work unsocial hours: early mornings and evenings cleaning offices, evenings and Saturdays in shops in restaurants, weekends and holidays in hospitals and nursing homes. While women may work such hours to accommodate the care of their children, family and social life are disrupted and the women are not recompensed for such disruption. Part-time workers are hired precisely to fill in the unsocial hours in many work places and, as we have seen, they are generally paid less than full-time workers.

Further disruption is caused because a part-time worker's hours of employment may fluctuate from week to week or day to day. While employers have applauded the flexibility of part-time work,[58] for many workers it means not knowing when there will be work or how long it will last. A bank worker described the problem for part-time workers: "Some people had their hours cut arbitrarily and without warning while others were forced to resign because their hours increased. Days off were changed without consultation or notice."[59] For women with children, making child-care arrangements under such circumstances is often a time-consuming and frustrating feat of scheduling and rescheduling.

More than one study has suggested that because of their shorter hours, part-time workers are more productive than full-time workers. This argument has been used to propose that employers would benefit from hiring more part-time workers.[60] While the increased productivity is advantageous to employers, what does it mean for the part-time workers? It means that they work faster. Part-time workers are often hired to deal with business peaks, including lunch times at restaurants and busy downtown stores, Saturdays in department and food stores, and so on. As a consequence, many are expected to work at a fast pace of work throughout their working hours, without the ups and downs of activity of a full-time job. This problem is aggravated by the lack of meal and coffee breaks. Full-time workers on an eight-hour day must obviously be allowed breaks, but part-time workers may be employed for their three- or four-hour shift without a rest. One article in an employer's magazine noted that part-time workers are "the answer to coffee breaks."[61]

Many part-time workers have very little security in their jobs. Indeed one major reason that they are employed, according to employers, is because of this flexibility. Part-time workers can be called in for work and then let go without notice or termination pay. The advantages of part-time flexibility are summarized in Weeks' study of business views:

> Lay-offs are cheaper and less likely to damage the morale of other workers. In direct employment of part-timers, the company can cease to call in a particular employee without any required notice of termination or pay in lieu. If employers are using a temporary help service, a Business Week journalist comments, "You can send back a person who doesn't work out, and you don't have to give notice."[62]

Such flexibility is hardly as advantageous to the part-time workers as it is to the company. Moreover, many part-time workers are casual or temporary workers and have no job security whatsoever.

Work Today, None Tomorrow — Casual Part-Time Work

Some part-time workers are employed on a permanent or regular basis with the expectation of work over an extended period of time. The clerical worker employed from 9:00 to 12:00 for five days every week and the cashier who works every Thursday, Friday and Saturday are regular part-time workers. However, there is evidence that many part-time workers are not regularly employed, but work on a casual or temporary basis. They may be listed on a call-in list, and called to work on occasional days to cover for the sickness of regular workers or to meet brief business peaks. Others work part-time on a temporary basis, employed for part of the week but for just a few weeks or months. For example, extra sales clerks work evenings and weekends in stores for the month before Christmas. . . .[63]

Is all this casual work serving the needs of part-time workers? Do part-time workers want temporary jobs? From the limited evidence available it would seem that while a proportion of part-time workers do seek temporary jobs, a far greater proportion are actually employed on a casual basis. Each month in its labour force survey, Statistics Canada asks unemployed workers whether they are seeking full-time, part-time, permanent or temporary work. Temporary work is work undertaken for less than six months duration. In 1981, of unemployed workers seeking part-time work, 22% stated that they were looking for temporary jobs.[64] It would seem from the limited evidence available that while 22% of part-time workers may seek temporary jobs, from two to three times this proportion of part-time jobs are actually casual rather than permanent. In other words, many part-time workers who are now employed on a casual basis would prefer permanent part-time jobs.

Moreover, the lack of permanent part-time work may be particularly detrimental for married women with children. While overall 22% of unemployed part-time workers are seeking temporary jobs, important differences appear in the breakdowns by age, sex and marital status. Of single men under 25 who are unemployed and wanting part-time work, 27% say that they want temporary work. For single women under 25, the proportion is similar at 25%. However, for married women aged 25 and above only 3% say they are seeking temporary part-time jobs.[65] Thus, while young and single people are more interested in temporary part-time work, 87% of married women over 25 seeking part-time work want permanent positions.

But I Want to Work Full-Time — Involuntary Part-Time Work

It has been argued that because part-time work is cheap labour it is used by employers to replace full-time jobs, forcing workers into part-time jobs and underemployment. By this process, the increase in part-time work has been connected to the economic crisis and high unemployment rates. . . . It is important to mention here that a significant proportion of part-time workers would prefer to have full-time jobs.

In 1981, 17% of all women part-time workers and 20% of all men part-time workers said that they were working part-time because they were unable to find full-time jobs. Because there are far more women than men who work part-time, this meant that 184,000 women were underemployed compared to 83,000 men.[66] It is not surprising that so many more women than men are affected by the lack of full-time jobs. Part-time work is highly concentrated in occupations that have been traditionally dominated by women. Consequently, it is largely women who are forced unwillingly into part-time jobs. Of the 267,000 workers who in 1981 were working part-time because they could not get full-time jobs, 70% were women. Involuntary part-time work may be particularly disastrous for women, who even in their full-time jobs are low paid compared to men.

Summary

Part-time workers are largely confined to the lowest levels of low-paid job ghettos where they are paid less and provided with fewer benefits than their full-time counterparts. They may find themselves working at a constantly rapid pace during unsocial hours for which they receive no financial recompense. When they have served their purpose, they may be laid off, or simply not recalled, without notice, pay in lieu or severance pay. Part-time workers have little job security, particularly those who work on a casual basis. Almost one out of every five part-time workers would prefer full-time work and 70% of these underemployed workers are women.

Under such circumstances it seems hardly likely that part-time work will "allow individuals to work at jobs they find interesting and rewarding" or that it will enable women "to keep up their job skills," as one study has suggested.[67] It is even less likely that part-time work will "help women to achieve equality of opportunity in employment," as the Royal Commission on the Status of Women suggested.[68] Part-time workers are not even provided with the pay, benefits and conditions of work of full-time *women* workers, quite apart from the discrepancy between women and men on these issues.

Conclusion

It has been argued that part-time work may undermine progress towards equality for women in general.[69] The cause of this is not only the exploitation of part-time workers in the labour force. It has also been related to the domestic role of women. Two concerns have been raised:

— Part-time work may be regarded as an alternative to day care and used to undermine pressure for improved services.

— Part-time work may reaffirm women's responsibility for domestic work by enabling women to perform all the housework and child-care tasks in the home.

On the first issue, the fact that opponents of day care may suggest that part-time work is the solution to child care is no reason to oppose part-time work. Many other arguments have also been used to avoid increasing day-care facilities and this one must be countered like any other. In fact, the provision of day care is so appallingly deficient that the unmet demand could hardly be satisfied through part-time work. Too many mothers work full-time and will continue to do so. Moreover, it is obvious that the children of many part-time women workers need supervised day care no less than those with mothers working full-time.

It has been argued that part-time work will reaffirm women's domestic role by enabling women to carry their double burden rather than being relieved of it. A preferred alternative to part-time work has been proposed: shorter working hours for all workers so that men and women could share in household responsibilities. There are real problems with such an argument. First, changes in the labour market have no necessary relationship to the socially-determined role of women. While it is true, of course, that women who work part-time have more time for household tasks, we also know that when women work full-time it does not alleviate their domestic labour. Women work in the home whatever their hours in the labour force. Likewise, whatever their hours in the labour force, men do not work in the home. There is no reason to suppose that shortening the working hours of men, from 40 to say 30 per week, will cause them to use the additional time for domestic work. In fact, there is evidence that they will not. During this century men's hours of paid work have been reduced substantially, but we have yet to see the results in more nearly equal sharing in the home. While shorter working hours for all workers would have many desirable consequences, it is not clear that greater equality between men and women would be one of them.

Even if regular full-time hours were dramatically decreased, to 30 hours per week, for example, part-time workers are employed for fewer hours than this. The 13.5% of workers in the labour force considered to be part-time by Statistics Canada are all employed for less than 30 hours per week, and the average employment for part-time workers is 15 hours per week.[70] Moreover, as part-time work has been increasing over the last 30 years, the usual full-time hours of work have been declining simultaneously. It is not apparent that even much shorter full-time hours would meet the needs of those who presently work part-time.

There seems little reason why shorter full-time hours and part-time work should be perceived as alternatives rather than as complementary. If a goal for the future includes shorter full-time hours with men and women sharing housework, it might also encompass part-time work undertaken as often by fathers as by mothers of young children.

Since some advocates of women's rights have argued that because part-time work reaffirms women's domestic role it should be restricted or eliminated, one further point needs to be made. The problem is that part-time work, dominated as it is by women, is a symptom of women's domestic inequality rather than a cause of it. Eliminating part-time work would take away one means women have of alleviating their unequal situation, while leaving intact all those inequalities and problems which make women want to work part-time. It is small comfort to a woman with pre-school children, no day care and insufficient income to tell her that she does not need her part-time job but better day care. To say that mothers and fathers should share childrearing is an abstraction for the woman who wants to spend some time with her child and whose husband has never changed a diaper.

Remarkable powers have been attributed to part-time work, so let us be clear about what it cannot do either by its presence or its absence. Part-time work cannot resolve the lack of day care, responsibility for housework, the stressful nature of low-paid, low-status work, or the need for fathers as well as mothers to take part in childrearing. Such problems require housework and child care to be equally shared between men and women and supported by community services, an end to the ghettoization of women's work in the labour force and shorter working hours for all workers. The struggle to obtain real equality for women involves all of these factors and more, and part-time work is no substitute for gains in these areas.

However, the general restriction or elimination of part-time work proposed by some will not produce more day-care centres, more nearly equal sharing of child care, the equality of women in the labour force, or a shorter work week. What it might do, given the current pressures upon women, is force some mothers out of the labour force and entirely into the domestic role, while others, under extreme financial pressure, would work long and stressful hours.

Is part-time work good or bad? It is neither entirely. While many women who work part-time are exploited, women continue to want part-time work because of the social and economic pressures in their lives. Until these social and economic inequalities are removed, any policy of generally eliminating part-time work may only cause further hardship to women with young children. However, if part-time work as it now exists is further expanded, it will only serve to worsen women's position in the labour force, increasing ghettoization, low pay and lack of benefits.

Notes

1. Women were 72% of part-time workers in 1981. Canada, Statistics Canada, *The Labour Force*, Cat. No. 71-001, December 1981, 112, table 87.

2. Canada, *Report of the Royal Commission on the Status of Women in Canada*, 1970, 104.

3. Ibid., 105.

4. Harry Mackay, "Part-Time Work in Canada", submission to the Canada Employment and Immigration Advisory Council (Ottawa: Canadian Council on Social Development, September 1980), 4–5.

5. Canadian Advisory Council on the Status of Women, "Part-Time Work: A Review of the Issues," brief to the Canada Employment and Immigration Advisory Council (Ottawa, November 1980), 17.

6. Harry Mackay, "Part-Time Work in Canada," 6.

7. La Coalition (CSN, CEQ, SFPQ, SPGQ, FQII, FSPIIQ, Action-travail des femmes, Ligue des femmes du Québec, Au bas de l'échelle, Carrefour des associations de familles monoparentales du Québec), Press release, "200,000 femmes dénoncent le piège du temps partiel," (Montreal, 8 December 1981), 1.

8. Public Service Alliance of Canada, "Part-Time Employment," Discussion Paper, mimeographed (Ottawa, October 1981).

9. André J. Beauchamp, "The Sham of Part-Time Work," *Perspective CUPW* (Canadian Union of Postal Workers), January 1981.

10. Canada, Statistics Canada, *Vital Statistics*, Volume 1, *Births, 1975 and 1976*, Cat. No. 84-204, 13, table 6. In 1976, the latest year for which figures are available, the fertility rate was 1.8 children per woman.

11. Canada, Health and Welfare Canada, unpublished data from *Survey of Consumer Finances 1980 (Income 1979 – Economic Families)*, microdata tape.

12. Meg Luxton, "Taking on the Double Day," *Atlantis* 7, 1 (Fall 1981), 15–16.

13. Health and Welfare Canada, unpublished data from *Survey of Consumer Finances*.

14. Manitoba, Department of Labour, Women's Bureau, "A Study of Part-Time Employment," August 1976.

15. Canada, Health and Welfare Canada, National Day Care Information Centre, unpublished estimates for 1982.

16. The exclusion of middle income families from daycare centres has been reported by two studies: Laura C. Johnson, *Who Cares? A Report of the Project Child Care Survey of Parents and Their Child Care Arrangements* (Toronto: Community Day Care Coalition and the Social Planning Council of Metropolitan Toronto, November 1977), 88; Saskatchewan, Social Services, "Summary of Day Care Needs and Demands in Saskatchewan 1978," 1 June 1980, 16.

17. Alberta, Social Services and Community Health, "Interprovincial Comparison — Day Care Facilities, Licensed Full-Day Program," study conducted by Price Waterhouse Associates, August 1980, Exhibit 7.

18. Laura C. Johnson, *The Search for Child Care*, Project Child Care Working Paper No. 3 (Toronto: Children's Day Care Coalition and the Social Planning Council of Metropolitan Toronto, January 1978); Donna S. Lero, "Factors Influencing Parents' Preference for, and Use of, Alternative Child Care Arrangements for Pre-School-Age Children, Final Division" (Guelph, Ont.: University of Guelph, 1981).

19. Canada, Health and Welfare Canada, *Status of Day Care in Canada*, 1980, 8.

20. Laura C. Johnson, *Taking Care: A Report of the Project Child Care Survey of Caregivers in Metropolitan Toronto* (Toronto: Children's Day Care Coalition and the Social Planning Council of Metropolitan Toronto, April 1978), 79.

21. Ibid.; Ontario, Ministry of Community and Social Services, "Family Benefits Mothers in Metropolitan Toronto," 1973.

22. Johnson, *Taking Care.*

23. Ibid., 21.

24. May Nickson, "Preliminary Report on Working Mothers and Their Child Care Arrangements in 1973," (Ottawa: Statistics Canada, Labour Division, January 1975), table 10; Ontario Ministry of Community and Social Services, "Family Benefits Mothers"; Saskatchewan, Social Services, "Summary of Day Care Needs," 17.

25. Health and Welfare Canada, *Status of Day Care*, 8.

26. Martin Meissner et al., "No Exit for Wives: Sexual Division of Labour and the Cumulation of Household Demands," *The Canadian Review of Sociology and Anthropology* 12, 4, Part 1, November 1975; Susan Clark and Andrew S. Harvey, "The Sexual Division of Labour: The Use of Time," *Atlantis* 2, 1 (Fall 1976), 46.

27. Martin Meissner et al., "No Exit for Wives," 436.

28. Sylvia Shimmin et al., "Pressures of Women Engaged in Factory Work" *Employment Gazette* 89, 8 (August 1981), 348.

29. Ibid., 347.

30. Pat Armstrong and Hugh Armstrong, *The Double Ghetto* (Toronto: McClelland and Stewart, 1978).

31. Ibid., 33.

32. Ibid., 38.

33. Jeanne H. Stellman, "Occupational Health and Women Workers: A Review," *Labour Studies Journal* 6, 1 (Spring 1981), 18.

34. Ibid., 18.

35. Ibid., 19.

36. Health and Welfare Canada, unpublished data from *Survey of Consumer Finances*, 1980.

37. Saskatchewan, Department of Social Services, "Survey of Child Care Preferences," April 1980, 4.

38. Health and Welfare Canada, unpublished data from *Survey of Consumer Finances*.

39. Statistics Canada, *The Labour Force*, December 1981, 113, table 88.

40. Ibid., 123, table 98.

41. Carol Reich, "A Study of Interest in Part-Time Employment Among Non-Teaching Employees of the Board," Toronto Board of Education, Research Department (Toronto, September 1975); Michèle de Sève and Simon Langlois, "Les hommes et les femmes dans la fonction publique québécoise" (Québec, Éditeur officiel du Québec, 1978).

42. Canada, Statistics Canada, Labour Force survey Division, unpublished data, 1981. See Appendix 1.

43. Ibid.

44. Armstrong and Armstrong, *The Double Ghetto.*

45. Wendy Weeks, "The Extent and Nature of Part-Time Work in Hamilton, Survey Results of Selected Hamilton Businesses—1978," prepared for the Community Permanent Part-Time Work Committee (Hamilton, September 1980), table 40.

46. Ibid., table 41.

47. Ibid., tables 44, 47 and 48.

48. Marianne Bossen, "Part-Time Work in the Canadian Economy," Labour Canada, (Ottawa, October 1975), 68–69; Wendy Weeks, "Part-Time Work: The Business View on Second-Class Jobs for Housewives and Mothers," *Atlantis* 5, 2, (Spring 1980), 76–77.

49. Wendy Weeks, "Part-Time Work: The Business View," 73.

50. Statistics Canada, Labour Force Survey Division, unpublished data, 1981. See Appendix I.

51. In 1981 the Statistics Canada low-income lines for one person ranged from $5,949 in rural areas to $8,045 in urban areas, for two-person families from $7,775 to $10,614 and for three persons from $10,412 to $14,198. Information from the National Council of Welfare, Ottawa.

52. Gord Robertson, "Part-Time Work in Ontario: 1966 to 1976," Employment Information Series Number 20 (Toronto: Ontario Ministry of Labour, Research Branch, August 1976).

53. Jennifer Hurstfield, *The Part-Time Trap: Part-Time Workers in Britain Today*, Low Pay Pamphlet No. 9 (London: Low Pay Unit, December 1978); John D. Owen, "Why Part-time Workers Tend to be in Low-Wage Jobs," *Monthly Labor Review* 101, 6 (June 1978).

54. Wendy Weeks, "Part-Time Work in Hamilton," table 28.

55. Canada, Statistics Canada, *Employee Compensation in Canada*, Cat. No. 72–169, 1978, 46, table 1.

56. Saskatchewan, Department of Labour, Research and Planning Division, "A Comparative Study of the Provision of Selected Non-Wage Benefits to Part-Time and Full-Time Employees in Rural Saskatchewan April to June 1974," October 1975.

57. Ibid., ix.

58. Wendy Weeks, "Part-Time Work: The Business View," 73.

59. The Bank Book Collective, *An Account to Settle. The Story of the United Bank Workers (SORWUC)* (Vancouver: Press Gang Publishers, 1979), 29.

60. Jane Schwartz, *Part-Time Employment* (New York: Alumnae Advisory Center, 1964); Carol Greenwald and Judith Liss, "Part-Time Workers Can Bring Higher Productivity," *Harvard Business Review* 51 (September-October 1973); William B. Werther, "Mini-Shifts: An Alternative to Overtime," *Personnel Journal* 55, 3 (March 1976), 130.

61. Wendy Weeks, "Part-Time Work: The Business View," 75.

62. Ibid., 73.

63. The proportion of part-time workers employed regularly is just 26.6% of all those who do part-time work when those who are employed temporarily or occasionally or are on call-in lists for casual work, are also figured in. See Wendy Weeks, "Part-Time Work in Hamilton," tables 8, 10.

64. Statistics Canada, *The Labour Force*, December 1981, 123, table 98.

65. Ibid.

66. Ibid., 113, table 88.

67. Harry Mackay, "Part-Time Work in Canada," 5, 14.

68. Canada, *Royal Commission on the Status of Women*, 104.

69. Québec, Conseil du statut de la femme, "Le travail à temps partiel: une mesure d'égalité en emploi ou d'inégalité en emploi . . . ," September 1982, 40–41.

70. Statistics Canada, *The Labour Force*, December 1981, 109, table 84.

INDEPENDENCE VERSUS PARTISANSHIP: DILEMMAS IN THE POLITICAL HISTORY OF WOMEN IN ENGLISH CANADA†

SYLVIA B. BASHEVKIN

Feminism, like other reform movements, has emerged during periods in which the society of which it is a part tolerates searching self-criticism in the belief that purposeful change can bring about indisputable improvement. Invariably in such cases, some people take the questioning further than anyone had initially intended. Québécoises, for instance, starting off to protest, with men in the 1960s, the subordinate role of francophones in Quebec and of Quebec in Canada, went on to identify and then protest the subordinate role of women in the nationalist movement and in French-Canadian society. They, along with women elsewhere in the country (also committed to societal rejuvenation), ended up questioning the family, sexual conventions and roles, language, and the distribution of power. Such emphases differ from those of "first-wave" feminism, reflecting contemporary women's greater participation in the labour force, the separation of sexuality from reproduction, the higher divorce rate and the incursion of the state into ever more aspects of our lives.

However, like their earlier counterparts, contemporary feminists have been torn as to how to effect the changes they would like to see in women's lives. Some have created alternative institutions, run by women themselves, to deal with the unmet needs of female Canadians. Women's health collectives, feminist bookstores and newspapers, houses for battered women and their children, feminist labour unions are all attempts to compel modifications in the terms on which conventional institutions deal with women. To alter the impoverished symbolic representation of women, feminists have analysed and criticized all forms of media as well as traditional bodies of knowledge, and, where possible, have begun creating their own art, literature, and scholarship, taking women's points of view into account. All such activity has made an impact. Many more Canadians have become self-conscious about language, support equal pay for work of equal value, and acknowledge that men ought to take their share of domestic responsibilities. Labour unions have begun tackling subjects such as sexual harassment and day care for members' children. In their quest to see the world through women's eyes, feminists, while not convincing everyone, have identified issues that have touched a nerve even in those whose first response is to oppose feminism.

Institutions tend to be resistant to change, however, and the state has not been an unqualified advocate of equality for women, especially where such reforms would challenge vested interests. The growth of government, which over the past hundred years has taken responsibility for increasingly intimate aspects of its citizens' lives (many feel inappropriately so in the case of women), ensures that politics is one arena in which feminists need to do combat. But a dilemma, which Sylvia Bashevkin traces to the beginning of Canadian women's participation in public politics, has emerged. Bashevkin describes it as the "tension between independence and partisanship." Should women adhere to a position of "political independence which could guarantee both organizational autonomy and purity," so that their goals would not be watered down by male politicians with little interest or knowledge of women's issues, or should

†Sylvia B. Bashevkin, *Toeing the Lines: Women and Party Politics in English Canada* (Toronto: University of Toronto Press, 1985): 3–32.

they embrace "conventional partisanship which might better ensure their political influence and legislative success" but perhaps at the expense of carefully thought-out programs and policies?

Lobbying, one traditional way of inducing legislators to adopt a specific group's point of view, has been given more attention by women in recent years, although they lack the financial resources of business groups. The National Action Committee on the Status of Women continuously prods legislators to pay attention to women's issues, while other groups have emerged to ensure the enshrinement of equal rights for women in the Canadian Charter of Rights and Freedoms, to inform government commissions of the impact of pornography on women, and to pressure crown corporations into hiring females for "male" occupations and positions.

The success of lobbyists, however, ultimately depends upon having reliable allies as elected legislators. Bashevkin, in Toeing the Lines: Women and Party Politics in English Canada *(1985) from which this chapter is taken, explains how women in English Canada have been marginalized within the party system, and hence why there are still so few women in the country's legislatures. Although integration into male-dominated political parties has met with only limited success, Bashevkin is not optimistic about the prospects for an independent feminist politics in a party-based parliamentary system. Too many levers of power operate only from within the traditional parties, and outsiders remain at a substantial disadvantage if they choose other methods of influencing government policy.*

Yet for all the difficulties in finding an effective way of making their voices heard, women cannot afford to leave the politics of the public sphere solely to male direction. Decisions taken within city councils, provincial legislatures, and the House of Commons critically influence women's lives. Even the alternative institutions that women have established for themselves are usually dependent upon funding from some level of government. Bashevkin notes in her book that there is some evidence that politically active women are especially likely to support feminist issues like day care and equal pay for work of equal value. Certainly the efforts of Canada's three major national parties to recruit female voters, party members and, occasionally, candidates, have brought some important developments, notably the proposal for homemakers' pensions by the Conservative government in 1985. Experience in every party from the Social Credit to the Parti Québécois indicates that an independent feminist lobby within the party is essential if women and their particular interests are not to be subsumed to the demands of a male agenda.

> The Women's Good Government League . . . stands on the principle of cooperation and is assured that women can best serve their country by keeping out of parties and away from the party machines.
> *Woman's Century,* 1918[1]

> I couldn't open my mouth to say the simplest thing without it appearing in the papers. I was curiosity, a freak. And you know the way the world treats freaks.
> Agnes Macphail, 1949[2]

The political experiences of women in Canada have been shaped by many influences, some of which are related directly to women, and others of which emanate from broader political processes and structures. Existing research on female political involvement has interpreted these experiences in reference to two main sets of factors, one psychological, including conventional patterns of gender role socialization, and the second structural, involving discriminatory practices within party organizations.[3]

While this prevailing focus upon role constraints and structural limitations reveals some of the obstacles to female political activity, it has obscured an important historical dimension within the political development of English-Canadian women. Boldly stated, the ideological and organizational dilemmas surrounding female enfranchisement in English Canada provide a critical and widely neglected perspective on subsequent political experiences in this culture. In the following discussion, we shall argue that early feminism and suffragism in English Canada were part of a broader progressive challenge to the traditional two-party system and, furthermore, that these movements became locked in the horns of a trying political dilemma: on the one hand, early women's groups were attracted toward a position of political independence, which could guarantee both organizational autonomy and purity; on the other hand, they were drawn toward conventional partisanship, which might better ensure their political influence and legislative success. Taken together, this tension between independence and partisanship within the context of a changing party system helped to define the parameters of women's political history in English Canada for many decades. A similar dilemma, in fact, continues to shape the development of contemporary English-Canadian feminism, as well as the broader relationship between women and the present party system.

In practical terms, this tension between independence and partisanship has limited the exercise of effective political power by women in English Canada.[4] Ironically, even though females in some regions had the right to vote — primarily in local school board elections — as early as the eighteenth century, and although many were organized into such party affiliates as the Toronto Women's Liberal Association prior to the formal extension of the franchise, few entered the electorate as politically skilled or equal participants.[5]

This situation resulted in part from the ideological position adopted by mainstream suffragists, which began with the assumption that females would spread a mantle of purity from their private domestic sphere to the public, political domain. In the words of the *Woman's Century*, quoted above, new women voters were advised to avoid the corrupting, immoral party organizations and to adopt an independent, non-partisan route to national influence. The limitations of this strategy, as applied within an essentially partisan, parliamentary system, combined with women's co-optation into separate auxiliaries within the two major parties, are reflected clearly in Agnes Macphail's commentary on life in the House of Commons. More than fifteen years after the formal extension of the federal franchise, Macphail remained the sole female member of parliament, a "freak" who reluctantly symbolized a continuing distance between women and political power in Canada.

What was the organizational and ideological background to this dilemma between independence and partisanship? To what extent has the subsequent political history of women in English Canada been shaped by early feminist experiences? And how have women recently begun to question and to challenge their lack of political and especially partisan influence? These are the main questions which inform our discussion of the political history of women in English Canada.

Origins of the Movement

The formal beginnings of the suffrage movement in English Canada are generally dated from the founding of the Toronto Women's Literary Society in 1877.[6] Composed primarily of well-educated and professional women of the Protestant middle classes, the Literary Society disguised its suffragist leanings until the 1880s, when Dr Emily Stowe, her daughter (Dr Augusta Stowe-Gullen), and a number of other activists established the Canadian Woman Suffrage Association and a series of similarly directed organizations.[7]

Much of the ideological and organizational strength of English-Canadian suffragism developed as a result of ties between this movement and other reform groups which operated during the turn-of-the-century period. As indicated by Carol Bacchi's research on major suffragist leaders, the movement attracted many men and women who were also affiliated with temperance, urban improvement, and civic education activities. Organized pressure for the vote was thus allied with a broader reformist response to the rapid pace of in-dustrialization, urbanization, and the perceived decline of traditional values in many Western societies, including Canadian.

In addition, women in Toronto and the western provinces were particularly influenced by feminist and suffragist initiatives in other Anglo-American democracies; they frequently merged elements of the American and British movements with an essentially moderate, non-militant approach which was reflective of English-Canadian culture more generally.[8] Moreover, Canadian feminists also benefited from the increasing opportunities available to middle-class women in education, professional employment, and volunteer work, and thus shared a growing international commitment to broadening their own political rights.[9]

What rationale did English-Canadian suffragists offer in pursuit of the vote? The historical literature on this subject demonstrates a number of important divisions within the movement, particularly along generational and ideological lines. As in the American case, English-Canadian activists included an older "hard-core" minority which sought to challenge the discriminatory treatment of women in virtually all facets of social life, including education, employment, political rights, and, most importantly, the family.[10] Believing that females justly deserved the same degree of individual independence that had accrued to males, "hard-core" feminists, such as Flora MacDonald Denison, campaigned outside the more moderate, reformist mainstream of "social femin-ism" in English Canada.[11]

TABLE 1

Legislative Changes Affecting the Political Status of Women in Canada

Jurisdiction	Date of female enfranchisement[a]	Legislative sponsor	Date of eligibility to hold office	First woman elected
Man.	28 Jan. 1916	Liberal gov't	28 Jan. 1916	29 June 1920
Sask.	14 Mar. 1916	Liberal gov't	14 Mar. 1916	29 June 1919
Alta.	19 Apr. 1916	Liberal gov't	19 Apr. 1916	7 June 1917
B.C.	5 Apr. 1917	Liberal gov't	5 Apr. 1917	24 Jan. 1918[b]
Ont.	23 Apr. 1917	Conserv. gov't	4 Apr. 1919	4 Aug. 1943
Canada	24 May 1918, full female franchise[c]	Union gov't	7 July 1919	6 Dec. 1921
N.S.	26 Apr. 1918	Liberal gov't	26 Apr. 1918	7 June 1960
N.B.	17 Apr. 1919	Liberal gov't	9 Mar. 1934	10 Oct. 1967
P.E.I.	3 May 1922	Liberal gov't	3 May 1922	11 May 1970
Nfld.	13 Apr. 1925[d]	Conserv. gov't	13 Apr. 1925	17 May 1930[b]
Que.	25 Apr. 1940	Liberal gov't	25 Apr. 1940	14 Dec. 1961

a   Denotes date of royal assent.
b   Denotes victory in by-election.
c   The Military Voters Act and the Wartime Elections Act, which both received royal assent in September 1917, enfranchised women who were British subjects and who had served in any branch of the military, or who had a close relative serving in the armed forces of Canada or Great Britain.
d   According to this 1925 legislation, female voters had to be age 25 or over to vote, while men could vote at age 21. This disparity was rectified by the Terms of Union of Newfoundland with Canada, 1948.

SOURCES: Catherine L. Cleverdon, *The Woman Suffrage Movement in Canada* (Toronto: University of Toronto Press, 1974) and Terence H. Qualter, *The Election Process in Canada* (Toronto: McGraw-Hill, 1970), 9, 52

The ideological and organizational pivot of Canadian suffragism thus resembled its "social feminist" counterpart in the United States, which linked "suffrage and temperance and other crusades, such as civil service reform, conservation, child labour laws, mothers' pensions, municipal improvements, education reform, pure food and drug laws, industrial commissions, social justice and peace."[12] "Maternal" or "social" feminism in English Canada was, as its name suggests, predicated upon a fundamental belief in the necessity for social reform and for women's participation in this process. Unlike more radical "hardcore" arguments, it elevated Protestant social reform above demands for legal emancipation and claimed that the granting of the vote to women was essential for general social improvement.[13]

The manner in which organized feminism developed held important implications for women's relationship to the Canadian political system. For much of its history, the core of the movement remained in Toronto, which served as the headquarters for such groups as the Dominion Women's Enfranchisement Association and the Canadian Suffrage Association. While claiming to be nationwide, these organizations actually "had few affiliates and even less control outside Toronto" — where, ironically, the initial legislative successes of the movement were achieved (see table 1).[14]

The regional divisions and conflicts which characterized other Canadian social movements thus affected suffragist organization in an especially damaging manner, since the latter needed to operate on a region-by-region basis in order to secure the provincial franchise, while it also required an image of national influence in order to achieve the vote federally. These organizational demands were not easily reconcilable; as Catherine L. Cleverdon points out: "The small but valiant bands of women found it necessary to concentrate their political efforts upon their provincial governments, and this undoubtedly militated against the successful formation of any truly nation-wide suffrage association."[15] Indeed, in the absence of such a national organization, suffragists relied heavily upon alliances with older, established, and generally conservative women's groups, including the Woman's Christian Temperance Union (WCTU), the Federated Women's Institutes, and the National Council of Women of Canada (NCWC).[16] Particularly in the case of the NCWC, which formally endorsed enfranchisement in 1910, suffragists gained an important element of national visibility and credibility, at the same time as they became dependent upon increasingly moderate, social feminist strategies which were acceptable to the NCWC leadership and similar coalition partners.

The organizational features of Canadian suffragism thus held important consequences for the momentum of the movement. Cleverdon's historical study offers abundant evidence regarding its episodic or "fits-and-starts" development; enfranchisement organizations were established, activated, and then receded into dormancy and were reactivated with great frequency. As rapid legislative progress was made in one region, particularly in the western provinces during the years 1914–17 (see table 1), it was expected that a growing momentum would carry the cause from coast to coast. This sense of momentum, however, over-shadowed the fact that the women's movement remained small and weak in national terms. Moreover, its affiliates in Francophone Quebec and Atlantic Canada were particularly slow to develop, meaning that the organizational strength of the movement existed outside of those areas where women's traditional roles were most constraining and, in the view of many activists, most in need of legislative reform.[17]

Social Feminism and the Parties

The major political effects of early feminist history in English Canada, however, concern women's relationship with the established party system. In common with other reformist movements of the early twentieth century, including those which embraced labour and agrarian interests in the western provinces, major streams within Canadian suffragism rejected the evils of "partyism" in favour of an independent, virtually suprapolitical posture.[18]

This rejection of conventional partisanship grew out of a broader distrust of established political structures, which was reflected quite generally in Western Canadian progressivism. As described in the classic study by W.L. Morton, leading progressive farmers and trade unionists supported direct or populist democracy, based upon citizen-initiated legislation, referenda, and recall propositions.[19] Many progressives believed that political corruption and the absence of regional and group representation under existing arrangements resulted from party control over political nomination and election procedures. In the words of Morton, progressives endorsed a populist system to replace conventional representative democracy, in order to "break the hold 'bosses' and 'machines' serving the 'invisible government' of the 'interests' were alleged to have on the government of the country."[20] Many suffragists, especially in Western Canada, shared this belief in the intrinsically corrupting, immoral, and impure character of established party institutions.

One of the most vocal critics of this system was Nellie McClung, a nationally prominent suffragist and social feminist who was especially active in both Manitoba and Alberta. McClung's diary recorded her initial impressions of party politics, gathered during a Liberal campaign meeting which she attended in rural Manitoba during the 1880s. Women in the audience were exhorted by provincial Premier Thomas Greenway "to see that their menfolk voted and voted right and this he said (so even we could understand) meant voting Liberal."[21] After two questions regarding women's rights were ignored by the chairman, McClung left the meeting with a firm belief that politics was "a sordid, grubby business. . . . I do not want to be a reformer."[22]

McClung's subsequent exposure to WCTU activities and to Women's Press Club and Local Council work in Winnipeg led toward a reversal of this early view regarding reform. As a suffrage activist in the Political Equality League during later years, however, McClung reflected many elements of her older anti-party attitude. In fact, like many American social feminists, she merged a progressive critique of party politics with social reform arguments in favour of female enfranchisement: "If politics are corrupt, it is all the more reason that a new element should be introduced. Women will I believe supply that new element, that purifying influence. Men and women were intended to work together, and will work more ideally together, than apart, and just as the mother's influence as well as the father's is needed in the bringing up of children and in the affairs of the home, so are they needed in the larger home, — the state."[23] Politics was thus perceived by McClung and many of her allies as housekeeping on a grand scale. If women could introduce order, morality, and purpose to the domestic household, then they could surely extend this positive influence to "the larger home, — the state." The evils of partyism would finally be superseded, following female suffrage, by a reform-oriented system of good government.

Aside from the utopian expectations which were generated by this approach, and which were particularly significant in the decades after 1918, McClung's argument was important because it cemented the alliance between mainstream social feminism, on the one hand, and parties which were anxious to co-opt progressive interests — including women — on the other. In the Prairie region, which is useful for illustrative purposes, McClung established what might be termed an "arm's-length alliance" with the pro-reform Manitoba Liberals in 1914, on the basis of an agreement that the latter would introduce suffrage legislation once they defeated the governing provincial Conservatives. The Liberals lost the subsequent election despite the efforts of McClung (who noted that she "never even took car fare from the Liberal party. . . . I am a freelance in this fight") and others, but later won power in 1915.[24] The party indeed sponsored suffrage legislation following its election, as did the Alberta

Liberals for whom McClung campaigned successfully as a provincial candidate in the 1921 elections.

Perhaps the most troubling aspect of this alliance was its effect upon newly elected suffragists: McClung, for example, grew increasingly uncomfortable in her role as an "independent" MLA within a distinctively partisan caucus and legislature. Believing in the need for non-partisanship, however, McClung voted her conscience in the Alberta house, which generally meant crossing party lines to support government (UFA)-sponsored legislation. The frustration which greeted this direct exposure to political and especially parliamentary decision-making, combined with McClung's defeat in the subsequent provincial election, was echoed across Canada as other suffragists and similarly minded reformers entered the party-dominated system, only to find that their broader structural and issue (especially prohibitionist) objectives were marginalized by the very parliamentary system which they had set out to transform. Despite their formal commitments to political independence, therefore, suffragists soon discovered that they were wedged within the same partisan political system which they had earlier promised to eliminate, or at least transcend.

The Federal Franchise

The difficulties associated with operating within an established party system and, at the same time, maintaining a critical distance and independence from that system are evidenced clearly in events surrounding the granting of the federal franchise. While legislation to enfranchise widows and unmarried women was presented as early as 1883 by Sir John A. Macdonald, it was not until after provincial suffrage was enacted in Ontario and the western provinces that this issue received serious consideration on the federal level.[25] Suffrage thus reached the national agenda at the same time as women's contribution to the World War I effort was becoming increasingly evident, and when the Union government of Prime Minister Robert Borden faced a major electoral and political challenge concerning the issue of conscription.

While the basic facts of the conscription crisis are relatively well known, only limited attention has been given to the organizational dynamics of Canadian suffragism during this period and their relationship to wartime legislation. One source of internal conflict among English-Canadian feminists existed long before 1917, since it dated back to older generational and ideological differences between radical "hard-core," represented by the Canadian Suffrage Association (CSA), and more moderate "social," including the NCWC, WCTU, and National Equal Franchise Union (NEFU), elements in the movement.

Racism, conscription, and the war itself further divided feminist ranks during the period of World War I. As demonstrated in historical research by Gloria Geller and Bacchi, the political or hard-core stream represented by the CSA generally resisted appeals to Anglo-Saxon superiority and purity which were inherent in government-sponsored legislation to permit a limited female franchise in 1917.[26] CSA activists also tended to be urban pacifists who remained suspicious of the government's motives in introducing the Wartime Elections Act. In the words of the CSA president, Dr Margaret Gordon, this proposal constituted "a win-the-election measure. . . . It would be direct and at the same time more honest if the bill simply stated that all who did not pledge themselves to vote Conservative would be disfranchised. This might be satisfactory to some but it is not a Canadian-born woman's ideal of free government, nor can anyone who approves of this disfranchise bill claim to represent Canadian suffragettes."[27]

By way of contrast, the more conservative mainstream of English-Canadian feminism — and particularly the members of its elite — were more willing to adopt racial and patriotic (that is, pro-war) arguments in their pursuit of the franchise. Bacchi points out that the four activists who surveyed women's opinions regarding full versus partial federal suffrage (on behalf of the prime minister) were all married to Conservatives. In addition, it is notable that such pro-reform Liberal women as Nellie McClung agreed with limited enfranchisement and expressed racial and patriotic views in support of this legislation.[28] Mainstream social feminists, and most notably the presidents of the NCWC, NEFU, Imperial Order Daughters of the Empire (IODE), and the Ontario WCTU, thus endorsed what Cleverdon terms "one of the most bitterly debated and controversial measures in Canadian history."[29]

The Wartime Elections Act, which received royal assent on 29 September 1917, ultimately enfranchised only those women who were British subjects of age 21 and over, and who had a close family member serving in the Canadian or British armed forces. In political terms, the effects of this bill were as predicted, since newly enfranchised women helped to re-elect the pro-conscription government of Prime Minister Borden. Furthermore, once established in its new term, the Union government convened a Women's War Conference in Ottawa and enacted full suffrage legislation in 1918.[30]

While these developments suggest that Canadian women made successful use of the federal party system, it is important to recognize that their 1918 victory entailed major political costs. First, and probably most important for the future relationship between women and political power in Canada, the key arguments of both hard-core (equal rights on the basis of political justice) and social feminists (social reform incorporating the vote) were marginalized in the federal debate, which centred more directly around conscription and the electoral viability of Borden's Union government. Therefore, both the women's rights and social reform concerns of Canadian feminism were wedged outside the main national agenda, such that federal suffrage was largely achieved through a series of political choices made by, and in the interests of, the government of the day. Suffragists thus found themselves formally empowered within, but substantively distant from, the very system of national party government which they had long distrusted.

Second, the federal victory and subsequent enfranchisement bills in Atlantic Canada left organized feminism with no clear strategy for future action. It is to these post-enfranchisement dilemmas that we now turn our attention.

The Aftermath of Suffrage

As in the United States, many women voters in English Canada entered the electorate expecting a social and political millennium. The ideology of social feminism, which emphasized the pure reformist motives of women, promised a restoration of traditional moral values in both the home and the state. This commitment to uplifting was not easily translated into practical action on a mass scale, however. As Nellie McClung reflected during the 1930s, "We were obsessed with the belief that we could cleanse and purify the world by law. We said women were naturally lovers of peace and purity, temperance and justice. There never has been a campaign like the suffrage campaign. . . . But when all was over, and the smoke of battle cleared away, something happened to us. Our forces, so well organized for the campaign, began to dwindle. We had no constructive program for making a new world. . . . So the enfranchised women drifted. Many are still drifting."[31]

As McClung observed, the divisions within suffragist ranks which had existed throughout the early decades of the twentieth century deepened during subsequent years. In many regions, feminists and other newly enfranchised women split politically along demographic lines which had conventionally divided men. In this manner, class, ethnic, occupational, regional, and rural/urban differences shaped female political perceptions and often obscured earlier visions of a single emancipated womanhood, united in its goals and experiences.

On an organizational level, these internal cleavages became increasingly visible. Research by Bacchi, for example, reveals the fragmentation surrounding Canadian efforts to establish a separate woman's party in the years immediately after federal suffrage.[32] In 1918, a number of social feminists in the NEFU founded this party, with the stated goal of extending their political gains as enfranchised women. While the objective of consolidating earlier achievements was probably shared by many feminists, a separate party strategy under the leadership of pro-war, anti-labour, and generally Conservative-affiliated women from Toronto met with less than solid support. Not surprisingly, the Woman's Party was frequently condemned as being urban, elitist, and a Conservative front group. Its failure to develop as a viable and autonomous political organization paralleled the fate met by a similar National Woman's Party in the United States, where females were also wedged by established lines of party organization, political ideology, and social class.[33]

What distinguished English-Canadian from American feminism, however, was the absence of strong national organization following enfranchisement. Mainstream social feminists in the United States recognized the importance of political education and a cohesive social reform lobby at the state and federal levels; in 1920, they launched the non-partisan National League of Women Voters (NLWV) to fulfil this mandate.[34]

With the important exception of British Columbia, English-Canadian suffragists established few ongoing organizations following enfranchisement, and women generally floundered politically as a result. It was widely believed, including by such prominent social feminists as Nellie McClung and Louise McKinney, that Canadian women voters should return to their homes after World War I and, using their domestic environment as a base, work to mobilize public opinion around such issues as the minimum wage and industrial working conditions.[35] Unfortunately, the organizational structures necessary to achieve systematic results were generally lacking.

One notable exception to this pattern developed in British Columbia, where social feminists continued to remain active in politics following provincial enfranchisement. As a group, BC suffragists employed their alliance with the provincial Liberals in order to retain significant legislative influence through the late 1920s. In fact, the path adopted by BC feminists, which involved transforming the suffragist Political Equality League (established in 1910) into the post-suffragist New Era League, coincided with similar national efforts in the United States, where the pro-vote National American Woman Suffrage Association became the League of Women Voters following 1920.

Many of the major policy concerns of the New Era League paralleled those which had motivated earlier suffragist activities. As summarized by Elsie Gregory MacGill in the story of her mother's social feminist involvement, the main priorities for reform legislation in BC included prison and family law reform; infant protection; industrial health and safety; minimum wage legislation for women; mothers' pensions; a Juvenile Courts Act; and improved public health, library, and education systems.[36]

The ability of BC feminists to ensure government sponsorship and passage of this legislation was related to two factors: first, a number of active suffragists, including "high Tory" Helen Gregory MacGill, became party members after the provincial Liberals adopted woman suffrage in their platforms of 1912 and following.[37] In addition, the fact that Liberals in the Prairie provinces also favoured and ultimately enacted female enfranchisement legislation (see table 1) led active suffragists to join the party and to establish the BC Women's Liberal Association during this same period.[38]

Second, alongside their partisan ties, social feminists in BC retained an independent women's network through such groups as the New Era League. After a prominent suffragist and founder of the Women's Liberal Association, Mary Ellen Smith, was elected to the provincial legislature in 1918 and later appointed Minister without Portfolio in 1921 (thus becoming the first female cabinet minister in the British Empire), feminists outside the legislature began to channel their reformist concerns through Smith to the provincial government.[39] Smith's position in the Liberal cabinet, combined with the ability of social feminists in BC to retain some organizational continuity following enfranchisement, thus ensured the passage of significant reform measures, including mothers' pensions and a Minimum Wage Act.[40]

With their active ally inside the chambers of government, social feminists in BC found that many reform bills received favourable reception during the critical first decade after suffrage. However, this successful combination in BC of partisan alliances, including the election and cabinet appointment of an active feminist woman, with politically independent and effective women's organizations became the exception rather than the rule for many years following 1918. Indeed, as evidenced on the federal level during the 1920s, women's rights to vote and to hold public office generally had minimal effects on the broader political system.

The Problem of Public Office

Despite the early successes of the Dominion Women's Enfranchisement Association in electing two women to the Toronto School Board in 1892, the election of females to public office was not a high priority for mainstream social feminism in English Canada. According to Bacchi, efforts to elect women faltered as older hard-core feminists became increasingly outnumbered by moderate social reformers, who attached relatively little importance to candidacy and office-holding. In fact, many social feminists questioned how the bulk of married, child-rearing women could devote themselves to any career outside the home, including politics. In the words of one activist, there were "plenty of 'unmarried women and widows, and married women with grown-up children' " to work in elections and run for office.[41]

In light of this prevailing view, it is not surprising that relatively few women contested public office, and even fewer held elective office, in the years following formal enfranchisement. On the federal level, for example, only four women were nominated as candidates in the 1921 general elections, representing 0.6% of the total federal candidates for that year.[42] The sole woman elected to the House of Commons in 1921 was Agnes Macphail, a 31-year-old unmarried schoolteacher who represented the rural Ontario riding of South-East Grey.

Macphail's political career, including her experiences as an MP and subsequently as an Ontario MPP, is important not only because it confronted many of the psychological and structural obstacles generally faced by women in politics, but also because it reflected a more specific tension between partisanship and independence in the political history of women in Canada. In terms of general barriers to elite-level participation, the nomination, election, and legislative tenure of Agnes Macphail had much in common with the experiences of other women in Canada and elsewhere. For example, like many female candidates in competitive ridings, she had to defeat ten males to win nomination initially, and then withstood strong protests from both the constituency organization and electorate at large because of her gender.[43] In Macphail's own words, "It took strenuous campaigning for two months just to stop people from saying, 'We can't have a woman.' I won that election in spite of being a woman."[44]

Once she had defeated the incumbent Conservative MP in South-East Grey, Macphail's entrance to the House of Commons was treated on the social or women's pages of the Canadian press, where her wardrobe and personal style were closely scrutinized.[45] This treatment as a new MP encouraged Macphail to adopt an increasingly critical perspective toward her own political experiences, even though she had not been active previously as a feminist or suffragist.[46] First, and very importantly, Macphail's legislative work suggested to her that progressive men were not immune to the general biases of males against females in politics, since J.S. Woodsworth (at the time a Labour MP from

Manitoba) once confessed: "I still don't think a woman has any place in politics."[47] Second, Macphail learned that few policy concerns raised by Canadian feminists received serious attention within legislative bodies. She therefore worked diligently on family allowance, equal pay, and women's prison issues, even though her initial priorities had concerned the rights of Ontario farmers.

Third, Macphail's experiences as a provincial and federal legislator led her to speak publicly about continuing obstacles to female political involvement. During the 1930s, she rejected at least one proposal which would have guaranteed female representation on all new CCF committees, arguing that women could not demand special considerations on the basis of gender.[48] Nevertheless, she believed strongly that males would not easily concede or even share control over political decision-making. In a 1949 article entitled "Men Want to Hog Everything," Macphail foreshadowed the more recent observations of Liberal MP Judy LaMarsh: "The old ideas of chivalry justify men in thinking of women as a rather poor choice in human beings. Put her on a pedestal, then put pedestal and all in a cage."[49]

What was specifically Canadian about Macphail's experience, however, was the extent to which her own career reflected ongoing political tensions between partisanship and independence. Most notably, Macphail was elected on the platform of the United Farmers of Ontario, a primarily agrarian-based rural organization which rejected conventional "partyism" in favour of direct group representation in the House of Commons.[50] Her role as a parliamentarian was therefore independent of the two established national parties, which did not elect woman members other than the spouses of former (male) MPs until the 1950s, at the same time as it was related to ongoing efforts to challenge Liberal and Conservative dominance through a progressive labour/agrarian coalition at the federal level. Ultimately, the parliamentary alliance with which Macphail was associated formed one basis for the Co-operative Commonwealth Federation, established in 1932.

Macphail's political impact as a legislator was thus constrained by many of the same factors which had affected early feminist activism in English Canada. Like the suffrage movement itself, Macphail rejected conventional partisanship and established her legislative career outside the parameters of mainstream party politics. While this "anti-partyism" was consistent with Macphail's progressive beliefs, just as it coincided with the reformist tenor of Canadian suffragism, such a position tended to limit her influence within an essentially partisan, parliamentary system.

On the other side of the coin, Macphail's commitment to political independence was complicated by a need to form coalitions in order to challenge conventional two-party dominance in English Canada. In Macphail's case, a parliamentary alliance with pacifists and Western Canadian socialists eventually cost her the seat in South-East Grey, since the constituents of this rural riding were unsympathetic toward many of the political partnerships and causes with which their MP was associated.[51]

Moreover, Macphail's ability to fashion an independent position around the rights of women was hampered by both consciousness and organization during this period: not only was there limited understanding of gender inequality and its implications, but also most established organizations of Canadian women were ideologically opposed to the broader political views held by Agnes Macphail. Notably, Macphail was generally viewed as an agrarian progressive and, ultimately, as a leading Canadian socialist and pacifist. Her statements in support of the Glace Bay miners and against Canadian military academies, for example, were vehemently denounced by IODE, the Women's Canadian Club, and other established groups which had staked out a role as the legitimate and representative voices of Canadian women.[52]

It was not until the relatively legalistic matter of female appointment to the Senate was broached that Canadian women began to overcome these internal differences and to pursue a more unified, coherent political strategy. In fact, the judicial victory associated with the Persons Case in 1929 resembled closely the efforts to establish a royal commission on the status of women nearly forty years later, as well as the subsequent constitutional changes won by Canadian women in 1981. It is to the issue of Senate appointments that we now turn our attention.

The "Persons Case"

The issue of women's eligibility for Canadian Senate appointments, which centred around legal interpretations of the word "persons," came to public attention during the year following full federal enfranchisement. In 1919, the first president of the Federated Women's Institutes of Canada, Edmonton police magistrate Emily Murphy, received unanimous support from her organization for a resolution which encouraged the government of Canada to appoint a woman to the Senate. The NCWC and the Montreal Women's Club passed similar resolutions, which were subsequently rejected by the federal Conservative government on the basis of a narrow constitutional reading of the word "persons."[53] A specific nominee to the Senate was suggested by the Montreal Women's Club, which endorsed Judge Murphy on the basis of her suffragist and social feminist efforts in co-ordination with Nellie McClung, Henrietta Muir Edwards (an activist in the Alberta branch of the NCWC), provincial UFA legislator Irene Parlby, and former Alberta legislator Louise McKinney.

One difficult problem which confronted Murphy and her supporters grew out of partisan divisions among Canadian women. According to Rudy Marchildon, attempts to have the "persons" issued raised at major party conventions during the 1920s were unsuccessful, largely because many women's groups (including the Montreal Women's Club) were composed primarily of Liberals who objected to petitioning the then-Conservative government. Once the Tories were defeated federally, fears that a newly elected Liberal government might appoint British Columbia MLA Mary Ellen Smith to the Senate prevented many Conservatives from actively pursuing the "persons" issue.[54]

Fortunately for the cause of female senators, Emily Murphy learned in 1927 of an obscure provision in the Supreme Court Act which permitted interested parties to request constitutional interpretation of points under the BNA Act. She then enlisted the support of her four suffragist colleagues from Alberta and, on 19 October 1927, all five women petitioned the Supreme Court of

Canada. Since their legal expenses were assumed by the federal government, Murphy's group selected a prominent Toronto lawyer, Newton Wesley Rowell, to present the case both in Ottawa and, subsequently, before the Privy Council in London. Rowell had strongly supported woman suffrage during his term as Liberal Opposition leader in Ontario, and his wife had served during that same period as the first president of the Toronto Women's Liberal Association.[55]

Despite the well-sustained arguments presented by Rowell in Ottawa, all five Supreme Court justices who heard the case concurred in the following judgment, delivered on 24 April 1928: "Women are not 'qualified persons' within the meaning of Section 24 of the BNA Act, 1867, and therefore are not eligible for appointment by the Governor General to the Senate of Canada."[56] The solicitor-general in the federal liberal government, Lucien Cannon, supported by Quebec special counsel Charles Lanctot, had successfully argued that the original intent of the BNA Act was strictly for men, as "qualified persons," to be appointed to the Senate. The federal government position also maintained that if a more liberal and contemporary interpretation were to be attached to "persons," then such changes would require legislative rather than judicial action.

Undeterred by this defeat in the Supreme Court of Canada, and by the failure of the federal justice minister to introduce amending legislation as promised during the 1928 parliamentary session, Judge Murphy made plans to present her case in London. On 18 October 1929, approximately two years following an initial petition to the Supreme Court of Canada, the Judicial Committee of the Privy Council announced its decision that women were indeed persons and thus eligible for appointment to the Senate. This decision was greeted with "much gratification" by Judge Murphy and her allies, who believed that the "persons" judgment at last conferred "full political rights" upon the women of Canada.[57]

In the years following 1929, neither Emily Murphy nor any of her four colleagues was appointed to the Senate. Apparently, their feminist activities and, in the case of Murphy, Conservative family connections eliminated them from consideration by a Liberal government which was unwilling to risk the political costs which might be attached to such nominations, especially in the province of Quebec. The Senate thus became for women what it had long remained for men, namely a regionally and religiously balanced Upper House which rewarded loyal party activists rather than non- or minimally partisan social reformers.

Not surprisingly, then, the first woman to be appointed to the Senate was a well-known Ontario Liberal, Cairine Wilson, who was nominated in 1930 by the King government. Unlike Murphy, McClung, or other feminist women who had entered into alliances with the Liberals, Senator Wilson was a seasoned and reliable partisan who had led the Eastern Ontario Liberal Women's Association, the Ottawa Liberal Women's Club, and the National Federation of Liberal Women. Her father was a wealthy Laurier Liberal from Montreal, who had also held a Senate seat.

Aside from these obvious political credentials, Senator Wilson was an uncontroversial social choice as the first woman in the Upper House. She had raised a large family, was active in church and charity work, and believed firmly in traditional moral and family values. For example, when asked in one interview about her interest in serving on the Senate divorce committee, Wilson replied "that she had no such ambition, and that she had been so busy with her home and her babies she hadn't time to think about divorce."[58]

The press response to Wilson's appointment echoed conventional views regarding the civilizing influence which women would bring to public life. The new senator was predicted to become "a charming and hospitable hostess" in Ottawa, a welcome "adornment" to the city and the nation's Upper House.[59] In the words of a *Maclean's* journalist, Senator Wilson was "for all of her wealth and social prestige and political distinction . . . first, last, and always a woman — a wife and mother of eight children."[60]

The second woman appointed to the Senate was also a party stalwart who had served on the national executive of the Conservative Women's Association; Iva Fallis, from Ontario, was nominated in 1935 by the Tory government of R.B. Bennett. It was not until 1953 that additional women were appointed to the Senate, and not until the 1970s that two publicly prominent women, Thérèse Casgrain and Florence Bird, were named on the basis of their independent, non-partisan contributions to improving the status of women. The latter appointments were more closely related to the second wave of women's rights activism in Canada, discussed below, than to the premature expectations of political equality which accompanied victory in the Persons Case.

Between the Movements

In the years following federal enfranchisement, social reform legislation during the 1920s, and the Persons Case, most Canadian women reassumed the traditional domestic responsibilities which they had performed prior to World War I. The world Depression played a major role in limiting the number of jobs available to either men or women, and prevailing beliefs that whatever work existed should go to male breadwinners had an especially devastating effect upon female employment throughout the 1930s.

As women re-entered the home, frequently with the blessings of such prominent feminists as Nellie McClung, they helped to shape a society which was considerably different from that of earlier years. Perhaps the most significant change affecting women after 1920 was the increased level and acceptability of both female education and employment. As Mary Vipond demonstrates, growing numbers of single girls — and especially those of the middle classes — were encouraged during this period to develop career goals for the years prior to their marriage. A sound formal education was viewed as one critical element in such development since, over the longer term, "a well-educated woman would be a more capable, more self-confident, and therefore a *better* wife and mother."[61]

The household itself was also transformed during this period, as manufacturers introduced new "labour-saving" inventions to the marketplace. A wide array of new devices, from electric irons and toasters to dishwashers and sewing machines, was advertised as the cure for domestic drudgery. Married women could thus devote the bulk of their energies to the family, and particularly to the declining numbers of children who were born following 1920. As reflected in mass circulation magazines of the day, women were expected to develop a more trained and intense approach to their child-rearing responsibilities.[62]

This modernization of the domestic household, combined with increased opportunities for female employment and education, held differing political implications for middle- and working-class women. In the former case, the inter-war years were generally characterized by organizational continuity within such groups as the NCWC (established in 1893), the YWCA (established in 1894), and the Canadian Federation of University Women (CFUW, established in 1919). These voluntary associations, along with the newer Canadian Federation of Business and Professional Women's Clubs (established in 1930), remained actively committed to the social reformist goals which had earlier motivated mainstream English-Canadian feminism. Similarly, the various women's associations within the two older political parties continued to operate through the 1930s, and to promote in general an auxiliary or supportive role for women in politics.

By way of contrast, these same years were a time of considerable ferment within the Canadian left, and particularly among women on the left. Research by John Manley on the Ontario CCF, for example, suggests that some working-class women rejected both the conventional feminist model of moderate social reform, as well as the traditional partisan model of women as ancillary political workers and primary social and fund-raising organizers.[63] The Women's Joint Committee, which existed in Toronto for approximately six months during 1936, was a forerunner of more recent efforts to establish politically assertive women's groups within the major parties. Although the committee was weakened organizationally by a willingness to co-operate in "united front" activities, it strongly endorsed leadership training programs for party women, publicly accessible birth control clinics, equal pay statues, and other progressive positions on policies of specific relevance to Canadian women.[64]

This ferment among women on the left, as well as the expansion of voluntary organizations among middle-class women, was temporarily interrupted by the events of World War II. Wartime mobilization drew hundreds of thousands of Canadian women into the armed forces, defence industries, service sector, and agriculture.[65] Child-care facilities and special tax provisions were established to encourage married women in particular into the wartime labour force.

Following the end of hostilities, when women's employment was no longer deemed to be "of national importance," most day-care centres were closed and federal tax statutes reverted to their traditional format.[66] As in the years after World War I, women were expected to surrender their jobs to returning veterans — an arrangement to which most willingly consented — and to resume their domestic duties. Therefore, despite assumptions that wartime employment would permanently alter the status of women in Canada, it generally served as only a temporary break with conventional gender role norms and expectations.[67]

An important new influence upon the experiences of post-war women, however, was the economic prosperity and sense of confidence which pervaded North American society during these years. As in the decade after World War I, middle-class women in particular were pressured to consume on behalf of their households, and to provide emotional and personal comforts to their upwardly mobile husbands and "baby boom" offspring.

The conflict between these domestic pressures and conventional role responsibilities, on the one hand, and the social experiences and expectations of women outside the home, on the other, held important political consequences for later years. That is, as middle-class women were exposed to broadened educational and occupational opportunities, many of which resulted from an enlarged service sector necessary to operate the modern welfare state, they confronted an official as well as informal ideology which was grounded in older, increasingly outdated social values. This contradiction between the post-war "feminine mystique" of contented and conventional domesticity and a growing sense of personal restiveness and questioning provided one basis from which the second wave of women's rights activism developed in English Canada.[68]

A renewed feminist movement also grew out of post-war activities on the Canadian left, where the gap between egalitarian socialist ideology and internal party practices — noted earlier by Agnes Macphail and others — continued to widen. As highlighted by Dean Beeby in his study of the Ontario CCF, relatively few members of the party's political elite were females, even though the organization claimed to represent the interests of all women (notably, the provincial caucus became the first in Canada to introduce equal pay legislation, in 1949).[69] Moreover, the CCF in Ontario employed the bulk of its female membership in social, fund-raising, canvassing, and publicity work, a pattern which was reinforced following the appointment in 1942 of a separate women's committee. While the professed goal of this committee and a subsequent Status of Women Committee (established in 1947) was to increase female party involvement at all levels, such groups frequently evolved into auxiliary-type associations which specialized in consumer price monitoring, bazaars, cookbook projects, and other activities of a stereotypically feminine nature.[70]

This continuation of conventional role norms and power arrangements within the organized left provided an important groundwork for subsequent radical and socialist feminist movements in English Canada.

The Renewal of Canadian Feminism

The renewal of organized feminism in English Canada is often linked with the establishment in 1960 of Voice of Women (VOW), a non-partisan, grass-roots association which was formed to oppose nuclear arms testing and weapons proliferation. From the outset, VOW remained a loosely organized group whose main goal was "to unite women in concern for the future of the world."[71] The membership of VOW reached approximately 5,000 in 1961, and its leadership included a number of women who were later instrumental in efforts to establish a royal commission on the status of women (Helen Tucker, Thérèse Casgrain) and to pressure for implementation of the commission's recommendations in a national action committee on the status of women (Kay Macpherson).

While VOW thus provided "a significant training ground" for future status of women activists, it also offered valuable lessons in the political tensions which continued to confront independent women's organizations.[72] In 1963, when Prime Minister Lester Pearson reversed his position on the stationing of Bomarc missiles in Canada, VOW split internally over a response to his decision. Activists asked:

> Could one swallow the Liberal decision and still campaign against nuclear weapons without its constituting an attack on the party? The majority decided that such a swallow would gulp away VOW credibility. The organization attacked the policy. . . . Many members disagreed; some because they wished to support and vote for Liberals, some because they were convinced that the loss, apparent or real, of an apolitical posture would destroy VOW's effectiveness. Others argued that is was one thing to oppose policies in general, but quite a different and disturbing thing to oppose particular leaders on specific matters. To these latter, open disagreement with father-figures was a new and terrifying sensation.[73]

Voice of Women's external credibility and internal unity suffered a great deal because of this split, since what survived of the organization was increasingly labelled as politically marginal, a captive of the radical left. Despite its claims to political independence, therefore, VOW became wedged by broader partisan conflicts which shaped the debate over war, peace, and specifically the Bomarc missiles. The transcendence of party politics, promised during the first decades of this century by mainstream suffragists, thus remained problematical within VOW during the 1960s.

The apparent lesson which was drawn from VOW's internal fragmentation was that Canadian women could best coalesce around one carefully circumscribed, relatively non-partisan concern, namely an official inquiry into the status of women. Demands for such an inquiry came to light publicly on 5 January 1967, when CFUW president Laura Sabia was quoted on the front page of the Toronto *Globe and Mail* as threatening to march some two million women on Ottawa, unless the federal government agreed to establish the Royal Commission on the Status of Women (RCSW).[74] Despite this seemingly sudden and, particularly for Canada and Canadian women, provocative statement, the discussion of women's status had continued for a number of years within older, middle-class women's associations, including CFUW, the YWCA, and Business and Professional Women's Clubs.[75]

As in the earlier example of the Persons Case, events surrounding the royal commission suggest that disparate groups and individuals could indeed organize around one narrow, well-defined objective. As summarized by Cerise Morris, Laura Sabia employed her position as CFUW president to call together the representatives of some thirty-two other groups, who agreed in June 1966

TABLE 2

The Establishment of Major Canadian Women's Organizations, 1960–83

Date	Organization	Main purpose
July 1960	Voice of Women (VOW)	"To crusade against the possibility of nuclear war"[a]
April 1966	Féderation des Femmes du Québec (FFQ)	To pressure for legislative reform and a Council of Women
June 1966	Committee for the Equality of Women in Canada (CEW)	To pressure for establishment of a royal commission on the status of women
February 1967	Royal Commission on the Status of Women (RCSW)	"To inquire into and report upon the status of women in Canada"[b]
March 1969	New Feminists, Toronto	"To awaken the consciousness of women as to the nature and extent of their oppression as women"[c]
September 1970	Report of the Royal Commission on the Status of Women	"To recommend what steps might be taken . . . to ensure for women equal opportunities"[d]
January 1971	National Ad Hoc Committee on the Status of Women in Canada	To pressure for implementation of Royal Commission recommendations
April 1972	National Action Committee on the Status of Women in Canada	(Replaced Ad Hoc Committee)
February 1972	Women for Political Action (WPA)	To increase female political participation and political education at all levels of government
May 1973	Canadian Advisory Council on the Status of Women (CACSW)	To report on women's concerns to the Minister Responsible for the Status of Women
February 1979	Feminist Party of Canada	To establish a political party with a feminist perspective
January 1981	Ad Hoc Committee of Canadian Women	To achieve equality for women in the Canadian Charter of Rights and Freedoms
January 1983	Canadian Coalition against Media Pornography	To protest the portrayal of women in First Choice Pay TV

a Kay Macpherson and Meg Sears, "The Voice of Women: A History," in *Women in the Canadian Mosaic*, edited by Gwen Matheson (Toronto: Peter Martin, 1976), 72.
b Terms of Reference, reprinted in *Report* of the Royal Commission on the Status of Women in Canada (Ottawa: Information Canada, 1970), vii.
c Lynne Teather, "The Feminist Mosaic," in *Women in the Canadian Mosaic*, 331.
d Terms of Reference, vii.

to form "a new national women's organization concerned solely with the status of women — Committee for the Equality of Women in Canada (CEW) and, through this vehicle, to press for the establishment of a royal commission."[76] Supported by a strong editorial which appeared in the July issue of *Chatelaine*, a leading women's magazine, and by the broad-based coalition represented in CEW (which included VOW, NCWC, IODE, YWCA, Business and Professional Women, and the newly formed Fédération des Femmes du Québec), Sabia and sixty-four of her colleagues presented the Liberal minority government with a brief requesting the formation of such a commission in September 1966.[77]

During this same period, both women who then held seats in the House of Commons pressured the Liberal cabinet to establish a royal commission. One was New Democrat Grace MacInnis, the daughter of former party leader J.S. Woodsworth, who had modelled herself as a youth after Agnes Macphail.[78] When MacInnis probed the government's plans on the floor of the House, she generally received facetious and non-committal replies to her questions.[79]

A considerably more influential MP in these matters was Judy LaMarsh, who held the secretary of state portfolio in the Pearson cabinet. Like Agnes Macphail during the 1920s and 1930s, LaMarsh reluctantly became a consistent supporter and initiator of women's rights legislation: "No matter how little a suffragette by temperament, circumstances gradually forced me into the role of acting as spokesman and watchdog for women. If there had been a dozen women in the Cabinet, that wouldn't have been necessary, but I had to carry out this dual, unasked for, entirely unofficial, and unpaid role."[80] LaMarsh's pressures within Cabinet, combined with Sabia's organizational abilities and statements to the press, began to take effect by the winter of 1967. On 3 February 1967, Prime Minister Pearson announced the formation of a commission, to be headed by well-known journalist Anne Francis (Florence Bird).[81]

Despite numerous doubts about its usefulness and, particularly in the case of LaMarsh, its legislative impact, the royal commission was critical in helping to define publicly the issue of women's status in Canada.[82] Many academic researchers, older women's associations, newer status of women groups, and private individuals contributed to the hearings and final report; approximately 470 briefs in total were presented during the four years following its establishment. Press coverage of the commission process also ensured its visibility, as did the publication of a well-written, well-organized *Report* which provided one of the first systematic overviews of the contemporary female condition in Canada.[83] In all, 167 recommendations were listed in the final version, which was presented to Prime Minister Trudeau in December 1970.

In historical terms, it is difficult to distinguish the impact of the RCSW from the influence of concurrent developments on the Canadian left. Unlike women's rights activists associated with the royal commission, many of whom were middle-aged members of older voluntary organizations, females who were attracted to the Canadian left during the 1960s tended to be younger, more politically radical, and more doubtful regarding the significance of formal legislative reform. Few of the latter presented submissions to the RCSW, since a commonly held belief on the left was that the transformation of basic social and economic structures in Canada was necessary in order to eliminate what radical women increasingly identified as a problem of sexual oppression — in contrast to the prevailing liberal conception of unequal opportunity.[84]

The emergence of a more radical, women's liberation movement in Canada can therefore be linked to the experiences of females on the left and, more specifically, to their treatment within such New Left groups as the Student Union for Peace Action (SUPA).[85] In common with some CCF women of the 1930s and following, female SUPA activists took issue with their assignment to clerical and fund-raising tasks, in light of the fact that men were deployed as leading political strategists, speakers, and decision-makers on the left. This rejection of conventional role norms by younger women produced a variety of practical and philosophic responses, ranging from radical feminism, which identified the origins of female oppression in biologically determined gender roles, to socialist and Marxist feminism, which generally focused upon the relationship between class structures and the institutions of the left, on the one hand, and women's social and economic position, on the other.[86]

Throughout most of the late 1960s and early 1970s, older women's rights and newer women's liberation groups competed for media attention, social legitimacy, and the loyalties of Canadian women. Signs of a possible rapprochement between the two sides appeared in 1972, however, at the Strategy for Change conference which formally established the National Action Committee on the Status of Women (NAC).[87] As an umbrella organization embracing widely disparate groups, NAC set out to see that the major recommendations of the royal commission were implemented, and that the various concerns of its constituent members were presented to parliamentary committees, task forces, and the public at large. From the outset, NAC's mandate was explicitly non-partisan; it was to argue forcefully and independently on behalf of Canadian women.

In the following year, the Canadian Advisory Council on the Status of Women (CACSW) was established. As suggested in the *Report* of the royal commission, this council was charged with the task of undertaking research, developing programs and legislative proposals, and consulting with existing organizations in the area of women's rights. However, contrary to the commission's recommendation, CACSW was made responsible to a single cabinet minister, namely the Minister Responsible for the Status of Women, rather than to Parliament as a whole. This jurisdictional matter became the basis for a major conflict between the Liberal government and women's groups during constitutional discussions in 1981, when the ability of the advisory council to represent independently the concerns of Canadian women was called into serious question.

The Problem of Political Strategy

The *Report* of the royal commission, published in 1970, highlights a wide variety of inequalities affecting women in Canada. One of the most troubling of these was the relative absence of females in positions of political influence and, more specifically, the weak representation of women in Canadian provincial and federal legislatures.[88] As British Columbia MLA Rosemary Brown reflected in the wake of both this report and her own political experiences, "to talk of power and to talk of women is to talk of the absence of power as we understand it today."[89]

The organized response of Canadian women to this situation has been complex and at times conflictual, encompassing both politically independent and partisan strategies. One early effort to increase female representation at elite levels was the Toronto-based Women for Political Action (WPA), a non-partisan organization established in 1972. Following a series of articles in *Chatelaine* magazine which highlighted the obstacles facing women in politics, and which presented profiles of "105 potential women MPs," a number of activists in Voice of Women (including Kay Macpherson) and the Ontario Committee on the Status of Women (including future MP Aideen Nicholson) established WPA as a focal point for the growing national network of politically active feminists.[90]

Although a key priority of WPA was the election of more females to public office, there were frequent disputes within the group regarding the best means toward this end.[91] In 1972, prior to the announcement of a federal election, many WPA members favoured the nomination of independent women candidates who, following their election, "could independently set up a caucus in the House of Commons."[92] This position in support of independent candidacies was in fact pursued by WPA in 1972, when the organization fielded two of its members in the Toronto federal ridings of St Paul's (Macpherson) and Rosedale (Aline Gregory). While both campaigns mobilized large numbers of newly active women and, particularly in the case of Rosedale, introduced feminist collective organization and consciousness-raising to federal electioneering, neither was successful in winning a parliamentary seat.

These electoral defeats, combined with the inroads which other women appeared to be making in established party organizations, led many WPA members away from political independence and in the direction of traditional partisanship. In the words of one activist in Aline Gregory's campaign, "There were a lot of people who took the message from these experiences that we should all join the established parties, and become conventional political participants. . . . In the years following 1972, many women indeed joined parties."[93] As more WPA members became active and committed partisans, however, the group's mandate to remain politically independent became increasingly irrelevant to its core constituency. Therefore, until about 1979, WPA existed as little more than a Toronto post-office box address, sponsoring occasional conferences (including a 1973 "Women in Politics" session with Rosemary Brown as keynote speaker) and campaign schools.[94]

The partisan identifications adopted by WPA veterans and other feminists who chose to participate in mainstream party politics were generally New Democratic and, particularly on the federal level, Liberal.[95] Within both parties, feminist activists made impressive gains by the mid-1970s, as task forces and new women's rights organizations were established (the NDP Participation of Women Committee and the Women's Liberal Commission were created in

1969 and 1973 respectively) and as more women became visibly influential, particularly as holders of major party and public office.[96] Notably, in 1972 three Liberal women were elected to the House of Commons from Quebec; they included Monique Bégin, who had served as executive secretary to the royal commission and as an activist in the Fédération des Femmes du Québec. In 1974, five more Liberal women took office as federal MPs, including Aideen Nicholson, who had largely built her campaign organization within the Ontario Committee on the Status of Women.[97]

The mid-1970s was also a very hopeful period for women in the NDP. On the federal level, a 1974 women's convention in Winnipeg served as the starting point for a feminist-oriented leadership campaign by Rosemary Brown.[98] As a backbencher in the British Columbia NDP caucus, Brown made a strong and credible showing against interim federal leader Ed Broadbent. In addition to marking the first campaign for major party leadership by a woman in Canada, this 1975 convention also elected Joyce Nash as the first female president of a major federal party organization. In short, the gains made by Liberal and New Democratic women during the early and mid-1970s suggested that political influence was indeed accessible to all hard-working and committed partisans, regardless of gender.

This promise began to fade, however, as growing numbers of feminists questioned the policy changes which had been effected during the decade since the establishment of the RCSW. Such issues as equal pay, pension reform, abortion, day care, and sex role stereotyping in education and the media remained largely ignored by both provincial and federal governments through the 1970s, even though detailed reports and legislative proposals had been prepared by status of women groups (including NAC) and internal party task forces and women's organizations.[99]

A sentiment thus began to build by the late 1970s that women's advisory councils, notably on the federal level (CACSW), as well as women's associations within the parties were too traditional in their composition and strategy to provide effective political leadership in these important issue areas. In addition, the partisan and personality conflicts which developed in such groups as NAC suggested that a systematic, coherent response to government inaction was unlikely to develop within "independent" women's organizations.[100]

Alongside these frustrations regarding policy influence, Canadian feminists also questioned the progress which had been made in electing women to public and party office. The weak showing of Conservative leadership candidate Flora MacDonald was particularly disappointing, since MacDonald had received considerable moral and financial support from many women who were not Conservatives. While her campaign thus captured the imagination of many politically minded feminists, its sixth-place finish at the 1976 leadership convention suggested that major obstacles continued to impeded women's participation in elite-level politics.

The establishment in February 1979 of the Feminist Party of Canada, coinciding with the revival of Women for Political Action and early discussions regarding a women's bureau in the federal Conservative organization, reflected the extent to which politically active women had begun to reconsider their accomplishments. One early statement by the Feminist Party expressed this malaise in terms of developments during the sixty years following the federal enfranchisement: "Since that time, women have indeed increased their attempts to become elected representatives — the number of women seeking federal office rose from 4, in 1921, to 137 in 1974. But the number of women who won seats in those 53 years rose only from one to nine. The dismal prognosis is that, at this rate, we will need another 842 years to achieve equal representation at the federal level."[101] The response of Feminist Party founders was to create their own "political party with a feminist perspective."[102] This goal was complicated early on by fragile internal alliances (that is, Conservative status of women activists combined with radical feminists in a single organization), and by the announcement of two federal elections within approximately one year of the new party's establishment.

Ultimately, the Feminist Party was a short-lived coalition which made little direct impact upon female participation in Canadian politics. Like the activities of Women for Political Action in 1972, however, its establishment symbolized the continuing attractiveness of independent women's organizations to many feminists, including those who only later recognized their limitations within a partisan, parliamentary system. Moreover, the existence of WPA, the Feminist Party, and other similar groups pointed toward an underlying discontent among many women regarding their numerical representation and policy impact within the Canadian political process.

Women and the Constitution

The longstanding political discontent of many Canadian women crystallized around a single issue — constitutional change — during the years 1980–82. Some English-Canadian feminists felt a particular stake in the renewal of a constitutional federalism, since they had sent letters and telegrams of support to the "Non" forces, and especially to activists in the "Yvette" movement, during the 1980 Quebec referendum campaign.[103] The success of the "Non" forces in this referendum, combined with the imminent defeat of the U.S. Equal Rights Amendment, suggested that Canadian women would need to play a major role in discussions over future constitutional arrangements.

Systematic input by women's groups into the constitutional process, however, came only after prolonged disputes with the federal government, and within these same women's organizations. Much of the public debate over women and the constitution followed a request by the Minister Responsible for the Status of Women, Lloyd Axworthy, that the federal advisory council (CACSW) cancel its planned conference on this subject. Axworthy advised that such a conference could prove politically damaging to the Liberal government, and a majority of council members — who were generally "safe" Liberal appointees — supported his view. In the words of one approving member, "I say that it's about time we started playing games the same way government plays games. We should start being nice to them. So if this conference is going to be an embarrassment, let's play it their way and cancel it."[104]

Doris Anderson, who had worked previously as editor of *Chatelaine* and run unsuccessfully as a federal Liberal candidate in 1978, opposed Axworthy's intervention and resigned from the presidency of CACSW on 20 January 1981. Her unwillingness to cancel the conference provided an unexpected turn of events for Axworthy and his supporters, as well as for many women who had long doubted the value of the federal advisory council. On an organizational level, Anderson's resignation prompted the formation on 21 January of the Ad Hoc Committee of Canadian Women, which later held its own highly successful constitutional conference in Ottawa on 14 February.[105] The Ad Hoc Committee relied upon a diverse base of volunteer support, similar to that which had been employed earlier in the Persons Case and in efforts to create a royal commission. This visible core of support, which again developed around a single, well-defined political issue, later helped to ensure the inclusion of an equality rights clause in the new constitution (section 28).

In political terms, however, the 1981 constitutional crisis tended to exacerbate older tensions between partisanship and independence among Canadian women. Just as a number of Liberal activists felt betrayed by the resignation of Doris Anderson,[106] so many others who were less identified with the party believed that they (along with Anderson) were the victims of government — and especially Cabinet — manipulation.[107] These perceptions of betrayal and manipulation were deep-seated and spilled over into other organizations which were also associated with the constitutional process. In the National Action Committee, for example, one assistant to Lloyd Axworthy sponsored a contentious resolution on the Charter of Rights, which was approved after dubious political manoeuvrings.[108] As retiring NAC president Lynn McDonald observed in the wake of these events, "Women's organizations, with their fragile interparty compositions, have been sorely tried by the Constitution debate."[109]

Recent conflicts concerning a new federal constitution thus reflect the ability of Canadian women to form narrow issue coalitions across party lines, at the same time as they demonstrate the fragility and temporary nature of these alliances.[110] In fact, the decline of the Ad Hoc Committee following parliamentary approval of section 28 suggests that ideological unity and organizational continuity remain elusive goals in English Canada. Women's political history in the 1980s thus continues to be enmeshed in a complex and uneasy tension between non-partisanship and independent feminism, on the one hand, and the demands of a party-structured parliamentary system, on the other.

Notes

1. *Woman's Century*, 1918, as quoted in Jean Cochrane, *Women in Canadian Politics* (Toronto: Fitzhenry and Whiteside, 1977), 37.

2. Agnes Macphail, "Men Want to Hog Everything," *Maclean's Magazine*, 15 September 1949, 72.

3. For a concise treatment of constraints upon female political participation, see Jean J. Kirkpatrick, *Political Woman* (New York: Basic Books, 1974), chap. 1.

4. A useful definition of political power is provided by Robert Putnam, who suggests that power constitutes "the probability of influencing the policies and activities of the state." See Robert D. Putnam, *The Comparative Study of Political Elites* (Englewood Cliffs, N.J.: Prentice-Hall, 1976), 6.

5. See Catherine L. Cleverdon, *The Woman Suffrage Movement in Canada* (Toronto: University of Toronto Press, 1974).

6. See Carol Lee Bacchi, *Liberation Deferred? The Ideas of the English-Canadian Suffragists, 1877–1918* (Toronto: University of Toronto Press, 1983), 26. Cleverdon, *Woman Suffrage*, 20. reports that the Toronto Women's Literary Club was established in 1876.

7. These subsequent organizations included the Canadian Woman Suffrage Association (CWSA), established in 1883; the Dominion Women's Enfranchisement Association (DWEA), founded in 1889; and the Canadian Suffrage Association (CSA), established in 1906.

8. On the international ties of the Canadian suffragists, see Deborah Gorham, "English Militancy and the Canadian Suffrage Movement," *Atlantis* 1 (1975) and "Singing Up the Hill," *Canadian Dimension* 10 (1975).

9. Richard Evans, *The Feminists* (London: Croom Helm, 1977).

10. The terms "social" and "hard-core" feminism were introduced in William L. O'Neill, *Everyone Was Brave: A History of Feminism in America* (New York: Quadrangle, 1971). A similar distinction between the "expediency" and "justice" claims of American suffragists was made earlier in Aileen S. Kraditor, *The Ideas of the Woman Suffrage Movement* (New York: Columbia University Press, 1965).

11. See Deborah Gorham, "Flora MacDonald Denison: Canadian Feminist," in *A Not Unreasonable Claim: Women and Reform in Canada*, edited by Linda Kealey (Toronto: Women's Press, 1979), 47–70.

12. J. Stanley Lemons, *The Woman Citizen: Social Feminism in the 1920s* (Urbana: University of Illinois Press, 1973), ix.

13. On the role of maternal feminism in Canada, see Linda Kealey, "Introduction" to *A Not Unreasonable Claim*, 1–14.

14. Bacchi, *Liberation Deferred*, 35.

15. Cleverdon, *Woman Suffrage*, 111.

16. The pivotal role of these women's organizations is discussed in Veronica Strong-Boag, " 'Setting the Stage': National Organization and the Women's Movement in the Late Nineteenth Century," in *The Neglected Majority*, edited by Susan Mann Trofimenkoff and Alison Prentice (Toronto: McClelland and Stewart, 1977), 87–103; and Wendy Mitchinson, "The WCTU: 'For God, Home and Native Land,' " in *A Not Unreasonable Claim*, 151–67.

17. See Cleverdon, *Woman Suffrage*, chaps. 6 and 7.

18. Allen Mills summarizes this position in his study of J.S. Woodsworth: "In Woodsworth's view what was wrong with Parliament was the partisan system that destroyed the independence of the average Member of Parliament. . . . Government, he felt, should not be party government but a committee of the best minds." See Allen Mills, "The Later Thought of J.S. Woodsworth, 1918–1942," *Journal of Canadian Studies* 17, 3 (Fall 1982), 80.

19. W.L. Morton, *The Progressive Party in Canada* (Toronto: University of Toronto Press, 1967).

20. Ibid., 16.

21. Candace Savage, *Our Nell: A Scrapbook Biography of Nellie L. McClung* (Saskatoon: Western Producer Prairie Books, 1979), 26.

22. Ibid., 27.

23. Ibid., 83.

24. Ibid., 95.

25. On the early debate over federal enfranchisement, see Cleverdon, *Woman Suffrage*, 105–18; and Bacchi, *Liberation Deferred*, 134–9.

26. See Gloria Geller, "The Wartime Elections Act of 1917 and the Canadian Women's Movement," *Atlantis* 2, 1 (Autumn 1976): 88–106; and Bacchi, *Liberation Deferred*, 139–43. On the background to this period, see Ceta Ramkhalawansingh, "Women during the Great War," in *Women at Work: Ontario, 1850–1930*, edited by Janice Acton, Penny Goldsmith, and Bonnie Shepard (Toronto: Women's Press, 1974), 261–307.

27. Dr Margaret Gordon, as quoted in Geller, "Wartime Elections," 104.

28. See Savage, *Our Nell*; as well as Carol Bacchi, "Race Regeneration and Social Purity: A Study of the Social Attitudes of Canada's English-Speaking Suffragists," *Histoire sociale/Social History* 11 (November 1978): 460–74.

29. Cleverdon, *Woman Suffrage*, 129.

30. See Geller, "Wartime Elections."

31. Savage, *Our Nell*, 171.

32. See Bacchi, *Liberation Deferred*, 129–31.

33. One major difference between the two cases, however, was that in the United States, the Woman's Party grew out of "hard-core" feminist activities, while in English Canada, it developed from the social feminist NEFU. On the American experience, see Susan D. Becker, *The Origins of the ERA: American Feminism between the Wars* (Westport, Conn.: Greenwood, 1981).

34. See Lemons, *The Woman Citizen*, chaps. 2–9.

35. See Savage, *Our Nell*.

36. Elsie Gregory MacGill, *My Mother the Judge*, with an Introduction by Naomi Black (Toronto: Peter Martin, 1981).

37. Ibid., 104.

38. Diane Crossley, "The BC Liberal Party and Women's Reforms, 1916–1928," in *In Her Own Right: Selected Essays on Women's History in BC*, edited by Barbara Latham and Kathy Kess (Victoria: Camosun College, 1980), 229–53.

39. Smith was initially elected as an Independent in 1918, replacing her deceased husband who had sat both provincially and federally as a Liberal. She was re-elected in 1920 and 1924 as a Liberal.

40. See Crossley, "BC Liberal Party," 234–5.

41. Bacchi, *Liberation Deferred*, 32. On the reluctance to pursue public office among Western Canadian suffragists, see L.G. Thomas, *The Liberal Party in Alberta* (Toronto: University of Toronto Press, 1959), 177.

42. See Liane Langevin, *Missing Persons: Women in Canadian Federal Politics* (Ottawa: Canadian Advisory Council on the Status of Women, 1977).

43. According to Macphail's biographers, the local UFO riding executive "was besieged by protests" concerning its choice of a candidate during the 1921 campaign and asked Macphail to resign. See Margaret Stewart and Doris French, *Ask No Quarter* (Toronto: Longmans, Green, 1959), 56.

44. Macphail, "Men Want to Hog Everything," 72.

45. See Stewart and French, *Ask No Quarter*.

46. In the words of Stewart and French (ibid., 38–9), Macphail "never took any part in the battle for votes for women. . . . She was so absorbed in farm problems and cooperatives that the struggle seemed a long way off. She was never a formal feminist, nor even an informal one in the conduct of her life. She blamed women as much as men for the inferior position of the female citizen."

47. Macphail, "Men Want to Hog Everything," 72.

48. According to Stewart and French (*Ask No Quarter*, 170), Macphail walked out of a CCF Women's luncheon with the words, "I'm sick and tired of all this 'woman' business. In all the time I've been in the House of Commons I've never asked for anything on the ground that I was a woman. If I didn't deserve it on my own merit I didn't want it! That's all I have to say."

49. Macphail, "Men Want to Hog Everything," 72. LaMarsh's memoirs were published in 1968 by McClelland and Stewart under the title *Memoirs of a Bird in a Gilded Cage*.

50. See Doris French, "Agnes Macphail, 1890–1954," in *The Clear Spirit*, edited by Mary Quayle Innis (Toronto: University of Toronto Press, 1966), 179–97.

51. Ibid., passim. A major snowstorm on the day of the 1940 federal elections also damaged Macphail's chances for re-election.

52. See ibid.

53. For details of this background, see Rudy G. Marchildon, "The 'Persons' Controversy," *Atlantis* 6, 2 (Spring 1981): 99–113.

54. See ibid., 103ff.

55. Rowell's activities as Ontario Opposition leader are summarized in Cleverdon, *Woman Suffrage*, 35–44. It is notable that Murphy learned of this provision through her brother, an insightful Ontario lawyer with Conservative political ties.

56. Marchildon, " 'Persons' Controversy," 106.

57. Ibid., 111.

58. John Leslie Scott, "Our New Woman Senator, The Honourable Cairine Wilson," *Maclean's Magazine*, 1 April 1930, 97. See also A.R. Way, "From Time to Time in the Queen's Name: The Story of the Honourable Cairine Reay Wilson" (MA thesis, Carleton University, 1984).

59. Scott, "Our New Woman Senator," 98, 97.

60. Ibid., 97.

61. Mary Vipond, "The Image of Women in Mass Circulation Magazines in the 1920s," in *The Neglected Majority*, 118; emphasis in original. On the idea of educated motherhood in the United States during this period, see Sheila M. Rothman, *Woman's Proper Place* (New York: Basic Books, 1978).

62. See Vipond, "Image of Women."

63. John Manley, "Women and the Left in the 1930s: The Case of the Toronto CCF Women's Joint Committee,' *Atlantis* 5, 2 (Spring 1980): 100-19.

64. See ibid., 111-13.

65. Ruth Pierson, "Women's Emancipation and the Recruitment of Women into the Labour Force in World War II," in *The Neglected Majority*, 125-45.

66. Ibid., 142. Under federal tax statutes, relaxed during World War II, husbands are unable to claim a married status exemption if their wives are employed for pay.

67. Ibid., passim.

68. Betty Friedan, *The Feminine Mystique* (New York: Dell, 1963).

69. Dean Beeby, "Women in the Ontario CCF,1940-1950," *Ontario History* 74, 4(December1982):258-83.

70. See ibid., 275-9.

71. Kay Macpherson and Meg Sears, "The Voice of Women: A History," In *Women in the Canadian Mosaic*, edited by Gwen Matheson (Toronto: Peter Martin, 1976), 71.

72. Cerise Morris, " 'Determination and Thoroughness': The Movement for a Royal Commission on the Status of Women in Canada," *Atlantis* 5, 2 (Spring 1980), 6.

73. Macpherson and Sears, "The Voice of Women," 75.

74. Barry Craig, "Women's March May Back Call for Rights Probe," *Globe and Mail*, 5 January 1967, 1.

75. See Lynne Teather, "The Feminist Mosaic," in *Women in the Canadian Mosaic*, 308-10.

76. Morris, " 'Determination and Thoroughness,' " 11. According to Laura Sabia, "The CFUW generally worked on scholarship funds, white-glove tea parties, and the like. They were a very proper and academic group . . . whose membership and executive frequently objected to my activities on behalf of the royal commission. One member even wrote to me and said that she was handing in her membership card because we were becoming too militantly feminist. Of course, when my statement about a march on Ottawa appeared in the *Globe and Mail*, the CFUW women were just appalled." Interview with Laura Sabia (15 March 1983).

77. See Doris Anderson, "Let's Find Out What's Happening to Women," *Chatelaine*, July 1966, 1. The CEW brief was compiled by a Toronto lawyer, Margaret Hyndman. On the chronology of this period, see Morris, " 'Determination and Thoroughness,' " 8-14.

78. See Macphail, "Men Want to Hog Everything," 72.

79. See Morris, " 'Determination and Thoroughness,' " 14.

80. LaMarsh, *Memoirs*, 292.

81. Bird's account of the royal commission is presented in *Anne Francis: An Autobiography* (Toronto: Clarke, Irwin, 1974), esp. 294ff.

82. In her *Memoirs* (301), LaMarsh observed, "There seems no one now within Government circles who is interested in seeing its recommendations take legislative form."

83. See *Report* of the Royal Commission on the Status of Women in Canada (Ottawa: Information Canada, 1970).

84. One radical brief presented to the royal commission in June 1968 was prepared by Bonnie Kreps. See Kreps, "Radical Feminism I," in *Women Unite! An Anthology of the Canadian Women's Movement* (Toronto: Canadian Women's Educational Press, 1972), 70-5.

85. See Judy Bernstein, Peggy Morton, Linda Seese, and Myrna Wood, "Sisters, Brothers, Lovers . . . Listen . . . ," in *Women Unite!*, 31-9.

86. For a useful clarification of these various streams within the feminist movement, written from a Marxist perspective, see Charnie Guettel, *Marxism and Feminism* (Toronto: Women's Press, 1974).

87. The highlights of this conference are documented in a 1974 film by Moira Armour, entitled *The Status of Women: Strategy for Change*.

88. See *Report* of the RCSW, chap. 7.

89. Rosemary Brown, "A New Kind of Power, 1973 Address to Women for Political Action," in

Women in the Canadian Mosaic, 291.

90. See "105 Potential Women MPs," Chatelaine, October 1971, 33ff.; and Barbara Frum, "Insiders' Tips on How to Get Women Elected," Chatelaine, October 1971, 38.

91. It should be noted that, between 1968 and 1972, Grace MacInnis was the sole female MP in Canada.

92. This idea was advanced by Kay Macpherson at the Strategy for Change conference in 1972, where "Ms. for M.P." buttons were sold. See Armour's film, The Status of Women.

93. Interview with Margaret Bryce (14 March 1983). Similar interpretations of the period following 1972 were presented in interviews with Kay Macpherson (18 March 1983) and Helen Lafountaine (25 February 1983).

94. Interview with Margaret Bryce (14 March 1983).

95. An important exception to this trend was Laura Sabia, who ran as a Conservative candidate in the 1968 federal elections and 1981 Spadina by-election.

96. In March 1971, for example, Prime Minister Trudeau appointed a three-woman task force "to investigate and report on the priorities which Liberals and others gave to the Royal Commission recommendations." See Report from Liberal Party Task Force on the Status of Women to LPC Consultative Council, dated October 1971.

97. Interviews with Aideen Nicholson (11 September 1982) and Lorna Marsden (18 March 1983).

98. Interviews with Kay Macpherson (18 March 1983) and Muriel Smith (7 July 1982).

99. On the general absence of legislative progress, see Ten Years Later: An Assessment of the Federal Government's Implementation of the Recommendations Made by the Royal Commission on the Status of Women (Ottawa: Canadian Advisory Council on the Status of Women, October 1979). The recommendations of the LPC Task Force on the Status of Women were also shelved (see note 96, above), according to at least two of its members. Interview with Esther Greenglass (17 March 1983) and note from Jan Steele to Esther Greenglass, dated 30 July 1973.

100. Interviews with Laura Sabia (15 March 1983), Lorna Marsden (18 March 1983), and Esther Greenglass (17 March 1983).

101. Feminist Party of Canada, "Towards a Canadian Feminist Party," April 1979.

102. Ibid.

103. The "Yvette" rally of about 15,000 women in Montreal, and a series of smaller gatherings of federalist women during the referendum campaign, were organized in response to statements by the PQ Minister of State for the Status of Women, Lise Payette. In March 1980, Payette stated that the period of the obedient little "Yvette" of Quebec schoolbooks had passed and compared women who voted against sovereignty-association to passive "Yvettes." Furthermore, she commented that the leader of the "Non" forces in the referendum campaign, Liberal Claude Ryan, was himself married to an "Yvette." See Evelyne Tardy, "Les femmes et la campagne référendaire," in Québec: Un pays incertain (Montreal: Québec-Amérique 1980), 184–203.

104. CACSW member Florence Ievers, as quoted in Marjorie Cohen, "Editorial: The Need for Independent Feminism," Canadian Forum, March 1981, 4.

105. According to most accounts, approximately 1,300 women attended the Ad Hoc Conference. See Anne Collins, "Which Way to Ottawa?" City Woman, Holiday 1981, 12; and Chaviva Hosek, "Women and the Constitutional Process," in And No One Cheered, edited by Keith Banting and Richard Simeon (Toronto: Methuen, 1983), 280–300. Additional studies of women and the 1982 constitution include Penny Kome, The Taking of Twenty-eight (Toronto: Women's Press, 1983); and Sandra D. Burt, "Women and the Canadian Charter of Rights and Freedoms" (paper presented at Canadian Political Science Association meetings, Vancouver, 1983).

106. Interview with Lorna Marsden (18 March 1983).

107. See Collins, "Which Way" and Cohen, "Editorial."

108. See Elizabeth Gray, "Women's Fight to Get in from the Cold Political Wind," Globe and Mail, 30 January 1981, 7.

109. Lynn McDonald, "The Charter of Rights and the Subjection of Women," Canadian Forum, June–July 1981, 18.

110. A more recent example of such a coalition is the Canadian Coalition against Media Pornography, formed in response to Playboy programming on First Choice Pay TV in 1983.

FURTHER READING

This bibliography of recent materials in Canadian women's history is not exhaustive. Instead it is intended as a jumping off point, a concise summary of those sources to which the reader can go for more information or for detailed bibliographic aid. Where good bibliographies exist, we refer to them rather than repeating their contents. We emphasize materials which have appeared since 1980, since *True Daughters of the North* by Beth Light and Veronica Strong-Boag covers earlier publications very thoroughly.

Bibliographies and Historiographical Essays

Listed here are those books and articles that broadly survey the literature of Canadian women's history. Bibliographic aid on specific topics can be found in relevant journals, monographs, and essay collections. We do not include guides to archival holdings or the bibliographies printed by individual libraries that will be of use to many readers.

Cohen, Yoland. "L'histoire des femmes au Québec 1900–1950," *Recherches sociographiques* 21, 3 (September–December, 1980): 339-45.

Conrad, Margaret. "The Re-Birth of Canada's Past: A Decade of Women's History," *Acadiensis* 12 (Spring 1983): 140-62.

Light, Beth, and Veronica Strong-Boag. *True Daughters of the North. Canadian Women's History: An Annotated Bibliography*. Toronto: OISE Press, 1980.

Pierson, Ruth. "Women's History: The State of the Art in Atlantic Canada," *Acadiensis* 7 (Autumn 1977): 121-31.

Prentice, Alison, and Susan Mann Trofimenkoff, eds. "Selected Bibliography: 1980–" in *The Neglected Majority: Essays in Canadian Women's History*, vol. 2. Toronto: McClelland and Stewart, 1985.

Silverman, Eliane Leslau. "Writing Canadian Women's History, 1970–1982: An Historiographical Analysis," *Canadian Historical Review* 63, 4 (December, 1982): 513-33.

Strong-Boag, Veronica. "Raising Clio's Consciousness: Women's History and Archives in Canada," *Archivaria* 6 (Summer 1978): 70-82.

Van Kirk, Sylvia, ed. "Canadian Women's History: Teaching and Research," *Resources for Feminist Research* 7 (July 1979): 5-71.

Walsh, Susan. "Studying Women at Home and Abroad: A Bibliographic Guide to English-Language Sources, 1970–1982," *The Journal of Educational Thought* 17, 2 (August 1983): 187-200.

Journals

Following are the major history journals in Canada and the major women's studies journals in Canada, the United States, and Great Britain. All regularly include useful bibliographic guides to new materials as well as relevant articles. Regional historical journals such as *Acadiensis* and *Saskatchewan History* are also worth consulting for their less frequent but often useful attention to women's history. We also recommend watching for publications from the Canadian Advisory Council on the Status of Women/Conseil consultatif canadien de la situation de la femme and the Canadian Research Institute for the Advancement of Women/Institut canadien de recherches sur les femmes which make bibliographic as well as substantive contributions to the development of women's history in Canada.

History
Beaver
Canadian Historical Review
Histoire sociale/Social History
Journal of Canadian Studies/Revue d'études canadiennes
Labour/Le Travail (formerly Labour/Le Travailleur)
Revue d'histoire d'Amérique française

Women's Studies
(i) Canadian
Atlantis
Canadian Woman Studies/Les cahiers de la femme
Resources for Feminist Research/Documentation sur la recherche féministe
(ii) International
Feminist Review
Feminist Studies
International Journal of Women's Studies
Signs
Women's Studies International Quarterly

Monographs

To date, collections of essays on various subjects by a large number of contributors are more common in the field of Canadian women's history than are full-length monographs by one or two authors. We include here those recent studies with the broadest scope of inquiry.

Armstrong, Pat, and Hugh Armstrong. *The Double Ghetto: Canadian Women and their Segregated Work*. 2nd ed. Toronto: McClelland and Stewart, 1984.
Bacchi, Carol Lee. *Liberation Deferred? The Ideas of the English-Canadian Suffragists, 1877–1918*. Toronto: University of Toronto Press, 1982.
Bashevkin, Sylvia B. *Toeing the Lines: Women and Party Politics in English Canada*. Toronto: University of Toronto Press, 1985.
Brown, Jennifer S.H. *Strangers in Blood: Fur Trade Company Families in Indian Country*. Vancouver: University of British Columbia Press, 1980.
Le Collectif Clio. *L'Histoire des femmes au Québec depuis quatre siecles*. Montréal: Les Quinze, 1982. Also available in English as *Quebec Women: A History*. Toronto: Women's Press, 1986.

Cruikshank, Julie. *Athapaskan Women: Lives and Legends*. Canadian Ethnology Service Paper, No. 57, Ottawa: National Museum of Man, 1979.

Fowler, Marian. *The Embroidered Tent; Five Gentlewomen in Early Canada*. Toronto: Anansi, 1982.

Gillett, Margaret. *We Walked Very Warily: A History of Women at McGill*. Montreal: Eden Press, 1981.

Johnson, Laura C., and Robert E. Johnson. *The Seam Allowance: Industrial Home Sewing in Canada*. Toronto: Women's Press, 1982.

Luxton, Meg. *More Than a Labour of Love: Three Generations of Women's Work in the Home*. Toronto: Women's Educational Press, 1980.

Phillips, Paul, and Erin Phillips. *Women and Work: Inequality in the Labour Market*. Toronto: James Lorimer, 1983.

Pierson, Ruth Roach. *Canadian Women and the Second World War*. Ottawa: Canadian Historical Association Historical Booklet, No. 37, 1983.

Pierson, Ruth Roach, with Marjorie Cohen. *"They're Still Women After All." The Second World War and Canadian Womanhood*. Toronto: McClelland and Stewart, 1986.

Silverman, Eliane Leslau. *Last Best West: Women on the Alberta Frontier, 1880–1930*. Montreal: Eden Press, 1984.

Strong-Boag, Veronica. *The Parliament of Women: The National Council of Women of Canada, 1893–1929*. History Division Paper no. 18. Ottawa: National Museums of Canada, 1976.

Van Kirk, Sylvia. *"Many Tender Ties": Women in Fur Trade Society in Western Canada, 1700–1850*. Winnipeg: Watson and Dwyer, 1980.

Essay Collections

Much of the best work in Canadian women's history is appearing in essay form. The following volumes collectively constitute an excellent guide to the state of research and reflection in the field. They frequently include useful bibliographic guides as well.

Acton, Janice, et al., eds. *Women at Work: Ontario 1850–1920*. Toronto: Canadian Women's Educational Press, 1974.

Briskin, Linda, and Lynda Yanz, eds. *Union Sisters: Women in the Labour Movement*. Toronto: Women's Press, 1983.

Fahmy-Eid, Nadia, and Micheline Dumont, eds. *Maitresses de maison, maitresses d'école: Femmes, famille et éducation dans l'histoire du Québec*. Montreal: Boreal Express, 1983.

FitzGerald, Maureen, Connie Gruberman, and Margie Wolfe, eds. *Still Ain't Satisfied. Canadian Feminism Today*. Toronto: Women's Press, 1982.

Franklin, Ursula Martius, et al. *Knowledge Reconsidered: A Feminist Overview*. Ottawa: Canadian Research Institute for the Advancement of Women/Institut Canadien de recherches sur l'avancement de la femme, 1984.

Kealey, Linda, ed. *A Not Unreasonable Claim: Women and Reform in Canada 1880-1920s*. Toronto: Canadian Women's Educational Press, 1979.

Latham, Barbara, and Cathy Kess, eds. *In Her Own Right: Selected Essays on Women's History in B.C.* Victoria: Camosun College, 1980.

Latham, Barbara, and Roberta Pazdro, eds. *Not Just Pin Money: Selected Essays on the History of Women's Work in British Columbia.* Victoria: Camosun College, 1984.

Lavigne, Marie, and Yolande Pinard, eds. *Les femmes dans la société québecoise: Aspects historiques.* Montreal: Boréal Express, 1977.

————. *Travailleuses et féministes: Aspects historiques.* Montreal: Boréal Express, 1983.

Miles, Angela, and Geraldine Finn, eds. *Feminism in Canada: From Pressure to Politics* Montreal: Black Rose Books, 1982.

Parr, Joy, ed. *Childhood and Family in Canadian History.* Toronto: McClelland and Stewart, 1982.

Prentice, Alison, and Susan Mann Trofimenkoff, eds. *The Neglected Majority: Essays in Canadian Women's History.* 2 vols. Toronto: McClelland and Stewart, 1977, 1985.

Documentary Studies

Included here are only major book-length collections and studies, but readers are reminded that *Atlantis, Canadian Woman Studies/les cahiers de la femme* and *Beaver* publish individual documents of considerable interest for the history of Canadian women.

Binnie-Clark, Georgina. *Wheat and Woman.* Introduction by Susan Jackel. Toronto: University of Toronto Press, 1979.

Cook, Ramsay, and Wendy Mitchinson, eds. *The Proper Sphere: Woman's Place in Canadian Society.* Toronto: Oxford University Press, 1976.

Jackel, Susan, ed. *A Flannel Shirt and Liberty. Emigrant British Gentlewomen in the Canadian West 1880–1914.* Vancouver: University of British Columbia Press, 1982.

Light, Beth, and Joy Parr, eds. *Canadian Women on the Move, 1867–1920.* Toronto: New Hogtown Press and OISE Press, 1983.

Light, Beth, and Alison Prentice, eds. *Pioneer and Gentlewomen of British North America.* Toronto: New Hogtown Press, 1980.

McClung, Nellie L. *In Times Like These.* Introduction by Veronica Strong-Boag. Toronto: University of Toronto Press, 1972.

Salverson, Laura. *Confessions of an Immigrant's Daughter.* Toronto: University of Toronto Press, 1981.

Smith, Elizabeth. *A Woman with a Purpose: The Diaries of Elizabeth Smith, 1872–1884.* Introduction by Veronica Strong-Boag. Toronto: University of Toronto Press, 1980.

CONTRIBUTORS

Sylvia Bashevkin teaches political science at Erindale College, the University of Toronto. She is the author of *Toeing the Lines: Women and Party Politics in English Canada* and articles on contemporary Canadian politics.

Mary Bishop's long volunteer service to the national and international birth control movements was recognized in 1984 by the Lifestyle Award from the Ministry of National Health and Welfare. She received a B.A. in 1935 and an M.A. in 1971 and has been associated with the Faculty of Medicine at the University of British Columbia. She is the author of numerous articles on birth control.

Margaret Conrad, a founding editor of *Atlantis: A Women's Studies Journal*, has been a faculty member in the history department at Acadia University since 1969. As a member of the Maritime Women's Archives Project, she has written several articles on the history of Maritime women.

Anita Clair Fellman teaches in the Women's Studies Program at Simon Fraser University. Co-author, with Michael Fellman, of *Making Sense of Self; Medical Advice Literature in Late Nineteenth-Century America*, she is now studying the politics of individualism in the "Little House" books of Laura Ingalls Wilder.

Eleanor Leacock is an anthropologist teaching at the City College, City University of New York. Her many essays on North American Indians and on the cross-cultural status of women are to be found in such collections as *North American Indians in Historical Perspective* and *Myths of Male Dominance*.

Graham Lowe teaches sociology at the University of Alberta. He has published widely on a range of topics in the sociology of work, and is currently involved in a study of youth employment, underemployment, and unemployment. The article reprinted here won the Marion Porter Award in 1980 from the Canadian Research Institute for the Advancement of Women.

Jan Noel, presently a doctoral student in history at the University of Toronto, is investigating the temperance movement in Pre-Confederation Canada.

Lilianne Plamondon has lectured at various times at Laval University, at the University of Quebec, and at Duke University. She has published articles in the *Dictionary of Canadian Biography* and in various editions of the *Quebec Yearbook*.

Patricia Rooke is associated with the Department of Educational Policy and Administrative Studies at the University of Calgary. With R.L. Schnell, she has written a wide range of articles and several books, including *Public Figure, Private Woman: Charlotte Whitton, 1896-1975*.

Joan Sangster teaches Canadian and women's history at Trent University. She is the author of many articles on women and socialist politics in Canada, and of a forthcoming book, *Women on the Canadian Left: Women in the CCF and Communist Party 1920–1950*.

R.L. Schnell teaches in the Department of Educational Policy and Administrative Studies at the University of Calgary. Co-author with Patricia Rooke of numerous books and articles, he has also been the recipient of many scholarly awards and fellowships, including a Killam Resident Fellowship in 1983.

Christina Simmons was a postdoctoral student at Dalhousie University when she wrote the article reprinted here. She now teaches history at a college of the University of Cincinnati, and is pursuing her interests in the shifting definition of female sexuality in twentieth-century America and in the popular history of the United States.

Veronica Strong-Boag teaches history and women's studies at Simon Fraser University. The author of numerous publications in Canadian women's history, including, with Beth Light, *True Daughters of the North. Canadian Women's History: An Annotated Bibliography*, she is currently writing a volume entitled *"Janey Canuck": Canadian Women between the Wars*.

Sara Brooks Sundberg has taught secondary social studies in Minnesota and Wisconsin. Recently she was employed as project historian for an architectural/historical survey of Chippewa Falls, Wisconsin and at present is researching a bibliography on frontierswomen from Minnesota, Iowa, and Wisconsin.

Susan Mann Trofimenkoff is a member of the Department of History and the Vice-rector Academic of the University of Ottawa. Her many publications include *Action Française. French Canadian Nationalism in the 1920s* and *The Dream of Nation. A Social and Intellectual History of Quebec*. She is now writing a biography of Thérèse Casgrain.

Sylvia Van Kirk teaches history and women's studies at the University of Toronto. She is the author of *"Many Tender Ties": Women in Fur Trade Society in Western Canada, 1670–1870*, and numerous articles on fur trade social history and women's history including "What Has the Feminist Perspective Done for Canadian History?" in *Knowledge Reconsidered.*.

Julie White graduated with a M.A. in Social Administration from the London School of Economics and has worked for a number of years as a freelance researcher on women's issues. She is the author of many articles on Canadian women's participation in trade unionism and in part-time work as well as of the book *Women and Unions*.

Anne Woywitka is an Albertan pioneer who has written a number of articles on the province's early history. Her interviews with long-time residents of Alberta have helped preserve a part of Canada's heritage that more traditionally trained historians have frequently ignored.

1 2 3 4 5 135525 90 89 88 87 86